TALKING FOR BRITAIN

TALKING
FOR
BRITAIN

A Journey through the Nation's Dialects

Simon Elmes

PENGUIN BOOKS

PENGUIN BOOKS

Published by the Penguin Group
Penguin Books Ltd, 80 Strand, London WC2R 0RL, England
Penguin Group (USA) Inc., 375 Hudson Street, New York, New York 10014, USA
Penguin Group (Canada), 90 Eglinton Avenue East, Suite 700, Toronto, Ontario, Canada M4P 2Y3
(a division of Pearson Penguin Canada Inc.)
Penguin Ireland, 25 St Stephen's Green, Dublin 2, Ireland
(a division of Penguin Books Ltd)
Penguin Group (Australia), 250 Camberwell Road,
Camberwell, Victoria 3124, Australia (a division of Pearson Australia Group Pty Ltd)
Penguin Books India Pvt Ltd, 11 Community Centre,
Panchsheel Park, New Delhi – 110 017, India
Penguin Group (NZ), cnr Airborne and Rosedale Roads, Albany,
Auckland 1310, New Zealand (a division of Pearson New Zealand Ltd)
Penguin Books (South Africa) (Pty) Ltd, 24 Sturdee Avenue,
Rosebank 2196, South Africa

Penguin Books Ltd, Registered Offices: 80 Strand, London WC2R 0RL, England

www.penguin.com

First published 2005
5

Copyright © Simon Elmes, 2005
All rights reserved

By arrangement with the BBC
BBC logo © BBC, 1996
The BBC logo is a registered trademark of the British Broadcasting Corporation
and is used under licence.

The moral right of the author has been asserted

Set in 10/12.5 pt Monotype Columbus
Designed by Andrew Barker
Typeset by Rowland Phototypesetting Ltd, Bury St Edmunds, Suffolk
Printed in England by Clays Ltd, St Ives plc

Contents

Preface

'Not *daps*, plimsolls!' The voice was my mother's, and yet again she was swinging into action to correct my schoolboy talk. It wasn't an angry voice, merely an insistent one. Because my mother, like so many just-postwar parents, was keen to make sure her son didn't grow up using local dialect words and a local accent. This was Bristol in the 1950s.

And from everything I've heard since, my case was typical. The writer and distinguished social commentator Richard Hoggart is on record as saying that there was a real fear when he was growing up in Yorkshire of what was referred to as 'sinking' in class terms; correct language and a refined accent (though in Hoggart's family not Received Pronunciation apparently, more what he called a 'Marshall and Snelgrove' Yorkshire accent, after the then famous department store) were easily acquired robust defences against that unhappy fate, and didn't cost a penny either.

It wasn't quite snobbery – not for me the elocution lessons imposed on many a contemporary youngster of upwardly mobile parents. But this was the era of U and non-U, of the writer Nancy Mitford's railing against in-appropriate language, and in my house we made sure we went to the 'lavatory' and used 'napkins'. 'Phone for the fish-knives, Norman,' intoned John Betjeman in his famous catalogue of linguistic social faux-pas, 'as Cook is a little unnerved', inveighing against supposedly lower-class usage – in the 1950s, it was okay to rid someone of vernacular speech.

So it was that to my lifelong regret I grew up purged of any of those characteristics that instantly mark out a Bristolian in a crowded room; like the heavily accentuated 'r' and the constantly uplifted ends to sentences (now a national feature, though stemming from Bondi not Bedminster). But what I really missed acquiring was the famous Bristol 'l'. Bristolians love this strange, unique phenomenon that adds an 'l' sound to hanging vowels, and enjoy the laughs that it often provokes.

So they're rather proud that one of the city's foremost public venues, named after out great nineteenth-century monarch, is known throughout the city as the Victoria*l* Rooms. And then there was my lovely neighbour Bob, who was something quite big in local telecommunications and who was about to go out to set up a new telephone system in Port Harcourt. 'Where's Port Harcourt, Bob?' 'Nigeria*l*,' said Bob, with his habitual guffaw, quite unabashed.

In fact, I think it was moments like that which first kindled my fascination with accent and dialect. I loved it; loved the energy, the confidence, the unapologetic distinctiveness of it all. And I loved the inherent sense of fun that Bristolians have with their speech. Like the local joke, passed into legend now, but nonetheless absolutely the genuine article, which has one chap complaining of bad TV reception (not uncommon in our hilly city). 'It's the aerial,' comes the repairman's reply. 'Well, just fix it,' says the unfortunate viewer, crossly. 'No,' remonstrates the by now equally irritated TV man, 'it's not the aerial on your roof, it's the area*l* *where* you live. Bad reception area*l*.'

Over the past nearly twenty-five years, I've had the good fortune to be able to carry out for the BBC a series of investigations into the joys such as these of regional speech across the country. Throughout the middle of the 1980s, the tireless field-worker of the Survey of English Dialects, Stanley Ellis of Leeds University, and I travelled Britain uncovering stories of local language for BBC Radio 4 which we called *Talk of the Town, Talk of the Country*. Fifteen years later, for the millennial celebrations of 2000, Melvin Bragg and I traced *The Routes of English*, again for Radio 4 across what has now grown to twenty-six programmes, with regional English as the focus of many of the programmes. These broadcasts, together with the earlier recordings of the SED, have been an invaluable archival source for the present volume.

Coming up to date with the Voices project – the most elaborate and complete popular examination of our vernacular ever undertaken – you can see in almost forensic detail how the powerful emotional connection between how we speak and where we live is evolving in communities right round the British Isles right now. *Talking for Britain* attempts to bring together the very best of all these investigations into a sort of linguistic and social panorama of how this country is conversing with itself in the first years of the new millennium – and how it got there.

I have many people to thank for their help in the preparation of this book. Top of the list is Dr Clive Upton, soon to be Professor of Modern English Language at the University of Leeds. Clive has been part of the Voices project from its inception, and it's his intellectual and academic rigour, long hardened in the disciplines of the Survey of Regional English which he heads, and its predecessor, the Survey of English Dialects, that have given the project its status, validity and authenticity. Clive it was, too, who first suggested it might be worthwhile putting together a popular book about dialect: for this – and for the beautiful yet deceptive simplicity of the word prompts used by the Voices field-workers – I am deeply indebted to Clive.

Alongside him in a photo-finish are my BBC co-conspirators on Voices, Faith Mowbray and Mick Ord. Faith runs the new media dimension of the project and is a powerhouse of talent, focusing the whole Voices team's endeavours with a devastating mixture of charm, determination and diplomacy worthy of the finest foreign embassy. Mick is Project Director of Voices and one of the nicest people I know. He's been tireless in persuading the recalcitrant, encouraging the discouraged, organizing the disorganized and in keeping the whole Local and Regional Radio and TV project bubbling away. Huge thanks too go to Mick's chosen 'audio-gatherers' (as they soon became known), who sallied forth to capture the responses of ordinary men and women to such seemingly unpromising questions as 'What do you call the long, soft seat in the main room of a house?' They stuck at it, even when lulled into eye-closing somnolence by a particularly garrulous speaker, or when – only occasionally – the conversation flowed like clotted cream, congealing into unyielding silences interrupted only by a forced 'OK, then, next question . . .'

My thanks go also to the School of English at the University of Leeds, and, in particular, to Professor Vivien Jones, for giving me permission to make use of the vast recorded resources from the Survey of English Dialects, and to the BBC Archive for similar access to the landmark series on language (*Talk of the Town, Talk of the Country* and *The Routes of English*) that Radio 4 has broadcast in the past twenty-five years. To the many academic experts on different aspects of regional usage – too numerous to mention individually – who contributed powerfully to these programmes, and who have kindly allowed me to quote them freely, I am very grateful.

Likewise I salute the dozens of literary and other sources that have helped give my amateur delvings into dialect substance and authority. Again there are too many to list in full, but David Crystal's *Cambridge Encyclopaedia of the English Language*, Martyn Wakelin's *English Dialects, An Introduction* and not least the latest edition of the twenty-volume *Oxford English Dictionary* have been immeasurably useful books. *Talking for Britain* is the product of the computer and Internet age, and it's worth noting that the boundless resources for the student of vernacular English now available online – from slang chatrooms to official dialect society sites – have made possible, for example, the instant elucidation of opaque aspects of contemporary speech that previous generations would have scoured libraries for months to achieve.

Finally there are three sets of people without whom not one word of this book would have been written: firstly my editor at Penguin, Nigel Wilcockson, who kept me from wandering off the shining path of clarity too frequently for comfort and who kept my spirits aloft when crises of all dimensions blocked the way. To my old friend Stanley Ellis, formerly of Leeds University and the cajoling interviewer on almost all of the archival documents quoted here from the original Survey of English Dialects, I offer my gratitude for a quarter-century of instruction and enlightenment about dialect. Stanley's deep linguistic wisdom and his love of the British landscape – the people who live in it and who describe it in their talk – inspired me to pursue my own long fascination. Lastly I owe infinite thanks to my family – to my children Jocelyn and John for allowing me to monopolize the conversation (and the computer), and above all to my wife Liz for encouraging me every inch of the way, coping with my moods and putting up with my months of solitary confinement as the manuscript took shape.

Oh, yes, and to the thousands of you – from Craigavon to Clapham, from Dundee to Dungeness and from Bon-y-maen to Barrow-in-Furness – who are proud of where you come from, of what you do, and of the words and accents you use to describe it: to you, the voices of Voices go the thanks of all of us on the project . . . You are the real experts.

Introduction

Words, the building blocks of the English language, the wherewithal to express emotion, describe events and create imaginative worlds, have always fascinated. Chaucer, Milton, Shakespeare, Swift . . . the hundreds of names that make up the canon of the world's greatest writers in English all play with words and delight in their ambiguities and resonances. But it was the great *Dictionary* of Dr Johnson, published in 1755, that really focused attention on those building blocks in a way hitherto undreamed of. Here was a set of formal definitions, a list of standard terms and meanings, that represented the English language and offered a form of regulation for it, drawing its illustrations from the literary monuments of the past.

Nearly 200 years earlier, in 1589, the writer George Puttenham had recommended in his *Arte of English Poesie* that the best type of English was 'the vsuall speach of the Court, and that of London and the shires lying about London', but his voice was relatively small and the time was not ripe. From the moment, however, when Johnson launched his mighty *Dictionary* on a society keen to put some order into what had become an overgrown garden of language, the notion of correctness, of a preferred form for words and syntax, took firm hold.

Thenceforth the notion of 'standardization', of some form of absolute gold standard of English to which one could aspire, was widely accepted and is still much referred to today. In fact, as Professor David Crystal has observed, the term 'Standard English' is often bandied around without clear definition of what is meant. Certainly it's not a question of accent: Standard English is a variety of our language that can be spoken with any number of accents. Rather it's a matter of grammar, vocabulary, spelling and punctuation: Standard English is a variety, too, which is widely understood and held in high esteem within society.

The corollary to this tide of 'correctness' that gained momentum in the eighteenth century was, of course, that other forms were inferior and improper. And though Britain has never resorted to the type of corrective and linguistically legislative Academy that the French created and still hold dear (despite the passionate advocacy of Jonathan Swift for 'some Method . . . for *ascertaining* and *fixing* our Language for ever'), there has always been a fierce debate between those who would prescribe a 'correct' form that should be aspired to, and those who prefer to let language take its course.

For the prescriptivists, dialect is by definition inferior as it deviates from the standard and any such deviation or error is to be deprecated. For descriptivists, the almost infinite regional variants simply enhance the richness and variety of our great language. Whichever side you took then (and the arguments still rage), by the Victorian age the many hundreds of varieties of regional English to be found in Britain began to be more widely acknowledged. From one end of the country to the other, amateur linguistic sleuths and more formal academic enquirers collated, assembled and annotated them in a welter of glossaries, word-lists, commentaries and collections.

For a record of the way earlier generations spoke in the outlying corners of the country, linguists rely on a relatively small trickle of documents, two notable examples being Nowell's *Vocabularium Saxonicum* of 1659, with its early forms of Lancastrian English, and, a century and a quarter later, the work of Francis Grose (*A Provincial Glossary*, 1787). This latter drew together a number of diverse sources and is an important early collection of dialect usage to which I refer regularly throughout this book.

However, as I say, a few years after Grose's *Glossary* appeared, specialist lexicons and the study of local English begin to abound, like the obscure list of so-called 'Montiaghisms' of William Lutton, collected near Portadown in Northern Ireland around 1840, or the many wordlists gathered in the mining industry in north-east England, such as Frederick Dinsdale's *Glossary of Provincial Words Used in Teesdale in the County of Durham* of 1849. The culmination of all these local lists and small-scale scholarship was the great work of Joseph Wright, his *English Dialect Dictionary* published in 1904, which is still the source of many of the definitions of regional words to be found in the *Oxford English Dictionary*.

In more recent times, Harold Orton and Eugen Dieth undertook from the fastness of the University of Leeds the greatest twentieth-century investigation of the state of regional English in their Survey of English Dialects (SED), whose field-work was carried out during the 1950s and early 1960s. This mapped for the first time the great differences between the pronunciation, vocabulary and syntax of the regions of England, quoting wherever possible elderly inhabitants of principally rural areas which were deemed to reflect the oldest and most marked reservoirs of dialect than extant. The recordings of dialect in context that accompany the formal field-work add real colour and depth to the exhaustive and systematic point-by-point lexical and pronunciation survey. For the amateur these old discs capture not only the sound of words now frequently lost from regular use but also fascinating vignettes of a rural Britain from the Edwardian and Victorian eras, aural snapshots of unpaved roads and horse-drawn ploughs and carters carrying bales of woven cloth to market in the nearby city.

Some of these recordings – like that of the Cumbrian midwife with her tales of stillborn babies and the rigours of home delivery in the early twentieth century – emphasize just how far removed from any notion of 'Standard English' dialect could be fifty years ago. In fact I listened dozens of times over to the elderly woman from 'Snuffy' 'Arrod (Great Harwood) in Lancashire and her tale of shenanigans in the churchyard in the early hours without ever fully being able to understand every syllable she uttered.

Yet this woman was telling her story in her rich Lancastrian at precisely the same time as BBC announcers like Alvar Lidell and John Snagge were seen as a standard to which to aspire: 'BBC English' represented clarity and simplicity, as accurate and precise in its vocabulary, grammar and syntax as it was in the facts the speech was communicating. Additionally, the accent and pronunciation of 'educated' men and women epitomized by BBC English were viewed as an absolute standard, from which any local variation, regional terminology or irregular syntax were seen at best as quaint and often formally as 'wrong'. It's an attitude that runs like a deep seam through the way we think about and discuss our spoken language.

How 'wrong', then, were the SED's midwife or cotton worker? Is dialect 'inferior'? Is a regional accent somehow 'less good' than a more neutral one? This is where the big battle between prescriptivists and descriptivists gets nasty. I have spent many happy hours of my BBC career reading and replying to letters about the linguistic style of broadcasters. If a well-known performer, such as the *Today* programme's John Humphrys or James Naughtie, were to split an infinitive, use a plural verb after a collective noun ('Parliament are . . .') or commit some other perceived solecism, the letters would flood in.

And not just for 'grammatical errors'. Susan Rae, a BBC radio announcer, following in the footsteps of Lidell and Snagge, was some years ago subjected to much public criticism for her warm Scottish accent and only recently returned to Radio 4 after several years' absence. Tolerance for variation from a perceived norm can still be very low, particularly in the former temple of perceived 'neutrality', the news-reader's chair.

To measure the depth of this seam of 'rightness' and 'wrongness' in speech, you have only to take more or less any of the 250 or more interviews carried out for the Voices survey during the course of late 2004 and early 2005. It comes up over and over again; a plaintive cry about schoolteachers who 'beat the dialect out of me', the tale of parents – frequently mothers – who still today tell their children to 'speak properly' and not use slang or rough words, the story of self-correction when speaking to superiors or on the telephone (the familiar 'telephone voice' phenomenon that many people admitted to).

Clearly, attitudes to accent and to an extent to regional vocabulary have much to do with feelings about social class, and a 'purer', less regional speech has for 200 years been seen as the essential concomitant of self-improvement. Not for nothing the rash of elocution brochures and booklets that appeared in the nineteenth century featuring such forlorn and neglected linguistic personalities as 'Poor Letter H'.

Happily, *Talking for Britain* takes no such issue with correctness or otherwise. The richer the diversity, the happier I am, whether it's in the old, rich and well-honed forms of Yorkshire dialect Voices recorded, for example, in Castleford and the North York Moors, or in the rapid-fire urban talk of Belfast, Dundee or Salford, thickened up by city streets and young people in a hurry.

A word about how these many voices were captured for posterity. During the winter and spring of 2004/5, over fifty field-workers operating out of BBC Local Radio stations, and broadcasting centres in Belfast, Glasgow and Cardiff, set out with questionnaires to interview groups of men and women from their area. The groups ranged from taxi-drivers to crane-drivers and bus-drivers, from dockers to drinkers in a gay bar and even one set of historic battle re-creationists. Ages were equally widespread, though young children were not canvassed, while as many as 250 different points across England, Wales, Scotland and Northern Ireland were targeted.

Interviews ranged in length from about forty-five minutes to two hours; some were tightly packed with linguistic detail, others meandered delightfully round the intricacies of the speakers' lives, stopping to take in particular dialect terms when the moment arose. In every case, however, the 'audio-gatherers' asked the members of the groups to fill in and talk about a sequence of forty specific definitions for which they sought the speakers' natural vernacular or regional equivalent. Some were simple: *What do you call your father, mother, grandfather, grandmother, a baby, a male/female partner?* and so on. Others started with a more elaborate definition, such as: *What do you call a young person in cheap, trendy clothes and jewellery?* or *What do you call the narrow walkway between buildings?* Then there were questions about the home: *What's the long soft seat in the main room? What do you call the toilet? Or What do you call the main room in your house with the TV?*

At first sight many of these questions appear rather simplistic, obvious in fact. But subtlety is the game here and having listened to several hundred hours of the Voices interview material I have been astonished at how such a simple question as *What do you call someone who's left-handed?* or *What do you call running water smaller than a river?* can unblock a whole lifetime or changing language and anecdotes to back it up ('I was always called cack-handed at school' . . . 'I was always told off for using my left hand' . . . 'I used always to say "burn" but now I tend to use "stream"' . . . 'We used to swim in the brook and my friend caught polio' . . .). Mystification greeted questions like *What do you say for 'to play a game'?*, with responses like 'To play – what else?' Yet in Yorkshire almost everyone interviewed by Voices knew that to 'laik', or 'laik out' was a standard local expression.

But that 'long, soft seat' question even left me puzzled. Certainly, some preferred 'sofa' and others 'settee'; I collected a number of 'couches', especially in Scotland, and even the odd 'chaise longue' and 'Chesterfield'. So far, so unsurprising. I was unprepared, therefore, for the variant that came storming through from the north Midlands, where, for many, this familiar piece of domestic furniture was – uniquely in my experience – a 'sofee'. Interesting to note, too, the current huge range of words to emerge from the Voices survey in response to the question about 'young person in cheap, trendy clothes and jewellery'. Just as the first interviews were being conducted, the popular press was full of coverage for a relatively new term that describes fairly accurately this sort of person: 'chav'. Inevitably, therefore, 'chavs' abound in the survey. But they were joined by a host of others: 'spides' and 'hoods' in Northern Ireland, 'scallies' in Liverpool, 'charvers' in Newcastle, 'neds' in Glasgow and 'trevs', 'townies' and 'wannabes' in many other places. In Bradford-on-Avon, Wiltshire, Voices was assured they were called 'Trobos' because they come mainly from the county town, Trowbridge.

Then alongside such wonderful old local usages (still just about surviving) as 'ferntickle' for freckle and 'erriwiggle' for earwig, Voices recorded the nation-beating triumph of a handful of modern slang terms that have passed into almost everyone's lexicon: 'knackered' for tired (despite the frequent observation that it was a rather vulgar word), 'chuffed' for pleased and 'loaded' for rich. There were some surprises too: the spreading use of the originally northern word 'keks' for trousers, as also 'strides' (surprisingly widespread) and 'pants' – though it seems this is indigenous usage and not borrowed from the US. The influence of television, and particularly of shows such as *Only Fools and Horses*, *Coronation Street* and *Big Brother*, was evident among young people's choice of words for good, attractive and unattractive ('minging' and 'minger' were national standards for the latter amongst this age-group).

On the other hand I was astonished to find the huge variety of terms in regular use round the country for left-handed. (Are you 'clicky', 'keggy', 'caggy-handed', 'cloddy-handed', 'corry-fisted', 'pally-jukered', 'carry-pod' or merely 'cack-handed'? And that's simply a sample.) Equally varied and colourful were the range of words for a walkway between houses, which is a 'jennel', 'ginnel', 'twitchel', 'jitty', 'snicket', 'alley', 'close', 'entry', 'wynd', 'backsie', 'eightfoot' or even 'tenfoot' depending on where you live.

Words are on the move as well: a number of expressions being adopted by younger people in many parts of Britain (e.g. 'bredren', 'blud') originated in the Afro-Caribbean or Asian communities but now simply exist as further additions to the range of attractive and fashionable word-choices available to a generation for whom bhangra and rap are the regular soundtrack to their lives. Voices is perhaps the first national survey systematically to track that linguistic and social evolution.

Language, they say, is a river constantly moving, constantly replenished. This book can only tap a few litres of that river and bottle them for examination. Because as sure as English will still continue to flourish across the world, by the time you read it, there will be a host of new terms flooding out of their localities to join the mainstream.

And the river, never still, will have moved on.

I : CORNWALL

Language in a Landscape: Cream of Cornish

There was always a satisfying complexity to life in Cornwall. Of course, situated as it is in the south-west of these islands, with the Gulf Stream engulfing it, with powerful tides driven on by the full force of the prevailing south-westerlies (not for nothing is a rain bonnet called a 'sou'wester'), the gentle climate, sandy strands and rocky romantic coves were always going to be a magnet for visitors. But before the tourist hordes in search of blue lagoons and magic pixies overwhelmed normality, life in Cornwall always contained a pleasing mix of fish and grain – of seafaring and husbandry. Add the gleaming seams of tin that weave through the granite of these tough old uplands and the bleach-white kaolin beds that provided clay for the china industry, and Cornwall was kept busy.

Some 400 years ago, one notable visitor to the county was Richard Carew, who in 1602 published his still fascinating *Survey of Cornwall*. Opinionated and grand, Carew none the less captures a real flavour of this south-western corner of Britain:

> Touching the temperature of Cornwall, the ayre thereof is cleansed, as with bellowes, by the billowes, and flowing and ebbing of the Sea, and therethrough becommeth pure, and subtill, and, by consequence, healthfull.

In keeping with the spirit of the Renaissance, Carew's compendium of Cornish life spans the geology, geography, customs, beliefs and occupations of the county. He notes for instance that:

> the Tynners digge a conuenient depth, and then passe forward vnder ground, so farre as the ayre will yeeld them breathing, which, as it

beginneth to faile, they sinke a Shaft downe thither from the top, to admit a renewing vent, which notwithstanding, their worke is most by Candle-light. In these passages, they meete sometimes with verie loose earth, sometimes with exceeding hard Rockes, and sometimes with great streames of water . . .

The linguistic bedrock of the county also runs deep: a Celtic tradition that has close connections with Welsh and Breton. It's been estimated that more than three-quarters of Cornish place-names are of Celtic origin (the remainder being derived from Old English or Norman French). 'By *Tre*, *Pol*, and *Pen*, You shall know the Cornishmen,' observes Carew, quoting what was for him already 'the common by-word':

They partake in some sort with their kinsmen the Welsh: for as the Welshmen catalogize *ap Rice*, *ap Griffin*, *ap Owen*, *ap Tuder*, *ap Lewellin*, &c. . . . So the Westerne Cornish, by a like, but more compendious maner, intitle one another with his owne & his fathers christen name, and conclude with the place of his dwelling. Most of them begin with *Tre*, *Pol*, or *Pen*, which signifie a Towne, a Top, and a head.

In fact, Carew is a bit hazy with his Celtic roots as *pol* refers not to 'poll', a head (cf. poll-tax), but to 'pool' or 'lake'.

The Celtic linguistic tradition was ground down by English supremacy such that Kernowek, the Cornish language, hasn't had a native speaker for two centuries or more. Modern enthusiasts are staging an effective revival linked in great part to the strong and vocal nationalist lobby, yet the living link with the Celtic language that throve west of the Tamar was lost long ago.

Richard Gendall, an honorary research fellow at the Institute of Cornish Studies at Exeter University whose work on the linguistic history of Cornwall is unequalled, says that the Cornish language lost ground westwards from the Tamar: over a period of about 800 years, English, in the form of the Wessex dialect, gradually encroached from the east over the river that marks the county boundary and moved down the peninsula:

The further west you go the less emphasis there is on the Wessex English and the greater emphasis on anything that has survived from the Cornish language. [East Cornwall represents the bastion of English influence] and in the west you get more Celtic words coming in. In mid-Cornwall you get a mixture of the two.

As in so many parts of these British Isles, it's the map and the names scattered across it that tell the linguistic story. To the east, the identities of the villages, towns and hamlets are English in origin, places such as Stratton and Ashton and places with names ending in -bury and -ford; to the west, the names they bear are Celtic, Cornish. Yet it's the detail that really reveals the history. So while the town of Bodmin reflects its Celtic roots (*bod meneich*, monks' dwelling), the adjoining moor remained largely unsettled and, says Gendall, has Middle English names:

> you get places like Bradford there, right in the middle, which only means 'broad ford', but that's a Middle English name. And then around what we shorten to 'lannson' but which you might call 'lawn-ston' [Launceston], there's a great spearhead of Cornish names which have just stayed there and haven't been obliterated.

Not surprisingly, given their meanings, *tre*, *pol* and *pen* crop up regularly in the place-names too, so there's a long list of places with names like *Tre*sillian, *Pol*perro and *Pen*zance.

Cornwall is a place of huge change. As much as anywhere in the British Isles, the old livelihoods that Richard Carew observed in 1602, and which continued without much disturbance for at least three and a half of the following four centuries, have undergone radical alteration. Overwhelmed by tourism ('emmets', ants, is the well-known disparaging term for the visitors) and the (highly profitable) sale of farm-workers' cottages to wealthy absentee second-home owners or incomers, which have driven many off the land, the agricultural tradition of Cornwall is being swamped. Fishing is subject to quotas and caps, and though there's good fish to be had, the fleet has dwindled. China clay still continues to be exported in large quantities, but the last tin-mine in Cornwall, South Crofty, kept alive at huge cost for years, finally fell silent in 1998 with an inrush of water, though plans to reopen it as a working mine are constantly mooted as the price of tin fluctuates upward once more.

The language too has been pushed and pulled over the centuries. During the Reformation, the 1549 Act of Uniformity imposed the Book of Common Prayer in English, replacing the old Latin prayer book, across the land. This proved particularly unpopular in south-west England and especially in Cornwall, where many at that time spoke only Cornish. The Prayer Book Rebellion ensued, in the course of which 4,000 people died and English forces moved wholesale into Cornwall.

Gradually, English displaced the Cornish tongue westwards so that fifty years after the rebellion, when Carew was writing, it had retreated as far as Truro. He reported:

> as the Cornish names hold an affinity with the Welsh, so is their language deduced from the same source, and differeth onely in the dialect. But the Cornish is more easie to bee pronounced, and not so vnpleasing in sound, with throat letters, as the Welsh. 1 2 3 4 In numbring they say, *Wonnen, Deaw, Tre, Pidder. Durdatha why*, is 'Good morrow to you'. *Trenestatha*, 'Good night'. *Fatlugan a why*: 'How do you?' *Da durdalathawhy*: 'Wel I thanke you'. A sister, they call *Whoore*: 'a whoore', *whorra*: 'a priest', *coggaz*: 'a partridge', *grigear*: 'a Mare', *cazock* . . .

But Carew notes that the English language:

> hath driuen the same into the vttermost skirts of the shire. Most of the Inhabitants can [know] no word of Cornish; but very few are ignorant of the English . . . The English which they speake, is good and pure, as receyving it from the best hands of their owne Gentry . . .

Though if their English grammar was pure, the way the Cornish pronounced it Carew cared little for:

> they disgrace it, in part, with a broad and rude accent, and eclipsing (somewhat like the Somersetshire men) specially in pronouncing the names: as Thomas they call, *Tummas* & *Tubby*: Mathew, *Mathaw*: Nicholas, *Nichlaaz*: Reginald, *Reinol*: David, *Daavi*: Mary, *Maari* . . .

Carew may not have liked the local pronunciations, preferring the company of the well-spoken gentry, yet isn't it amazing to hear in these 400-year-old transcriptions the real sound of Cornish popular speech preserved?

But as he notes, the number of native Cornish speakers was still shrinking, till a hundred years later, according to Richard Gendall, only

4

the very tip of the peninsula had any sizeable population of people who naturally used Cornish:

> Doctor Edward Lhuyd from Wales was actually invited to Cornwall to look at the language and try and save what remains there were. He spent four months with a team of men going about all over the place – he even got himself arrested: they thought he was a spy. And he noted down that the language was only known in the coastal parishes of what we now call West Penwith and Kerrier. So really all the very western parts of Cornwall still had Cornish going in 1700.

Famously, the last speaker of Cornish is recorded as Dolly Pentreath, who died in 1777, but she did have some English, and the palm of last monoglot speaker of Cornish belongs, it seems, to one Chesten Marchant, who died in 1676 at Gwithian.

But just as the spark of summer brushfires may continue to linger deep in the peat of Bodmin Moor long after the flames are put out, so the vocabulary of Cornish was by no means extinguished with the death of Dolly Pentreath. As I show elsewhere in this book, closed communities are perfect breeding grounds for vernaculars and Richard Gendall claims that there's evidence from the end of the nineteenth and the early twentieth century to suggest that fishermen still continued to count their catch in the language.

The dialect of Cornwall became the rich repository for the Celtic language, blended with plenty of English terms and all delivered traditionally in a broad and angular accent that often leaves the uninitiated bewildered. But whilst study of the old language has flourished in recent years and Cornish has been recognized officially as one of the minority languages of the United Kingdom, the past decade has seen perhaps the biggest shift Cornish *dialect* has undergone.

Stanley Ellis, the tireless field-worker for the Survey of English Dialects who spent more than a decade taking a meticulous and detailed linguistic X-ray of regional speech fifty years ago, came to Cornwall in March 1963. That notoriously hard winter had barely finished and the people of Egloshayle near Wadebridge were full of it, with comparisons to the worst winters of the First World War. The speaker here – we don't now know his name – had recollections of that far back, and reckoned the summer was set to be a fair one following the big freeze. He had few strong dialectal markers, apart from the ubiquitous 'r' sound (the 'burrds' whose nest-building would point to a fine summer to come – 'it's a bit arrly yet', though). But his weather lore had a nice Cornish touch as he affirmed 'red sky at night' meant '*sailor's* delight'. The man was a country-man through and through, with his complex explanations of hedging and stone-walling ('you see quaat a lot uv it araound'), yet compared with the other speaker Ellis recorded that March day, thirty miles east at Altarnun near Launceston, his speech was only lightly Cornish.

The Altarnun man's talk was, in keeping with the SED's objectives, as old and as broad as possible, and like the old recordings I've listened to from Suffolk and Lancashire, from Yorkshire, Somerset and elsewhere, it reflects a richness of accent and style of delivery that's rare in England now outside particular communities in the big cities, though, as you can read later in this book, still quite common in Scotland and Northern Ireland. The man's 'a' sounds in particular dominated his delivery, and if he didn't naturally use particular Cornish or Celtic-root words, his habit of sounding normally unvoiced consonants was very characteristic (see Chapter 2 on west of England speech for a detailed discussion of this phenomenon). So 'sometimes' became 'samdaahms' and 'rightaway' something like 'raat-aweaay'. And when he spoke about lambing, the ewes were in his accent 'yaws', legs were 'lags' and the verb find, 'faand'. In fact, so broad was he, that even after repeated auditions I found it hard to capture every detail of his description of road-mending in the 'awl deaays':

> Rough roawds; yeears ago when ah wus young, the stawn [stone] was put an the roawds. Ah mahn [mind = remember] the furrst steamrawller comin du Bolvenderr [Bolventor, three miles down the road] when ah wus aba' twel yerr awl [about twelve years old]. 'Arrses [horses] would tramp dem een [tramp them in] and ruwd-men'd rake 'em een [the road-men would rake them in] when they get chaance, liyke. 'T isn' laak 'tis t'daey. Ah spose 'twerre abaht sixty yerr ago first steamrawller come in this parish.

Has this depth of regional speech now been lost for ever in Cornwall? It's of course hard to tell, since whilst the last speaker was very broad indeed, his companion from Egloshayle speaking on the same day in 1963 was not. However, as you can read in the 'Voices' and 'Snapshot' sections in this chapter, there is plenty of evidence to suggest that though very broad speakers are still to be found – like the Voices group from Bodmin Moor – the old talk, as they put it, is 'bein' dahluyted'.

The Voices Survey: Cornish Speech in the Twenty-First Century

One of the problems Cornish speech faces is one of image. Along with many of the West Country variants, it has long been tarred with the brush of rural slowness. Les Lean, a former china clay employee, recalled in 2000 for Melvyn Bragg's radio series about dialect, *The Routes of English*, how he'd been ridiculed in the army for his accent and had sought to eliminate his rhotic ('r'-emphasized) regional speech: 'They used to laugh every time you'd say things,' he admitted, with a shrug, 'when I used to say about "sweating rivers" and things like that. Or they'd laugh at your 'r's; and you stopped saying it like.'

That Cornwall, a corner of England 300 long miles from London, has for centuries been one of the least prosperous parts of the country hasn't helped. On the other hand adversity, says the Cornish politician, poet and cultural champion Bert Biscoe, has shaped the way the inhabitants observe and talk about their world:

> The Cornish are an island people to all intents and purposes, and therefore they have that sense of having to carry on no matter what the pressures, no matter what the tragedy. You know, after the storm's blown you walk down on the beach and you never know what's going to be washed up on the shore. You've got to be prepared to think, 'Oh hell what are we going to do about that? Right, okay, we'll do it, let's get on.'

It's a solidarity that Biscoe extends to the way one Cornishman speaks to another, coupled with a certain wry humour: 'I think Cornish people use their dialect to accentuate their sense of themselves when they're with each other. But underpinning it all there's always that sense of irony, that sense of dryness.'

> We'm a rehce [race] on our own. I mean it's nat'rel the way we talk, ennit. Yeah, well 'tis Cornish ennit. We was borrn 'eere, no airs or graces . . .

The Sound of Cornwall

It is sad but true that the broad Cornish accent, full of nubbles like scalded cream, is being diluted somewhat these days. But when you do find it, as Voices did on Bodmin Moor, it still gurgles satisfyingly. Most obvious is the heavy, characteristic and ubiquitous 'r', a thick stratum running right through the granite of Cornish dialect: 'arr' (' 'tis arrd' – it's hard). It's also often darkened by the ritual voicing of normally unvoiced consonants, turning 't's into 'd's, 'p's into 'b's and 'f' into 'v'. So 'party' becomes the heavier-sounding 'pardee' ('Tip the Button', an old Cornish game, was 'Tep the Buddon') and 'done for' sounds more like 'dunver'.

As usual, vowel sounds carry many of the accent indicators and all play musical chairs to an extent: short 'i' can become the duller 'uh' sound making 'morning' 'morre-nun' (with a heavy 'r', of course) and 'will' turns into 'wull', to rhyme with Hull; 'i' is also regularly sounded like a short 'e', so 'bit' becomes 'bet' and the game of 'whist' goes 'west'! The open 'eh' sound of 'there' dims to that 'uh' sound too: 'thurr' (rhyming with standard 'purr').

In November 2004, Ken, Clive, Ruby, Cyril and Barbara, a group of elderly Cornish men and women from remote Bodmin Moor gathered to reflect – with a rich dose of Bert Biscoe's irony and dryness – on how Cornish is changing:

> 'Latterr yearrs, I don't think there's so many people arauynd speak as we dioo. The nyoocomers that've moved een, we gadda jawb [got a job] t'pick up some a theirr worrds, an' they 'ave got the same with us. 'S like the gutt'rin' on yuh roof, ennuh. To us i's the ''launder''. Well, you 'ave an autsider come in, say, ''Well your launder need fitten'', 'n' they'll look blank ut yuh, 'n' say ''Whoss tha'?'' '

'Launder' is the traditional old Cornish mining term for a wooden or steel trough used to carry water, for example to the buckets of a water-wheel, which has transferred to mean any form of guttering.

Dealing with outsiders has always been a sensitive issue for the Cornish, fearful of being thought ignorant, slow, rustic. To counter this, the Bodmin group admitted to diluting their regional speech and adopting a form of Received Pronunciation. 'Cutting up' they call it: 'We used to

8

The snap and crackle of Cornish is provided in no small measure by what in standard English pronunciation is the long 'eye' sound which here opens out to more like long 'aa' – 'skive' (to truant) is 'skaav', 'while' is 'waal' and 'lie down' something like 'laa daouwn'. Also shifting positions are the sounds 'ee' and 'ay', so if a Cornishman threw a ball, he would ' 'aive et at 'ee' – heave it at you.

And that brings me to 'theeing' and 'thouing'. In Yorkshire, this is still a fairly commonplace old form of 'you' ('tha naas' – you know). In Cornwall too they use it, but in West Country style – so Humphrey Bogart's famous 'Here's looking at you' comes out ' 'Ere's lookn at 'ee'. There's a real feeling of going back in time with features like this, as with the way 'it was' is here very frequently shortened to 'twas' – 'twoddn' in the negative. Another shortening, involving the dialectal form of the verb to be, is also fairly common: 'we *am*' shortens to 'we'm'; similarly 'they' turns up – as it does from Bristol right across much of the south-west – in the 'wrong' place, so 'go to they' is often heard instead of 'go to *them*'. It all helps give classic Cornish its patina of deeply rural antiquity.

say, "Aw he's 'cutt'n' up" – try'n' t'be a bi' bigg'r'n I be, yuh know, bi' posher like! – "Ark! Muther'z cutt'n' up!"' But it's not just a matter of mutual comprehension – linguistic variation here is also a courtesy; says another: 'They speak posh; you caan't speak rough, can 'ee?'

But it's not long before mutual suspicion of how local and visitor each is being thought of by the other surfaces, led by one particularly eloquent member of the group:

'Becuz 'ey 'ear us wiv our accen' they fink we've go' nothin' between our earrs, like. Jus' becoz they'm come from a posh arear, they think they'm better edjicated and they kinda wanna talk dauwn to us. They say, "What a different language!" – well I say, "We'm liv'n on the moors!" I think they thinks we're a bi' thick somtaams, bu' when they muyve off [move off], we think they'm a bit thick! I'ss a bit loik two cans a pain'. Ah min if yuh keep 'em sep'rut you keep 'em the same colourr, but if you starrt mix'n one wiv anuvver, you'm gonna be slowly dahluyted [diluted] into a completely diff'rent colour. And tha'ss wha'ss 'app'nin' to arr language, like.'

9

Note the repeated classic Cornish syntactical forms 'they'm', 'you'm' and 'we'm' for 'they are', 'you are' and 'we are', and the complex 'oo' sound that has elements of 'a', 'u' and 'y' in it: 'muyve' for 'move' and 'dahluyted', 'diluted'. But also in this passage there are several instances of what linguists call 'TH-fronting', for instance in 'wiν anuννer [with another]', where the 'th' becomes a 'v' sound, the lower lip pressed to the edge of the upper teeth. It's a feature especially of south-eastern and vernacular London speech that's now found across the country, particularly among younger people.

The opportunity to share the pleasure of words recalled, of times remembered, brings from this farming group on Bodmin Moor memories of shared excitement and hilarity. As the recollections come into sharper focus, so does the dialect. The statutory enquiry from the survey about local synonyms for 'trousers' elicits a story of a wedding where new trousers ('bought up Liskeard') were 'six inches too short'. These were the days when trousers were still 'breeches' and 'leggin's' or 'Yorks' ('Uncle Jim wore Yorks'). As for the women, one of the group affirmed proudly that she never wore trousers:

'Ah woul'n' be foun' dead in 'um. Ah always wore a skurrt. An' I
always wear a pinnay [pinafore]. Ah'm neverr withou' mah pinnay.
[After all, with trousers] you don' know if 'tis a man or a woman then,
do 'ee?'

This group were the broadest interviewed in the new survey, and the oldest. They are a close-knit older group who'd never moved far from their farming community in some of the wildest parts of the county. Classic elements of Cornish dialect come naturally to these men and women – 'cheel' for baby, to which one adds the colourful 'li' 'le tacker', a term found also in Devon dialect and extensively in Australia, while for them a 'trendy person in cheap jewellery' was 'all peint 'n' powderr, ennit?'

Although their accent was very broad, the syntactic structures were typical of old Cornish and you could sympathize with the visitor who failed to understand entirely what was being said, in fact the range of regional lexical items was relatively small. A parallel group, younger, more socially mobile, from Mawla Methodist Church just north of Redruth, were equally at home with 'wisht' for unwell and offered the classic Cornish expression 'wisht as a winnard' to back it up (though they couldn't say what a winnard was – it is a bird, a redwing, captured on the map near St Columb Major in the place-name Winnard's Perch).

'Wisht as a winnard' is still clearly part of a quite widespread older person's lexicon as it turns up near St Austell in the speech of Les Lean and his friends as recorded in 2000 by Melvyn Bragg. Another bird simile still with a certain currency was offered to the new survey by another church group, from St Feock, when asked for a synonym for annoyed: 'mazed' (pronounced with a long open first vowel 'mehzd') and 'maze' were for these people familiar Cornish words (and were again cited by Les Lean in 2000 and by the Mawla group in 2004), but here found also in the expression 'mazed as a curlew' – 'mehzd uhza kurrloo'.

To hit hard for the Bodmin farmers was to 'scat'. It also meant you had no money – 'gone scat' means 'bankrupt' – and if somebody were 'scatty like' they would be 'not quite the full pound' (not very bright). In Mawla, 'scat' turned up again, though it had a number of additional derogatory senses: local rivalry meant that Chasewater people were 'scat-ups' (an indelicate reference to diarrhoea: ''E's go' the scats') and to be lagging 'one scat behind'.

The Mawla group was a mix of the fairly broad local voice and the adoptive incomer. So the real local, Brian, regularly came up with the greatest number of native Cornish terms: 'clicky-'anded' for left-handed. The same word was also chorused as one by the Bodmin Moor group and by the St Feock team, one of whom added:

'I mean I used to bunch flowers an' I can 'ear my dad sayin' you're clicky-'anded, maid, you are! And I'd say, "Well, how?" And 'e'd say "Cos you're doing it in your left 'and. You should be doin' it in your right 'and." Holdin' the flowers in my left instead of my right.'

Likewise 'maid' (as here) used to address a young woman is still widespread today, though always as an older, quainter usage. Back in 2000, Les Lean remembered, 'I always call my sisters maid now; I always refer to maid. Yeah, I always say to 'em: "all right, maid?"' And when Les's niece started to howl, it never 'cried': 'My sister used to have a daughter that was crying a lot and she'd say, "If you don't stop cryin' for nothing, I'll give you something to squall for."' 'Squall' – real Cornish dialect meaning 'to cry'.

In slightly less tearful vein, 'teasy' (pronounced with a soft 's') is known and used across Cornwall amongst the middle-aged and elderly to mean moody. Les was formerly a 'kettle boy' in the china clay industry and had as an early duty to prepare the other men's pasties for their crib, or snack: 'Sometimes if I didn't get 'em hot or get 'em ready and the fire weren't going right they didn't like it very much, and they'd get teasy on me, teasy.' Brian from Mawla offered yet another animal simile here: 'teasy's nadder [teasy as an adder]', bad-tempered:

> 'I say "teasy 's nadder" because adder'll bite you ev'n na goo' moo'
> [even in a good mood], won' un? If you step on 'e, 'e'll bite you.'

The 2005 survey also interviewed three young stylists from Creations Hair Salon in Truro, whose rich and articulate opinions you'll find elsewhere in this chapter (see the 'Snapshot' section). They are modern Cornish women with a much wider range of vocabulary who broadly have rejected the older dialect in favour of a contemporary vernacular. Yet they too readily came up with 'teasy' – 'she's a bi' teasy . . .' – though it was more likely to be their mother who asked, 'Whass ma' 'er with you, why're you teasy?'

But when one of the trio offered 'henting' for pouring rain (it's 'henting down' – a standard Cornish dialect term), there was complete surprise amongst the hairdressers, particularly from the incomer who'd moved to Truro from Yorkshire: 'You not heard of that before? Gaw, henting down, that's what I'd say! It's tha' orrible misty rain . . . soaks you through.' Using old Cornishisms was clearly not the way they preferred to speak.

Nor I guess would they be comfortable with such old-fashioned yet still widely heard terms as 'handsome' (pronounced ''ansum') meaning not simply 'good-looking' but more broadly 'good' and often heard as an affectionate term of address – Brian from Mawla talked about 'my 'ansum'. Likewise, the use of 'some' to mean 'very' ('some poorly' was quoted by the St Feock's group) is still widespread. 'Some handsome' is still regular usage amongst older Cornish.

'Dreckly', however, the Creations trio knew all about. 'Dreckly' is one of those Cornish terms that learners of foreign languages refer to as 'false friends'. It doesn't mean what it appears to, i.e. 'directly' or 'immediately':

'It means "later" – my dad says it. Say yuh said to me, "You comin' over in a minute?"; I'd say, "I'll be over there dreckly"; which could mean in the next hour or two, or "I'll be down in a bit". It's a real Cornish thing.'

So much so that it became a bumper sticker that the hairdressers had noticed round the streets of Truro: CORNISH PEOPLE DO IT DRECKLY ... Familiar though it is, it still catches incomers out, as the one outsider from Mawla admitted:

'I asked if somebody would do something and they said they'd do it "dreckly". I stood patiently waiting and waiting and they never arrived and then I was told that "dreckly" meant "sometime later when I've finished what I'm doing" ...'

Repeated in these survey interviews right across the country is the phenomenon of the loosened tongue, and our Cornish sample is no different. So as the conversation flows, so does the richer, less standard vocabulary. At Mawla it was a discussion about what they would call a 'stream' that turned into a gusher:

'We allus used to call it a "brook" when we was kids. "Brook" be a "small stream" – we used to go down there fishing for whatever – an' we used to drink it when we were kids. And now you know what goes down there, there's no way I'll stick my finger in it ... ! [It's allegedly polluted.] Different to an "adit"; an adit comes down from a cave. My grandparents used to live from the water they got from an adit and that flowed into the brook but that was very clean. I remember goin' down Cambrose with dad on a Sunday night with a bath, fill'un up from the adit, takin' i' 'ome for mum to do the washin' on Monday. I dunno if that was exactly an adit; I think they used to call it a chute. It is a spring, like, innit? Come out of the rocks ...'

'Adit' is a very old word associated with the watercourses that Richard Carew detailed so precisely when describing Cornish tin-mining:

They call it the bringing of an Addit, or Audit, when they begin to trench without, and carrie the same thorow the ground to the Tynworke, somewhat deeper then the water doth lie, thereby to giue it passage away.

13

Derived from the Latin *aditus*, access, it's a common term in mining today meaning a horizontal shaft, and became widely known in Cornwall through the tin industry, where adits were used both for extracting ore and for drainage.

'Chute' on the other hand is a very particular Cornish usage quoted again amongst the Bodmin group, along with another mining word, a 'leat', an artificial channel for water (and not far removed from those launders I quoted earlier). But at Mawla, there was no stopping the reminiscences – and the local terminology – now:

> 'That water was pure, lovely. Down Rail Bottoms, there was a chute there that came out the wall, we used to go down there "cricking", you know picking up sticks for the fire, twigs off the tree for the fire. We used to take a cup with us an' 'ave a drink from the chute on the way up.'

Les Lean, the ex-clay worker from near St Austell unsurprisingly could quote a range of industrial terms that had passed into wider Cornish usage, like a 'dubber', a sort of pick for breaking down the clay, and a 'buttonhole launder': 'a channel of wood down the side of a tank containing clay,' he explained. The men would 'bal' a nail, rather than hammer it in, and if a job was well executed it was a 'fitty job': '. . . a good job, real fitty job'.

But many of Les's early years were spent close to the land, living in a railway carriage, close to the moors:

> 'And up in the top, you know what you call bracken, we call vuhrns [verns]. They always refer to vuhrns. They used to be out cuttin' vuhrns for their bed and for the pigs, you know – straw – vuhrns for the bed at night.'

Fields would be marked with the heaps of soil that indicate the burrowing of 'wants' or moles, and for Les, the moor too has always been a source of wild fruit:

> 'Last week I went up top the downs where I used to live and we picked some "urts". And I went home and had a urt tart; what you find up on the downs.'

'Urts' are bilberries to older Cornish folk.

Language particularities have a curious way of engraving themselves on the mind, and one of the features of the contemporary survey has been the many stories of usage that struck the hearer as unusual, unfamiliar and, frankly, odd – once heard, never forgotten and to be swapped with relish amongst friends, as here, in Mawla:

'Down here, when you bring the washing in you "pick" it in (not "bring" it in). I wondered for a minute what they meant by pick it in . . .'

To which a nurse in the group, who meets all sorts in Casualty, responds with a guffaw:

' 'e was a patient and he was getting a bit wound up an' I 'eard somebody say, " 'E's wound up like a Torpoint chicken" and I'd never heard of that one before. She said, "I don't know what's the matter with 'im, 'e's wound up like a Torpoint chicken" . . .'

At St Feock Methodist Church, the tangy local expression that tumbled out from family memory when asked for a synonym for hot stemmed from that other great Cornish working occupation, on the sea:

'My dad used to say " 'tis all for eatin' pilchards"; it meant it's gonna be hot and the pilchards were gonna come in: good for fishin'. Fishermen'd go out down Newlyn an' all and catch the pilchards – don't get pilchards these days – an' I suppose they came in when it was hot . . .'

As fewer people today enjoy Cornish pilchards, once hymned in the pages of Richard Carew's *Survey*, so too the expressions and words associated with them dwindle. But read the Cornish Snapshot that follows, and you'll find that the regional linguistic trail – like a vein of silvery Cornish tin – doesn't simply peter out, it merely switches direction . . .

A Cornish Snapshot: Delerios and Disbehavin'

Barely twenty-five miles as the crow flies separate the town of Truro from Bodmin Moor, yet the conversation of two gatherings of Cornish men and women surveyed in late 2004 for the Voices project reveals a linguistic gulf that might just as well be 250 miles wide. In part it's a question of generations – the group gathered on Bodmin Moor are old enough to be the grandparents of the three young stylists from Creations hair salon in Truro. Yet the differences run far deeper than age.

The first thing to strike the listener is accent. Not all of the actual words the moor-dwellers Barbara, Ken, Cyril, Clive and Ruby use are old and traditional – asked how they'd say they were cold, they use words that are completely standard. The pronunciation though renders them intensely local: ' 'Tis cawld, freezin' ennit?', ' 'Tis better [bitter] . . .' Similarly, their term for to play truant (a feature that frequently marks out one region from another) is in fact found right across the land. But the way these people say it, it's almost new-minted: the intonation takes on a sing-song modulation mid-word and 'skive' lengthens and darkens its vowel to become 'skaiuv'.

In Truro, meanwhile, Shareen and Rachel won't have any of it:

'I do like the Cornish accent but my dad's Cornish accent is absolutely hideous. I think it's horrible. I thin' he talks qui' common. He swears a lo' an' e's go' a very very broad Cornish accent. I don't like i'. But then Rachel's parents are Cornish and I think they speak grea'. I love their accents. But my dad's grates on me.'

Setting aside familial feelings, the acceptance of older Cornish speech is still somewhat grudging, and the accents that these three women share barely have a trace of the county about them. They all speak the same, roughly standard, casual English, a sound found widely across Britain, studded with glottal stops yet not markedly 'Estuary' – there's no real London twang about their talk. There's little in fact to point to where they come from at all – one of the three is actually an incomer, from Yorkshire. So when asked for a vernacular synonym for 'hot' Emma comes up with 'Maftin'; really ho' 'n' swea'y, but my mum's broad

Yorkshire . . .' she adds by way of explanation. And indeed 'mafting' is still widely reported from that county.

For this group two words dominate – and they're words that turn up in the speech of younger people in many parts of the country, from the south-east of England to the north-west. And they both mean roughly the same; they are 'minging' and 'hanging'. They are both derogatory or negative terms meaning approximately 'bad' – bad-looking, badly drunk, feeling bad, etc. So the Truro hairdressers, when asked what they say when they're not feeling well, offer:

' "Rough – rough as rats [according to the Yorkshire-born Emma]".
Got that from down 'ere. And "hangin' ", "mingin' ": if I was drunk, I was hangin' last night . . . Or she looks hangin' – don't look attractive. So mingin' an' hangin' are the same thing, really.'

More often the second of these is pronounced 'angin', though not by this group: a bunch of youngsters from Manchester became very indignant that in their usage the word definitely had no initial 'h': 'NOT hangin', 'angin'!'

Perhaps unsurprisingly amongst this Truro trio of enthusiastic clubbers, for whom sizing up the relative attractiveness of people they meet is routine, the range of words for 'ugly' was extensive, most of them found nationally: 'skank', 'rank', 'rough', 'dobra', 'mingin'' and 'muntin''. This last was a new one to the Yorkshire woman: 'When I first heard "she looks muntin' " I was like: "What the hell does that mean?" ' To which her friend responds, 'But our "muntin' " is like you say "maftin' ".' And while she's on unfamiliar terms, she throws in ' "dross" and "fusty" which to us don't mean anythin' '.

'Mong', 'monger', 'moose' are how they'd describe a guy whom they didn't find attractive, though 'They 'ave to be reely reely unattractive to say "mingin' " or "muntin' " – they'd 'ave to be pre' 'y rank.' Fine distinctions here, and when pressed, Rachel, Shareen and Emma admitted they even rated men on a scale of 1 to 3: 'Look at that 3 at the bar . . . !'

These three women offer a perfect example of the modern need for adaptability in language. No longer happy to use one register at home and another – perhaps more formal – at work, they have a whole portfolio of styles and variants. Slang laced with a few regionalisms, a 'telephone voice' they use for official communication with strangers and a professional vernacular in the confines of the salon. And they are finely attuned to which variant belongs where:

> 'I speak totally differently depending on who I'm talking to.'
> 'Yeah, like now you sound really posh, you've got your "hairdresser's voice" on now . . . like a "telephone voice".'
> 'I talk differently to my parents or get a whack round the chops, a backhander. My mum: it's like talking to your teachers at school. They don't understand the lingo. If you speak slang to my mum, it's like, "What the hell does that mean?" Like if I said, "I got mingin' lass night." Like, "You what? Come again?" She doesn't understan' i'. Whereas my dad's a bi' more laid-back so he'd jus' be, like, "Yeah, whatever".'
> 'If you're with a client you gotta think what you're sayin'. [In the salon] it's easy to slip up as well an' say some random words. I could say "I go' pissed righ' up this weekend", but would this other client mind hearin'?'

Shareen, Rachel and Emma take great delight in language – they invent code terms when they want to keep a surprise party event secret and love to play with words as a normal part of conversation. Listen, for example, to the way they talk about money – and the lack of it – 'skint':

> 'Skin' as you like – I'm skin' as you li' this wee'. [Or] I've go' a full-on lack of "delerios" this week . . . "delerio-shortage" this week.'

'Delerios', pronounced a little like 'delirious' but with a longer second syllable ('dill-*ear*-ee-ohs'), are, it seems, a form of imaginary currency. And if you're rich, you're:

> 'loaded, minted, plenty of delerios, rollin' in i', rakin' i' in. [Describing a rich-looking guy:] I be' 'e's go' plen'y of delerios [I bet he's got plenty . . .]. Be' 'e's min'ed. Be' 'e's go' a few shee's [sheets], like. I ge' tha' off my dad. If some'ing wuz a hundred pounds, even though notes are £5, £10 and £20, he'd say "Gawd, there's a hundred sheets." My brother uses that: "Gaw, that's like a hundred delerios for tha'." Sheets is another one, definitely.'

Back on Bodmin Moor with Barbara, Ken, Cyril, Clive and Ruby, not so very different memories of family discussions and punishments elicit a

similar warm glow of nostalgia. Yet in the smiling recollection of hard-
ships shared, the brutality of corporal punishment meted out for misbe-
having – or as these old country people all regularly call it, 'disbe'avin''
– seems to belong (together with the old Cornish pronunciations) to
another era entirely, not simply fifty years ago.

Listen, too, for how in these strong regional accents the ringing 'rr'
is joined by the 't' that becomes a 'd' sound before another vowel
('forrgedd et'); also notice how 'it' and 'stick' sound more like 'et' and
'steck' and syllables run into one another: 'twuddn' 'ard' – 'it wasn't
hard':

> 'If we disbe'eihv [misbehave] duyrin' the wik [during the week] father
> wud neverr coll [call] us to attention. But we'd 'ave the punishmen' in
> the baath, in the tin baath, Sadurrdeh naat [in the bath, Saturday
> night] frum mutherr: mutherr wud give us the steck [stick] – she
> wunnt forrgedd et [wouldn't forget it]. Twuddn' 'arrd. Bu' then yiu
> kniuw yiu woz in trouble Sadurrdeh naat if yiu disbe'eihvd. Cos
> faather wunnt say nuthn to uz. "Naouw, boiyz!" [Now, boys!] – thass
> all faather wud seyh. But mutherr wunnt furrget. No. [She'd use] a li'l
> ol' stick orr summun [a little old stick or something], orr slap with 'er
> 'an', when we ge' ou' the baath.'

Once started, the stories gush like a Cornish stream:

> 'Well Tom mah bruthrn me, in Poust Awfess [= when Tom my brother
> and me were in the Post Office], there wuz a li'l crook [= hook] in the
> ceilun an' there wuz a li'l thin steck therre, an' ef tha' wun a come
> douwn [and if that one had come down], we kniuw we wuz gunna 'ev
> i' on ar 'aendz [we were going to have it on our hands], yeah . . . We
> olwiz [always] kniuw ef we disbe'eihvd.'

'You can tell the difference with the young Cornish to old Cornish,
definitely,' observe the Truro hairdressing trio. 'Old Cornish is really,
really broad.' ('A bit farmerish, a bit common', according to the one
who's originally from Yorkshire.) 'But young Cornish – it's still an
accent.' But here's the rub: they acknowledge that many people seem
routinely to associate a broad accent with being less acute, and this
prejudicial view leads them to some somewhat startling conclusions:

'the only people who sound educated are posh nobs who speak very upper-class and proper English; that sounds educated. You wouldn't expect to hear somebody who is dumb-as-you-like speaking very proper; you wouldn't expect it. You would expect somebody who is really unintelligent to speak a bit more common. And I think the Cornish accent is singled out a bit in that respect.'

In contradistinction, the final word in this chapter goes to a champion of Cornwall and all things Cornish, Bert Biscoe, who's also from Truro:

'Many of the young and not so young people now feel very self-conscious about themselves as the result of these pressures, and I think that self-consciousness has contributed to a kind of economic malaise. But without the Cornish there wouldn't have been much of an Industrial Revolution and in those days we were the cock of the walk. So I think that we need to get ourselves back into the mind set where we value ourselves for what we are and for our values, for the way we want to live.'

A Cornish Glossary

adit a mining term for a horizontal shaft opening out on to a hillside or valley floor often used for drainage. First recorded by Carew in his *Survey*. From Latin *aditus*, access

bal a tin-mine, derived from the Cornish word *bal*, a group of tin-workings. Also, to hit (e.g. 'to bal a nail'). From a generally obsolete meaning of 'ball', to strike or thump

bal-maidens (in a tin-mine) women working at the surface

caggled covered with filth, oil

cheel a baby

clicky-handed, clicky left-handed, hence 'clumsy'

clunk to swallow (with difficulty). From Scandinavian *klunk, klunka*, to gulp

crib a (miner's) snack, (packed) lunch; from Cornish *cribbon, crevan*, a dry hard crust (east Cornwall)

croust, crowst a (miner's) snack. From French *croûte*, crust (west Cornwall)

dreckly in a while ('directly')

eckemoule a tomtit (also **hickeymore, heckmoyle, eckymollar**)

emmet an ant (by association, tourists). From Old English *aemete*

fitty good, suitable, correct. A corruption of 'featous', 'featy'. From Middle English *fetys*, handsome, well-formed

forthy rude, impudent, forward. From 'forth' (forward) but in the sense of 'outspoken'. First noted in the sixteenth century

grammersow a woodlouse, millipede

(h)andsome, 'ansum fine, excellent, beautiful. **Me 'ansum** is a term of affection or greeting

(h)entin' down pouring with rain; perhaps from 'hent', to strike, hit

knack to cease production (e.g. 'the bal's knacked', the mine's closed). Perhaps from *knack*, to deal blows

lampered exhausted

launder originally a mining term meaning a trough for carrying water, frequently to the buckets of a water-wheel. By association, 'domestic guttering'

leat a mining term meaning (like 'launder') an open watercourse, noted in texts from the late sixteenth century. From Old English *waeter gelaet*, water-conduit

lerrup, larrup, lerrups a blow; to hit hard, beat, thrash. Found in dialect in East Anglia and south-west England from the early nineteenth century

maid a girl, daughter. A form of direct address: 'Maid . . .'

man-engine a mining term for the machine which lowered miners into deep shafts

manshons, manshuns small loaves

maze(d) mad, annoyed, in a temper. To 'maze' meant to 'put out of one's wits' and dates back to medieval times; perhaps from Old English *masian*

meesy-y-mazy confused, puzzled

nuddick the nape (of the neck). Also found as **nuddock** and **niddick**. An old south-west England dialect word

oggy a pasty, pie; **tiddy oggy** potato pie or pasty

rigged up in a state of excitement. Perhaps from 'rig' meaning 'to play the wanton' recorded in Elizabethan times

scat break, smash, knock. To 'go scat' means to go bankrupt. Recorded in south-west English dialect in 1837, meaning 'to break in pieces'

some very (e.g. 'some handsome')

spence a cupboard (e.g. under the stairs). The word is found in the works of Chaucer (1340–1400); from Old French *despense*

squall cry (of a baby etc.), to scream loudly. Imitative of the sound of a cry

stagged overworked

stream the clome do the washing up. 'Clome' is crockery, and derives from Old English *clám*, mud, and by extension 'potter's clay' and so 'earthenware'

swailing burning (e.g. gorse) on moorland. An old word, with roots in Anglo-Saxon

tacker a (lively) child

teasy annoyed, irritable. Noted as a dialect word from the mid nineteenth century ('taisy'); from Old English *taesan*, to tear to pieces

trig support, prop up (e.g. 'trig up the launders'); to make firm, secure. Recorded from the late sixteenth century

urts whortleberries, whorts. A south-western dialectal form of 'hurt', hurt-leberry. Sometimes spelled 'eerts'

verns bracken, fern. From Old English *fearn*. South-western English pronunciation replaces 'f' with 'v'

vuzz furse

want a mole. The word exists in many forms in regional and old English

want-hill a mole-hill

wap moody (as in 'got the wap')

wayzgoose a scarecrow

wheal a tin-mine. Cornish word *huel*, a mine, first recorded in the 1830s

winnard a redwing (e.g. 'wisht as a winnard'). Ultimately related to the German *Vogel*, bird

wisht sickly, thin, wan, sad. The origins of the word are obscure

2 : THE WEST OF ENGLAND

Language in a Landscape: Wess Vinglun

It was the Bristol-born writer Derek Robinson who coined the phrase 'Wess Vinglun' to describe that portion of the United Kingdom stretching from Hampshire and Wiltshire in the east, along the M4 corridor, spreading slightly north to encompass Gloucestershire but above all heading south and west through Somerset, Dorset, Devon and Cornwall. 'Wess Vinglun' is how Bristolians refer to this area, and though Devonians will shout, 'What about Plymouth?' and Somerset folk will cheer for Taunton, it's Bristol that's the south-west's unofficial capital. It's the biggest urban area in the region and stands like a sentinel on the M4 and the M5 for travellers heading to the holiday honeypots of the coasts and the moors from all points east and north.

In this chapter I'll be looking at what makes the speech of this area both special, individual and internally richly varied, taking in the urban drawl of Bedminster in Bristol but concentrating on the countryside, from Hardy's Wessex to the cracking 'vuzz-bushes' celebrated in Dartmoor talk; Cornwall has its own Celtic language complexity and its own section in this book.

One feature that dominates the landscape both topographically and linguistically is the countryside: green fields, winding roads and villages. In spite of plenty of urban busy-ness besides Bristol's – from the now defunct heavy industry of railway Swindon in the east to naval Devonport in Plymouth to the west – this is overwhelmingly a rural area; Somerset had a coalfield, too, though you'd hardly know it now. And it's a rural sound, dominated by the unmistakable west of England 'r' that predominates. 'Mummerset' and 'Loamshire' are just two of the not particularly attractive names for the equally not particularly convincing attempts by second-rate actors to impersonate the sound of the south-west. All oo's and arr's.

'People can be very insultin' abou' our accen',' protested a pair of Plymouth women to the Voices interviewer recently, 'like carrot crunchers, sort of thing. We're claessd as thick: "Have you got a bit of straw in your mouth"; it's very insultin'.' And 78-year-old Joan went further: 'I could hit 'em between the eyes [when they go] "Oo arr, mi dearr". It dun saound righ' at oll.'

And it isn't. Yet growing up in Bristol, I recall that my schoolmates – most of them from city homes – themselves indulged in a very similar sort of simple-minded discrimination. A young lad in my class was a farmer's son from north Somerset who had a farm accent and (these were the days of the radio soap's patriarch *Dan* Archer) had the misfortune to be called Daniel. He was persecuted mercilessly till the teachers put a stop to it for what was perceived as his country boy tones. It's a quality that the Bristolian Derek Robinson has remarked upon, laughingly ascribing it to the lack of bracing climate in the south-west: all those warm, wet westerlies producing a lazy and uninvigorating, sluggish sort of speech, slow and easy-going.

Setting aside any environmental effects, many of the characteristics of the speech of the bottom left-hand corner of England are as old as the villages that populate it; they date back to the Anglo-Saxon conquest – both the words themselves and the sounds with which they are produced. There is in Devon and Somerset a little influence from the Celtic west, but it seems that the River Parrett in Somerset was the boundary to that influence, felt most strongly of course in the once monolingual Cornish-speaking areas of the peninsula (see Chapter 1, 'Language in a Landscape: Cream of Cornish'). As so often, you can take your cue from the map: look at Widecombe in the Moor, the famous Dartmoor village celebrated in the old song about Bill Brewer, Jan Stewer, Peter Gurney, Peter Davey, Dan'l Whiddon, Harry Hawke and Uncle Tom Cobbleigh and all, 'Widdecome Fair'. Today's tourist trap village has an ancient Anglo-Saxon pedigree, the name meaning 'willow-valley' – *withig-cumb* in Old English – and with its modern form already very much in place by 1461, when it is recorded as 'Wydecomb yn the More'.

Other places with equally antique names reveal the mixed parentage of their earliest settlers, so to take a handful at random, Tavistock, not far from where the Voices team made some of their Devon recordings for the latest survey, has elements of Old (Roman era) British (Tavy – a river name, also in Petertavy and Marytavy) and Old English: a *stoc* was a place, a farm or even a monastery. It comes up in place-names right across these southern counties in a number of formations: *Stog*umber, *Stog*ursey and Kew*stoke* in Somerset, *Stock*wood in Dorset and *Stock*leigh English in Devon (the 'English', incidentally, comes from one Gilbertus Anglicus who held the village in the thirteenth century).

From Sherborne in Dorset (Old English, bright stream) to Stroud (marshy land overgrown with brushwood) in Gloucestershire, the deep roots of the culture in the south-west of England are plain to see on every road atlas to this day. To listen to the *sound* of true West Country speech is another journey through time. It's a trail that spans at least six centuries, as the dialects here still preserve some of the known pronunciations of Middle English (the language Geoffrey Chaucer used for his *Canterbury Tales* in the 1380s and that preceded what's called 'Modern English').

You can trace this path using just one characteristic linguistic feature, such as the frequently quoted hardening (or 'voicing') of unvoiced consonants like 'f' and 's', and 'th' and 'sh'. Thus in medieval England 'varmer' and 'voal' would have been not just *regional* pronunciations of 'farmer' and 'foal' but the standard way in which those words (despite being written with an 'f') would have been said. Likewise 'see' would generally have been pronounced as 'zee' and 'thatch' with a voiced sound as in today's 'that'. Abundant evidence in texts clearly shows that what is now considered a regional variation was the Middle English norm.

But in medieval England the myriad local vernaculars were under threat from the written standard emanating from the capital, and by the time we get to the *Letters* composed in the mid fifteenth century by John Shillingford, Mayor of Exeter in Devon, the often colourful and vivid texts show very little sign of having been written by a local man:

> Worthy siris, ryght feyne ffrendis and ffelows, y grete yow well alle, doyng yow to understonde that on Wendisday next after Corporis Christi day, as ye knowe right well, after vj atte clokke yn the mornyng y rode oute of Exeter to London warde; the Saterdey next

ther after at vij atte clokke by the mornyng y came to London, and so
to Westminster, and ther mette with my lord Chaunceller . . .
(Shillingford to his Fellows, 24 May 1448)

On the page, at least, the London form of English had prevailed.

Yet what people actually *said* in Exeter was clearly still rich in accent
and local vocabulary. Because very shortly after Shillingford was penning
this letter to his colleagues, the High Master of St Paul's School in
London, Alexander Gil, was having a right old go at the accent of the
very Devon whose capital Shillingford administered, complaining about
the pronunciation of 'sit' as 'zit' and 'thirteen' as 'throttin'. He didn't care
too much either for the local words he'd come across, such as 'vang', to
take or accept, and 'sax' for knife.

A further 150 years on, when Shakespeare's Edgar in *King Lear* adopts
a West Country accent, once again it's those famous voiced 'f's and 's's
that he chooses to feature, as well as another characteristic that we tend
not to hear today but which was around for many centuries, the aspiration
of the letter 'i' at the beginning of words, such as 'I'll':

Good gentleman, go your gait, and let poor volk pass. And 'chud ha'
bin zwagger'd out of my life, 'twould not ha' bin zo long as 'tis by a
vortnight. Nay, come not near th'old man; keep out, che vor' ye, or
ise try whither your costard or my ballow be the harder. Chill be plain
with you.

Almost exactly 150 years after the first performance of *Lear*, Samuel
Johnson unveiled his *Dictionary* and the age of the great lexicographers
was upon us. Now there was considerable enthusiasm for standardization
and 'correct pronunciation' led by the scholar (and father of the playwright Richard) Thomas Sheridan. But it fell to another scholar, John
Walker, formally to set down in his *Pronouncing Dictionary* of 1791 those
same regionalisms:

There is scarcely any part of England, remote from the capital, where a
different system of pronunciation does not prevail . . . In
Somersetshire they pronounce many of the flat instead of the sharp;
thus for *Somersetshire* they say *Zomerzetzhire*; for *father*, *vather*, for
think, TH*ink* and for *sure*, *zhure*

Voices was recording exactly these same regional sounds 203 years later, in the age of the iPod and the internet: 'There wuz a varmerr . . .', 'This old lady 'ad a varm . . .'. They certainly weren't ubiquitous and tended to be limited to remotest Devon and amongst the older informants, but the pronunciation was strongly and robustly alive. There was a sense, though, that perhaps you had to look a bit harder for it now than twenty years ago, when Stanley Ellis taped this man for the BBC talking about an old farm labourer he remembered. Don Hill, a hedger, had really broad talk, with a stony, angular accent typical of his native north Devon, merrily twisting vowels and hardening up a veritable chorus of those unvoiced consonants – 'k' in 'hayma*k*ing', 'f' in '*f*or' and 'be*f*ore', 'p' in 'peo*p*le', 't' in 'quar*t*er', 'go*t* *t*o' and 'be*tt*er' and 'th' in '*th*en':

I bin ayemeggin vorr peoble bivor naouyw, an' 'bout quarrder ti vor, ee'd tekk out is watch an ee'd say, 'Woll us goddy beddarr well gwaan in den' . . .

['I've been haymaking for people before now, and about a quarter to four, he'd take out his watch and he'd say "well we [got to] better well go on in then'.]

North of the river Avon in south Gloucestershire, an even more marked form of voicing was captured by the Survey of English Dialects fifty years ago: an old man, when asked the time, offered 'a'pass *dr*ee [half past three]'. In his speech, alongside more widely found south-western characteristics, the 'thr' cluster of sounds hardened regularly to a very clearly sounded 'drr'; he also referred to '*dr*rippunce 'aeip'ny [*thr*eepence ha'penny]'. I think you'd be hard pushed to find an extreme form like this one nowadays.

In Dorset, closer to London still, the features of this sort of old, deeply rural speech are tending to fade markedly too. Thomas Hardy had a wonderful ear for the talk 130 years ago of what he called Wessex – his name for that county – and throughout his novels captured the authentic sound of West Country conversation. In this short section of dialogue (describing a drowned man) taken from *Under the Greenwood Tree*, his second novel, published in 1872, notice (in addition to voiced 'voot' for 'foot') the use of 'en' where standard English would use 'him'. It's another classic feature of this region's rural talk and one Voices was still capturing very recently:

'Men looked at en; women looked at en; children looked at en; nobody knowed en. He was covered wi' a sheet; but I catched sight of his voot, just showing out as they carried en along.'

Hardy's time was also the moment when enthusiasm for recording dialect became widespread – Joseph Wright's *English Dialect Dictionary* was only thirty years away – and, as I show elsewhere in this book, Victorian collectors in quite large numbers were noting down regionalisms right across Britain: Devon dialect even became a subject of hot debate in the *Pall Mall Gazette*'s letters page in January 1870, to which an unnamed 'Devonshire Man' wrote:

> I have repeatedly heard 'leery' for empty, 'drang' for press, 'fang' for take, 'rin' for run, 'to' (zu) for at, &c. &c. Even the personal pronouns 'er' and 'ihn' (for he and him) are still in much common use among the peasantry as to have given rise to the Cockney joke that in Devonshire they call everything *her* except a tomcat . . .

Notice that 'fang', meaning to take, had thus survived in Devon dialect for 400 years since Alexander Gil noted it down (he had it as 'vang') and I suspect that the writer's 'ihn' is identical to Hardy's 'en'. Leaping forwards to today, at Buckland in the Moor on Dartmoor we found people who still use 'leery' to mean empty and, by extension, hungry (not 'fearful' as in general usage): 'Go up [the hill for lunch] leery; feelin' a bit leery . . .' Find the appropriate speakers in these parts and there's a real sense of time standing still.

Right across the region, the other most sharply focused historical feature is rhoticity, that tolling 'r' sound. This is a real piece of English linguistic bedrock, jutting up out of the speech of the twenty-first century like a Dartmoor tor. Stanley Ellis of the Survey of English Dialects sketched its history when he wrote about the speech of the region for the BBC twenty years ago:

> That 'r' sound is believed to be the original Saxon 'r'. Certainly 'r' was sounded in English in the Middle Ages in words like 'tu*r*n' and 'fa*r*m' and 'ho*r*se': the fact that we have it in the spelling confirms that. The 'r' was there in standard English pronunciation at least up to the time of the first emigrations to the American colonies and when later it

disappeared in standard English speech it continued to be used by
Americans and Devon and western men . . .

The examples are everywhere across the south of England, town and
country, from Bristol to Wiltshire to Hampshire to Cornwall, and north-
wards into Oxfordshire and Gloucestershire: the Survey of English Dialects
recorded this old man in Latteridge (south Gloucestershire) in 1956 sounding his 'r's merrily: 'somwurr [somewhere]' and 'Werrs bin do then?
[Where's [you] been to then?]'; in fact, if you don't sound your 'r's, you're
still often the exception. By way of illustration of the persistence of this
sound, here are three short extracts from interviews taken across the last
fifty years, all talking about that other typical West Country feature, cider.

At the little west Somerset village of Stogumber in the valley between
the Quantock and Brendon hills, Stanley Ellis set down his tape recorder
in July 1956 in the home of a farmer and cider-maker. As so often, the
conversation nostalgically turned to former, apparently sweeter days, the
man's speech littered with another West Country staple that's still heard
in town and country, 'in they days':

> An' in they days 'aay use tuh meik [they used to make] some
> beuootiful saydahrr, an' we use tuh drenk et too! Oh Lordy, yehs! But
> as ay say everything 'ave olterrd, see. Use te'enjoy it – plenny saydarr
> drunk!

Three decades later, in August 1985, Ellis found himself once again
talking cider, thirty odd miles to the south of Stogumber, in a corner of
south Devon inland from Budleigh Salterton and Exmouth. Again, it was
time for old men to reminisce, 'r's to the fore – 'saaidrr', 'yurr [year]',
'everr', 'beerr' – though the vowel sounds are slightly different here in
south Devon, more open and further back in the mouth, with many 'aa'
sounds: 'ahve' for 'I've' and 'aan an' aff' for 'on and off'. Worth noting
also, incidentally, the particular usage here of 'now' to mean 'still':

> Ayve bin drinkin' saaidrr since aye wuz three yurr oul, an' ahve bin
> drenkin it aan an' aaff everr sence. An aye still laaks saaidrr, oul
> varrmouse saaidrr – aye preferr it to beerr naouw!

Ellis makes the point that the rhoticity and the vowel changes here are
not unrelated: 'The quality of that Devon "r" is so different from the "r"

sound of standard English. It's spoken with the tongue pulled back, and its effect is felt on sounds round it.'

Coming bang up to date, a group of residents from the Exmoor village of Dulverton gathered for their Voices interview in November 2004, less rosy-tinted this one. Again you get a somewhat different pronunciation of 'soider' and the accents were generally much less marked, unsurprisingly as a couple of the group were incomers. But the rhotic 'r' was still the norm:

'Yearrs an' yearrs of dedicated soider drinkin: you'd end up with a bloody great nose with bits in it. An' you could always tell the soider drinkerrs by the breath . . .'

Finally, a brief urban excursion – I look in greater detail at the sound of the West Country city in the 'Voices' section – to listen to what happens to that 'r' when articulated by city lips. In the West Country's capital, Bristol, it's very strongly voiced. A gliding and intense sound, it's made quite far back in the mouth compared with much of the rest of the city's accent, which is relatively thin and can sound quite mumbly. What can happen in a city though is that, faced with a really marked Bristol 'r', issues of class and old social prejudices can often and quite quickly rear their heads.

Just like the farming parents of my school friend Daniel whom I mentioned at the beginning of this section, this Bristol mother sent her daughter Tina to an independent secondary school, where her strongly sounded and typical 'r's were much less the norm. Predictably enough, the old rustic jibe (that those Plymothians I also quoted earlier so objected to) was ready to surface:

'A lo' a people up therre tawks rill toffee-nose to arr way uv tawkin. We've 'ad lo'ss uv laffs when she furrss starrtid a' Cliftn 'lgh Skooaw. A gurrll fouwn' u' wun niyte an' she sai', "Arr you a farrmerrz wiyfe?" I koon ge' ouverr tha', laiyk. 'n' I sai', "Wha' jew mean?" Shi sai', "Neverr errd nohb'dee tawk li' you biforr!" '

['A lot of people up there talks real toffee-nosed to our way of talking. We've had lots of laughs when she first started at Clifton High School. A girl phoned up one night and she said, "Are you a farmer's wife?"

I couldn't get over that, like. And I said, "What do you mean?" She said, "Never heard nobody talk like you before!" ']

A quick glance at the glossary will show how rich the region is in specifically local terms, words frequently with as long and rich a heritage as the accent with which they're pronounced. Yet some are now as rare in these shires as the golden oriole or the waxwing and in the next section I show to what extent – as so many of our informants have repeatedly said to their interviewers over the years – West Country dialect really isn't like it was 'in they days'.

The Voices Survey: Out of the Orchard, into the Street

There's piskies up to Dartymoor, and tidden good ye zay there baint
I've felt 'en grawpin' at me heart, I've heard their voices calling
    faint . . .

Piskies – little people – thatched cottages, villages buried in deep combes, country lanes overarched with trees. The appeal of the west of England constitutes one of this country's most enduring idylls, with high wind-scoured moorland to set off the softness of the valleys and somewhere distant, a glimpse of blue horizon. The tourist stereotype of Devon and Somerset, Dorset, Wiltshire and to an extent Hampshire owes much to romance and sentimentality. It's got a long pedigree: tourists have been exploring the landscape for generations. The myths were both spun and elaborated by figures such as the romantic poet Coleridge, who famously wrote his mystical 'Kubla Khan' near Porlock, and R. D. Blackmore, whose tale of love and death set on Exmoor, *Lorna Doone*, has been another mainstay of the region's romantic connections. Unsurprisingly, today's tourism mavens never tire of using this tradition to keep the economy spinning happily (the Coleridge Trail and Doone Country are always near the top of local listings). And though it's easy to scoff and regret a lost 'innocence', the reality is that tourism plays a vital part in local economics.

It also does much to dilute the purity of the local speech. A few local words get seized upon and hardened up into tourist items in their own right (like those 'piskies' in the old dialect verse at the beginning of this

The Sound of the West Country

There's something about the sound of West Country talk that, a little like Yorkshire, makes people think they can 'do' it. The reality is of course that there isn't just one accent. All though do have common features: from Hampshire and Oxfordshire in the east right down to Devon and Cornwall they exhibit rhoticity, that's to say 'r's are sounded in places where in standard English they're silent: 'cider' comes out with slightly different vowels, depending on the county something like 'saydarr', 'soiderr' and 'saaidrr' but the voiced 'r' is pretty consistent throughout. In Bristol, however, the 'r' sounds different when surrounded with pinched flat vowels, compared with full-throated Devon, where I've heard the *Daily Mirror* newspaper quite literally called the 'Dailee Murrr'. I describe the way 'f', 's', 't' almost everywhere become 'v', 'z', 'd' in the historical section of this chapter, but again the contribution this makes to the overall 'tune' here can't be underestimated, giving it a deep, gravelly quality.

In this region, as so often, the vowels shift round: short 'i' becomes 'e', so 'pick' sounds like 'peck': ' 'Aouw's trex?' would be a normal greeting. In Devon the vowel in 'ore' often opens up to 'are': 'marning' is what comes before noon.

section). Other terms, usually associated with farming and with the land it depends on, either become marginalized as methods evolve, or are overlaid by more universal words that incomers will readily comprehend. As I show elsewhere, regional speech frequently occupies a sort of liminal territory, looking inwards (towards those in the know) and locking out (the outsiders). When the outsiders outnumber the insiders old regional talk is threatened.

Voices met a group of middle-aged and elderly Devonians in one of Dartmoor's loveliest and literally most chocolate-boxy villages, Buckland in the Moor, thatched cottages and old square-towered St Peter's clustered under the hillside. This group, Dave, Derek, Cyril and Ena, all have broad accents, share farming as a thread through their lives, but come from different corners of the area. Typical features are their voiced 't's, their marked 'r's and the way they cluster and shorten syllables – 'gawn' for 'going', 'traan' for 'try and'. Dave, the broadest of the group, also has the very distinctive narrow 'u' sound typical of north Devon which starts with a long 'oo' but ends with a twist a little like the French 'u' in 'tu' –

Perhaps the most distinctive vowel is that in 'cow', which, at its broadest, can modulate around three separate sounds, which I've tried to represent on the page as 'aou'. So one speaker described 'the gorrse aout in full flaouwerr'; likewise in urban Bristol clouds become 'claouwds'. And there too the 'o' sound in 'home' can get stretched to 'ouw': the big theatre in the city, the Hippodrome, gets called the ' 'Ippadrouwm'.

There are a number of local particularities which I've detailed in the text, but the region shares many non-standard parts of speech and verb conjugation. So 'in they days' and 'talk to we' are both found widely in town and country, as is ' 'em' for him, her or they ('wannum?' = wouldn't they?); 'I doos' is standard Bristolian for 'I do'. 'Thee' – usually 'ee' in the west – still turns up among older speakers and a Bristol snooker player was challenged once with the question: 'Thees cassn't potun, casst? [You can't pot it, can you?]'.

But it is the various tunes and rhythms of West Country speech that differentiate and individualize local accents. Flat and slurred with lengthened vowels for the cities, very up-and-down in the rural areas, especially in Devon. As one man told Voices: 'We're praouwd of owurr language – ah knaw someone said we tolk slang bu', bah gaw', tis goouyd staff!'

'moved' is pronounced 'muyvd' and 'who' something like 'oouy'. Interesting too the way the 'v' in the word 'Devon' ritually moves from being a fricative ('v') to a plosive ('b'), which was something all four tended to do. They also all concurred that incomers were the main cause of linguistic change locally:

> 'A lodd uvit uz gawn, the Dabn lingaw, bicuz peepluv muyvd in th'area oouy dawn wawnta ev this thing – We getem awn the caouncil, we getem in evree facetuv laaif an theyrr traan te teach us the way tuh speak but if youy be Dabn, you stell speak Dabn.'

> ['A lot of it is going, the Devon lingo, because people have moved in(to) the area who don't want to have this thing – we get them on the council, we get them in every facet of life and they're trying to teach us the way to speak, but if you be Devon, you still speak Devon.']

This sort of social mobility isn't of course entirely new. Twenty years ago, an elderly resident of south Devon, Annie Annings, was already charting huge changes compared with the isolation that kept local Devonians resolutely local before the war: '[Then] we 'ad everything, as you might say. We didn't 'ave to go to [Budleigh] Salterton to get what we wanted; we 'ad grocers, bakers, shoemakers, blacksmiths and two butchers as a matter of fact.' To get to the local towns of Exeter or Exmouth a handful of miles distant she had to get Paine's the carrier to take her.

And outsiders were not welcome – being 'local' actually meant not coming from beyond the locality – as the hedger Don Hill remembered in his very strong accent (complete with that 'b' for 'v' shift again: 'sebn' for 'seven'). He should know – he was one:

Twas all cluwse-knet [close knit], an', b'lieve me, an outsaiyder you was like poison. En fact ah 'ave yearrd 'em seay ef a fellow went courrdeng [courting] in the nex' parish 'e was thought very, very lauw [low], ef 'e went outuv 'is parish to go courrdeng. An' ah met up with kwaat a bid uv that in naantin thurdy sebn [And I met up with quite a bit of that in 1937].

Those old days, fondly remembered with a wry smile, feel just so very long ago, yet, in Buckland in the Moor in 2004, Voices found exactly the same story within living memory, though now there are only two residents who were born in the village: outsiders completely outnumber them, 'with all sorts of accents'. Dave, who was born in Buckland, uses the same archaic word 'courting' as Don in his anecdote of an amorous 'closed shop', sounding more like a scene from *Tess of the d'Urbervilles* in its rustic antiquity than the latter half of the twentieth century:

'En fact when gurruls starrted coourtin' age they wouldn' allow young men comin' from the next village aouyt: they used t'ave a clawsed shawp and ef they did coom en they used to put them en a dungy wheelbarrer and wheel them touy the boundary and tep 'em ouyt an send 'em oom [tip them out and send them home].'

The range of local vocabulary this elderly group was able to offer was predictably the largest captured in the south-west by Voices. Many of the terms, though, belong to a way of life completely swept away in the course of the last fifty years, when for instance peat fires burned brightly in the farmhouse 'Debn grate' and a free supply of fuel was to be had up on Dartmoor: 'Ma father used to go up awn the moor cuttn *veggs* – *veggs* is peat,' Dave recalled. It was a tradition that was already disappearing back in 1963 when the Survey of English Dialects came to Widecombe in the Moor: 'Uss used tuh coll et *veggs*, cot about a thouysun adeiy [us used to call it *veggs*, cut about a thousand a day].'

At Dulverton in Somerset on the southern edge of Exmoor, Voices gathered a group of mixed long-resident incomers and locals. By contrast, old dialect terms were thin on the ground here, the intonation patterns very standardized with little trace of a traditional rural 'tune'. But they could unearth a handful of older variants like 'peart' and 'snarty' for cold. And, as I've found throughout the UK, vernacular words often double up and do service in a number of contexts ('scundered' in Northern Ireland for instance and 'minging' among young people everywhere), so 'peart' they used to mean annoyed as well. A couple of farm terms persist here – 'yet up' for to get hot (silage is said to be 'yetting up') and 'yaws' for ewes. One of the non-natives remembered with a smile how she was caught out shortly after moving to Dulverton when the vet tending her flock asked her:

> ' "All yaws?" And I said, "Oh yes". And 'e said, "I thought that was a ram over there!" I said, "Oh yes, that is a ram." "Well," he replied, "I thought you just said they were all yaws!" '

Local food and festivals have their own special words and the Buckland in the Moor group still enjoy a 'frawze' (pronounced 'frawsee') or 'tay [tea] an' pasties' which traditionally, they said, should here be made from mutton and apple: 'tiddy oggy' – a delicacy enjoyed on both sides of the Tamar. This group also still talk about a baby as a 'cheel', playing truant as 'ferniggling' and of sunshine and showers as 'catchy weather', pronounced of course 'cadgy'.

From Buckland to Plymouth is only a matter of five miles or so, yet when Voices made the quick dash down the A386 it was into a different landscape and linguistic world. Here was a contemporary city speech, known as Janner, having as much in common with the tones of urban Bristol a hundred miles away to the north and west as with the talk of the Dartmoor farm. In fact one of the group was upset frequently for being taken for a Bristolian: 'People thought I came from Brist*aw*,' she said, using the Bristolian 'dark' 'l' that I'll explain in detail at the end of this section. Christine, Lee, Joan, Paul and Karen are all Plymouth locals, ranging in age from early thirties to nearly eighty, and though Paul was the hardest to follow it was as much the result of his diction as of his relatively strong accent. Some of the group admitted to a tinge of Cornish in their accent – Plymouth lies on the county boundary and all knew and used the expression 'dreckly' (see the 'Voices' section in Chapter 1) for 'in a while' – but the overall impression was that of a west of England urban speech style.

Again exactly as found in Bristol, the phrases they'd naturally use to greet someone are 'Ullo, my luvver!' and 'Ullo, mi burrd!' and Paul's pronunciation of the local Plymouth landmark Royal Parade as 'Rawl Prade' was so close to Bristolian as makes no difference. Likewise 'yes' was said 'yass' and in general 'a' in the middle of words was always short – 'laff' for 'laugh' and 'haff' for 'half' as in the larger city. One feature that perhaps marks these Devonians out as city dwellers compared with their country cousins five miles away at Buckland is their lack of the typical rural intonation. The 'song' of a language is almost impossible to represent on the page and I don't intend to attempt it, yet in many cases it is what above all characterizes someone as belonging to a particular area or dialect group. In rural Devon it's a combination of a sing-song tune with lots of open, gravelly low notes. Amongst our Plymouth group, on the other hand, the tune has a town flatness that doesn't feel particularly typical of the county, more outer London than Ottery St Mary, and for me at least it's what makes these speakers feel less distinctively local.

But it also has a lot to do with the actual range of words they use. For example, on the Voices list under 'happy' these Plymothians offered the now standard national form 'chuffed'; 'tired' was 'knackered'; and 'without money' was 'brassic' (reputedly from rhyming slang 'boracic lint' = 'skint' and again found, with variations, right across urban Britain). However, 'drunk' brought from Paul – along with 'steamin' ', ' 'ammered' and 'pessd uz a farrt' – 'skimmershed'. At least that's how he spelled it, but further research throws up 'skimmished' reportedly derived from 'iskimmish' (also 'drunk') and which, according to a website devoted to the collection of inebriation terms, has been around since the 1700s. 'Skimmish' is said to be tramps' slang for beer.

Joan, who's seventy-eight, perhaps predictably came up with the greatest number of specifically local terms – 'mazed' for insane (recognized by the older members of the group, but news to the pair in their thirties) and 'wish' meaning unwell and also spelled 'wisht', both found widely in Cornwall (see Chapter 1, 'A Cornish Glossary') and most interestingly 'shrammed' for cold. 'Shrammed' is still reported today right across southern England, from Hampshire to Wiltshire and even appears in a list of Bristol dialect terms. The dictionary records it in dialectal use as early as 1787 – 'I am shram'd to death – I am dead with cold' – and Thomas Hardy uses it in the poem 'The Fire at Tranter Sweatley's':

> Then tender Tim Tankens he searched here and there
>> For some garment to clothe her fair skin;
> But though he had breeches and waistcoats to spare,
> He had nothing quite seemly for Barbree to wear,
> Who, half *shrammed* to death, stood and cried on a chair
>> At the caddle she found herself in.

This group from Plymouth were not as broad as some we've surveyed in Voices, and not the most accented we found in the south-west, but they were considerably more so than a quartet from Swindon in Wiltshire who demonstrated quite graphically (as with the young Punjabi women from Leeds – see Chapter 8) how local pressures shape the way our speech develops as much as our own families. This group were mixed Anglo-Polish, the father a first-generation immigrant and still speaking fairly broken English with no distinguishable local qualities at all. His two daughters on the other hand had a mixed accent with elements of south-eastern and outer London and a tinge of rural – the 'r' being the main giveaway. The only regional variant that they offered was for alleyway (a favourite item for linguistic surveys and one that in 2004/5 has yielded 'twitchel', 'ginnel' and several others). For these Swindon women, it's 'backsies' – back alleys. 'Took 'im down the backsies . . . we alwiz used to meet down the backsies . . . Always police in the backsies.'

If Swindon is these days too close to London and the M4 corridor to be able to hold its own with a truly distinctively local way of speaking, this certainly isn't true of Bristol. A city with a population of close to 400,000, it's the economic hub of the region. But over the twenty years since Stanley Ellis came to capture the sound of Bristol talk, there have been major shifts in the way the city works. In 1985, he recorded some rich samples of Bristolian amongst the employees at the WD & HO Wills No. 1 Factory in East Street, Bedminster. Now the factory has closed and the tobacco industry, for so long a staple of inner-city employment, has left town along with Bristol's central docks, the employment transferred elsewhere.

Factories are wonderful places for the nurturing of local talk. They have their jargon and their routines, their regular meal breaks when the chat flows, and they frequently have a spirit of 'everyone in the same boat' kept alive by jokes and gossip.

Thus the tobacco workers Ellis recorded described warmly 'that feelin' of belongin'' to the factory and the 'Bemminster' part of the city: 'I bin brough' up a few stree's away. Mi nan lives 'ere . . .' The talk was heavy with the glottal stops common in city speech ('brough' up', 'stree's') and with that rich Bristolian 'r'. Also on display were two of the ways a Bristolian deals with a -y at the end of words: either lengthened – 'factory' for example routinely becomes 'factree' – or flattened with a slightly dreary-sounding 'ay': 'communitay' and 'Dickay' in place of 'community' and 'Dickie'. (Both of these pronunciations Voices also picked up in rural Devon, so they are clearly not purely a city phenomenon.) One cigarette maker, Carol, grappling with a malfunctioning machine that had just produced a three-metre long Embassy, explained that the process was entirely mechanized: 'The machine doos it forr you, i' oll ge's weiyghed u' ackerut, look [it all gets weighed up accurate, look]'. 'Doos' rather than 'does' is still the vernacular form of the verb – 'I doos', 'he doos', 'they doos'.

Today in Bristol, the only heavy industry still thriving is what is known as 'Filton', from the outer suburb where the British Aerospace factory continues to build wings for European Airbuses. This was where Concorde was constructed and it remains a source of civic pride and rich local vernacular, described by Ellis as 'a cranky, crazy, crab-apple tree of language and with the sharpest, juiciest flavour I've heard for a long time'.

Also going strong since those field recordings of twenty years ago is Pat Dallimore. She's carved out a career for herself on local radio with pithy commentaries delivered in her characteristic gurgle of Bristolian speech. Pat as a typical city-dweller speaks fast, running her words together, with that rising questioning inflexion that used to be more or less limited to Bristol and Belfast but that has, with the popularity of American and Australian soap operas, become an international phenomenon known as 'Upspeak'. This Bristolian intonation has a much longer pedigree and is completely distinct from any of the other south-western speech tunes, such that, whatever the many points of similarity amongst these western dialects, 'Bristol Upspeak' is still sure to mark you out.

The other real Bristolian giveaway that Pat triumphantly has is the famous – or notorious – Bristol 'dark' 'l' that gets attached to hanging vowels at the ends of words, particularly 'a' and 'o' sounds. They say it's why the city, formerly known in documents as *Brycgstow* (Old English, the site of the bridge) is suddenly recorded around 1200 as 'Brist*oll*'. The Bristol novelist Derek Robinson once recalled an old Bristolian who'd served in the First World War rattling off the countries in which he'd served: 'Africa*l*, Persia*l*, Syria*l*' and even, with a particular sense of precision that inserted the sound *within* a word, 'A*l*rabia*l* and Mesa*l*potamia*l*'.

So here, as a grand finale to this linguistic progression from the cider orchards of Devon to a council house in the Knowle West district ('Naw Wess' in Bristolian), is Pat Dallimore on her first visit with husband Jim to the 'opera*l*'.

'Aye din p'tickly wan'r see 'n oprul, bu' Jim did, bicuz Jim fanciz isself uz a bi' v'un oprul singerr, see. An' aye thing kwuz *Toscal* arr summuh. The woomun 'oo wuz singin' i' – wossa wummun 'a' sings in opral? Woss err neym? She ain' a primmuhdonnal isshee? – She's a primmuhdonnal.'

['I didn't particularly want to see an opera, but Jim did, because Jim fancies himself as a bit of an opera singer, see. And I think it was *Tosca* or something. The woman who was singing it – what's a woman that sings in opera? What's her name? She isn't a primadonna is she? – She's a primadonna.']

A Western Snapshot: Trevs and Trobos

Doran, Joe, Vicky and Zoe are sixth-formers at Bradford-on-Avon in Wiltshire. A casual listener would barely notice a trace of accent, local or otherwise, though they're very conscious of one. Voices listened as they talked eagerly about accent and localness, both their own and those voices they heard in this comfortable corner of the county eight miles from Bath. Was it 'Bath' (short 'a': 'Baeth'), for example, as in the local vernacular, or Received Pronunciation 'Baath'? All four used the RP form by preference: 'If you've got an accent you're automatically labelled as coming from [somewhere] and I wouldn't want to be.' If the quartet have one quality uniting the way they speak it's a slightly slack-jawed combination of youthful public school-ese blended with that outer-London accent which was first identified as what he called 'Estuary' English by the linguist David Rosewarne in 1984.

Unlike so many of their contemporaries interviewed for the Voices project, this group are self-conscious about accent and don't want to be pinned down: 'I hate it,' said one, 'my grandparents had a Somerset accent.' Maybe because of their age or background – they have had fairly mobile short lives already – they don't see dialect particularly as a badge or a source of local pride but simply as something that can cause embarrassment. Zoe recalled:

> 'I was driving back from Nottingham, and went to the old Burger King and there was a girl working there and she had the strongest accent ever and I swear that she was going "dadandanda" [SUNG], like that. And she wasn't – she was just asking, "Do you want ketchup with that?" but I couldn't understand her and I didn't know what to say and you feel really awkward.'

At their most positive, the group could only offer lukewarm support to being defined regionally by the way they sounded. 'I keep slipping,' said Joe, 'and I used to get quite embarrassed about it 'cos I'd say "trouwserrs" and correct myself. But I don't care; I think it's quite nice to have a bit of an accent.' As they admit, however, few people they bump into have much of an accent in what has become in recent years, despite the presence of important local industries, a fairly elderly middle-class town: 'I don't hear people talking like that round here.'

What you need in order to communicate effectively is the *appropriate* style of speech. If the folk you brush up against daily are farmers and sheep dealers from nearby, you'll speak much the same way as they do; mutual understanding, as in the cliché, literally is 'talking the same language'. So these sixth-formers, mingling regularly with a relatively narrow social grouping, have styled their speech accordingly. It's one of the most powerful forces driving language change: compare these two comments from the young women from Plymouth that we met in 'Out of the Orchard, into the Street'.

> 'I must admit I do tend to tone [my accent] down when I go somewhere else because people can't understand me; unless I'm with people I know really well when I can speak as I want.'

> 'Workin' for a lot of years in the public sector I've had to slow down and pronounce things sli'ly diffrun' [slightly different] so people can understand [me]. When you're dealin' with caouncillors an' managers an' things you do have tuh, no' posh i' up, bu' speak clearerr, otherrwise you don' ge' taken seeriuslee in your worrk.'

Despite their lack of marked regionalisms, the Wiltshire students are, however, very attuned to language, sensitive to proprieties (they're uncomfortable with swearing) and have a good stock of personal vernacular culled from their friends, from television programmes they like or simply invented by themselves:

> 'To "barry-out" from the way Barry White used to talk – it was a bit like snoring. We got it off a group of people from the Lake District . . .'

Thus, in common with a vast number of young people round Britain, they'd use 'minging' for ugly (attributing it to the popularity of *Big Brother* on TV), as well as those other derogatory slang words 'munter' and 'moose'. For left-handed, their term wasn't (as for the elderly Devonians from Buckland) 'clicky' or 'couchy', but simply the widely used 'cack-handed': 'There's a computer game where you choose to be "cack-handed" or "right-handed,"' observed one. They did use one regionalism that's found above all in the Bristol area and in parts of south Wales, the word for plimsolls:

to almost every Bristolian they're 'daps'. Though Joe, born in Rugby, still calls them by their northern name, 'pumps'.

However, what really engaged their linguistic enthusiasm was the Voices question about local terms for 'young person in cheap and trendy clothing'. Immediately local rivalry was to the fore, just as it is all over the country (Lurgan vs Craigavon, Ashington vs Stakeford, Mellor Brook vs Blackburn to name three), and for these Bradford-on-Avon dwellers, it was the nearby county town, Trowbridge:

> 'You can talk to any young person anywhere and they have a word for it: "pikey", "chav", "trev" and "townie", "Trobos" [Trowbridge], "nobs", "gudgeons" . . .'

The forum spreading this new vernacular like wildfire across the UK is the internet: there are acres of server-space devoted to the exchange in chat-rooms by youngsters of slang words for what they see as social undesirables. It's oneupmanship in the cyber age: pour scorn on someone by classing him a 'chav', a 'trev' or a 'townie' – I've heard all of these during the Voices survey, often many times over – and you feel superior. 'Trobos', though, are really local, the Wiltshire equivalent:

> 'Lots of people go through a stage of wearing these sorts of clothes and we do judge them as a group: they're a "trev". By giving something a label you know whether it's approachable or something you think you should stay away from. And if you see a group of lads that you think, "Oh they're all 'trevs' ", you're not going to walk around on your own if they're around. You'd go a different way or something; you would judge them by their looks. I think Bradford is full of "Trobos" or "trevs": [they] would beat you up and steal your mobile.'

Fascinating to compare this account of street life in twenty-first century Bradford-on-Avon with the following tale of a not-so-dissimilar stand-off that happened perhaps seventy-five years ago. It's interesting both in the parallels and in the contrasts. The rivalry's barely changed a jot, but listen to the broad Wiltshire accent: 'lave' for 'leave', 'atwum' for 'at home', 'wawlk' for 'folk'. It's full too of those voiced consonants (see 'Wess Vinglun') 'th' in 'dthree [three]', 'f' in 'vor [four]' and critically – if you want to understand the insult perpetrated by the 'sparks' – 'p' in 'blauw [plough]'.

It was recorded by an old man from twenty-five miles away at Aldbourne in Wiltshire in 1939 and tells the story of what happened when he went up to London with his mate Horace Shepherd, who insisted on wearing his countryman's clothes. Not a good idea in a London pub filled with 'young sparks', the 'Trobos' or 'trevs' of the time:

> 'Arry worr 'is smock: I tawld 'im to lave it atwum, boot ee 'ould bring't. We went into a pob an' there dthree uh vor young sparks askt 'Arry te show un 'ow th' blauw wurrkt. So 'e brings un down on the floor, wallop! Larrd 'ow eye laeffd. 'Serve the' righ'!' says 'Arry. 'We Wiltshurr wawlk allus gets urr own baeck!'

> [Harry wore his smock: I told him to leave it at home, but he would bring it. We went into a pub and there three or four young sparks asked Harry to show them how the plough worked. So he brings one down on the floor, wallop! Lord how I laughed. 'Serve them right!' says Harry. 'We Wiltshire folk always gets our own back!']

A West Country Glossary

I have indicated particular county usages where relevant

acker a friend. Somerset usage; the jazz musician Acker Bilk, born in Pensford, Somerset, took his professional name from this dialect word

areal an area. In Bristol dialect words and names with a final 'a' or 'o' sound are susceptible to the addition of an 'l'-like sound (cf. 'Handel's oratoriol Messiah'l')

backsie, -ies an alley behind houses. From 'back-alley'; Swindon, Wiltshire usage, late twentieth century

baint (there) isn't, aren't. From 'be' and 'ain't' (isn't): 'tidden good ye zay there baint' (it isn't good you say there aren't); Devon usage

batch a hillock. Buckland's Batch and Cambridge Batch are the names of two small hills in north Somerset

bis, bist 'Are you'. Bristol dialect form of the verb to be: 'I be, you bist, he be . . .'; as in the phrase, 'bist comin' tonight?'

blare to weep. Dorset dialect from Old English *blaren*, to cry, weep, probably imitative; found from fifteenth century

bock to mess up. Contemporary Plymouth slang, e.g. 'don't bock my hair'

cast, cassn't 'can you?', 'you can't'. Bristol dialect, interrogative form of the verb 'to be able'; (presumably originally from 'canst thou?', 'thou canst not'), as in 'thees cassn't potun, cast?', 'you can't pot it [the ball], can you?'

catchy changeable (weather). Devon dialect, perhaps from the obsolete meaning 'occurring in disconnected bursts', 'changeable' – 'a *catchy* wind'

cheel, cheal a baby. Devon usage (from 'child')

cidered up drunk

coochy, couchy, cauchy left-handed. Devon dialect usage; G. A. Cooke's *The County of Devon* (*c.* 1820) noted 'couch-pawed' or 'handed', meaning awkward, left-handed

coopy/croopy down to crouch down, squat. Bristol usage, possibly from 'croup', hindquarters, but cf. 'twti-down', crouch down: South Wales valleys Anglo-Welsh dialect

dap to bounce (e.g. a ball), or bound along. Somerset, Bristol usage; origin obscure

daps plimsolls, soft rubber shoes. The word is found as far east as Wiltshire and in parts of South Wales, essentially though Bristol, Somerset dialect: possibly related to 'dap', above

dibs money. Slang usage; in early nineteenth century, 'dibs' were tokens used in card games in place of money

doos 'do'. Bristol dialect form of the verb 'to do': 'I doos', 'he doos', 'they doos'

drexy falling to pieces. Devon dialect; possibly from 'druxy', descriptive of decaying timber; of uncertain etymology

ferniggle to play truant

frawze a special meal or feast. The term is found from Hampshire to Cornwall; a 'waygoose' or 'wayzgoose' was an outing often followed by a frawze (pronounced 'frawsee'), a treat

grockle a visitor, tourist. Modern usage, from the children's comic, *Dandy* and its cartoon *Danny and His Grockle*; according to research by the OED, 'grockle' was adopted by a Torquay man as a nickname for a regular visitor he knew; the term gained currency during the 1960s because of a popular film, *The System*, which was set in Torquay and in which the term was extensively used

gurt, girt big. Somerset, Bristol, Dorset usage; from 'great'

'isself himself. Bristol usage

Janner the dialect of Plymouth. The term, of disputed origin, refers to someone born by the sea; in naval parlance, from the west of England, specifically Plymouth

jonnick, jannock, jonnock, jenick true, the truth. Recorded from early nineteenth century, it has multiple formations and is found throughout the west of England. Meanings include 'pleasant', 'outspoken', 'honest' and 'generous'

leary, leery empty, hungry. Francis Grose in his 1787 *Provincial Glossary* first noted the word in this sense; Wilkinson Sherren's *The Wessex of Romance* from 1902 notes it with the meaning 'hungry', 'unladen'; from Old English *laere*, empty

lover, luvver a term of endearment. 'My lover' is Bristol usage, but also found quite widely in the West Country

mazed confused, flummoxed, insane. To 'maze' meant to 'put out of one's wits' and dates back to medieval times; perhaps from Old English *masian*

peart cold, annoyed. Devon dialect

piskies pixies. Local Devon pronunciation

pitch to settle (exclusively of snow). Standard Bristol usage: 'I think it's going to pitch tonight'

pook a heap of new-mown hay that has been cut and turned ('tedded') and is awaiting gathering into ricks or stooks. Derivation unknown, in use from early eighteenth century

shrammed freezing cold. A dialect term found across south-western England; the antiquary Francis Grose records 'shrammed' as Wiltshire dialect in his *Provincial Glossary* of 1787: 'I am shram'd to death; I am dead with cold'; from shram, scram, 'to shrivel with cold', Old English *scrimman*, shrivel

skimmished drunk. From 'iskimmish', 'drunk', allegedly in use since the 1700s; 'skimmish' is said to have been tramps' slang for beer

teddies potatoes. From 'taties' but with voiced dental in mid-word

tidden it isn't

tiddy-oggy a pasty or potato pie, in Devon made with pork or mutton and apple; naval slang for a rating from Devonport (Plymouth)

to as in 'where's 'e to?'. In Bristol dialect, questions of location are given additional specificity by the routine addition of 'to': 'werr's yorr Fiestal to?' would be a normal Bristolian enquiry about a missing vehicle.

uddent wouldn't. Bristol usage as in ''e udden' do daa'' ('he wouldn't do that')

un, um it, them. As detailed in the text, the routine substitution of 'un' and 'um' (or 'em') for it and they, them has a long pedigree

veggs peat. Old Devon dialect

verns bracken. Old English *fearn*. South-western English prounciation replaces 'f' with 'v'

vitty, viddy correct, proper (cf. Cornish dialect 'fitty'). Cooke recorded the term in his *The County of Devon* in c. 1820

vuzz, vuzz-bush furze. Sherren's *The Wessex of Romance* of 1902 records the term; as in the dialect verse '. . . like vuzz-bush fires in swailin' time'

wannum 'wouldn't they'. Verbal usage from (especially) Devon; see 'um' above

way fore and **back fore** left and right. Voices reported these terms as old Devon dialect from at least fifty years ago

wish(t) sickly, thin, wan, sad. The origins of the word are obscure

yaws ewes. West Somerset pronunciation

yet up heat up (cf. the Lancastrian transition from 'head' to 'yed')

3 : LONDON AND THE SOUTH-EAST

Language in a Landscape 1: An Ear for the Estuary

'Ladies and gentlemen, we are now on our final approach to London's Heathrow Airport. Crew, prepare for landing.' The 747 has floated in high above the Essex marshes, a weak sun catching ripple and creek. Clumps of buildings along tiny waterways are replaced by sprinkles of houses grouped at crossroads and farm buildings with acres of yellow oil seed rape ballooning round them. Now there are snaking curves and closes of houses looping out and around the villages, low-slung hangars and smudges of industrial roadways camped on the outskirts. Almost imperceptibly, the predominant green turns grey, and the ranks of roofs and roads take over, the occasional oblong football field with matchstick floodlight gantries the only green now.

The plane banks and suddenly the majestic eastern sweep of the Thames rolls into vision, white cowls of the Thames Barrier, mushroom-capped Millennium Dome and then, west along the river, the parade of power and British pomp. Tightly belted passengers strain towards windows to catch a glimpse: there's St Paul's, Big Ben . . . Shading off into the mist to the south, as the plane once again rolls lazily round in its stacking-circuit, are Surrey and Kent and, beyond, somewhere further south, Sussex and the channel coast. This is the miracle of being two miles high over London: one short five-minute sweep and we've encompassed the lives and the language of nearly 20 million people.

The poet Craig Raine once described Belfast seen from the air as being like a radio with the back off, but a plane's-eye view of London is a procession – albeit a miniature one – of the richness and the diversity and, quite simply, the bigness of the British capital. And the same goes in many ways for the way London and the south-eastern corner of the

47

UK speaks. Describe London's language and you are in some senses cupping an ear to the world. Have you ever stood with your ears tuned in outside a London Underground station listening to the chatter of voices emerging into the daylight? It's like plugging in to the interpreters' room at the UN, though with time-zones: an army of African night-workers swapping stories in French as they come off shift into the gloom of a winter's dawn, the taciturn exchanges of a cohort of handsome young Poles in spattered overalls knocking off at five after setting to rights the plumbing of WC2. And the South Africans and the Somalis, the Bangladeshis and the Bahrainis, all with their own sound and social centre, a multiplicity of London ethnic villages scattered across the Greater London lozenge.

Head out on the sprinter trains north and south and there's another swathe of accents and languages, no less diverse, only with a different, even more tidal rhythm to their day. The briefcases flood in for nine-thirty and ebb at six, west and north from Paddington, Marylebone and Kings Cross, south and east from Victoria and Waterloo and London Bridge. It's an extraordinary cycle of living, and although many whom Voices has interviewed in the north of England, in Scotland, Wales and Northern Ireland, have been quick to complain that south-easterners never talk, preferring to lock themselves away behind their iPods and *Evening Standards*, the fact is that when they do, Londoners love to rabbit on. To 'rabbit' of course is a notable piece of Cockney rhyming slang that's entered the wider vernacular: 'rabbit and pork – talk'.

So how to capture a real sense of this bewildering diversity and volume of voices that speak for and about the capital and the counties around? It's almost impossible. Yet amid the many accents, there is a common base-note that's today shared by the majority of those who live in this corner of England. It's not Cockney, though it shares elements with the old traditional speech of inner London. Nor is it Received Pronunciation (RP), at least in the conventional sense of some form of relatively regionally unmarked accent. It was recognized in print by a young linguist called David Rosewarne in 1984. He called it 'Estuary English' and the term, neatly alliterative, became indelibly associated with a form of accent and to a certain extent of vocabulary that was the hallmark of the Thatcher years.

Whilst the cliché of the East End barrow-boy turned investment banker was undoubtedly overstated, the status accorded to such successful entrepreneurs, for whom where you came from and how you spoke were no longer relevant, was real enough. What they all spoke, it seemed, was a form of Cockney, altered and flattened and now found well beyond the sound of Bow Bells. David Rosewarne defined it in his seminal article in the *Times Educational Supplement* as:

> A variety of modified regional speech . . . a mixture of non-regional and local south-eastern English pronunciation and intonation. If one imagines a continuum with RP and London speech at either end, 'Estuary English' speakers are to be found grouped in the middle ground.

In fact, though the phenomenon was real enough, Rosewarne's coinage lay relatively undisturbed within the world of linguistic analysis until well after Mrs Thatcher left Downing Street. It was a sequence of newspaper articles, including one on the front page of the *Sunday Times* in March 1993, that propelled the term out into the mainstream. Radio and television also now brought the sound into the front room, particularly in the mouths of comedians such as Ben Elton and Paul Merton. Back in the 1980s, when Stanley Ellis, veteran of the Survey of English Dialects, took his surveying microphone out on to the streets of the capital, he none the less recognized the linguistic species in its natural state:

> This is the way [London speech] is moving everywhere, making a new kind of London accent, a Cockney accent that forces its way east to Dagenham out to Harlow and north to Luton, overriding the older tones of the countryman.

Ellis pointed out that this new London sound had flattened the harsh 'a' of a Cockney's 'round' – 'raaend' – to something more like 'raound'; and the 'ay' sound that in old London speech would ritually be pronounced 'eye' was also softened: 'basically' was 'baye-sickly' not 'bye-sickly':

> The powerful swinging zappiness of the London accent continues to expand. North and south of the river the move goes on, into Kent and Surrey as well as into Essex and Hertfordshire, the punchy talk sweeps out with the people.

Now you can visit many parts of the UK and find traces of the Estuarial revolution well established. Although it's by no means all-pervasive, its

49

effects on traditional regional speech may be powerful and dynamic, as the Voices survey shows. It includes points of pronunciation, such as the widespread use of glottal stops (by no means restricted to Estuary, of course) and, more markedly, the phenomenon known as 'TH-fronting'. This ungainly expression refers to the replacement of the 'th' sound in words like 'mother' and 'father' by a 'v', so producing 'muvver' and 'faaver'. 'TH-fronting' has long been a well-known feature of Cockney, too, but today it's also part of pronunciation from Cornwall to Cumbria.

This way that the capital has of leading by example is nothing new. As the language developed, the earliest dominant form of Old English was that of Wessex and of the then capital, Winchester, where West Saxon dialect ruled (as opposed, for example, to the northern variety, Northumbrian – see Chapter 10). As Middle English developed through the early-medieval period, the main influence on standard written English came from the east of the capital, which was now London, from Essex and Norfolk speech. Then, around the end of the fourteenth century, powerful and wealthy incomers from the east Midlands, from Northamptonshire and Bedfordshire, begin to arrive in large numbers in London and to bring their regional speech with them. Henceforth, it's the English of the east Midlands (Mercian) that predominates in the capital. In Westminster, the so-called Chancery scribes reproduce documents in their thousands – this was the pre-Caxton early fifteenth century when photocopying was done by hand, letter by letter – and their formulations and spellings now came with the style and syntax of the counties north, not east, of London. Their choices of how to write English (favouring, for instance, 'such' rather than 'sich' or 'swiche' or a number of other possibilities) set the pattern for the era of (written) Modern English that was dawning.

Now the Devonian, John Shillingford, mayor of Exeter, would write sentences in perfectly formed 'Chancery Standard' English:

> The Bysshop taried at Excetre fro Fridey yevynsonge tyme yn to a Monedey erly yn the mornynge. The Maier wayted apon his gode lordship at alle tymes . . .

Not a trace there, and barely a flavour elsewhere, of Shillingford's native south-west in his carefully kept journals. As far as the written standard was concerned, London set the pace.

In some ways, the teeming complexity of the modern capital is just as it has always been, outsiders constantly swelling the population and bringing their diverse linguistic influences to bear: it's said that East End speech wouldn't be as it is without the long history of Jewish, Irish and many other new arrivals making this corner of London their own. So, too, in medieval times. Then, the relatively great social mobility brought about by the Crusades, the many religious pilgrimages at home and abroad, and the power of the great universities and the inns of court and, not least, too, the magnet of the royal court turned London into a medieval melting-pot. Its population in the fifteenth century was large at 40,000, but a century later had grown to five times that size, with one in twenty of the population of England resident here.

The end of the sixteenth century was a time of awakening interest in conformity and excellence in language: now London was seen as setting the pace, not simply *de facto* but by preference. In 1581 Richard Mulcaster, headmaster of the Merchant Taylors' School in the capital, wrote championing the English language above scholarly Latin, and within the same decade George Puttenham's *Arte of English Poesie* was declaring that the best type of English was 'the vsuall speach of the Court, and that of London and the shires lying about London within lx. myles, and not much aboue'.

Puttenham was frank about dialect and class, and his 1589 strictures about the vulgarity of regional speech ring down the ages with an authentic critique that every elocution-mad parent, every self-improving careerist, right up to these early years of the twenty-first century will recognize. The preferred language of the poet (he called it 'our Southerne English') should be, he said, limited to those who lived south of the Trent, avoiding:

> that which is spoken in . . . any uplandish village or corner of a
> Realme, where is no resort but of poore rusticall or uncivill people.
> Neither shall he follow the speech of a craftes man or carter, or other
> of an inferiour sort, though he be inhabitant or bred in the best towne
> and Citie in this Realme, for such persons do abuse good speaches by
> strange accents or ill shapen soundes, and false ortographie.

By the early 1600s the residents of the City of London had become so distinctive a band of citizens as to merit a name, a name which remains to this day, Cockney. A noted scholar, John Minsheu (pronounced 'Minshew'), who was a self-proclaimed 'professor of languages' and also responsible for a dictionary of English and Spanish, in 1617 published a book called *Ductor in Linguas, the Guide to Tongues*, in which he offered the now-famous definition:

A *Cockney* or *Cockny*, applied only to one borne within the sound of Bow-bell, that is, within the City of London.

Minsheu was keen to provide an etymology for the strange name:

. . . which tearme came first out of this tale: That a Citizens sonne riding with his father into the country asked, when he heard a horse neigh, what the horse did the father answered 'the horse doth neigh'; riding farther he heard a cocke crow, and said 'doth the *cocke neigh* too?' and therefore Cockney or cocknie, by inuersion thus: *incock*, *incoctus*: raw or vnripe in Country-men affaires.

Unlikely. In fact, according to the *Oxford English Dictionary*, 'Cockney' comes from Middle English *coken ey*, 'a cock's egg', with the meaning 'a (misshapen) egg'. Thence by a somewhat winding path it came to be applied to an indulged or 'soft' child, which was then widened to mean an 'effeminate person', which in turn was used as a term of abuse by people of the country for town-dwellers (who were deemed 'soft' compared with hardy rustics). Finally, Cockney came to be the term for an inhabitant of one specific town, the city of London.

In the eighteenth century, Thomas Sheridan, father of the famous playwright Richard Brinsley Sheridan and author of a number of works about language, offered (in his *Course of Lectures on Elocution* of 1762) the following linguistic snapshot of the capital:

In the very metropolis two different modes of pronunciation prevail, by which the inhabitants of one part of the town, are distinguished from those of the other. One is current in the city, and is called the cockney; the other at the court-end, and is called the polite pronunciation. As amongst these various dialects, one must have the preference, and become fashionable, it will of course fall to the lot of that which prevails at court, the source of fashions of all kinds.

The speech of the ordinary Londoner – and beyond – finds no favour:

All other dialects, are sure marks, either of a provincial, rustic, pedantic, or mechanic education; and therefore have some degree of disgrace annexed to them.

The ever-censorious Sheridan laments the way people drop their 'h's ('one defect which more generally prevails in the counties than any other'), a trend he notes also among the provincial gentry. He particularly censures Londoners for the way they pronounce 'w' as 'v' and vice versa ('vinter' for winter and 'vell' for well are two examples he quotes), which to me recalls a Dickensian landscape of rough and ready characters saying things like 'a werry merry Christmas'. Take, for instance, the cabbie hailed by Mr Pickwick in the 1836 novel:

> 'He lives at Pentonwil when he's at home,' observed the driver coolly [of the waterman who fetched the cab], 'but we seldom takes him home, on account of his weakness.' 'On account of his weakness!' reiterated the perplexed Mr Pickwick. 'He always falls down when he's took out o' the cab,' continued the driver, 'but when he's in it, we bears him up werry tight, and takes him in werry short, so as he can't werry well fall down; and we've got a pair o' precious large wheels on, so ven he does move, they run after him, and he must go on – he can't help it.'

What a fascinating sidelight this exchange offers on the language of immediately pre-Victorian London: not just 'werry's in profusion but 'Pentonwil' for Pentonville and 'ven' for when.

Today, there's a tendency to celebrate the riches of East End speech: Cockney rhyming slang, for all the fakery that's associated with many of the expressions (do East Enders really call a 'geezer' a 'Bacardi Breezer' or is that just a bit of two-bit Mockney linguistic invention: 'Wanna nice bi' o' rhymin' slang, guvnor?') is seen as fun and wholesome. So it comes as something of a shock to realize just how frowned upon Cockney once was. The poet John Keats grew up in stables where his father worked on Finsbury Pavement, a street in Islington, north London. It was a birthright that served him ill, certainly in critical terms: 'a young Cockney rhymester' was the dismissive description used of him in a vituperative review in 1818. Continuing in the same vein, the article made a number of scathing references to him and his fellow poets of what the writer dismissively called 'the Cockney school of poetry'. The critic (John Gibson Lockhart) referred to:

> the rising brood of Cockneys . . . the meanest, the filthiest, and the most vulgar of Cockney poetasters . . . uneducated and flimsy striplings . . . without . . . learning enough to distinguish between the written language of Englishmen and the spoken jargon of Cockneys . . .

and so on. As George Puttenham's observations at the end of the sixteenth century prove, plebeian accents have long been an integral part of social snobbery – Shakespeare no less uses regional accents to mock. By the middle of the nineteenth century, the strictures and sneers of Sheridan, Lockhart and others had encouraged a minor flood of self-improvement manuals, with titles like *Poor Letter H – Its Use and Abuse*, which ran to forty editions, and *Harry Hawkins' H Book* and *Mind Your Hs*. A cartoon in *Poor Letter H* shows a gentleman of quality doffing his hat to a haughty, scowling woman in long skirts. In his hand is a giant letter H, and the caption reads: 'Please Ma'am, you've dropped something'. Even in the late twentieth century, such sensitivities were still abroad in the capital. Stanley Ellis, in his survey of 1989, heard a tale that neatly illustrates the persistence of the Londoner's self-consciousness about how he speaks:

> The extremes of Cockney pronunciation – saying 'shaa-ap!' [shut up!] and 'raand' [round] and the glottal stop are looked upon as things which you must not say because our street is better than theirs: we don't go on like that. We were on the beach at Southend and a woman cuffed our kids and shouted 'be'ave yourself you're a' Saafend naouw no' Limeaahse' [Limehouse, in the East End].

Nearly twenty years after that comment, Voices in 2004/5 has picked up many similar concerns across Britain. And yet in London there's clearly a bit of a shift going on as Estuary English and TV shows such as *EastEnders, Only Fools and Horses* and *Big Brother* have to an extent 'legitimized' or at least made fashionable the capital's way of speaking. And that huge social and cultural churn that I described at the beginning of this chapter is undoubtedly making a difference too. Alongside the Somali, the Hindi, the Urdu, the Polish, the Turkish, Bengali and all the other dozens of languages that are heard right across the capital you can hear the same men, women and children speaking a fully fledged London vernacular, complete with glottal stops, 'h'-dropping and slack-jawed city vowels (see the 'Sound of...' section for details). It was there when Stanley Ellis interviewed a shop-keeper, Pranjit (but 'Paul' to his customers), twenty years ago and it's truer still today. The powerhouse of the London voice is unstoppable.

Language in a Landscape 2: Beyond the Smoke

This power is also felt as London suburb shades off into green field in every quarter of the compass. The Survey of English Dialects didn't visit London because their interest lay in rural speech, yet they came pretty close in Essex and Kent and elsewhere. These recordings from the late 1950s and early 1960s are for the most part interviews with farm-workers. Listening to their tales of horse-ploughing, of harrowing and mowing, you sense that it's more than simply forty years that separates the lives and language they're describing and the world of *Footballers' Wives* and chavs.

Here's a ploughman, interviewed in July 1961, who still measured a day's work in *roods* ploughed: 'You were supposed to do foive roods – there are four roods to th' iker' (a rood is a quarter of an acre). It's a voice from another world, but it's linguistically interesting, though, too. Because the man comes from Doddinghurst, barely five miles beyond the M25, on the road to Chelmsford: listen in his indelibly rural accent to sounds that are from the same stable (like 'iker' for 'acre', and elsewhere 'ti-dye' for 'today', and 'chines' for 'chains') as the pure London accent fifteen miles south-west:

> Horses were loik maen. If they were braough' up on the laend, and bro'e in to u' [broke into it], they knew exaec'ly what you was gonna do, sem as you did. But if you braought a taan 'orse daouwn an' put tha' on the plaouw, tha' was sor' a silly: di'n't know what to daoo [didn't know what to do]. But a horse wha' was braough' up on the coun'ry knew prac'ly as much about the job as the maen did. He bin braought up into it from a caoult [colt]. Bu' you couldn't larn a taan 'orse [learn = teach a town horse] once 'e bin a London.

His vowels are harsh and open, particularly his 'a', like a Londoner's: 'laend', 'maen' for 'land' and 'man', and his 'town horse' becomes a pure

Cockney 'taan 'orse'. Lots of glottal stops, too: 'sor' a silly [sort of silly]', 'braough' up [brought up]'. There are city-like elisions: 'prac'ly' in place of 'practically', as well as some 'h'-dropping ('orse') and the very London 'a' for 'to' ('bin a London [been to London]'). And yet alongside these features are a few Essex characteristics that Voices heard in the eastern end of the county that are closer to East Anglian speech: 'it' comes out as 'ut' ('bro'e into u'') and 'go' as 'goo'.

In other Essex tapes from the SED, many similar traces turn up, but with the emphasis more on the rural than the urban – that 'oi' for 'eye' sound that the Doddinghurst ploughman has is everywhere: 'foive [five]', 'noin o' clock [nine o'clock]', 'toid-up [tied-up]', and swinging round north of London in Hertfordshire 'toimaday [time of day]'.

Move south of London into Sussex and forty years ago the SED could still find eloquent speakers of true rural dialect: listen to this man's southern rolling of his 'r' sounds, a feature completely alien to London speech. His memories go back decades, to before the First World War, and in his accent and pronunciation (he actually does use a 'b' at the front of 'delinquents') he's very much the old countryman, complete with crusty views of 'today's youth':

> Ah don' thing they'rre 'appierr than we were, ar else therre wunt be all this 'ere juvnile bilinquuns would therre? We neverr use' t'ave none o' tha'. We used to [work hard] an' we used to go ou' 'n the fiel' an' 'ave a game a cricket or some'ing jus' forr a li'le racriaytion. But naow people all wan' carrs an' all this rollin' about all o'er the pleaice. Neverr sa'isfied.

By 1985, when Stanley Ellis took his tape recorder out into rural Berkshire, men who spoke like this had become few and far between. He noted what was being referred then to as 'the revolution of sameness' that was spreading around London. This was the Estuarial flood that had engulfed the villages and towns along the railway line out of London like Wallingford, Cholsey and Blewbury. In this last village he met an old countryman, Claud Corderoy, whose resinous accent had the 'r's and the 'oi' sounds that mark him out as a local of this corner of England. Blewbury even twenty years ago was expanding hugely, part of the westward development of factories and research laboratories along the M4 and railway corridor from London that had begun more than a generation earlier:

You'rre looked upon as an owd coun'ry yokel 'oo knaws nothing, in many cases. But o' courrse it's the boo' on the other foot. These peop'le – quoite nice people, naturally, go' a ci'y and coun'ry loif be'ind 'em – they thin' the village's gonna be the same, but big city an' a small village is a differen' loife al'ogetherr. An they dawn' ge' accustome' to i' and they think it's *us* thass wrawng.

The incomers filled up the new estates, nobody knew anybody any more and the old sense of community was dying:

Yew knew everybody. That was one of the great things about it. And people alwiz aout in theirr garrdens. An' everybody 'ad a cheerry wurrd fer ye, ' 'Allo, Georrge, 'allo, Tom; wha' dyou think on i' this morrnin?' People they come an' go so much morre awfen naouw – we got one or two different estates – if anybody's been there three or four years, they bin 'ere a long toime, whereas beforre: bred an' borrn in the village, stayed in the village.

And one of the incomers, Maureen, noted that the way children at the village school were speaking even then, twenty years ago, sounded very London – an early pointer to the Estuarization of the Home Counties:

You don't hear children speaking [with a Berkshire accent] now. It's now what I call a London accent. Not necessarily Cockney, a bit like mine with a bit of this and a bit of that all sort of thrown in together.

So is the onward march of Estuary unstoppable? Are we all in time to be victims of the revolution of sameness? I'm tempted to think not. The results of the Voices survey in London and south-east England, that you can read later in this chapter, suggest there's some dogged resistance by the older forms and a lot of energy among the newer vernaculars. As Stanley Ellis wrote, emphatically, at the end of his survey of the evolving Berkshire dialect in 1985:

How sad? Not on your life! I'm telling a story of what's actually happening to a language, and the last thing I want to do is to imply that something is dying and is not being replaced by something equally living. Don't forget that we *all* have an accent and if you live in west London you have one as well. It's the powerful social effect of this particular style of speech that's at the moment changing life-style and language.

The Voices Survey: London and the South-East – Who Says We All Speak the Same?

Is the revolution of sameness going to encompass all of us as it forges along? I don't think so, for as it spreads I'm sure it'll splinter. It will form local enclaves which will promote more and yet newer local changes. So I'm sure that at the street level people in twenty years will still be arguing about speech east or west of the greater London boundary.

Stanley Ellis wrote those words at the end of the 1980s, when he surveyed the language of London for the BBC. Has his prediction that sameness would be resisted been fulfilled? Voices interviewed a range of men and women across the region, from Hackney in north London to Clapham in the south, from Gravesend in Kent on the south bank of the Thames estuary, to further up the coast at Maldon in Essex. In the west, Voices went to neighbouring Reading and Purley in Berkshire, forty or more miles from London and not too far from the Wallingford and Cholsey area surveyed in 1985. Then right down in the south of Kent, twenty miles east of Hastings, the team heard from the crew of the Dungeness lifeboat. It's a whirlwind tour of south-east England and one that a little echoes the sweeping circuits of that aircraft on its final approach to Heathrow. In our linguistic overflight, I'll be taking in very different sorts of people, too, from an Afro-Caribbean group in Reading, to a traveller couple from Kent, some Essex teachers and a family from Berkshire.

I'll start, though, in north London, in Hackney, where John, his wife Marion and a teenage friend, Jessica, are talking about the changing sound of Cockney. John is convinced there's a north–south divide in the accents, with the Thames as the boundary:

'Ah faind yangsters from saaf Landun still tolk more Cocknay dan yangsters from nawf Landun would. Ah can tolk to a bloke maybe of twenty-foive, from saaf Landun that would tolk lak ma dad. We tolk very awl-fashion' Cocknay, whereas now you don't fin' i' a lo' in nawf Landun. This side of the Thames, pu' it tha' way.'

According to one expert, this sort of difference (which he noted two decades ago, so it can't be changing that fast) may be ascribed to the great homogeneity of south London communities, the north having traditionally absorbed a greater mix of outsiders. Whatever the truth, it's worth pausing a moment to inspect John's pronunciation. To my ear, he has a pretty classic (he calls it 'old-fashioned') Cockney accent. The 'u' sound in 'youngsters' and 'London' itself becomes hardened into a harsh, open 'a' ('yangsters', 'Landun'). 'South' and 'north' are pronounced 'saaf' and 'nawf' complete with TH-fronting ('f' for 'th') and there are plenty of glottal stops ('fin' i' a lo' [find it a lot]'), as well as a tendency to distort other vowels – that rustic Essex 'foive' turns up here, and the 'y' stretches and flattens to 'ay' ('Cocknay'). Jessica has this last characteristic even more markedly: she calls the 'narrow walkway beside a house' an 'allay' and her grandmother is 'grannay', while Marion describes her grand-children as 'lavvlay' – 'Katie's two gehls are lavvlay.' 'Gehls', incidentally, is the typical pronunciation of the word 'girl' in London speech, and it's heard very widely – Mary from the Gravesend group declares herself 'a propuh Ken' gehl [a proper Kent girl]', but none the less she's one who speaks like a Londoner.

In the example I quoted above, John also illustrates another typical Cockney trait, but one that's not always heard: the hardening of 'th' to 'd' ('than' to 'dan', in this case). This was most evident amongst the survey groups in Gravesend, where the traveller family, though full of words from the Romany tradition and very fluent in that language, none the less had very marked south-eastern features in their speech. Take this example from Frank, who's full of these 'd's for 'th's – 'dat', 'dough', 'dere' for 'that', 'though' and 'there':

> 'Ah fin' a lot of the people dat has bin born in Ken' – dough we're some maals away from London – dat a lo' of the peepaw does tawk loik Cockneys. Dat par' I can't make eaou' [That part I can't make out]. Dere is some people dat tawk loik Ken' peepaw what lives in Ken' bu' there's a lo' a peopl' 'a' lives in Ken' tawk loik London slang. I foind a lo' of people from a long way away still tawk London.'

As he points out, there are many voices heard in this part of Kent, not from people who've moved out of town, but Kent born and bred, that sound very Cockney these days: 'That part I can't make out', he says. In fact, Gravesend isn't enormously far from London, only a little over twenty miles down-river from Westminster, yet the pervasive influence

The Sound of the South-East

A strong London accent has four main features: glottal stops ('butter' becomes 'bu''er'), the pronunciation of 'th' as 'v' ('with' becomes 'wiv'), the frequent omission of 'h' (' 'e's in 'ospital in 'Arrow') and a whole merry-go-round of vowel changes. The 'r' at the middle or ends of words is not sounded, so a Londoner puts his or her vehicle in a 'caah paak' where for a Devonian it would be a 'carr parrk'. There's also a tendency in London speech to swallow the 'r' slightly so that 'from' can sound sometimes closer to 'fwom'.

Words get crunched and run together, with the grunting 'uh' sound detectable everywhere, representing 'to' ('aw' a do [ought to do]'), 'with' ('alonga [along with]') and 'of' ('the sideatheaahse [the side of the house]').

But it's the vowels that most noticeably mark out the Londoner, and it's this quality that shows up, in diluted form, in the outer suburban, more generalized south-eastern form, sometimes known as 'Estuary'. The 'ay' sound that becomes 'eye' is the best-known, with all that *My Fair Lady* stuff about 'rine in Spine', but running it a close second is the 'ow' sound in 'house' and 'Southend' that becomes opened into a harsh 'a': ' 'aahse', 'Saafend'. The short 'a' vowel in 'Camden' and 'Lambeth' gets squeezed and nasalized more towards an 'e'

of the capital's style is unmistakable: 'loik' for 'like', 'maals' for 'miles' and the rest. Frank also has the so-called 'dark 'l'' that is often heard in these parts – 'peepaw' for 'people' (though, as you can tell from the transcription, he doesn't do it all the time). His syntax too is very characteristic of working-class London: 'there is some people that talk' and 'people what lives in Kent'; likewise the way he reduces the word 'that' to a solitary 'a' ('people 'a' lives . . .').

Mary, a non-traveller neighbour and Kent-born (though with a Londoner for a partner), has also noticed the way Gravesend has become very East End-sounding:

> 'My partner 'e says I tawk Cockney bu' I think doan'. I think I tawk Ken'ish. But I class meself as pure English Ken' gehl. Ef summun says t'me [If someone says to me], "Oh you tawk Cockney", I says, "Naow! I'm a propuh Ken' gehl." "Bu'," they say, "no, you're tawkin' Cockney", bu' t'me I doan'.'

('Caemdin', 'Laembith') while the 'uh' of 'London' itself sharpens up towards an 'a': Voices recorded people talking about 'Landun yangsters', though a London 'girl' would be a 'gehl' with the 'ur' sound trimmed to an open 'eh'.

There are some more subtle vowel shifts, too, like the 'y' sound at the end of a word that can become lengthened and flattened: 'Cocknay', 'allay', 'stroppay', while long 'o' and 'u' are sometimes stretched into diphthongs like 'gaoo' for 'go' and 'laooo' for 'loo'. It all gets rather complex-sounding to describe, but if you're in any doubt, just think *EastEnders*. It's worth noting, too, a subtlety about the glottal stops. They don't just turn up wherever there's a 't' to be dropped ('li''l'un [little one]' is the Londoner's term for a baby), but occur all over the place, replacing 'p' in 'people' ('peo'le'), 'k' in 'like' (Voices recorded 'ladyli'' for 'ladylike') and so on.

The tune of south-east England speech tends to be flat and urban; after all, it does spring broadly from the city, and there's not a great degree of rise and fall. It's noticeable listening to the old rural recordings made for the SED that the countrymen spoke markedly more slowly than city folk, with words coming in clumps rather than in the city-dweller's tumble of syllables that often run into one another. It's this slightly slurred, under-articulated, slack-sounding delivery that is part of the flavour of the broader Estuary accent too.

A striking feature of many of the Voices interviews has been the way in which specific accents and words are identified as belonging very narrowly to a particular village or town. 'They speak completely different and they're only two miles away', 'The townies aren't like us' are comments that show the club-like quality of a closed speech community, heard everywhere in the UK. And Londoners with their urban 'villages', their north of the river, south of the river rivalry, their inner and their outer suburbs are just as partisan and fiercely attached to their individual locality and culture as someone from a remote corner of rusticity. Listen to the way the Hackney group refer to the survey question about what they'd call a trendy person in cheap clothes and jewellery:

'Chigwell people or Laa'un [Loughton]. Yuh can 'ave someone wiv no' much mannay wolkin' along in cheap jooleree or yuh can 'ave someone thass go' a few quid bu' dun really know 'ow to dress, an' would juss loo' trashee. Maybe Chigwell people or Laa'un.'

So according to John and Marion, the residents of the Essex towns on the edge of greater London, like Chigwell and Loughton, are home to people with more money than dress-sense. 'Watch it!' warns Marion as John gets into his stride. John and Marion use few uniquely Cockney terms, though they offered 'threads' and 'garms' as synonyms for clothes, both well established words still in use, and the charming 'potless' alongside the standard 'skint' for being out of cash.

Jessica is two generations younger at least than John and Marion, and unlike them, she uses many of the new national vernacular terms: 'butters' and 'minging' for bad or ugly, a 'dog' for an unattractive woman. 'Butters', incidentally, she glottalizes ferociously: 'bu' 'ers'. Interestingly, though, Jessica has also adopted some of the new vernaculars swirling around in the capital, like 'bredren' for friend, absorbed from Caribbean slang:

> ' "Bredren" – a lot of people at my school say "bredrens", or "blud", or "blad": a lotta vem say that, not me personally. What you've heard from the younger myebe black tabs is "bruv" or "bro" or even "boss", but that's obviously more than we would use. My friends call me "beibe" [babe].'

With those thoughts still in mind, swing now sixty odd miles west to Purley in the western fringes of Reading in Berkshire to listen to Donna, who's twenty-eight, answering the same question about what she'd call a 'friend':

> ' "Mate", "spar": " 'E's my spar"; it's more of a black terminology, I think. " 'E's my spar" and they do the touch of the knuckles. I've got a few black friends an' it's jus', like, " 'E's my spar." I don't know what that means; it's just " 'E's my spar" and the knuckle thing, but I do think it's more of a black thing; I don't know woy.'

Donna is by no means as London as Jessica from Hackney or Mary from Gravesend, yet she displays some definite features of south-eastern speech like 'h'-dropping and 'woy' for why. But if her accent is more Estuary than Cockney (i.e. less markedly inner-city metropolitan and more broadly south-eastern), the way she's absorbed the fashionable jargon of other ethnic groups is similar to Jessica's and a very marked feature of the capital. And it's spreading via music fashion throughout the country.

Non-native British influences, like black music – rap, hip-hop and so on – are a powerful force on the language these days, giving huge energy to urban and young people's vernaculars (see the 'South-East Snapshot'). The exact process of assimilation is not straightforward, though; the route via music into the mainstream may come directly from the Caribbean, from New York or via the London black music industry. Americanisms, too, are often adopted by journalists in search of a 'cooler' tone of voice (I recall an article not so very long ago in a broadsheet newspaper that described the 'elevators' in a British hospital) and slowly the drip-feed is making a mark, albeit a small one. When mentioning 'pants' for trousers (a surprisingly widespread usage) Voices interviewees often remarked that this was 'also the American word'.

Additionally, the effect of hugely popular and influential television hits such as *Friends* and *Neighbours* is difficult to gauge but there's little doubt that it's being felt right across the country: the tip-up intonation pattern (known as 'Upspeak') adopted by many youngsters in Britain has, for example, frequently been ascribed to the influence of Australian soap operas.

One thing almost all the Voices groups interviewed across the south-east can agree on, however, is the London standard for grandmother: it's 'nan'. This is the response from Purley:

> ' "Nan", gotta be "nan", by order of Nan! Or "nanny": I refer to her as nanny when I'm talking to [my son].'

'Nan' is another element of south-eastern standard speech that's being widely adopted elsewhere in the UK. It's quintessentially the word for the capital, though, and was ubiquitous twenty years ago in the last survey ('Gary's nan knew my nan,' said one woman then commenting on the intimacy of East End living). In 2004/5, 'Nan, nanny, grannay, when you're very small, nana' were the Hackney group's responses.

Now I'm going to shift the scene south of the river Thames to Clapham. Clapham has many large houses and even the more artisanal streets have long been gentrified, the area laughingly known for a while (in fake imitation of all those Featherstonehaugh/Fanshawe pronunciations) as 'Claam'. Four-by-fours patrol the school run and au-pairs often live in, frequently with a car provided by the householder. This is a very different, essentially upper middle-class London, and one that offers yet another distinctive flavour in the capital's linguistic cuisine.

Charlotte, Alexandra and Juliet speak with a fairly standard RP accent, though some of their vowels are exaggeratedly 'posh': 'off' for example is stretched to 'awff' and 'out' is closer to 'ight' (as in 'light'). Above all, what marks this trio's speech are the intonation and stress patterns, emphatic and volatile: the word 'furious' (offered as a synonym for 'annoyed') is pronounced with heavy weight laid on the first syllable and very little on the remainder so that it sounds almost like '*fyure*-iss'. Their words, too, belong very much to their milieu: terms like to 'bear' ('my mother acshly caan't beaah . . .'), 'frightfully' (for very) and 'absolutely' (another reinforcing word) – 'absolutely hideous' is probably how they'd describe both something really ugly and a gruesome party.

So when the time came to ask for their word for 'grandmother', the response was perhaps unsurprising:

'Grandma or granny. What we *don't* say [is] "nan". My children find it very, very confusing when their friends sometimes describe or talk about their grandmother as "nan" – their "nanny" or "nan". Because they think of their nan or nanny as their "nanny", their au pair. Somebody who's employed to look after them. So they get very confused if someone says they're "going round to their nan's", and they're about nyeen-ti [ninety]!

And they think the nanny should be living in the home because she's the nanny and looks after them. Our nanny happens to live in the house. So they think that when someone's going round to see their nan, it's all veh ahdd [very odd].'

Conversely, the trio have a wonderfully eccentric selection of personal 'grandmother' terms: 'grandmummy' ('it's an awfully big mitheful'), 'guggie' and 'goom' ('my brother's wife is Polish and they call their Polish grandmother 'Babooshka', which ah think is raather nice – Lahvely, yah').

The speech of these Claphamites is just as idiosyncratic and individual in its accent and word-choice as any other in this book, determined by family and by a shared wider culture. Listen, for instance, to these reflections on their words for 'toilet':

' "Lavatri" or "loo". 100 per cent "loo". My mother won't have the word "toilet" used. And the children all say "toilet" now 'cos that's what they say at schools now, isn't it? And my mother ac'shly caan't beaah to heaah the wuhd "toilet". It's like a nail on a blackboard, she abs'lutely haytes it; it haats [hurts] her sensibilities.'

Now contrast the responses to the same question of the other south-eastern groups Voices interviewed. Hackney:

'"Toiluh'" or "loo". I just call it the toiluh', goin' to the toiluh': it's prob'ly no' very sophisticati' or ladyli'. But then when I'm gonna 'ave a baaff I say baaffroom.'

A middle-class family, Purley, Berkshire:

'"Loo", "shit'ouse", "dunny": that used to be in the bo'm of the garden. [I'd say] "Where's the porcelain pony?" and "I'm gonna water the 'orse". I think toilet is more polite . . .'

A group of teachers from Maldon, Essex, plumped for 'loo, lavatory' while the Dungeness lifeboatmen voted for 'toilet or loo; but the nautical phrase would be the head'. The travellers from Gravesend said 'toilet or baaffroom, but pani tan in Romany'. Finally in Reading, a group with roots in Barbados preferred 'men's room or lavatory'. But in a variant on the well-loved stories of outside dunnies and petties found throughout this book, they remembered the Barbadian equivalent '. . . the closet: it's a pit and you build a little house over it. Dey would drop a stawn and dependin' on how it sound, dey would know if it fillin up!' Yet even this story wasn't quite as colourful as the piece of lavatorial linguistic invention Voices heard about from Clapham:

'Course, my father called it "going for a George" because there was a hisemaster at Eton called George (or *Mister* George because they all called themselves by their surname) and he always used to disappear at regular times during the day. And the boys discovered that he was having a good poo on the loo, so they all used to call going to have a poo "a George".'

Listening to this range of accents and cultural backgrounds, it's perhaps no wonder that lavatory has retreated, toilet has become culturally pigeonholed and 'loo' has triumphed as the classless term of choice across the UK.

What emerges from the survey in the south-east is a broadly consistent sound for the speech throughout the region: old local accents (the Home Counties rural with rolled 'r' and country vowels like 'oi' for 'eye') have receded in the face of a new standard. Certain common words also find unanimity in this speech style: 'loo', as we've seen, but also 'chuffed' for happy and above all 'knackered' for tired (Marion, from Hackney: 'It's a good word "knackered", it says exactly what it's supposed to mean. You sit down and you think, "I'm knackered": I like "knackered"').

Yet there are still strong local variants of tone, of intensity of accent and of vocabulary. In the Snapshot, you can hear the very particular voice of Barbadian Reading, but this continuing individuality is to be found in most areas if you look hard enough: in the Hackney group with their pungent Cockney:

'We'd never ever ga aat [go out] on a Sat'di evenin' wivvout a free-piece saoo' [three-piece suit] on, usually mo'air, two-tone. We din't seem to drink too much: praps wha' yangsters spen' now on drink, we'd spen' on clo'es [clothes].'

Down the Thames at Gravesend, whilst the traveller family's accent may be pretty indistinguishable from John's in Hackney, their vocabulary, rich in Romany terms like 'cushty' (good), 'skimmished' (drunk) and dozens more, is as local to their tradition as Cumbrian or Cornish are to theirs.

And amongst the Dungeness lifeboat crew, there's plenty of individuality on offer when they're talking about things that really matter to them, like the weather:

'The "agger-jaggers": that's a Dungeness [term]. When the water's warmer than the air you get all this steam along the shore, like a fog. You'll steam in from the sea – and it can be nice and clear out there – into this mist, this low-lying sea mist that'll be close in to the beach and then half a mile up the road as well. And then as the sun gets up it'll all clear.'

Stuart, one of the crew, divides his time between the south coast and London, and he's had a chance to try out these local words in the capital: 'My friends from all parts up in London, when I describe it to them, they didn't know what I meant!' Likewise getting 'girted' by the tide:

'I mentioned that once or twice and they looked at me as if to say "What the hell are you on about?" It's just when you're trying to tow something very heavy and the tide sweeps you around, overpowering the boat.'

Then there are the many names for fish: 'flukes' (flounders) and 'scads' (horse mackerel), also known as 'policemen' and 'joe-bungers': 'They're useless sharp fish and they 'urt your hands when you're dealing with them. One of the dogfish family's called "smellies", 'cos they smell!'

Fish names, like the names given to birds and insects, are so often a mark of localness. But Stuart's experience of working away has given a different shape to his view of the world, and a linguistic horizon that now stretches the full length of the Garden of England away to the Smoke.

'The culture difference was quite remarkable; the hustle and bustle of London after bein' in Dungeness where there's one road, an' if you see four cars you'd be quite surprised. It definitely was a shock to the system.'

Stuart's is one of thousands upon thousands of similar experiences that have changed the shape of regional speech in the past half-century: thus his accent, noticeably not Cockney, but not particularly Kentish either, has more in common with Estuary than that of his local colleagues.

To find real evidence of the revolution of sameness, the Estuarial tide, you have to go much closer to London, and especially to those areas around the capital that have been since the first half of the twentieth century the settling points of the exodus that followed new industries out of town and sought wider spaces in which to live. The teachers from Maldon in Essex have watched it happen:

'I think most of our children spend so much time watching TV that their accents and the lazy way that they speak come from the bad TV programmes, which is of course what they enjoy. I always try to correct, things like "I done this" and the dropping of the letter sounds, the "t" and the "d", I correct those as well 'cos otherwise it doesn't help their spelling. They also have this inflexion at the end where they go up like a mad Australian all the time – and "like": they say "like" instead of a pause.'

Correctness. Laudable, of course, and what every self-respecting teacher is looking for. Yet at the same time, I can't help recalling the countless stories I've heard in the course of preparing this book of regret expressed for local broad accents flattened at school. I remember the laments for dialect driven out by over-enthusiastic teachers, unwilling to accept other than the norm, the national standard. Now it's always going to be a question of balance, and to be fair to Shelley, Jen, Jean and Linda they love distinctive words and encourage them when they hear them. But the Essex fringe they live in, like Berkshire, has it seems to me succumbed to a certain uniformity.

In the group from Purley, on the outskirts of Reading, the younger members repeatedly take their cue from television and radio, citing Chris Moyles, Denise van Outen and others who'd used phrases they'd copied. The accents, too, particularly those of the younger contributors, Donna and Daniel, were typically those that Stanley Ellis was noting amongst Berkshire schoolchildren twenty years ago: 'oy' for 'eye' ('my' sounds like 'moy') and 'eye' for 'ay' ('play' is pronounced 'ply') and that London 'gehl' for 'girl', too, along with much 'h'-dropping and glottalizing. The vocabulary, with the few exceptions I've already mentioned, is here, as amongst the teachers of Maldon, also completely routine: so drunk is 'pissed' or 'rat-arsed', attractive is 'stunnin' ', rich, 'loaded' and the main room a 'lounge' (pronounced with the unmistakable Estuary extended whine, 'laouwnge').

Where they and the other groups do markedly differ is on the regular question of the chav, the young person in cheap trendy clothes and jewellery. Sixty years ago, they were known as 'spivs' or 'drones'; now they're 'chavs', 'trevs', 'neds' and a host of other generally derogatory terms. In the south-east, Voices noted 'posers', 'yobs', 'wannabes', 'wideboys', 'saga-boys' (among the Reading Barbadian group) and 'spivs'. 'Chavs' were not mentioned or were felt not to fit the description, except of course by the Gravesend travellers, for whom 'chav' or 'chavvie' is simply Romany for 'child'.

In Clapham, on the other hand, they had a whole story to tell . . .

'He'd probly be a "yawbboe" [yobbo]: cheap jew'ry wud prob'ly be a "yawbboe".'

' "Taahts" [tarts] for girls – depends on what they're wearing;
"slag" or "slapper".'

'Could be a twelve-year-old who [shops at] Primark, but if she
looked nice I'd call her a "chick".'

'D'you know the twelve- and thirteen-year-olds are starting to
wear really short skirts, which people would call "pussy pelmets".'

'If a boy is wearing jewellery he's probably gay.'

' "Youth of today." My father would say, "Oh my God! Youth of
today!" '

Finally, a quick word about the feature of London speech that's
supposed to typify the Cockney, rhyming slang. Surf the web and you'll
find long and elaborate lists of rhyming expressions on the classic 'apples
and pears – stairs' model. But Voices heard it used unselfconsciously only
once, and then abusively, where the expression 'happy-go-likey' was
mentioned in connection with the Gravesend travellers, rhyming slang
for 'pikey' (a much disliked derogatory description of them). Some may
use it from time to time in a jocular way, others use it but get it wrong:
sixteen-year-old Jessica from Hackney claimed a friend of hers said, 'I'm
Marvin' for 'starvin' '; to which her friend John retorted that she'd got it
wrong – 'It's mean' a be "I'm 'Ank" – 'Ank Marvin [starvin']!' And then
added, 'Bu' you wouldn't know 'oo 'Ank Marvin is!'

Certainly rhyming slang is not a dominant feature as far as Voices is
concerned and the Hackney group, for example, actually find it embarrassing and artificial. As Marion and John so succinctly put it:

'It's something we never use, I've never used rhyming slang . . .
I fin' i' qui' embarrassing when y' 'ear people on the television
usin' i' . . .'

'I've go' a cousin 'oo uses i' and it's embarrassin'.'

'Yeah, it's a bi' old a' [old hat], 'cos the East End's a bit mul'icultural
naouw an' everyone looks a' 'im as if [he's mad]. Z'only aba' free
peoplina wuhl knows wha' e's tolkin' abah' [There's only about three
people in the world knows what he's talking about]. Migh' as well be
speakin' Welsh! Knaw wha' a min?'

A South-East Snapshot: Blingin' it in Reading and Cambridge

Amongst the riches brought by the Voices project is the opportunity to reflect and reminisce on lives lived, through the medium of language. And while it's true that nationally there is a general retreat from the older forms of regional speech, conversely within the cities and towns I've found a great deal of lively and dynamic new language going on. This is particularly true in places where the speech traditions of ethnically distinct communities are converging and mixing.

In the south-east of England, some of the most stimulating conversation emerged when a group of men and women with a family background in Barbadian or Bajan culture gathered in a home in Reading. Lyle and Myrtle are an older couple who came to Britain from the Caribbean island of Barbados in the 1950s. Their memories of lives lived on the island before they emigrated contrast with those of Kevin and Jeff both born here, and Jeff's brother Junior who, though born in the West Indies, has spent much of his adult life in the UK.

Lyle is full of stories about the old days in Barbados and offers a constant counterpoint of information and authority to the observations of the younger men. One of the first topics the group raised was the weather, when asked for what they said for 'hot' and 'cold'; Myrtle, always quick with metaphorical phrases, kicked off. 'In the West Indies, I'd say, "I feel as hot as fire."' The rest of the group chimed in: 'In Bajan I would say, "It's as hot as hell" or "I feel like I'm in the oven" or "What are you doin'? Trying to cook me?"' To which Lyle added sardonically, 'In this country it never gets hot.' To express the sort of heat experienced in Britain, he added, he'd be more oblique: '"It's a bit warm", "open the window, please" – people will get the message that you are hot!'

Most of the time, though, they were cold in Britain: 'frawzin', said Myrtle. 'Ice log' was the preferred expression – Lyle explained:

> 'I ge' "ice log" today – I go' frozen today. Tha' comes from workin' on a building site when everything's frozen up in the morning!'

The only time he could remember really feeling cold in Barbados was at the sea's edge at dawn:

'We were in the habit of gettin' up at four in the mornin' and bringing back some grit and some sand an' bottles of sea-*water*, because they would say that the sea-*water* could keep you purged, [would] clean your system. And we'd be runnin' and, on a few occasions awnly, I could hear my teeth knocking. And youda seay [you'd say], "It muss be cawl' like this in Englan'!" But for us, that's too cold!'

The culture gap was never far away from the conversation, and specifically when asked about what term the group would use to say they weren't well: 'Not feelin' vell today, I got bad feels: the Bajan general expression is "bad feels".' As Lyle explained:

'And it's become a joke, really, with the doctor because they will go ti doctor and doctor'll say, "Whass wrong wi you?" and they'll say, "I'm no' feelin good." And de poor doctor doan knaw what to do, he still caen't ge' down to diag*no*sin' what's causin' them trouble!'

When asked what they'd use to say they were annoyed, the group settled first on 'vexed'. Interestingly, it's a usage that has cropped up regionally, too, in the Voices survey, though in standard modern English it feels, I think, a little old-fashioned. The group agreed:

'That is awld English – "vexed", you stress it: this person's vexed with me; this person aggra*va*ted me. Vex' as hell – not just plain vexed, but he made me maad, he really loss screw face. If you're really vexed you're going to explode!'

At this point, let me introduce you to a couple of musicians living in Cambridge, some hundred or more miles away to the east and north. Jason and Mark, known as Lofty, are part Caribbean in their background too, but their speech style is pure Estuary, with an accent that has all the features of the outer London fringe. Their vocabulary has many of the typical terms of their generation – 'fit' for attractive, a 'wannabe' for the trendy young guy, though, unlike many, they used 'butters' not to mean *un*attractive, but for the reverse: 'Sexy, smooth and soft like butter,' said Lofty. But they also used terms that belonged to their world, like 'cotch', originally a West Indian term which has now become London slang for 'to relax', and 'bruck up' (unwell, or tired).

Voices caught up with them at about the same moment as the group in Reading and it's interesting that though in many ways their backgrounds and circumstances were quite different, and despite a physical distance between them that in traditional dialect terms would be sufficient to separate, say, a Yorkshire tyke from a Geordie, some of the parallels were striking. For Jason and Lofty, then, 'vexed' was the preferred term for annoyed, and again that 'screw face' notion: 'screwy' or 'screwin'' (looking at someone with your face screwed up, they explained).

Back to Reading, and the group is embroidering on their list of 'annoying' expressions:

> '"Don't mek me sin my soul today", and that means that that person is really angry and if you get in their way, they'll knock you out. Or "You tried my faith today!" You're trying me (my faith) so don't get in my way! That is very old English in Barbados.'

Now it's Jeff's turn to chip in:

> 'Also there's "trusting my faith": "Don't trust my faith too much", [meaning] don't overplay your hand. If you're trusting my faith, you're doing things that you knaw will anger me, but because I love you I'm not going to do them back. It's a warning: don't trust my faith too much because I might lose it.'

If the person who was testing your patience is a friend of yours, for the Reading team, he's your 'spar', your 'buddy' or your 'mate'. Lyle explained that he'd not used 'mate' until he came to Britain, but working on the buses, 'Your driver was always your "mate"', so he'd got used to saying it. 'Spar' is a crossover term that's now well known beyond the Afro-Caribbean community. Voices met it in Liverpool and in Purley, a stone's throw from Lyle and his friends, and Donna uses it with her black mates, you'll recall. In Cambridge, it turns up again on Jason and Lofty's list of terms for friend – along with some explanations:

> 'That's a "spar", "bredren", "breh", "blud": a lot of people call people that in the UK at the moment. Your spar is someone you spar with, like you go boxin', you spar with them; your friends and you spar. See, me an' 'im might know each other from young. Like when we were young we'd give each other a coupla fumps [thumps] or something. Thass where it comes from, it's that kind of relationship.'

Cut back to Donna and here's the rest of the picture filled in: 'It's just "'E's my spar" and they do the touch of the knuckles.' Over in Hackney, sixteen-year-old Jessica also had some of these terms in her vocabulary, 'bredren' and 'blud' specifically, words which were again mentioned in the Scousers' lexicon. One interesting addition to this list of 'friend'-terms (drawn I imagine from legal language) came from Lofty: 'co-dee'.

> ' "Co-dee" is like co-defendant. Like if [my friend] was in bovver and 'e needed my 'elp I'd be vere for 'im, and vice versa.'

Back in Reading, Voices asked the team for terms for playing, throwing and hitting. In general, responses to these questions have been patchy, with the older dialect areas providing a deal of variety, especially in words for hitting, while younger speakers have tended to use national slang standards like 'thump', 'bang', 'chuck' and 'lob'. The Barbadian group, though, had a huge range of words here. Playing in a metaphorical sense was 'mekking sport', according to Jeff: 'You're mekkin' sport! Bein' a bit of a comedian . . .', i.e. having someone on. Throwing was a serious matter for Lyle, his reference point being the game of cricket; unsurprising perhaps, given Barbados's glittering contribution to the game (Sir Garfield Sobers is a Barbadian). Lyle's word is 'pelt':

> 'If you're playing cricket wit a ball you pelt i' to the nex' perrson an' they'll catch it. I don't thraw i' to im, I pelt it at 'im. Or I pelt it to 'im. If I pelt it at 'im, I want to knock 'im awver [knock him over]. If I thraw it to 'im I want him to catch it so I send it in a reasonable way without force. An' if you're really mad you just "fling" it.'

As for hitting someone hard (with a ball, or not), Myrtle came up with a vivid metaphor:

> 'I'm goin to hit you so harrd you think the Devil harse [the Devil's horse] hit you! That is a really hard blaw; give you a harrd blaw.'

To which her husband adds an expression that he's never been able to trace (nor I):

> 'One of the things I used to hear my mother seay, and my father, is that they'll "hit you as hard as Max Millyarrd". And I never know to

73

this day what Max Millyarrd is supposed to be! But it meant you would get hit very harrd.'

They're all riveted now: Jeff is curious to find out if anyone knows the source of an expression he finds very evocative:

' "Moon run, de day catch it": I don't know what the hell it means; it's a great saying, though.'

Lyle explains that it means that your turn will come and your situation won't last for ever, though he's heard the expression in reverse: 'The day run, till night catch it.'

Words for 'unattractive' bring not a single 'minging' or 'munter' from this group. But Myrtle's back with some more striking images that then inspire the room:

'Ugly as a baboon; you're an empty monkey; rough as ever, man; ugly as a bad penny; ugly as a byled [boiled] ham.'

And finally, from Lyle:

'Not ugly facially but there's something ungainly: we say "obzocky", meaning "You just don't look right!" "Obzocky" is when you're [wearing] good clothes but still not right.'

'Obzocky' or 'obzockie' is in fact Trinidadian dialect for something that doesn't look quite as it should, ungainly, awkward or shapeless: 'those obzocky police vans,' wrote the author of an essay on Trinidadian life, describing ugly official vehicles.

It's not possible to list all the very many fresh and different words that Lyle, Myrtle, Jeff, Junior and Kevin were able to come up with in response to the Voices questions, but a few more of the most interesting were: for truanting, 'limeing' – 'That's a Trinidadian expression' (Jeff); for sleeping, 'have a foive [five]', 'pick up a ress [rest]' and 'goin' to shat-eye lan' [shut-eye land]', and for criticizing someone, 'cry someone down'.

The group conveyed the strong impression that certainly as far as the older members were concerned, their vernacular of choice still came from the culture of Barbados. The last word in this section, though, goes to the musicians Lofty and Jason, whom Voices met, you'll remember, in

Cambridge. They draw on a wider range of sources, Jamaican for instance ('picknee' for baby – also cited in Toxteth, Liverpool). But many are unsurprisingly terms that are rooted in black music culture, many of which are steadily finding their way out into the general lexicon. Terms like to 'bling it':

> 'You'd be goin' to the club that night to go an' 'ave a good time, but you'd be "on the bling" because you'd be bustin' all your shit. But the next day you've got to get up in the morning an' go down the shop to get your pint o' milk you didn't have the night before – but still with all your gold on and 'alf awake. *That* is blingin' it.'

A South-East England Glossary

agger(aggy)-jaggers a mist that forms along the sea-edge (Dungeness usage)

bad feels unwell (Bajan usage)

barnet hair. Cockney rhyming slang (Barnet Fair – hair)

blank to have an unsuccessful fishing trip: 'I blanked today'

bling flashy jewellery; used as metaphor: 'blinging it', 'on the bling', meaning something like 'go the whole hog'. Originally from Jamaican slang; 'bling-bling' allegedly refers to the imaginary 'sound' of light flashing from a gemstone

blud a friend. Perhaps from 'blood-brother'; contemporary slang, from West Indian usage

boracic, brassic broke, lacking money. Cockney rhyming slang (boracic lint – skint)

bredren, bredrin, breh a friend (from 'brethren', brothers). Contemporary slang, from West Indian usage

breeding pregnant: 'she's breedin''. Contemporary slang from Afro-Caribbean usage

bruck up unwell, tired. Contemporary slang; from Afro-Caribbean usage

butcher's a look: ''ave a quick butcher's'. Cockney rhyming slang (butcher's hook – look)

butters unattractive (British usage); also, attractive (see Snapshot). Contemporary slang, from West Indian origin

china mate, friend: 'all right, me old China?' Cockney rhyming slang (china plate – mate)

Cockney a resident of the city of London, according to John Minsheu (1617), born within earshot of Bow Bells; the vernacular speech of the city. From Middle English *coken ey*, a cock's egg. For detailed etymology, see 'Language in a Landscape 1'

co-dee a friend. London Caribbean slang; from 'co-defendant'

cotch to relax, sleep. London slang, from West Indian usage

cream-crackered knackered, exhausted. Cockney rhyming slang (cream-crackered – knackered); reported widely across UK as euphemistic usage for 'knackered'

crepes (a pair of) trainers: 'I'm gonna get me a pair of new crepes.' Afro-Caribbean usage

cushty, kushti good, in good order. Romany term, originally from Persian *kushi*, good

Estuary English the speech of the south-east of England based on the accent and style of the communities living around the Thames *Estuary*. Coined by David Rosewarne, 1984

garms, threads clothes. Old London usage (from 'garments'), but still in current use by teenagers: '. . . where all of the rude boyz get their buff garms'

girt to be caught by a powerful tide or surge of water: 'the tug was girted, capsized, and sank' (maritime accident report, 1976). Dictionary definitions suggest 'girted' refers to a ship being held too tightly by her cables ('a Ship is girted when her Cables are too tight, which prevents her swinging': *The Young Sea Officer's Sheet Anchor, A Dictionary of Sea Terms*, Darcy Lever (1808)

gorja a non-Romany (Romany term)

guv'nor a boss (London slang). From 'governor'

Hank Marvin starvin(g). Cockney rhyming slang (Hank Marvin – starvin'); Hank Marvin was the lead guitarist of the Shadows

heads the lavatory on board ship. Naval term, latrine situated in prow, or head, of ship; eighteenth century

kena a house (Romany term)

lime to play truant (Trinidadian usage)

loaf head, brains: 'use yer loaf, mate!' Cockney rhyming slang (loaf of bread – head)

mek sport to be kidding, joking (= 'make sport', Bajan usage); as in 'you mekking bare sport'

nan a grandmother

obzocky, obzockie ungainly, unattractive (Trinidadian usage)

on your todd alone. Cockney rhyming slang (Todd Sloan – own/ alone)

pani tan a bathroom (Romany usage). From *pani*, water, and *tan*, place

pelt to throw; standard usage, 'to assail with missiles' (Bajan usage in the specific sense of e.g. throwing a ball)

pikey a gypsy, traveller (racist term); a disreputable person (cf. 'chav'). From 'turnpike'

porkies lies: 'you bin tellin' porkies, aincha?' Cockney rhyming slang (pork-pies – lies)

potless broke, lacking money (London slang)

rabbit to talk. Rhyming slang (rabbit and pork – talk)

rood an old form of measurement of area: 40 square rods (1 rod = 5.5 yards); four roods = one acre

saga boy – a playboy (West Indian usage)

scad the Atlantic horse mackerel, *trachurus trachurus*

sinkers socks (old Berkshire usage)

skimmished drunk (cited as Romany term). 'Iskimmish', meaning 'drunk', allegedly in use since the 1700s; 'skimmish' is said to have been tramps' slang for beer

snatched cold. Claimed as Kent term, but also reported in northern England

spar a friend. Contemporary slang, from West Indian usage

trust my faith 'Don't trust my faith': don't push me too far (Bajan usage)

vexed annoyed (West Indian usage)

wannabe a poser, a trendy person (contemporary slang). The word is used in contexts similar to 'chav' and 'townie'; one glossary suggests it refers to a white person seeking to emulate black people to appear cool

4 : WALES

Language in a Landscape: Divided We Stand?

On a football field a few miles outside the Shropshire market town of Oswestry, young lads from the area are punting a ball about in the dusk. Shouts of encouragement from the coach ring across the practice field. It's an unexceptional scene: not the most obvious arena for bitterness and persecution. Yet here in these gentle fields we are in frontierland. 'Oswestry's renowned for fighting at night,' says one of the men watching from the touchline. 'It's gangs from over the border: they come to Oswestry for a bit of fisticuffs.' Chirk is a town on the Welsh side of the border and according to this young man there's little love lost between the young people from there and the English here, though when pressed locals are quick to deny the fighting talk and assure me that all is harmonious coexistence.

But border lands are strange places where rivalries and tensions surface in countries across the world, and even here, where Henry VIII's Acts of Union of 1536–43 have for centuries ensured that Wales and England have a shared destiny, the rules of the dividing line can still spell trouble. Particularly when one of the central planks of Henry's legislation was to outlaw the language of the indigenous people of the country, one of the oldest in Europe:

> The people of the same dominion have and do daily use a speche nothing like ne consonaut to the naturall mother tonge used within this Realme . . .

'Outlaw' is putting it accurately – Welsh was no longer permitted usage in the courts – though the wording was more graphic: the Act declared its intention 'utterly to extirpe alle and singular sinister usages and customs'. English and Welsh, with the long north–south border to share, were destined for an uneasy coexistence linguistically and culturally. Right down to the twenty-first century. On the football field near Oswestry, the coach gestures over his shoulder towards the pub down the road, the Bradford, which actually straddles the border. Here, he said, Welsh Sunday drinkers, deprived of their pints by dry Sunday laws, had until 2003 only to shift to the other bar, which lay geographically and legally over the border in England, in order to enjoy their alcohol.

But dividing lines aren't just cartographic or administrative phenomena. They're states of mind. Over the years I've spent many happy days in both north and south Wales and I was unprepared for the still visceral rivalry not just between Welsh and English but between fellow Welsh men and women that Voices disclosed, much of it rooted in language. Take for example the story of Deborah, who's spent all her life in the Welsh capital – born in Roath and now living in the Splott district – about a trip she'd made to the north:

> 'I did 'ave a negative response when I went into a shop and the lady just blanked me; so I asked 'er again what I wanted and she still blanked me; and in the end she did serve me. And we come out from the shop and we joined the people from the coach an' they were sayin' the same, and we said, 'Well, why?', an' it was because we were from Cardiff. I was shocked because [it was] Wales: we're all Welsh – I was really shocked. Apparently they didn't like that Cardiff was the capital and they did prejudge us by our accent to start with, but it was more boundaries. But I thought it was a bit strange they judged us by our accent first off, because we're just the same as them!'

A different accent, the other end of the country: a matter of boundaries, says Deborah. Now listen to Ann in Holyhead. Speaking in her soft, sibilant accent of the native Welsh speaker of the north of the country, she's passionate about her language, and while she's very gracious about the English and south Walians, there's little doubt in my mind she feels herself linguistically under attack from incomers, from other parts of Wales as well as from England, who can express themselves only in English:

'I like them to keep the Welsh language koin'. I think itss a pitsi to let it ko because it's one of the oltest lankuages. We'fe lost so much: let uss keep awer lankuage alive. We'fe lost so much when awur grandparents ad to gaw to school wearin' tags with "Welsh Not" on it. That is why I'm so strong to keep my Welsh lankuage alife today.'

Ann expresses a deeply felt grief for those unfortunate children who, in the wake of a parliamentary report on education in Wales of 1847, were forced by schoolteachers to wear wooden tags around their necks, with the words 'Welsh Not' or simply 'W. N.' branded into them. As crude and undignified as a dunce's hat, they were intended as a constant reminder, chiding the child to speak not in their native language but in English. This form of linguistic imperialism is a shocking barbarism to us today, yet it's perhaps worth remembering that the social and legal context was far harsher than today. This was a time when slavery was still a recent memory and when transportation to the antipodes was the natural penalty for even relatively minor misdemeanours.

Nevertheless, there's no doubt that for many hundreds of years the Welsh language was under extreme attack. Today, when levels of Welsh-speaking hover around 20 per cent of the population, the position is very different and there's positive encouragement for the linguistic and cultural diversity that Welsh offers. Yet the damage is to a large extent done, and the pressure of 55 or more million English speakers on the other side of Offa's Dyke is hard to resist. Particularly when one parent is English and speaks no Welsh. It gets Ann's goat:

'One thing that I feel quite strongly apout is that Welsh parents – maybe my son, my daughter – Welsh-speaking, married to an Englishman or an English girl: what right have they got to deprive their children of the Welsh language, living in Wales? What right have my children – an' I'm talking apout *my children* – of depriving my krandchildren of their mother language? . . . *Their* mother language?'

And, recorded four years ago, here's Ieuan, a Welsh sheep-farmer amid the flock he's selling across the border in Shropshire on his own dilemma:

I couldn't speak a word of English till I was about eleven. Never heard of it like. I was up in the hills like and it was never, never spoken in my local school. And the headmaster was a Welsh nationalist and I was grown up amongst Welsh nationalists. So it suits me. [But] English are coming in and they're trying to change our ways to suit them like. Remote cottages are being sold to English families, and we tend to converse with them in their language, and we gradually would lose our language if we continued. It's very important to start with the young kids: although my wife is English, my kids speak fluent Welsh, though we speak English in my kitchen if you like. Unfortunately, my wife has stuck to her language and I speak English to her, but if I'm ever with my kids like it's always Welsh.

Back on the nearby football field, there's another piece of linguistic barbarism going on: a young Welsh lad called Gareth is skulking around the back of the group. He's clearly sick and tired of hearing the endless jokes about sheep and the constant unsubtle mimicking of a sing-song Welsh accent: 'It's got serious undertones,' agrees one of the supporting dads, 'but, I mean, lads are always taking the mickey out of the one another, aren't they, and anything at all that is slightly different they pick on, not necessarily the language.' The youngsters' coach concurs: 'I'm English, and they do rag the Welsh, well, they all do; we all take the mick out the Welsh, don't we?'

This sense of boundaries, social, cultural and linguistic divisions, is of course not restricted to Wales. Elsewhere in this book I've for instance quoted the vehemence with which a young lad from Northumberland spoke about the rival gang from the neighbouring village two miles away. It's something that goes hand in hand with localness and expressing yourself in a specifically local manner. However, from the evidence of the recordings made not just recently but across the past twenty or more years, this sniping sense of difference – and of being prepared to express it quite openly – seems to be a characteristic feature of Wales. The 'opposition' may be the old enemy across the border, but it may equally come from closer to home. Here's Jeff, a man from the Rhondda but now holding a position of some public distinction in Anglesey, speaking very recently about how people still constantly make fun of his south Walian accent:

'People regularly say, "Pakistani, are you?" because my accent is still so south Walian. In the youth club I go, "Do you wanna cuppa tea?", an' they go, "Cuppatee! Cuppatee! Cuppatee!" – as if you're a Pakistani!'

And it's not just Jeff and his fellow south Walians who have reason to take offence at that bit of linguistic stereotyping, either. Cut to the south of the country, and to the Gower peninsula, that twenty-mile-long peninsula stretching westwards beyond Swansea. It's a tourist paradise, with golden beaches, caves and a long tradition of welcoming visitors. I spent several happy childhood holidays there fifty years ago. But what the outsider like me doesn't notice perhaps, at least first off, is that here you have yet another of these little territorial battlefields, where language and culture are marshalled either side of a divide.

Look at the map, of course and, as so often, the picture comes into sharp focus. Here in the north of the peninsula are Pen-clawdd, Gorseinon, Llanmorlais ... in the England-facing south, Bishopston, Oxwich, Parkmill and Southgate. The locals will even locate the spot where the language splits: they say it's an old road used in generations past by cocklers bringing their gatherings up from the coast to Pen-clawdd to sell, and known as Herman Lane.

Visiting the Gower in 1983 in search of these linguistic frontiers, Stanley Ellis, veteran of the Survey of English Dialects, met a man on one side of the boundary who clearly relished his distaste for the Welsh language, and indeed all things Welsh, albeit articulated in a strong Welsh accent:

> Welsh on't get ye anywhere! If you learn French, you gaw abroad an' it may be yuseful awver there. But where is Welsh yuseful? Awnly in Weels [Wales]. Let the Welsh people speak Welsh to their 'earts' content, but dawn't try to push it down other people's thrawts.

Here in the south of Gower, Stanley Ellis found people who still used expressions like 'Thee ust if thee cust, but thee cassn't [you would if you could, but you can't]', with a strong whiff of the south Somerset and north Devon that they confront across the water. Conversely, on the Pen-clawdd side of Herman Lane, Ellis met another embattled Welsh speaker who, just like farmer Ieuan in 2001 and Ann from Holyhead in 2004/5, felt he was manning the linguistic barricades:

> Luckily in this village there are plenty of people, friends and acquaintances. [We're] keeping back, keeping at arm's length this great onslaught that the English language is making upon me.

In Gower, twenty or more years ago, there were still strong memories of when Welsh was frowned upon: 'If they want to get on in the world they must know English,' confessed Alwyn, a passionate Welsh speaker, of the attitude that prevailed even within his own community. It was a stance reinforced in the schoolroom:

> The tendency to use English even among Welsh speakers arose because of school, you see. The major language in school was English and Welsh was very little used in school, very little taught in school.

The path of the Welsh language to the early years of the twenty-first century has indeed been a long and troubled one. The indigenous language of the country emerged around the sixth century after the withdrawal of the Romans from Britain (a form known as Early Welsh) and flourished as the speech of the territory across the ninth to eleventh centuries, from when a set of legal codes in Welsh, credited to a man called Hywel Dda (known as 'the laws of Hywel Dda'), as well as various pieces of verse have come down to us. This language is today called Old Welsh.

Following the Roman withdrawal, the Saxons had failed to expand westwards from England, and in the late eighth century the king of the midland territory of Mercia, Offa, ordered a huge earthwork or dyke to be built that's still visible today, running north to south from sea to sea the length of Wales. Offa's Dyke in essence established the dimensions of the land of Wales. With the Norman conquest of England, Wales was a target but proved difficult to hold and despite a number of agreements and treaties between the Welsh and English crowns remained disputed territory largely under the dominion of the rulers of the border territories or Marches, the so-called Marcher Lords.

Dr Robert Penhallurick, Head of the English Department at the University of Wales in Swansea, explains:

> The Marches were set up by the Normans as a way really of getting those parts of Wales that they wanted. The Marches don't only come down the traditional border between England and Wales, but the old Marcher Lordships extended into south Wales, through Glamorgan, through Gower and down into Pembroke, and the Normans also established fortresses in isolated locations through north Wales. It was

a way of containing the Welsh, and setting up a kind of transition area between Wales and England.

Despite the uneasy relationship between the Welsh and the would-be conqueror, the Norman presence none the less established a bridgehead for the English language:

> There's a long process of anglicization which began with the Normans, with the Lordships. The Normans established castles and set up the first towns and, as a result, English speakers were encouraged to settle in those areas: that's when the process of anglicization began.

During the thirteenth century, the Welsh attempted to organize the country into a unified principality, but with the defeat and execution of the principal participants in 1282–3 the country fell to the English King Edward I's forces and was thenceforth organized into six counties under the crown of England.

For many years, the Marches were a sort of buffer zone between Wales and England in which both cultures and languages mingled. Little surprise therefore that the day-to-day speech of both traditions reflects that coexistence, with Welsh words and constructions giving the dialect of English spoken in Wales its unique intonation, structure and lexicon. Meanwhile Welsh today has absorbed (to the distress of traditionalists and purists) many, many English terms and given them a Welsh form.

> In the early centuries after the Norman Conquest there was a lot of conflict, but also there was a lot of intermingling and we can see it even today: you'll hear Welsh spoken in Oswestry, you'll hear English spoken in Oswestry; so there's always been a lot of to-and-fro across this apparent frontier.

Following Henry VIII's Act of Union, although English was henceforth the only permitted idiom of officialdom (as Rob Penhallurick puts it, 'If you wanted to get on, you had to learn English, not Welsh'), for the vast majority of the population of Wales their native Welsh continued to be the natural means of expression. The publication in 1588 of the Bible in Welsh helped standardize and regularize the language, although as in English several dialects exist to this day. Despite the stranglehold of English on officialdom and despite the barbarisms I've mentioned earlier exercised in Welsh schools, religion (in the shape of non-conformism) and the development of Welsh-speaking Sunday schools did much to keep the flame of spoken Welsh alive. Dr Penhallurick offers some figures:

> Through the eighteenth century it was bolstered by Methodism, by the circulating schools of Methodism, and even through the Industrial Revolution Welsh was still in a very healthy state. Census figures from 1801 to 1901 show that by 1901 there were still at least half a million Welsh-speakers. But what had happened in the meantime was that the population of Wales as a whole had expanded greatly, so that whereas in 1801, 80 per cent of the population spoke Welsh, by 1901 only 50 per cent did. And I think it was that that then set the scene for what has been a very steep decline in Welsh-speaking throughout most of the twentieth century.

When Stanley Ellis came to Wales to survey the interface between the two languages nearly a quarter of a century ago, there was still much to be done to secure the future of Welsh. Since then, as a result of the 1993 Welsh Language Act, the languages have been granted equal status and the teaching of Welsh is compulsory in schools up to the age of sixteen, though the number of people born outside the country has continued to rise. There is too a great deal of teaching 'through the medium of Welsh' in the official phrase, helping secure the place of the language beyond simple linguistic study. Today, as I've mentioned, a fifth of Wales's three million people speak the language, an increase from the figure a decade or so ago.

Nic and Vernon, older members of a famous male voice choir from Flint, a fairly English corner of the country just across the water from Merseyside, have witnessed the reinvigorated spirit around Welsh:

> 'Is it cool to speak Welsh, with the youngsters comin' up now? Maybe not in this area but it will still survive in my own area of Caernarfonshire; it will survive there . . .'
> 'I think it will here as well because there's a Welsh school here and my friend's little grandson goes to this school now an' ah was ameized this Christmas when 'e came to see is *taid* an' 'is *nain* [grandpa and grandma] an' 'e sang a Welsh song; an' the pride comin' out of 'is side

– it was unbelievable! Long may it last; and the more children that go to this Welsh school an' keep our language going . . . I'm probably prouder now of my heritage, of my Welshness, than I was when I was a child! We've got guys in awer kwyer, people who travel from Warrington, that have never spawken Welsh all their lives but 'ave got more pride in the Welsh language than a lot of 'em have.'

Although knowledge of the language is reported right across the country the principal Welsh-speaking areas lie in the west and north-west. Almost all Welsh-speakers have English at least as a second language and it's not thought there are today any purely monoglot Welsh speakers. It's inevitable therefore that there's going to be a great deal of shared language. In the story I've just quoted for example, the Welsh terms for grandparents are dropped quite naturally into the tale by this first-language English speaker. And even in the towns of the south you'll find 'taid' and 'nain' regularly in use, as well as expressions like 'tŷ bach [little house]' for toilet (see 'The Voices Survey: A Shared *Hiraeth*'). The so-called 'Wenglish' of south Wales – the English dialect of the former industrial heartland of the country – despite being strongly English in its overall feel, possesses many words with Welsh origins and several direct borrowings (see Glossary).

The indigenous language is also responsible for two of the features of the English of Wales that are most imitated (and mocked), namely the melodic rise and fall of the voice pitch (usually called the 'sing-song' accent) and idiosyncratic expressions like 'come you over by here now', which are borrowings from Welsh syntax. Dr Robert Penhallurick has some other familiar examples:

When people say 'there's lovely', again it's a translation from a Welsh idiom: the Welsh word is 'dyna' – there's – followed by an adjective. The other thing that Welsh English speakers are well known for is the way they tack 'isn't it' on to sentences: 'We went shopping the other day, isn't it', which again sounds odd. But once again it's a direct translation of an idiom from the Welsh language [and] because of the way Welsh verbs are constructed, it's quite normal to have that sort of tag at the end of the phrase or a sentence. Then it gets transported into Welsh English.

Dr Penhallurick can also quote an interesting example of an individual word that made a long and tortuous journey firstly into Welsh (originally from Latin) and that's subsequently been reabsorbed into Wenglish: it's a favourite south Walian term 'cwtch', to snuggle down or hide. Starting with a Latin verb 'collocare' (to lay in place), the word travelled through French 'coucher' into Middle English as 'couch', which then becomes Welsh 'cwtsh', from which it's then routinely borrowed by English speakers in Wales as a useful and expressive term, spelled slightly differently: 'cwtch' (pronounced 'cootch').

> Another good example – it doesn't sound like a Welsh word but the word to 'keep', but being used in the sense to gather up and store away the crockery after washing up: to 'keep the dishes', which is a literal translation of Welsh 'cadw', meaning to keep or preserve, which is used in that sense in Welsh.

This was, as Voices heard, an idiom that tripped up Jeff, a south Walian non-Welsh speaker, when he went to spend a Sunday with his prospective north Walian mother-in-law:

> 'An' after we 'ad Sunday tea, she said to me, "Will you keep the dishes for me?" I said, "I don't wann'em. I enjoyed the tea, but I dawn't wanna dishes as well!" But she meant "put them away". I'd never 'eard of "keep the dishes"!'

In the wider world of English, there are just a handful of purely Welsh words in the mainstream (such as 'eisteddfod'), but several others are used in quotation and often with humorous or mocking intent, like 'yachy da' (an anglicized form of the toast meaning 'Good health': 'Iechyd da').

As I said at the outset, there's a great deal of rivalry and mickey-taking abroad in Wales. In 2004/5 Voices captured numerous examples of the time-honoured English-on-Welsh mockery that already 400 years ago was one of Shakespeare's favourite linguistic and cultural belly-laughs in, for example, *Henry V*. Here, the Welsh rustic Fluellen (complete with devoiced 'b' pronounced as 'p') is discussing the king with Gower in act IV, scene vii:

FLUELLEN Ay, he was porn at Monmouth, Captain Gower. What call you the town's name where Alexander the Pig was born!

GOWER Alexander the Great.

FLUELLEN Why, I pray you, is not pig great? the pig, or the great, or the mighty, or the huge, or the magnanimous, are all one reckonings, save the phrase is a little variations . . .

Compare that with this anecdote from real life in Bethesda, north Wales, in late 2004:

'Sometimes when I go on holiday people make fun of you an' speak in a fake Welsh accent; it's spiteful really. It's not the accent so much as because of the language itself. They hear you speaking Welsh and it's like "sheep-shaggin' " jibes an' everything, but that's not associated with the accent. That's just the language.'

But within a moment the young lad who's talking is himself having a pop at his fellow Welshmen, from the south:

'My brother's at university down there and every time he comes back up 'ere it's his south Walian accent and I cann't stand it. The enunciation I think: di-da di-da di-da da. We have a sexy rhythm [in north Wales], a nice smooth rhythm. Not like those bom bom bom . . .'

Even within south Wales, the accent is often a point of conflict. In Glynneath, Voices met Anne and her young nephew, David, who'd spent some time in Pembrokeshire, one of the historic pockets of Englishness (like south Gower) and known sometimes as 'little England beyond Wales'. In David's case the linguistic ragging became so serious that the boy felt obliged to conform to a more standard English accent, which he still retains. His aunt explains:

'You just wanted to sound the same as everybuddy else. Because mawst people in Pembrokeshire are from Birmingham: thass the mawst accent you ever year [hear] in Pembrokeshire, it's people from Birmingham. And his headmaster was from Merthyr actually an' ah went to a peirents' evenin' an' 'e said ti me, "Please meik 'im feel praud to be Welsh!" It was [just] that 'e got bullied saw much, he just 'ad ti cheinge 'is accent.'

Sad story, but for every one of these, Voices captured one in reverse. Again from the Valleys town of Glynneath, it was the tale of a colliery worker in the old days of mining who'd given up life underground to seek his fortune in London. But when he came back, says Idris . . .

'. . . 'e 'ad a posh English accent. An' when 'e went baack to the coyery [colliery] to worrk they soon put a nickname on 'im. 'E was David Evans before 'e went an' then when 'e kem back 'e was "Dai *Educated* Evans"!'

It wouldn't surprise me if Dai Evans's experience was rather like this young woman's, recounted to Voices by her dad in Flint: she lost out both ways, criticized for speaking with a Welsh accent and subsequently mocked for having adopted more standard speech:

'My daughter suffered quite a lot with her accent. She went as a nanny to London and she was with a Welsh famlee there. And the lady there tried to correct the children and her to say "baath" and "glaass". Boot consequently when she keime hawm her friends here used to ridicule 'er because she said "baath" and "glaass".'

As I've said, these entrenched divisions seem to be expressed more feistily in Wales than anywhere else I've described in Britain; and the more local the points of difference are, the more sharply defined. In Glynneath, Voices heard a long lament from Anne about the prejudice town-dwellers allegedly expressed towards her Valleys mining community when she left her village school for the secondary in Neath:

'We was awnly ninety of us wen' from the Vaalley to Neath Grammar Schawl: my surname usst to be Baker and the teacher usst to say, "Right, Baker, Farmer, Butcher, I'll put you three together!" They usst to treat us a little bit diff'rent 'cos we were from the Vaalleys. "Townies" we usst to coll 'em in them days. That doesn't occur now; thass oll gone. But we were chalk an' cheese, tawtally diff'rent. Townspeople in them deeys were more worldly wise 'an us and we were, like, backwud. Judgin' [us] because of our accent, an' because of our fathers were all workin' in the collieries.'

Yet overall, despite these strongly articulated grudges and jealousies, fears and frustrations, English and Welsh today seem to coexist remarkably comfortably within the new climate that thoroughly encourages linguistic diversity. Through many centuries of rubbing up against each other, the two traditions have been enriched with linguistic qualities drawn from both. In the Gower nearly twenty-five years ago for example, Alwyn Guy opined that he no longer used the 'proper' Welsh word for to play truant (a form of the verb to play, 'chwarae') but simply copied the English word, to mitch:

> 'Mitsio': we Welshified the name. Just as we can anglicize a Welsh name, we Welshify an English name. That's one of the sins I'm guilty of committing – I found it easier, less troublesome, to Welshify an English word than search for and use the correct Welsh word. 'Ffeindio' [to find] from finding, you see – [not] 'darganfod' – three syllable word. It's easier to say a two-syllable word: 'ffeindio', 'watsio' – to watch, and the simple Welsh word is 'gwylio'.

In the section devoted to the Voices survey, you'll see that such Welshification of English words is, to the dismay of purists, today still going strong. But enough of all this guilt and blame: languages are communication tools. It seems to me that if Welsh is still seen as an effective means of expression in day-to-day transaction while at the same time representing something culturally bigger and deeper, it must be alive and well – for all its embracing of imported terms from big brother across the border.

I'll end this section with a couple of comments from south Wales, firstly from the thoroughly English-speaking suburb of Swansea called Bon-y-maen:

> 'I'm ashamed of not being able to speak Welsh because 'tis an asset, it is really. I wish when I was in school I'd listened to the teacher more, so that I could speak Welsh more. It's part of our culture.'

And this, from the Gower:

> 'Very often a word is far more descriptive to use in Welsh: it seems to convey something more in Welsh. There are many Welsh words that haven't got the real English equivalent. Near enough, but not quite the same. "Longing": the English word "longing". Now the Welsh equivalent to that – or *better* than that – is "hiraeth". Well, by usin' the word, to me, bein' Welsh, it conveys more than the translated version of it. HIRAETH – do you feel it?'

The Voices Survey: A Shared Hiraeth

Voices surveyed a broad spread of locations across Wales in 2004/5, from Holyhead on Anglesey (Ynys Môn) and Bethesda on the edge of the Snowdonia National Park to Glynneath in the Vale of Neath in the south Wales Valleys, Bon-y-maen in Swansea as well as the Splott area of the capital, Cardiff. Mid-Wales was represented by Builth Wells and Newtown, near Welshpool, both in the county of Powys, while areas close to the border with England featured a group in Flint only a handful of miles across the water from Liverpool and, a little further south, from Wrexham.

As I've listened to these many hundreds of hours of interviews undertaken by the Voices survey across the UK, it's been very noticeable where the points of similarity lie, where a single vernacular term has tended to outdistance all others. So for 'tired' the national standard is now clearly 'knackered', and if you're 'pleased' you're most likely to admit to being 'chuffed'. Unattractive young people are 'mingers' or 'minging', and if you're drunk you're as like as not 'pissed'. Not so in Wales. Yes, Voices did of course come across all these terms, but it was to a far lesser degree than elsewhere and tended to be limited to the capital and to areas closer to the border with England.

So whereas young people right across the UK have tended to favour these modern slang terms, the group of youngsters in Bethesda on the northern fringe of Snowdonia, with the Welsh language firmly part of their culture, suggested for attractive the Welsh word 'del' (pretty) and for the opposite, 'hyll' or 'anffodus' (which means unfortunate). In fact, many of the vernacular alternatives proposed by Dewi, Katrin, Jenna, Dalyth, two Huws, Hayley and Hedd, especially the verbs, were the actual Welsh words. Thus for to throw they offered 'lluchio' and 'taflu', and for to sleep 'cysgu', as well as 'glawio' for to rain. Pleased was 'balch' (glad) and unwell 'sâl' or 'gwael'.

Like Alwyn Guy a quarter of a century ago in Gower, this group tend to adapt English words into Welsh rather than use the classical alternative. It's a question these days not of ignorance but of striking the appropriate attitude:

The Sound of Welsh English

To attempt to sum up the accent of a whole country within a couple of short paragraphs is in one sense a fruitless task: for a start, the south Walian accent is markedly different from that of the north. But there are none the less major common factors: both are of course typified by an intonation tune that rises and falls in a melodic fashion that's known as 'sing-song'. The core of this musicality lies in the way stressed syllables are given extra emphasis, combined with many elisions, which together impart a rolling rhythm to phrase and sentence: so 'everybody else' becomes 'EVry BUD YELse', with three heavy stresses and the intervening syllables correspondingly unmarked. By eliding the -y at the end of 'everybody', too, word divisions become less important than syllabic ones; Anne from Glynneath said, of her bullied nephew: 'he juss TAD ti CHEInge is AAKsent, an' issAD [he just had to change his accent and it's sad]'. As you can see, notating these stresses and syllabic divisions on the page is very difficult as it makes the text almost unreadable, so for the sake of intelligibility I have decided to mark up texts with word divisions in their normal places, irrespective of a speaker's natural elisions.

Typical pronunciation features of south Wales include a lengthening of other-wise short 'a': 'back' becomes more like 'bark', which I've indicated with 'aa' in quotations (as in the pronunciation of the 'Vaalleys'). The 'ay' vowel in 'hay' and 'change' tends to get tightened to more of a 'ee' sound which I've indicated either as 'ei' ('cheinge' in the quote above) or in the more acute examples as

'We do know the corract Walsh words for them, just we use the [English term] because it sounds more cool. We have so many English influences round us that we just tend to pick up English words and use English words but then our parents 'ave a go on us an' corract us all the time. Ev'ryone round 'ere speaks Welsh so iss not regarded as such a bad thing that we use English words for the Welsh language.'

Additionally, they said, using the correct dictionary term in Welsh sounded far too straitlaced for their conversational idiom: 'Proper formal Welsh wouldn't sound right,' observed one girl, 'it sounds as if you're reading a book if you speak proper Welsh.' There's a tendency therefore to append the verbal ending -io to English words in order to make them function as 'Welsh' verbs:

'ee' (Wales is transcribed as 'Weels'). The 'o' in 'know' and 'go' is shortened to a very clear 'aw' sound (think Rob Brydon), such that 'I don't know' comes out more like 'adawnaw'. Terminal '-ing' is often pronounced 'en', so 'saying' sounds more like 'sayen' (Voices recorded 'an old sayen'' in Builth Wells, 'boilen'' and 'rawsten'' for boiling and roasting in Glynneath). And ubiquitous is the insertion of a 'y' sound in front of a dropped 'h', such that 'here' is almost always heard as 'yer' or 'year': 'We're a bit stuck in the middle yeer,' said Rob from Builth Wells.

In north Wales speech, particularly in the principally Welsh-speaking areas, the accent and tune are strongly modified by the language. The tune is more staccato and less melodious, though still with the rolling rise and fall. But there's very noticeable 'devoicing' of voiced consonants, sometimes with added sibilance. So Ann from Holyhead says 'koin'' for 'going' and pronounces the 't' in words like 'pity' with a lisp-like 's' sound: 'I like them to keep the Welsh language koin'. I think itss a pitsi to lets it ko'. Also notable in the English of the Welsh-speaking areas is the way that 'r' is rolled, whereas all other parts of the country are non-rhotic, i.e. the 'r' is not sounded.

Finally, towards the north-east of Wales, in the Flint area, the local accent takes on a very distinctive flavour of Merseyside with trailing word ends and added sibilance, as it closes geographically on the cities just across the water. Nick from Bagillt near Flint says, 'I've been taken for a Scouser: very often the people say, "You're proper Scouse, man! You're not Welsh."' To which his response is simple – he simply starts speaking in fluent Welsh.

'I say "climbio" instead of "dringo", which means climb a mountain, not translating but just putting the Welsh accent in the English word. Like "cookio" instead of "coginio".'

Interestingly, too, there are levels of slang usage in Welsh as well. This group had two words for pregnant – the more popular, spoken form 'disgwyl', equivalent to Welsh English expecting (literally, 'waiting') and the formal Welsh word:

' "Beichiog", the Welsh word for it, I'd use that if I was writing it down, but speech is different to the way we write things down. It's not just the youngsters – everyone in my family just uses "disgwyl", my mum, my grandmother, everyone. That's what people use. We do know the Welsh terms for things like "disgwyl", which is "beichiog", but we just doan' use 'em.'

However, what I find interesting about these seventeen- and eighteen-year-olds is that while they clearly recognize that English is going to be part of their lives, especially in a more mobile world, they are happy to adapt fashionable English idioms like 'hanging' (for drunk, cf. the usage in Salford, Lancashire, noted in Chapter 7) in Welsh rather than simply revert to 'pissed' or 'hammered'. These were Jenna's words for 'drunk': '"Hongian" or "meddwyn": "hongian" means hanging, a term we use round here.' 'Meddwyn', incidentally, is the normal term for drunk in Welsh. Elsewhere, the Welshness was a little patchier: when they were short of cash these young people were 'skint', 'broke' or (odd this piece of rhyming slang in the wilds of Snowdonia) 'Larry Flint'. The toilet was 'tŷ bach [little house]', as frequently in Wales, though:

'We do have Welsh names for toilet but we just don't use them: "toiled", "tŷ bach"; my nain [grandmother] uses tŷ bach but I don't.'

Here in Bethesda, a friend was, as everywhere, a 'mate', though spelled and pronounced literally with a Welsh accent, 'mêt'. However, the local term for a 'trendy person in cheap clothes and jewellery' – elsewhere so frequently a 'chav', 'townie' or 'trev' – here is a 'common Jack' or 'CJ':

'My mum says "common Jack" – well, we call it "CJ"'s, like. "Common Jack" means like somebody common.'

Despite the many English words they were happy to borrow, the enthusiasm these youngsters evinced for their language and heritage was genuinely felt:

'Losing the Welsh would be losing something important to your personality. I've spoken Welsh, my parents have spoken Welsh, people have fought to keep it alive, it gives the Welsh people an element of uniqueness and we have something that the rest of Britain doesn't.'

Not far away across the Menai Strait, the older people of Holyhead expressed a similar passion for their native tongue, though Jeff, an outsider from the Rhondda, remembered how strange he felt when first he set foot in a Welsh-speaking area:

'When I moved up yer [here], I 'ad difficulty understandin' anybody
speakin' up yer and people 'ad difficulty understandin' me. But now I've
lived yer saw long, I think everybody up yer speaks normal an' when I yer
[hear] south Walians speakin' I think – "Duw! thass a funny accent!" '

The Holyhead group, Ann, Jean and Gary together with the incomer,
Jeff, tended to use the equivalent word in standard Welsh as their vernacular and, unlike the young people from Bethesda, they stuck pretty solidly
to the classic Welsh form: 'meddwyn' for drunk and 'beichiog' for
pregnant, 'gwallgof' for insane, 'chwarae' for to play, 'nain' and 'taid' for
grandmother and grandfather and so on. The trendy young person,
though, was a 'gwennie' ('That's old-fashioned,' commented one of the
group) and PE shoes were (in common with much of northern England
directly east across the border), 'pumps'.

Time for another anecdote of cultural confusion from the south Walian
Jeff:

'When I come up yer I used to listen to some boys in the youth club
an' thee were sayin' they wer gawn a get some "pumps", an' I said,
"A pump for what?" like, you knaw. I thought the were gawna get
a pump to pump the water auwt. An' then I found out they were
plimsolls or trainers, where I call em "daps". Now if I said "daps"
oop yer, you'd think I meant fish – a dap is a fish.'

And down in the southern parts of Wales, as well as across the Bristol
Channel, the word for those ubiquitous if unexciting pieces of schoolwear
is indeed 'daps'. It's a word that runs out of steam quickly the further
east and north you go, being unknown in the London area and the
Midlands. Mid-Wales, though, understands what 'daps' are: 'but nobody
wears daps any more: if you wear daps you're a bit of a dork really,'
commented the fifteen-year-old James from Builth Wells. In fact 'daps'
was offered everywhere in Wales except in Wrexham, though 'pumps'
and standard plimsolls were close alternatives.

Beyond the purely Welsh vocabulary that you might expect in areas
of the country where the old language still holds sway, there were some
interesting local usages: take the old favourite about the 'narrow walkway'
between houses. As I explain elsewhere, in the north of England this is
often called a 'ginnel', in the Midlands, a 'jitty', while 'tenfoot' is the

Humberside term. In Scotland it's frequently an 'entry' and this, curiously, is the word Voices heard in Flint, where Nic, a man with a strong proto-Scouse accent, commented:

> 'We always terrmed those as an "entry", whether you were goin' into it or coomin' out of it. If there was a speice between two sets of houses, an openin' between two terrace houses and we used to term that opening "an entry".'

'Entry' cropped up again in Wrexham, but down in the Valleys, in the Vale of Neath, the preferred word was either the standard-issue 'alley' (though pronounced with the inimitable long 'a' of the south Walian: 'aallee') or a piece of classic 'Wenglish': 'gwli', pronounced 'goolie' (a borrowing in this case from Welsh, but used specifically in English and which in Cardiff was anglicized to 'gully').

Anne, Christina, Mary, Idris and David from Glynneath, who mentioned 'gwli', exuded a real sense of the centred Valleys community of the old industrial heartland, though now fractured following the demise of coal. Idrys, the former miner, was full of tales from his pit days and explanations for mining sayings, such as 'cool head – sharp mandrel' ('mandrel' is the local 'Wenglish' term for a miner's pick) and 'the tools are on the bar', meaning work's finished for the day:

> ' "The tools are on the bar": that was a long bar, an' all your tools – your mandrel, your sledge, your shovel – they 'ad awls [holes] in 'em an' you'd slaiyde 'em on a bar an' you'd a lock at de end that if anybody 'a' to steal 'em then they'd a carry a lot: so you 'ad ten tools, ten 'eavy tools. So "the tools on 'e bar" was de finish of a shift.'

They also produced a long list of typical Valleys words and expressions, including 'trimming up' for decorating a Christmas tree, 'having a cwtch' (a snuggle-down – see the 'Language in a Landscape' section for the etymology) and 'it's pickin' [coming on] to rain':

> '[There was a Valleys] woman who went to live in Cambridge who said, "I'll 'ave to get the washin' in 'cos it's pickin'," an' they di'n't 'ave a clew [clue]. It's pickin' to rain.'

The group from the Vale of Neath also shared the Welshman's traditional love of nicknames. Although part of the standard caricature of

Welsh life, this custom has long genuinely existed and apparently still flourishes today. Nearly a quarter of a century ago, Stanley Ellis listened in the Gower peninsula to an involved explanation of the many different Tuckers who lived in the area ('and none of them related!'), each bearing a locating nickname. Another Gower man known as Dennis Haddy was, Ellis heard, individualized by his *wife's* name (Haddy = Harriet), while a certain Ben Thomas took the Welsh identifier 'Saer' after his profession of carpenter ('Ben Saer'), and the local baker, David Rhys was indeed – though I thought that name only turned up in fiction – Dai Bun.

The nickname tradition stems from the multitude of families sharing the same surname and a likewise limited number of preferred first names, and was recorded still in use by Voices this year: here's the ex-miner Idris remembering an old colleague:

> ' 'E usst to work up in the awpen-casst [open-cast] in Merthyr an' Dowlais top and 'e went by the neime Doug Doubler because 'e usst to do double shifts. Usst to gaw to work one deiy an' we wun't see im till the next deiy.'

In Builth Wells too 'a lot of people round here aren't known by their proper names: it's not Mr John Davies, it's "John Cwmbach" [a nearby village], or it's the "Morgan boys",' while the Anglesey group claimed there were at least 600 nicknames in Holyhead alone. David from the Flint interview group had followed his father's footsteps into law enforcement and 'was known as Dai the Cop because my father was a policeman'.

But this Welsh custom is far more than simply a whimsical fancy: for David it had real professional value:

> 'There were saw many Jawnses [Joneses] that you'd call 'em Jawnes the gardener, Jawnes the oil. Nicknames in Welsh came because there were so many people neimed the seime, saw [so] many Jawnses and Hugheses or Edwardses, and especially in the villages, in the outlandish villages. I was in the tops of the Denbighshire moors there and you had outlandish farms there, and they were all Mr and Mrs Jawnes to you, but y'ad to name the farm as well. Will Pengarth, Dafydd the Moor . . .'

One of the revealing features about 'localness' that the Voices survey has uncovered is that people frequently love to claim words as their own very narrow usage which are, in reality, found much more widely within a region, sometimes even nationally. In the case of the farmers from Builth Wells, for example, they staked ownership of the widely used expression 'I'll be home directly': 'That's a Radnorshire one, I'd say.' (Radnorshire is one of the old county divisions of Wales.)

More genuinely dialectal though was their 'Where beest you goin'? [where are you going]', though their supposedly local expression 'come by yer [come here]' is found a lot more widely than mid-Wales. Similarly, Voices recorded the Male Voice Choir members from Flint claiming the word 'tidy' (nice or attractive – 'We always used to say "Auw she's tidy" '), whereas in fact it's a usage found in many parts of the country and provided the writer John Edwards with the title for his well-known books on south Walian English, *Talk Tidy*.

But whether a term is in fact local or national matters very little to the speaker. What does concern him or her is that the word *feels* right, it feels part of them, seems in some way to belong. And this notion of an inclusive language that makes you part of a group, large or small, is critical to the way we develop local speech styles, wherever we are. In Wales there are two such words – Welsh words – that are quoted repeatedly throughout the Voices survey; they are 'hwyl' and 'hiraeth' (pronounced 'hooyl' and 'he-rye-th'). 'Hwyl' (which means spirit or fervour, as well as goodbye) embodies an indefinable sense of the homeland, of national identity that's caught up in the people and the landscape. The other, 'hiraeth', is that sense of longing or homesickness that Welsh men and women feel in their hearts when a long way from the Valleys of the south or the mountains of the north.

Now it may just be that this special sense of emotional attachment to a place, of longing and belonging, is much the same the world over – they make very similar claims to uniqueness, after all, about the German term *Heimat*. And maybe this sense of magical connection to a country and a culture is simply yet another of those myths of 'localness'. Yet I'd bet there's scarcely a single Welsh man or woman who doesn't recognize 'hwyl' and 'hiraeth' as representing something for them that's very special and very, well . . . Welsh.

To end this section, though, a little language tale for our times, re-counted to Voices by David, the student from Glynneath, who, you'll remember, bleached the Welshness from his accent to avoid being pilloried at school:

> 'A good friend of mine in college went to the mountains with his girlfriend, who was black. But she'd lived in Wales her entire life, and they went into a pub up in north Wales in the mountains. The barman said to her, "Why don't you get back to your own country?" So she ordered her entire round of drinks in Welsh! – An' [the barman] couldn't even speak Welsh!'

A Welsh Snapshot: Singing for Wales, Speaking for England

Flint is the little county town of Flintshire on the northern coast of Wales. To the west are the holiday beaches of Llandudno, Rhyl, Colwyn Bay and sunny Prestatyn, but although very much part of Wales, Flint lies just a stone's throw from Ellesmere Port and its oil refineries and car plants, ten miles from Birkenhead and a mere dozen from Liverpool. It's hardly Snowdonia nor yet the Valleys. But the group of men that Voices caught up with here embody much of the spirit of the country within whose boundaries they live. John, David, Vernon and Lawrence, always known as Nic, are proud senior members of the Flint Male Voice Choir. They've sung across Europe to audiences of as many as 80,000 and performed alongside Bryn Terfel and Mick Hucknall and were part of the Millennium night celebrations at the Dome. But despite their well-travelled lives, the four men are still firmly rooted in the area they've lived in most of their days, and in the speech communities to which they belong: David was born in Buckley, five miles south of Flint:

> 'And the accent in that little village is totally different to anywhere else in the county. I think this was mainly due to the influx of workers from the Midlands, working in potteries and brickworks in Buckley, and they had their own language. We spoke Welsh at home and my first real contact with the English language was when I went to school. I went to school in Buckley and it's all "thees and thous and dunna knaw . . . and 'old thee 'and up, old butt". That's how they spoke.'

David's father was a policeman and with his family in tow found himself being moved to different places all round the local area – Mold, New Brighton, Greenfield, places all within a radius of five miles, yet, says David, with widely variable accents:

> 'We went to live in New Brighton and the accent is completely different there from the Buckley accent, a softer Welsh accent. And then he moved to Greenfield and they never said "give me that", they'd say "gizzit 'ere" and words of that sort. And when I came to live in Greenfield I thought I was in a foreign land.'

Today, to an outsider's ear, David speaks with a gentle, not particularly marked Welsh accent. His fellow singer in the choir, Nic, on the other hand, sounds distinctly Liverpudlian. He's from Bagillt, a little place a mile and a half along the coast road west from Flint, but he ascribes his accent to the influx of Merseysiders in the 1940s:

> 'During the war when aall the Scousers came over heeah, we thought it wus pretty khool to try and khatch their Scaouse accent, liyke, ye knaw. We tried to think well, they're a li"le bit haader than oos, an' they did seem to be a li"le moore world-weary than we wear; sorta placid around heeah, an' they were boys who'd seen a lotta life even though they were only in their very early teens. Now this in my opinion did a lot in my area of Bagillt to lose the language – because we were brought oop speakin' Welsh – "nains" and "taids" and ooncles and aants, they spawk Welsh – we listened, we heard, we probably understood a lot of it, boot we didn't respond in Welsh. We wanted to be like the little 'ard-knock Scaousers.'

Note the way Nic aspirates, in true Liverpudlian fashion, his hard 'c' sounds (I've used an 'h' to indicate this in the text), thus he says 'khool' for cool and 'khatch' for catch (see also Chapter 9 that deals with Cumbria and Liverpool). Also worth underlining is how Nick pronounces his short 'u' sound (up, uncle, us). Unlike other parts of Wales, in this area so close to Lancashire it takes on the typically northern English 'oo' pronunciation ('oop', 'ooncle', 'oos'). Another of the features of the local speech in Flint is the rather harsh-sounding open 'a' sound that Nic has when he says 'aants [aunts]'. His friend and colleague John reckons it's ineradicable:

'My wife cooms from Chester and woon of the things she says, "I'll change you all this 'caa' and 'paak'." That's the Flint way of saying "car" and "park". But now she's changed and when I listen to her talking she's saying "caa" and "paak". She said, "I'll make you speak proper", but she never has and now she's speaking the same as me!'

According to David, TH-fronting (the pronunciation of 'th' in words like 'feather' as a 'v' sound), so typical of Cockney and general London vernacular, is now a sound often heard in the Flint area:

'Youngsters can't pronounce the letters "th": they make the sound "f" – firty fousand fevvers on a frush'es froat.'

Though another of the quartet is quick to claim that such pronunciations aren't particularly new; he recalled an old decorator friend who used to say that something was 'not worf bovverin' wiv'. Listening to this group speak is to hear a sort of linguistic crossroads in action; in the way they speak you can detect flavours of all the neighbouring accents, yet their words at the same time express a passion for Wales, for 'hiraeth' and for the traditional language. Says Nic:

'The area that we live in is so clawse to England, because England is only twenty minutes awei from oos, an' a lorra the language 'as been bastardized really – that is the correct word.'

There are, it seems though, some quite unusual turns of phrase that I've not come across elsewhere in my travels; from John, three examples:

'You don't coom *from* Flint, you coom *off* Flint. An' you get people sayin', "Aal yous lot coom with me; the lest [sic] of yer, stay where yer is." An' thee always seay, not the *way*, this is the *rawd* [road]; not the *way* I talk, it's the *rawd* I talk.'

This last recalls the similar Yorkshire usage in expressions like 'any road' (for anyway) and 'any road up', though I've not heard the simple substitution of 'road' for 'way' elsewhere, as in the phrase that David quotes here: 'That's naw rawd to talk ti yer mam [that's no road = way to talk to your mother]'.

In response to the Voices survey questions, this group from a linguistic point of confluence offer, as you might expect, alternatives that reflect their mixed heritage. So they will use the Welsh 'nain' and 'taid' for their grandparents and 'mam' for mother, 'nant' for stream. But for truanting, they suggested not 'mitching' or its Welshified form 'mitsian' but the Lancastrian 'wag': 'Come on, we'll play wag today.' One even said he mixed the two languages up thoroughly, sometimes saying to 'dodge' school, at others 'dodgio ysgol'. 'Starved' was the preferred term for cold (a very old usage and found in several regions of England): 'When the coal ran out they'd say, "Duw! Starvin'!"' And David came up with what was arguably the most colourful usage yet for to hit hard, to 'mollycrosh': 'If you were going to hit somewoon you'd say, "I'll mollycrosh yer!"' It seems though that this may be a Lancastrian import: one glossary that I've found lists the term as the more likely 'molly*crush*' and quotes it as being typical Wigan slang.

Perhaps because of where their territory lies, right in the angle between the two strong language areas of Lancashire/Merseyside and Welsh-speaking north Wales, the people of Flint seem to suffer both ways. So despite sounding really quite un-Welsh, Nic and Vernon say they have to put up with many of the stereotypical slurs cast upon the Welsh by some English people and by the south Walians on northerners:

> 'We've always been knawn by the south Walians as "the gogs" and soomtimes people feel insoolted by it – what's the gogs? The "gogledd" is the north, you see, an iss a well-knawn fakht that we are northerners. Boot at first you thought it was a bit of an insult by the south.'

> 'I feel they think we're a bit – to use a word that we use round ere – a bit "dorchy". "Dorchy" bein' simple or a bit slaw. An' [they say] how [the Welsh] can awnly handle sheep an' faaming. That does annoy me; but again we can alwiz coom back an' alwiz ge' woon better.'

A Wales Glossary

Note: only those pure Welsh terms that are referred to within the text or that have subsequently been adopted by the English-speaking community in Wales are included in this wordlist

ach-y-fi an expression of disgust or repugnance: means approximately 'ah me!' Used in English, from Welsh words (pronounced *a*cka vee)

anffodus unfortunate, regrettable, unlucky (= ugly, Welsh word, pronounced 'an*fodd*is')

balch glad, proud (Welsh word, pronounced 'bvalch')

beichiog pregnant (Welsh word, pronounced 'bay-schiock')

butty a friend, mate, colleague, one of a pair (Welsh English usage)

chwarae to play (Welsh word, pronounced 'whwara')

ciff, cyff unwell, under the weather (Welsh English term, pronounced 'kiff')

coggy-handed left-handed

coginio to cook (Welsh word, pronounced 'co*ckee*nyo')

common Jack, CJ a rough-looking individual (quoted by Bethesda group)

coopy-down to crouch down. Possibly related to Welsh 'twtio', to tidy; cf. Welsh English 'twti-down', to hunker down

cwm a valley (used in Valleys English, pronounced 'coom'; from Welsh word meaning valley)

cwtch to snuggle or lay down, a hollow place. Used verbally, 'cwtch' has a variety of meanings: to keep something hidden, to snuggle up close to someone. As a noun, equivalent to the Welsh word 'cwts' or 'cwtsh' (a recess or hollow), it can mean a cupboard under the stairs ('cwtch dan staer') or a coal-shed ('cwts glo'). Originally from Latin *collocare*, to lay down, via Old French *coucher*, to Welsh *cwtsh* and then to Welsh English 'cwtch'. Pronounced 'cootch'

cysgu to sleep (Welsh word, pronounced 'kissgi')

Dai David (Welsh diminutive of Dafydd)

daps plimsolls (used throughout south Wales, Bristol area)

darganfod to find (Welsh word, pronounced 'darr*ganv*od')

del pretty (Welsh word, pronounced 'dell')

disgwyl expecting, waiting (= pregnant; Welsh word, pronounced 'diskwil')

dringo to climb (Welsh word, pronounced 'dringo')

Duw! God! Expletive (Welsh word = God, pronounced 'dyou')

entry a narrow walkway between houses, alley (cf. Chapter 12)

ffeindio to find (Welsh word, adaptation of English *find*)

glawio to rain (Welsh word, pronounced 'gla-weo')

gogledd the north (of Wales – Welsh word)

gwennie a trendy young woman (old usage recorded by Voices in Anglesey)

gwli a narrow walkway, alley (from Welsh *gwli*, a gully, pronounced 'gooly'). The back lanes of miners' houses in the Valley communities were known as 'gwlis' or 'gullies'

hiraeth homesickness, longing (Welsh word, pronounced '*he*-rye-th')

hongian hanging = drunk (Welsh word, from English usage, pronounced 'hongyan')

hwyl spirit, fervour, also goodbye (Welsh word, pronounced 'hooyl')

hyll ugly (Welsh word, pronounced 'hich')

isn't it tag word, used irrespective of subject (from Welsh construction)

keep (the dishes) to put away (after washing up). From *cadw*, to keep, used in this sense in Welsh

llawchwith left-handed (Welsh word, pronounced 'schl-ow-ch-with')

lluchio, taflu to throw (Welsh words, pronounced '*ch*echio', '*tav*lay')

losins, loshins sweets. A south Walian term, from Welsh *losinen*, sweets

maldod, muldod indulgence or spoiling. A Welsh English word from the Welsh *maldod*, affectation or dalliance

mamgu, myngu grandmother (pronounced 'mungee'). A south Walian term, cf. 'nain' in north Wales; recorded by Voices in Neath area 2004/5

mandrel a miner's pick (Valleys usage, also elsewhere). From French *mandrin*, a part of a lathe; sixteenth century

meddwyn drunk (Welsh word, pronounced 'medthwy')

mitch to play truant, as 'mitching' or 'on the mitch'. From Old French *muchier*, to hide, thence to pilfer or hide from view, subsequently to play truant; sixteenth century

mitsian to play truant (Welsh adaptation of English *mitch*)

moithered, moidered, mithered confused, bothered (Welsh English usage, and more generally). Etymology uncertain, possibly related to 'muddle'; seventeenth century

mollycrosh, mollycrush to hit, whack. Perhaps from Lancashire usage – recorded in Wigan dialect glossary

nain a grandmother. Used particularly in north Wales English (from Welsh word, pronounced 'nine')

pick to rain to start raining, also 'pick *with* rain'. Welsh English usage, borrowed from Welsh *pigan*, to begin to rain

potch a mess, trouble; also verbal, to 'potch with' something: mess about with (Welsh English usage)

quat, twti down to squat or crouch down (cf. **coopy down**). From Welsh words *cwat, twti* (pronounced 'toottie')

sâl, gwael unwell (Welsh words, pronounced 'saal', 'gwyle')

sorry (in) his or **her heart** very sorry indeed (Welsh English expression)

taid a grandfather. Especially north Wales usage (Welsh word, pronounced 'tide')

tidy good, excellent; a 'tidy feller' is a decent person; to 'talk tidy' is to speak properly (and was the title of the definitive guides to Welsh English)

trim up to decorate, dress a Christmas tree

twp slow-witted. Welsh English usage (from Welsh *twp*, stupid, pronounced 'tup')

tŷ bach toilet (Welsh words = little house, pronounced 'tee baach')

Valleys, the the Valleys of the rivers Neath, Tawe, Taff, Rhymney, Sirhowy, Ebbw, Cynon and others that flow south from the Brecon Beacons and along which the mining and industrial communities of south Wales flourished in the nineteenth and twentieth centuries. The heartland of Welsh industrialization, the closely knit Valleys communities were also a focus for powerful political and social activism

Welsh Not a wooden neck-tag or tablet, variously incised with the words 'Welsh Not', 'W. N.' or 'Welsh N.', which was often required to be worn by Welsh-speaking pupils in the nineteenth century in order to promote the use of English in Welsh-speaking Wales, following a notorious parliamentary report on education in Wales of 1847

Wenglish the variety of English language spoken in (south) Wales. Term coined by John Edwards in his dialect studies *Talk Tidy*

where's it to? where is it? Valleys expression; cf. similar Bristolian usage (see Chapter 2)

yachy da Cheers! Good health! From Welsh words *iechyd da* (literally 'good health')

yer, year here, hear, ear. The pronunciation of unaspirated 'h' and initial 'e' as a 'y' sound is one of the most distinctive features of Welsh English

5 : THE MIDLANDS

Language in a Landscape: Ducks, Loves, Cocks and Flowers

You go out to the country from here and it's scarred and it's bent. The country looks as if it's been picked up and it's been put down and the miners have done their worst two hundred feet underground; so that there's no level field, there's no field that seems to be without its mineshaft. And all around here are people who have such a distinctive way of speech they really do stand out in speech and in a community.

The Midlands, characterized there by the tireless field-worker of the Survey of English Dialects, Stanley Ellis, who's spent more time than most raking over the slagheaps and spoil-tips of local language that litter the vast central belt of England. It's a region of fierce loyalties and strong opinions, of great history and massive change. It's been the theatre for some of this country's greatest creations of classic fiction – D. H. Lawrence memorably immortalized the coalmining life of Eastwood in Nottingham-shire, the landscape described by Stanley Ellis above. Arnold Bennett made Burslem, Hanley and the other kiln-girt communities of the Potter-ies the stage for his Potteries novels, like *Anna of the Five Towns* and the adventures of Denry Machin in *The Card*. And Alan Sillitoe's famous novel of working-class life of the Angry 1950s, *Saturday Night and Sunday Morning*, took Nottingham factory life as its stage. Hard graft and hard lives are the story of the Midlands and as I've observed in many places in this book, it's so often in the closed world of the factory, pit or village community that local talk takes deepest root.

It's a long industrial history too. The Midlands have seen two or three hundred years of productive work in forge and factory, in a land criss-crossed by canals built to serve the new industries and pockmarked, as still it was in the mid-eighties when Ellis visited, by the detritus and deep shafts of old colliery workings. But since his visit a great deal of this industrial energy has been knocked out of the Midlands. The Potteries are no longer smoky, Wedgwood and Royal Doulton are now manufactured in the Far East and Nottingham's Triumph Road factory, the manufactury of everyboy's dream – a Raleigh bicycle – and where the film of Sillitoe's novel was shot, fell to the demolition men in the summer of 2003. And in the years since Stanley Ellis visited Eastwood, the collieries that were the lifeblood of the region have almost all closed.

There's something very special about the heart of a country, furthest from coasts and those sea-borne linguistic influences that are so strongly felt throughout these islands. Here in the heart of the land, where manufacturing took root in the mid eighteenth century, a new future is being carved out. The old city centres, blackened by 150 years of factory smoke that I saw as a child in the 1950s, are now reborn, have been scrubbed up and repositioned in the modern idiom – Birmingham city centre is shaped by elegant squares, the old canal footpaths have been turned into romantic visitor attractions open for summer evening strolls between the old warehouses now tastefully translated to twenty-first century use. And many Midlands voices are different too, with the riches of the Indian subcontinent rooted firmly across the region, bringing bhangra and Bollywood to the heart of England; Caribbean voices too, for example in Nottingham and Birmingham.

The picture of this part of the country, so often sped past by outsiders (or as often crawled through on a typical jam-ridden journey) on the M6 motorway, is one of linguistic individualism and character almost unequalled in the country. There's huge variety, to begin with. East and west Midlands mark an age-old language division that is still audible to this day. In 1985, Stanley Ellis found students from Derbyshire marvelling at and uncomprehending of a young friend who'd joined them in class from across the divide in Nottingham, where the words were all different:

> 'E's from wrong said of brook; tha' meant 'e coom from oother said of [the River] Erewash, see. An' folks used to seay we shall 'a' to watch them: they've coom from over th'oother saide of brook.

He would say 'causey' for pavement, they protested, talk of a 'gennel' (pronounced with a soft 'g' as in 'gentle') for a narrow walkway between houses, where in Derbyshire they'd have used 'jitty'. And though the differences have been largely smoothed away across the past quarter-century – you'll find people quoting 'jitty' and 'gennel' in the same breath across pretty well the whole region, east to west, today – there are notable differences of accent. Contrast Birmingham speech, with its strongly urban drawl and heavily modified vowels, with what the locals admit to be the 'rough' talk of Mansfield forty miles to the north-east, where they don't think much of the talk of the region's biggest city:

> 'Ah'm not keen on it laike; ah can't stan' the Broommie language. Aw, it's a 'orrible accent, in't it? They probably think the same about arn [ours]!'

And it's true that people always seem to hold strong views for and against Birmingham's speech:

> People are defensive about Brummie, and you'll often hear people say that when they hear themselves on tape they cringe a bit. It is a bit anarchic, but it's people just using language as a tool to get the job done and not worrying too much about the niceties of grammar.

The speaker is Dr Clive Upton, currently a Reader at the University of Leeds and shortly to become Professor of Modern English Language there. He is himself a Brummie, and thus knows both the practicalities of the city's speech and the theory. He and other locals offer their take on the sound of Brum towards the end of this section.

As the comment from Mansfield indicates, the way they speak in England's second city is as different from other parts of the Midlands as, say, Geordie is from Yorkshire, as Norfolk is from Northants. But there are none the less also many shared features across the region, which historically made up one of the heartlands of Old English – the Mercian kingdom. Assertions of both the detail and distribution of Mercian Old English are necessarily somewhat vague. We're not talking about spoken English, naturally, nor yet – amongst the written documents – of vast libraries of texts. What has come down to us of the Midlands form of English that thrived in the eighth to thirteenth centuries is just a handful of texts. These include royal charters of the kings of Mercia, glosses (textual translations), collections of psalms (such as the so-called Vespasian Psalter, in which explanations of the word 'Alleluia' in ninth-century

Mercian are offered, written in a tiny but precise hand above the main text, which is, of course, in Latin) and the odd prayer.

We have little or no indication of how far the Mercian English area extended, though it's usually accepted that the northern boundary of the Mercian-speaking 'Midlands' was the river Humber. Mercian and Northumbrian Old English are often grouped together under a single variety, known as Anglian, while the other varieties of Old English were Kentish and West Saxon, the latter being the 'dialect' that prevailed in the then capital, Winchester.

As I explain in greater detail in Chapter 3, it's the Middle English dialect of the southern area of the Midlands (especially Northamptonshire, Bedfordshire and Huntingdonshire) that in the Middle Ages became the backbone of London English, and thence the national standard. Unlike the earlier period, the Middle Ages provide scholars with a wealth of literary and more prosaic texts (place names, legal documents and so on) from which to map the distribution of the many varieties of spoken and written (Middle) English that abounded. In 1387, a cleric, John Trevisa, writing in his local Gloucestershire dialect, translates the original Latin text of a famed 'universal history' or *Polichronicon* by Ranulph Higden. Trevisa's text is rightly famous for his critical assessment of the northern dialects and particularly that of York ('so scharp, slitting, and frottynge, and unschape, that we southerne men may that longage unnethe understonde'). But he also has an interesting comment to make in passing on the speech of Midlanders (he calls them, historically, 'Mercii' – Mercians). It forms, he says, a sort of bridge between north and south:

> For men of the est with men of the west, as it were undir the same partie
> of hevene, acordeth more in sownynge of speche [= pronunciation]
> than men of the north with men of the south, therfore it is that
> Mercii, that beeth men of myddel Engelond, as it were parteners of
> the endes, understondeth bettre the side langages, northerne and
> southerne, than northerne and southerne understondeth either [each]
> other . . .

In the late-fourteenth-century world of Middle English, too, it was in the north-west Midlands that an anonymous author, known now only after one of his works as the 'Pearl Poet', set down the epic tale of *Sir Gawain and the Green Knight*, which begins:

sithen the sege and the assaut watȝ sesed at troye
the borȝ brittened and brent to brondeȝ and askeȝ
the tulk that the trammes of tresoun þer wroȝt
watȝ tried for his tricherie the trewest on erthe . . .

[Since the siege and the assault was concluded at Troy
The city laid waste and burned to brands and ashes
The man that there devised the devices of treason
Was for his treachery tried, the truest on earth . . .]

Coincidentally, it was a sense of that millennial span of time that the Midlands novelist Arnold Bennett chose to evoke five or six hundred years later for the opening of his first published work, *Anna of the Five Towns*:

> Bursley, the ancient home of the potter, has an antiquity of a thousand years. It lies towards the north end of an extensive valley, which must have been one of the fairest spots in Alfred's England, but which is now defaced by the activities of a quarter of a million of people.

Bennett was born in the heart of the north Midlands, in Staffordshire (probably, according to scholars, not so very far from where the author of Gawain originated), in the middle years of the Victorian era, in 1867. Growing up in Hanley, one of the kiln-dominated Potteries towns that fashioned and fired the Empire's tableware, Bennett knew his industrial landscape, a landscape that had been transformed from rural tranquillity by the building of manufactures, the construction of canals and the taming of waterways. And just as the fictional Hanbridge and Bursley are each only a single syllable away from the real Hanley and Burslem that Bennett lived in and knew so well, so the fiction he wrote was rooted deep in the reality of that rapidly evolving Potteries townscape:

> Five contiguous towns – Turnhill, Bursley, Hanbridge, Knype, and Longshaw – united by a single winding thoroughfare some eight miles in length, have inundated the valley like a succession of great lakes. Of these five Bursley is the mother, but Hanbridge is the largest. They are mean and forbidding of aspect – sombre, hard-featured, uncouth; and the vaporous poison of their ovens and chimneys has soiled and shrivelled the surrounding country till there is no village lane within a

league but what offers a gaunt and ludicrous travesty of rural charms.
Nothing could be more prosaic than the huddled, red-brown streets . . .

And as in the Potteries, so too across the region: Birmingham, once a
sleepy market town with a reputation for metalworking, in the course of
less than a century became a modern industrial metropolis, one of the
great powerhouses of the Industrial Revolution. Josiah Wedgwood,
another son of the Potteries, built his legendary Etruria works in Stoke-
on-Trent in 1771. In the east Midlands, Nottingham's hosiery factories
flourished, despite the riots inspired by the Leicestershire machine-
breaker Ned Ludd (who may or may not actually have existed, but from
whom we have the term 'Luddite' today describing anyone resistant to
change). And throughout the Midlands men went underground following
the seams of coal. Two hundred and fifty years of grime and hard graft
settled over the Midlands, faithfully documented in his first novel of this
industrial transformation by Arnold Bennett:

> Out beyond the municipal confines, where the subsidiary industries of
> coal and iron prosper amid a wreck of verdure, the struggle is grim,
> appalling, heroic . . . On the one side is a wresting from nature's own
> bowels of the means to waste her; on the other, an undismayed,
> enduring fortitude. The grass grows; though it is not green, it grows.
> In the very heart of the valley, hedged about with furnaces, a farm still
> stands, and at harvest-time the sooty sheaves are gathered in.

Bennett had a decent crack at transcribing the dialect of the Potteries
too, one of the richest and most expressive in Britain, bred in the closed
environment of factory life and those narrow red-brick streets of tiny
houses:

> 'Nay, my lad. I'm owd enough to leave it to young uns.' 'What dost
> ask me for? Please thysen. I've nowt do wi' it.'

Bennett is no Thomas Hardy as far as dialect is concerned though, and
if the above sample begins to suggest localness with its phonetic spelling
of 'old' as 'owd' (which you'll find too in my modern transcriptions of
Midlands talk, e.g. 'grand owd blokes'), 'thysen' for yourself and 'nowt'
for nothing, there's no real attempt to catch the very specific quality
of the Potteries talk. Stoke dialect is now and has for centuries been as

rich and distinctive as any in the country: try this from Roy, a bus driver, talking in Chesterton in the northern part of the Stoke-on-Trent conurbation.

> 'Lass coopla weeks ah've bin workin' a' Crewe depot an' to me iss a foreign accent: when a ge' daown soomwhere laik Paahker's Reoad [Parker's Road] or Badger's Avenue 't'slike forinners tawkin to you. Y'aff t'ask them where th'wan' a go. The' caan't oonderstan' what aah'm on abaout an' it's awnly twelve miyle daown the reowd, an' it's completely different language altogether. Saound like faarmers when thee tawk to ye at Crewe. An it's "Hello, loov", in Stoke it's "Hello, doock." '

Roy's story is not untypical of the dialect picture right across the country: local is here, and the next village or town is a 'foreign land'. It's the old, old story that still reflects a time, not so long past, often still within living memory, when people rarely strayed more than a few miles from where they were born.

In his work on the buses, Roy moves about the local area every day and he's well placed to observe these minute shifts of accent and usage. In this case he hears a contrast between the vowel sounds of Stoke and Crewe, half a bus route away to the north. But also in the lexicon, because, as he and his companions at Stoke Speedway track where they were interviewed all agree, the term of endearment for Staffordshire people is 'duck' – or as I've routinely transcribed it, 'doock'. Go beyond the area and it's 'loov [love]'.

The mobility that started with the social shaking produced by the Second World War and that's continued at ever-increasing pace has tended to blur the boundaries of who says what, where. Workers were told 'on yer bike' after the industrial closures in the Thatcherite 1980s, multinationals and government departments have relocated more and more staff round the country, whilst nowadays many English villages are emptying of locals in retreat from rising prices and an army of cash-rich weekenders. Thus the old concentrations of unified, shared speech, of specific sharp local particularities of language have become diluted, the word boundaries smudged.

Yet in the Midlands, I get the strong impression – though I can't vouch for it scientifically – that the linguistic lines of demarcation that were set hundreds of years ago when communities first grew up around a ford, or a fertile valley or a newly discovered seam of coal remain more distinct than in many parts of the country. So that the old boundary, for example, that Roy observes when he takes the fares from his passengers who call him 'loov' in Cheshire and 'doock' in Stoke is still keenly felt.

That said of course, words are often claimed as much more local than they actually are. I guess it's an affirmation of belonging and ownership. For instance, the old 'duck' word, championed as uniquely local here in Stoke-on-Trent, is actually found across to the east in Derbyshire (*Ey Oop Mi Duck* was in fact the title of a well-known guide to Derbyshire dialect that was popular when Stanley Ellis came to the area in the mid-1980s), and also yet further east in Nottinghamshire. In fact the word seems to be a good definer of this north-central section of the Midlands. But because it's so local, 'duck' can sound strange to the outsider: it's used of men and women by men and women, irrespective of their relationship, just as 'love' is frequently used elsewhere in northern England, 'mate' in London and the south, and 'my lover' in Bristol. Fred, Roy's companion at the speedway, has turned the usage into a gag:

'I gaw into a fish an' chip shop in Kidsgrove – Leon's Chip Shop – an' there's a girl in there an she always says "Fish an' chips?" Ah said, "Yeah." "Sal' n' vinegar, doock?" So now go in an say, "Can ah 'ave a sal'-n'-vinegar-doock, please?" '

On the other side of the Midlands, the duck also flies. Ivan's a fireman from Kirkby in Ashfield and he's always calling people – men and women – 'duck':

'Ah coll my missus doock: "Coom 'ere, doock." Also on the station if we're playin' football an' soomwoon dooz a good shot at and: "Shot, doock!" an' it's not offensive. A man saying "doock" to another man – it's joost a phrase: "Shot, doock!" '

On the other hand, Ivan recounts that he inadvertently did it once on a visit to Newcastle and people were offended. It's a fine distinction:

'An' soomb'dy 'ead-bootted me oonce becoz ah colled 'em "loov". Ah were walkin' 'ome an' ah boomped into [a guy called Geoff]; 'e were a big blawke – 'e's a doostbin man naow – an' ah said, "sorry, loov" an' 'e turned raound an' nootted me square on the nawse [nutted me square on the nose].'

In spite of such encounters, these terms of endearment with a long pedigree are frequent and widespread across the Midlands: 'love', 'duck', 'flower' and even 'cock' – Voices heard all four in Mansfield (Notts) and 'cock' was also a favourite for Rita from Wolverhampton, at the other end of the Midlands: 'You do foind in the Black Coontry iss normally "cock": "Ullo, cock, 'ow are yuh?" '

To call a person 'youth', or more appropriately 'yowth' (the accent somehow eases away the juvenile connotations) seems to me to have a slightly different, more male-oriented usage, as, for example, a greeting to a workmate. It too turns up on both sides of that divide that linguists have sometimes remarked on between Derbyshire and Nottinghamshire, defined by the meanders of the river Erewash. Here's Ivan again from the Nottingham side:

' "Where did you end oop lass' naiyte, yowth", or "Where d'you end oop lass naiyte, doock?" Same thing – yowth or doock.'

And ten miles south-west of him, the Voices group from Belper in Derbyshire proposed 'Ey oop, yowth'; likewise again – and a good twenty-five miles further south this time – an old miner from Coalville near Leicester: 'Ey oop, yowth.'

This companionable Midlands term – and the others I've mentioned – flourished in the stifling confinement and dust of the underground workings, where your mate might one day turn out to be your saviour. Stanley Ellis captured the still living reality of Midlands pit-talk when in 1985 he visited the town of Eastwood, where, at 8A Victoria Street, D. H. Lawrence made his home, and which he made the backdrop for novels like *Sons and Lovers*. Ray Huthwaite was an Eastwood miner who knew from close up that vital need to watch out for your mate in the levels:

We used to 'elp woon anoother; it were comradeship alone. An it 'ad to be, because, same as when we was 'and-getting, it was a job where you'd got to be riskin' your laif every daey.

And there was one Sunday morning at Castle Colliery that Ray would never forget:

Wi could 'ear the coals beginnin' ter groan an' groomble. We usst to allus saey, 'We can 'ear flashers' in this area, an' it could be soomthin' laik three or four 'oondred yaads aweiy from yer, boo' yuh could 'ear i' in distance laik thoonder.

'Flash' is a word widely used in English indicating some sudden occurrence (a 'flash-flood' for instance). In the next part of Ray's tale, 'gobbings' (from 'gob') is coal-mining refuse, according to Smyth's *Treatise on Coal and Coal-Mining* of 1867:

An' then laiter on there was over forty yaads of coal gain [going] down an' ah thaought ah'd 'ad mi chips tha' daey. An' then when ye could see the gobbin's – tha's the area where the cawl's bin wehrked [the coal's been worked] – beginnin' ter coom th'oother said [side] of conveyer, tha' were the taim fer everybody to roon. We usst to shaat [shout] to woon anoother, 'Top weight's on, yowth, let's goow!' an' that was it. Then yer'd joos' feel woon maighty blasst uv ayer [you'd just feel one mighty blast of air] an' the face 'ud 'ave gone.

Now only a handful of pits remain open in Nottinghamshire, I imagine the life expectancy of words like 'gobbings' will be pretty well equal to that of the youngest man to have gone underground. That term 'yowth', which came so naturally to Ray nearly a quarter of a century ago, is also under threat in Eastwood, according to Gordon, whom Voices interviewed there. He came to the town to teach thirty years ago:

'I didn't like bein' called "yowth" boot everybody'd [go] "Ey oop, yowth", "Ow yer gooin on, yowth?" An' I was older than them so 'ow I could be a youth I don't know. Boot that's died out, I've not heard it used for ages, yet when I first came here in 1975 it was used all the time.

Now I've learned over the years that there are two features of local talk that one has to be particularly wary about, often asserted, yet often wrong. One is the claim to the extreme localness of a particular word or expression (usually the distribution is far wider); the other is of the mortality of words. So although 'yowth' is no doubt a term in decline in Eastwood, I doubt it's gone completely. 'Suckers' (or more accurately 'soockers') was claimed by some Eastwood children back in the 1980s as the local word for ice-lollies, yet exactly the same term is also in day-to-day usage across the county in Kirkby in Ashfield. Clearly, therefore, it's still very much alive, but how far around the Midlands 'suckers' is used it's difficult to tell – certainly the word is claimed by one glossary I've seen as Brummie dialect. The story the fireman Ivan recently told Voices (and which, incidentally, I've transcribed in this case with all his distinctive elisions in place, such as 'kemoop' for 'came up') clearly demonstrates, however, that it's not spread as far as the west of England:

> 'Went on 'oliday wi' me two soons lasst year down to Devon an' sev'nye'rold kemoop an' "Can I 'avenice cream, dad?" So ah giv'im a pan coi' [pound coin]; go in the shop, coom back all oopset, asaid, "What'sa matter?" 'E said, "Lady sen' me out the shop. Wu'n give me one, dad." Says, "Why no'? What ye asskfor?" 'E said, "Can ah 'ave a red soocker, please?" An she di'n't oonderstan' what 'e meant. Thought 'e was bein' rude.'

Ah, the joys of regional confusion: 'sucker' clearly implied some cheeky schoolboy talk as far as the Devon shopkeeper was concerned when all the lad wanted was an ice-lolly. It's tales like these, taken from the talk of young men and women right now that constantly give the lie to claims that regional vernaculars are dead, or even dying.

I'd in fact go further. It strikes me that Midlands dialects are still vigorously alive. Perhaps it has something to do with the fact that the seismic shocks undergone by Midlands industry that I mentioned earlier are still very recent and maybe the decline is about to accelerate. But from the evidence of the Voices survey in 2004/5 I'd say that the speech of those close, working communities is still holding, and linguistic boundaries, such as the one between 'duck' and 'love' that Roy the bus driver observed as he drove the route, are still audible.

There appears too to be some empirical evidence that the changes have been slighter here. Listening to Stanley Ellis's hundreds of recordings made across England in the 1950s and 1960s for the Leeds University Survey of English Dialects I've often noted how wide the gulf is, as a general rule, between the speech of around half a century ago and today. Not so though, it seems, in the Midlands. Here, of course, I enter all the normal caveats about the difficulties of comparison: it's very easy to chance upon, for instance, a broad speaker from today and a relatively unaccented one from 1957 and conclude that there's been little slippage. But given that the Survey's aim was to seek out older, broader representatives from rural areas where the speech is frequently slowest to change, I find it quite remarkable that in the recordings I've listened to, from Leicestershire, Rutland, Nottinghamshire, Staffordshire and Derbyshire, the shift away from stronger regional speech is very much less marked than in almost any other English region. I think, for example, of the Lancashire woman whose account of village life half a century ago still left my outsider's ears unsure of every word after replaying it at least twenty times. Or of the Cumbrian midwife's account of difficult deliveries that similarly had me reaching repeatedly for the rewind button.

In comparison, the account of laying a hedge from Lyddington in Rutland, recorded by Stanley Ellis in 1957, is clear and comprehensible, even down to the dialect words the hedger uses. In fact, it's not far off RP, except for the dropped initial 'h's, a tendency to sharpen the 'e' in words like 'hedge' towards 'i' ('hidge'), suggesting a whiff of not-so-distant Norfolk, and that clear stamp of Midlands and northern dialects, the 'oo' sound in 'cut': 'a lot of hoontin' done round 'ere ... a good 'edge cootter'.

The farmer from Markfield in Leicestershire with his account of sheep-worrying also posed few problems of clarity: ''E coot a stick out the 'edge ... an' 'e follered the dog 'om' ... ah phoned for the p'lice ...' The same goes for the Harby farmer with his tale of a fox, the Seagrave cheesemaker ('it tek about a gallon of milk to make a paand of cheese ...'), the Goadby wool-dealer ('this is a very naace clip of wool, an' wi'v' given you the top praaice for it ...') and even the markedly more 'northern' accent of the Nottinghamshire farmer talking about 'brekkin' 'osses [breaking horses]'. His 'affpass six [half past six]', 'god 'old of their teails [got hold of their tails]' and 'brot this 'oss [brought this horse]' for example are clearly more sharply accented than his equivalents in Leicestershire, but there are few comprehension problems, despite the rather crackly quality of the recording.

Near Retford (Notts), Ellis recorded a fruit farmer talking about his apple orchards. Same story here: his pronunciation of 'cookers' (cooking apples) is lengthened, he says 'ovver' for over, but the broadest he ever got was when he talked of the cropping performance of his trees: 'They started to beear, an' the' beear very 'eavy naa ...' Even in Staffordshire, where talk in the Potteries towns remains very strongly accented today (see 'The Voices Survey: The Neglected, the Not Nice and the New'), the 78-year-old farmer from near Tamworth that the SED recorded was delightfully easy to understand with his tales of traditional fairs: 'We used to 'ave the maypolin' an' go round singkin':

> Maypole Deay, it's a very noice deay,
> Please to remember the Maypole Deay!
> Dressed in ribbins, toid in a boow,
> See what a maypole oi can show!'

Surely in the pit-villages of Derbyshire, where the mining days are fading fast, there would be some really audible shifts of accent and vocabulary? Not so. This retired miner was eighty when he recorded his memories of pit-sense – knowing what's what underground – for Stanley Ellis fifty years ago. He cared little for the then new-fangled classroom-taught miner: 'He'll get 'is diplawma [and have] no practical experience whatever.' You had actually to work at the pit bottom to 'feel' a working, 'the state of yer rawdweays', for example:

> Soom'll stand withaat pins an' soom wawn't. Soom 'as to be timbered every yard, oothers ye can gaw on gawing an' not see a bar set in the pleeaice.

It's regional all right, but perfectly comprehensible and no broader than Ray from Eastwood recorded in the 1980s, or the Swadlincote ex-miner Alan's account of the indelible grime of the Derbyshire pits captured by Voices in 2004/5:

> 'When ye'ad a fortnight 'oliday it would tek a fortnight to get the moock right out yer eyes, from oop yer nose and in yer ears. Ye can wash yer, boot it would be working out yer eyes; you'd wash ears an' it'd tek yer a fortnight three weeks to clean yersen properly.'

Now compare this snatch of dialogue from Lawrence's *Sons and Lovers* from 1913. The miner Walter Morel is about to try and wash off that ingrained pit-dust, but is interrupted by his wife, Gertrude:

> 'What, are thee there!' he said boisterously. 'Sluthe off an' let me wesh mysen.' 'You may wait till I've finished,' said his wife. 'Oh, mun

I? An' what if I shonna?' This good-humoured threat amused Mrs
Morel. 'Then you can go and wash yourself in the soft-water tub.'
'Ha! I can' an' a', tha mucky little 'ussy.'

More than ninety years of Midlands talk, and barely a difference. It's a
very artificial comparison of course, and Lawrence's was a literary version
of the Eastwood twang, but perhaps revealing for all that.

No historical review of the language of the Midlands would be complete without evoking that other, rather different landscape forty miles
further south in the conurbation that is Birmingham and the Black
Country. You'll find detailed comparisons in the 'Voices' section of this
chapter and the Midlands 'Snapshot' focuses specifically on the language
of the region's capital. But the accent of this southern area is so different,
so urban, its intonation pattern so distinctive, that it deserves a particular
and separate mention. It's even given the language a word in its own right
– brummagem – which was used *contemptuously*, according to the *Oxford
English Dictionary*, of an article of Birmingham manufacture, especially a
counterfeit groat coin, a term that dates from as far back as 1691. Brummagem came to be applied to other manufactured goods, but the slightly
tawdry quality stuck to the products like the lacquer applied to 'brummagem' ware by Birmingham craftsmen, such that a further dictionary
definition reads: 'of the nature of cheap or showy imitation'.

> Birmingham has had a very bad press. People tend to think, I think, of
> a black smoky sort of place with a lot of heavy industry. Well,
> common sense will tell you that Birmingham isn't a centre of heavy
> industry at all – it's an assembly, tin-bashing place. I suspect part of it
> is that it's a bit too close to London to have a regional capital identity
> of its own. People haven't tended to accord it the sort of dignity that
> they accord to the big civic centres further north.

Dr Clive Upton of Leeds University comes from Birmingham and has
first-hand knowledge both of the way the local speech is perceived and
of how it functions from a linguistic point of view. The intonation is
idiosyncratic, an upwardly mobile drawl that seems to ensure that in
public consultations on 'favourite' accents, it always ends up pretty well
at the bottom of the heap, slugging the honours out with Liverpudlian.
Stanley Ellis came to Birmingham and the neighbouring Black Country

in the late 1980s to survey the sounds of England's second city rapidly transforming itself into a multicultural metropolis. He met, too, some of the older inhabitants who spoke with the broadest local accent, like Bette, who worked in the Bourneville chocolate factory:

> I down't think women were very well trayted in the Midlands. Oi think you were at the bottom of the peckin' ordah. You were expected to sty home an look affter the families whaal the min [while the men] droonk maost of theeir mooney awye. It was a very haad loife – you'd gow an clayne a poob for a cooupla bob. Boot that was what you were brought oop with.

A typical tale of hard-lived working lives, expressed in the unmistakable tones of Birmingham. Clive Upton says that the routine shifting around of vowels in the city's speech can sometimes induce confusion:

> I don't think there are any particular noises in Birmingham which are particularly aesthetically unpleasant. Pronunciation like the standard English 'ay' sound in 'rain' is more of an 'i' sort of sound in 'riyne'. And the 'i' sound in a word like 'fine' is an 'oi' and you'll hear that over and over again, the 'oi' sound. So 'fine rain' will be 'foine rine'. The 'oi' sound in 'spoil' will be an 'aoi' sound in 'spaoile', which is quite nice in that words like 'vice' and 'voice' will run together as 'vaoice' and if you hear someone say that someone's got a 'naoice vaoice' it'll be hard to say whether they've got a 'nice voice' or a 'nice vice'.

So in Bette's little story above, her 'i' is said more like 'oi', 'treated' becomes 'trayted' and the 'ay' sound in 'stay' shifts round to more of an 'eye' sound ('sty'). 'A' is a short sound, as throughout the Midlands, confirming the region's affiliation to the 'northern' group of accents, as does the 'oo' sound heard in Bette's 'poob', 'cooupla', 'boot [but]' etc. And Clive Upton notes another shift too:

> The 'o' sound in 'go' is more of an 'aow' sound. So if you run a few of those together you'll have someone giving 'a queek bairst on the xoylophaowne.'

Stanley Ellis has called the Brummie accent 'a proud, independent speech that knows very well it's one of the most unpopular talking vehicles that any English speaker uses' and even people from just outside the city limits but still, broadly, within the Birmingham conurbation often can't stand it. I guess it's just that old favourite again, the rivalry born of proximity. Listen to Steve, recorded in Birmingham (or as many locals pronounce it 'Birmingkham') by Voices, but by birth a Black Countryman from across the city line:

'The Birmingkham accent I don't like. In the Midlands you've go' the Black Coontray an' Birmingkham an' there's a massive divoide there bicos people in Birmingkham they're called "Brummies" or "0121ers" [the phone code] an' they ten' not to mix so mooch wi' the Black Coontray people, boot the Black Coontray – what you'll foind is they're the salt o' the earth, they're really noice people. [In] Birmingkham you ten' to get a lo' of imports, boot the Black Coontray people sorta joost sty over there.'

Stanley Ellis was very struck by the distinction, by this sharp dividing line that clearly separates the city off from the rest of that vast sprawl of housing and industry that constitutes the west Midlands:

Drive on the Dudley road a matter of three or four miles to 'Smerrick' and it's there before you. You won't find 'Smerrick' on any map as you go 'over the bonk': you might find 'Smethwick'.

Dudley lies five miles west of Smethwick and according to the local convention is the start of the Black Country; as one man told Ellis: 'Doodlay's gotta be the plyce. An' it's the area immediately sooraounding Doodlay that would be the Black Coountray in my estimytion.' Gary, another local, narrowed the area down: Edgbaston, Harborne, Northfield, Castle Bromwich, Coleshill, Sutton Coldfield and Solihull all belong to Birmingham:

Then you go north of Birmingkham an' you got Sandwell, West Brom, Tipton, Wednesbury, Bilston, all those are definitely Black Coontry accents. Boot then you go further to the north, you've got Aldridge, Brownhills, those are still Broommay, boot they 'aven't got the Broommay accent loik you 'ave in Moseley or anywhere like 'a'. Boo' they're no' Black Coountry either.

Wolverhampton, ten miles north-west of Birmingham city centre but still part of the built-up sprawl laced through by the M5 and M6 and their many junctions, is neither Black Country nor Birmingham, but as you can hear in the 'Voices' section, has an accent that comes from very much the same stock. It's the accent and the intonation pattern, says Clive Upton, rather than a very rich local lexicon or non-standard syntax, that characterize the speech of the west Midlands; and it's a sound that sometimes even proud Brummies find hard to take. As this local woman told Stanley Ellis in 1988:

> I watch the tellay, an oi see soombody interviewing a Birmingham person on the tellay and oi think God, that's awful!

The Voices Survey: The Neglected, the Not Nice and the New

Voices tackled the speech of the Midlands with enthusiasm and insight, the recordings – dozens of hours of them – bearing witness to some of the richest and most naturally used language I've heard, certainly in England. To my surprise, too, I've heard for the first time people here who actually dislike their own dialect, who think it sounds 'a bit rough'. And I've heard the refreshing stories of how old regional forms are being renewed and extended by young Midlanders with Asian and Afro-Caribbean roots. This, then, is just the cream of the recordings, featuring some of the more interesting words and expressions; those I haven't room for in this section I've included in the glossary.

I'll start in the south, in Wolverhampton, with Jan, Wolverhampton born and bred but who, until his untimely death, spent most of her life travelling with her soldier husband. Jan's one of those Midlanders who's very conscious of local linguistic difference, but isn't quite sure about whether she likes the Black Country sound:

> 'When you hear people on television or on the rydio from the west Midlands particularlay, oi do tend to cringe a little bit; oi think, "God, do oi saound loike that?" We do coom across as a little bit theek, oi must admit, with ar accent. Oi'm not ashymed of it, [though].'

Suggest that Jan comes from the big city ten miles away and she's mounting her steed and levelling her lance to defend Wolverhampton:

'They say, "Oh, you're a Broommay", [but] the accent to oos is
distinctly different. An' we don't like being called Broommies, actually.
If people call me a Broommie, oi saiy, "uh-uh, no way". Oi've got the
proide of being from Wolverhampton.'

These narrow local differences of pronunciation are claimed the length
and breadth of the UK. In this case, a handful of miles seems to be
critical: joining Jan for the Voices discussion are two young men who
came to Wolverhampton from far away, John from Chester and Craig
from Wales. They're used by now to coping with the local accent, but
find themselves completely at sea seven miles due south in Brierley Hill.

'If you go to Broierley 'ill you can't oonderstand a bloody word, can't
oonderstand what they're saying 'alf the toim, because they're even
more broader than what we are. Many a time I been over there,
assked for directions an' gone "OK, mate, cheers" an' gone on to the
next person an' ask 'im.'

For Jan, growing up in Wolverhampton was the familiar story of solidarity
in adversity expressed in the broad accents of the edge of the Black
Country:

'Wolverhampton when oi was little, maoust people were poor. An iss
the old cliché: we dinn 'aff to lock ar doors because we've got
noothin' for anybody to rob, anywye. Nyghbours ollwiz 'elped each
oother: if soomwon in the street was avin a byebee, there would be a
nyghbour 'oo would look after that lydie while she was 'avin the
byebee.'

Or 'babby'. That was the local alternative offered by these Voices
respondents; it's a Midlands standard and unquestionably the term to
use, though Afro-Caribbean groups favoured the word of West Indian
origin, 'picknee' (as also in Liverpool and in the London area). Amongst
the young women interviewed near Coventry with roots in the Asian
community 'babby' was much disliked:

'A lot of people around here say "babby", boot I hate i'. I' sounds
really tackay: "ma babby"; oh my God! It's common and I don't
like i'.'

The Sound of the Midlands

The accents of the Midlands are broadly northern in character, with the two tell-tale markers of the 'u' and 'a' vowels confirming this. 'Up', 'pub' and 'cup' are all therefore 'oop', 'poob' and 'coop' throughout the region, and the 'a' in 'bath' and 'last' is shortened to 'baeth' and 'lasst'. The east Midlands is what linguists call a non-rhotic area (the 'r' in 'cart' and 'bird' is not heard) while the southern and western counties tend to pronounce their 'r'. Shakespeare, growing up in Warwickshire, is famously supposed to have sounded 'r' in the middle of words.

The widest gulf is between the urban dialects of Coventry, Birmingham and the Black Country and the accents of Leicestershire, Nottinghamshire, Derbyshire and Staffordshire. The much imitated west Midlands accent with its droning 'tune' is often referred to as 'Brummie' but has a degree of variation across the area, with local differences (see 'The Voices Survey') between the city accent and that of the neighbouring Black Country (characterized by, for example, the comedian Lenny Henry's native Dudley speech).

But in both areas, alongside the intonation pattern, it's the way that the vowels are modified that typifies the pronunciation. The 'i' in 'night' and 'light' shifts to an 'oi' sound, so 'my night-light is quite bright' would sound something like 'moy noight-loight is quoite broight'. At the same time, the 'ay' sound in 'ray' and 'same' turns into 'eye'. Thus 'they may bake cakes' is on the lines of 'thy my byke kykes'. There are other vowel shifts too, including 'oh', which becomes more of an 'aow' ('no' turns into something approaching 'now') and

Amongst the ex-miners of 'Swad' (Swadlincote) in Derbyshire, discussion of what word they'd naturally reach for uncorked another memory of family hardship that's almost unbelievable now. The speaker is Alan, who was sometimes asked to account for his mother's periodic absences:

> 'Mi mam were always 'aving babies: "Where's Moll?" "She's 'ad anoother kid." Thirteen kids – twenty-six on oos in a four-bedroom 'ouse. Ah never 'ad a bed until ah was fifteen, never lay in a bed, till ar Maurice got married. 'E were ten year owder than me, an' ah took 'is place in the bed; never lay in a bed till ah were fifteen.'

Alan is eloquent when he reflects on his young hard life, and the fun

terminal -y, which is often 'ay' (e.g. 'particularlay', 'Broommay'). In the west Midlands, famously, final 'g' in words like 'among' and 'sing' is pronounced emphatically, which I've indicated in transcriptions with a 'k' (it's often heard too in the middle of words – so 'singkingk' and 'Birmingkham').

The sound of the north of the region is beginning to head off towards Yorkshire in the east and Lancashire in the west, and is in each case a pretty decent halfway house. Thus Nottinghamshire will elide 'the' and insert an eliding 'r': 'outar earshot o' t'missus, laike [out of earshot of the missus, like]' came from Mansfield, and 'gerra bag o' slack [get a bag of coal]' from Stoke. Across such a large region, there are inevitably a lot of fine differences in accent that I can't identify here, but it's noticeable that in the north Nottinghamshire recordings the 'eye' sound is sometimes pronounced more like 'oi', 'soomtoims', while in the Potteries accent of Stoke it's more of an 'aa' (as in the distinctive 'mar lady' for 'my lady', i.e. the wife).

Also a feature of the Potteries is the short 'i' in 'fifty, sixty' that opens out towards 'e': 'fefty, sexty' and 'ketchin' for kitchen, and the 'aa' in RP 'father' that becomes 'ay' as in 'fayther'. Voices heard that in Leicestershire too. 'Water' in Derbyshire and Nottinghamshire is 'watter', to rhyme with 'hatter' (the phrase 'watter is what ye wesh ye way' is quoted by experts as the typical Derbyshire rendering of 'water's what you wash yourself with'). Finally, certain sounds merge in this northern part of the region – Voices recorded the words 'shirt' and 'shot' in Leicestershire and Nottinghamshire being pronounced as 'shot' ('a clin shot' – clean shirt) together with the old dialect phrase 'shall thou': 'shot do that for me'.

youngsters got up to in this industrial landscape has similar echoes across the Midlands. This is Jan on childhood recreation in Wolverhampton:

'We ussed to swim in the coot when we was kids. We ussed to push the dead cats and dead dogs aside. The barges ussed to coom along. They ussed to throw loomps of caoul [an yell], "Get out yer little skit, get out!"'

The 'cut' – a man-made navigable waterway – is a classic feature of industrial landscapes throughout Britain, as was the coal that bargees threw at the kids in the water. For Roy and his friends growing up in Stoke-on-Trent, the cut was a playground:

'We ussed to build a rafft an' we ussed to say, "Where we geen?";
"aw, geen dawn t'coot on rafft." Boot it wadn' a c'nal, i' wuz a coot.'

And messing about in water was how Alan and his mates also loved to
spend their time, down at the local stream, or 'brook', a word favoured
by Voices respondents in many places, not with any particular poetic
connotation and just as polluted as the cut:

'We ussed t'swim in brook – dam the brook oop with sloodge [sludge]
an' swim in it; school 'olidays, it were a real treat. Woon lad caught
polio cos 'ere were rats in it, yaw see; finished oop in irons din't 'e? 'E
'ad polio through swimmin' in the brook. Used to be rats in it an'
frogs, dead dogs coom down. When dogs died they ussed to chook it
in brook. 'E couldn't walk an' 'e were wi' 'em for years – leg-irons to
'old 'is leg oop.'

The days of seeing young children struggling to cope with leg-callipers
are thankfully gone in the UK, but it wasn't the only occasion in these
Voices interviews when a sharp note from a past age brought me up
short. Take for instance the phrase that Jan and the Wolverhampton
team dropped into their conversation amid a fairly routine selection of
contemporary vernacular terms: 'brassic' for broke, 'minging' for unattractive and 'kip' for sleep; then suddenly:

' "If God spares me." "I'll see ya next week then, cock, if God
spares me." Obviously the yoongsters don't say that any more 'cos it's
an old-fashioned Black Coontry saying.'
'If you said to me, "See yer next Tuesday, then, Jan" an' I said, "If
God spares me", you'd think, "Is she gonna top 'erself?" Boot it is an
old Black Coontry thing that people'd say without givin' it anoother
thought.'

And how about this expression that I'd never come across before, from
the former china-worker Paul and his mates in the Middleport area of
Stoke-on-Trent, not far from Arnold Bennett's Burslem:

'Crimes o' Paris! When you can't think! We alwiz said tha' ant we?
Oow ay, Crimes o' Paris! It's when you're exasperated. Crimes o'
Paris, whatisname? It's like "bloody ell!" '

Paul, eighteen years 'in the pots', as he put it, was a rich source of local words with which he quite unselfconsciously peppered his conversation. He, like Midlanders from east and west, was very comfortable with the endearment term 'duck' (see 'Language in a Landscape'), but there was more:

'Most people use that: you can even talk to the lads, an seay, "Ey oop, doock, aaht all reaight?" Ah've used it very awften: "Thanks, doock." [Or] "Ey oop, soorry": it means "Hey oop, mayte". When ah wuz yoong at Biddulph Moor, [they'd say] to gain your attention: "Dust year, soorry? [= dost thou hear, mate]" '

This word 'sorry' or 'sorrey' is widespread in the north Midlands and was also reported from Belper in Derbyshire ('"Soorry" is a word they used to use a lot'), in Leicestershire and at Eastwood in Nottinghamshire, where they knew the word came from 'sirrah' ('"Arta goin wom?" [Are you going home?]. Sithee, soorry. And home was always "wom" '). Lots of regional detail here, including the use of 'wom' for home, which is a feature of the north Midlands that's shared with Lancashire dialect. Jan, the wife of Roy, the Stoke bus driver, told Voices:

'Ah say "wom". Ah never say "home"; ah always say, "Ah'm goin wom in a minute." '

Conversely, the other Jan, from Wolverhampton, twenty-five miles due south, is aware that the usage belongs slightly outside her area:

'Actually in Wolver'ampton, we say, "Ah'm goin' 'ome." A few moils oop the road they "gaw wom".'

Voices came across a number of very distinctive terms that had wide usage right across the region. Take 'bostin' and 'bosted' for example. The word has been around in dialect use for many years and was quoted by the authors of the Derbyshire dialect guide in the 1980s ('Ah'm bostin for a swag' – a drink). As other glossaries inform me, it comes from ' "bost" – to burst' (Potteries). And it's variously listed as 'bostin' – terrific, excellent, fantastic etc.' (Birmingham) and 'literally "bursting" but actually "very good indeed" e.g. "we 'ad a bostin time" ' (Black Country). In the Voices survey it therefore not surprisingly turned up in Wolverhampton (' "bostin"; it means wicked, fantastic: "a bostin night out . . ." "). At Stoke speedway track, Jan remembered the way her family used it:

> 'Ma grandfather's favourite phrase was "Coss keck a boll agains' a woll wi' y'ead till i' bost?" – "Can you kick a ball against a wall with your head till it bursts?" '

But 'bost' also has a somewhat different meaning: ' "bosted": it means she's oogly – "a face like a bosted clog" '; though the word derives here, surely, not from to burst, but to bust (break). That meaning of 'unattractive' or 'ugly' was very popular in Stoke:

> ' "Bosted"; a face like a bosted clog; " 'ell fire! she's bosted"; "she's got a face that'll freeze watter" . . . a "minger".'

How unexciting and unevocative the nationally used 'minger' feels amongst such colourful company as 'a face that'll freeze watter'!

Less widespread, but completely original and, as far as I'm aware, unique in the United Kingdom, is one particular Midlands usage for an item that's so familiar to most people that I often wondered whether Voices would discover any significant variation at all. The question asked of every interviewee in the country was: 'What is the name you use for the long, soft seat in the living room?' Nationally, the responses were pretty predictable: some prefer sofa, others, settee, still others couch. You get the occasional chaise longue and even in one case a Chesterfield. But what I'd not heard before and only encountered in the Midlands – in several locations – was 'sofee'. This was Ivan the fireman from Kirkby in Ashfield, Nottinghamshire:

> 'I've 'eard of "sofee" too. I always get bollocked for dropping coorry [curry] on t'sofee.'

It was quoted too in Stoke – twice, in different locations ('the old sofee') and down in Nottinghamshire amongst the Eastwood teachers:

> 'What became a "sofa" was always a "sofee": the miner wouldn't do anything till 'e'd 'ad an hour on the sofee.'

The Derbyshire group from Belper had also written the term amongst their responses: 'Ah put "sofee" . . . naow ah coll it a "sofa".' One member's 86-year-old mother had also completed the survey and she'd suggested an even older term, 'settle', evoking in my mind images of the Brontë sisters and Haworth Parsonage. In fact, as Alan, the ex-miner from Swadlincote also in Derbyshire, told Voices, in his cramped child-hood home (he was the man with twelve brothers and sisters, you'll recall) they'd also had a settle 'made outa wood with a squab on it' filled with ticking.

There were some terms on the Voices list which brought almost unanimous agreement from all the Midlands interviewees I've listened to. For 'left-handed', for instance, the preferred expression is almost always 'keggy-handed' or simply 'keggy'. A group of gay men from Nottingham used it ('I've got two keggy-'anded parents'), as did the allotment gardeners from Middleport in Stoke-on-Trent, the respondents from both Belper and Swadlincote in Derbyshire, and the old miners from Leicestershire. The Kirkby in Ashfield firemen offered (the almost identical) 'caggy' as an alternative, which was also the version the Wolver-hampton group used ('caggy-handed'). For the Eastwood teachers, the word was 'coggy', whilst at the northern boundary of the Midlands the Nantwich (Cheshire) group were also 'keggy' fans, though they also say 'gaggy-handed' and even '*gabby*-handed'.

That favourite place which also has so many regional variants across the country – the 'narrow walkway between buildings' – has, as I've indicated in the first section of this chapter, two standard terms in the Midlands: 'gennel' (with a soft 'g', cf. Yorkshire 'ginnel' where the 'g' is hard) and 'jitty'. Ivan, the loquacious Nottinghamshire fireman, says that for him there's a definite difference between them: 'gennel' is between houses within a terraced street, while a 'jitty' is at the *end* of a row. He'd say for example:

> 'Wen' daan this "gennel" an' there's an 'aase woon side an' an 'aase the oother side. Wen' daan this "jitty" an' there's awnly 'aases on woon side, then there's allotments or wha'ever.'

In Leicestershire, Horace and the other former miners also used 'jitty', but added that other widely used word 'entry', as well as another not infrequent northern usage, 'snicket'. Here, though, it belonged to their memories of going down the shaft to the pit-bottom:

'If ye were a bit early waitin' for the cages ye'd stay in the "snicket" –
a little bit of an alley-way – an' you used to go an' sit in there an' wait
for the cage to arrive.'

A final addition to this canon of Midlands 'alley' words, and one that's
less well known, though reported from Essex as well as here in the city
of Nottingham, is 'twitchel'.

The Midlands is also the traditional source of a word that's now gained
quite widespread currency in other parts of England, as detected by the
Voices survey: 'mardy', meaning moody or grumpy. As you'd expect,
almost everyone used it, from Wolverhampton ('mardy, misery arse,
misery goots'), Nottingham ('mardy, got a monk on. Kids are usually
mardy; they cry a lot'), Mansfield, Belper ('mardy, awkward boogger, got
t'monkey on their back; a mardy [person] is a bit of a whinger') to the
north-west of the region in Nantwich, Cheshire, where it wasn't the first
choice but did start a discussion:

'"He's got one on him", "mardy".'
'I used to think "mardy" meant "spoiled".'
'It could be both spoiled or in a bad temper, moody or sulking.'

In fact, as I note elsewhere in this book, 'mardy' and 'mard' derive from
'marred', the past tense of the verb to 'mar' or spoil, so it does carry both
meanings. Finally, head east and south of Nantwich towards the other
end of the Midlands and you can hear it too, from two groups whose
use of regional words is understandably less marked – young Punjabi
women and Afro-Caribbean teenagers, from Bedworth near Coventry
and Nottingham respectively. Their take on language is particularly
interesting and I return to it towards the end of this section.

The Voices question about truanting brought many familiar terms (bunk,
skive, nick, wag) but a trio of new ones: from the Nottinghamshire firemen
it was to 'cap' ('cap it, we used to cap school: "le'ss cap i' this afto!" '); in
Belper, Voices heard 'tag off'; and from the Potteries allotment-holders,
'bobbing off' ('I used to bob school regularly'). This is clearly a frequent
usage in the Stoke area as the local bus driver and speedway fan Roy knew
it too. It gave him a chance to indulge his passion for machines:

'We used to call it bobbin' it. I was down the scrap yard at thirteen,
drivin' a wagon when ah was fourteen – a petrol Bedford – 'stead o'

geein' t'school. Mi moother ussed to teik me t'school a' fourteen; kep' mark t'register an' back aat again i' 'bou' ten minutes, d'n the scrap yard working.'

It continually fascinates me how the recall of a single word from childhood has over and over again in this survey brought delightful anecdotes to back them up. Ask Roy's wife Janice, for example, about the shoes she wore as a child for PE (again a standard Voices question) and out tumbles this anecdote about what happened when she was cleaning her 'pumps' – the standard word for plimsolls in the Midlands and the north.

'Ah remember woon day ah'd to ge' mi poomps whaatend [whitened], and ah also 'ad to clean mi teeth. An' ah was doin' both the same things a' the seim taam, wan't ah? [wasn't I] An' ah pecked oop [picked up] mi toothpaste to clean mi teeth. An' ah wuz cleanin' mi teeth an' ah thought, "Euuuh! What the hell's tha'?" Ah'd pecked oop mi Meltonian shoe whaatenin' to clean mi teeth. Boot ah 'ad loovely white teeth!'

The Stoke-on-Trent area provided Voices with some of the best stories in the Midlands, perhaps because massive change has only really challenged the Potteries and pits relatively recently. Take this flavour of the town in carnival mood during the workers' annual break ('Potters' Fortnight: it were lasst week in June, fust week in July') from Paul, Tony, Norman, Peter and Norton, gardeners, whose ages range from early forties to seventies:

'It was called Stoke Wakes an' those that stopped at 'eome – if you went t'Blackpool ah think everybody in t'Pot'sies was there, that particular fortnaight – [but for] those that stoppt at 'eome, there wuz a Wakes, what they called a Wakes, in the meddle of Hanley. An' what would ye call a Wakes today? A fairground.'

Another fair was the 'Jam-Jar Wakes' ('If you wanted to ride on anything ye'd to take a jam-jar'). It was just before one of these holidays that Tony, a 65-year-old ex-miner, remembered watching as a young winding-engine man, keen to get away for his break, forgot that he had a last group of men in the cage at the bottom of the shaft when he brought it up for the last time:

'As soon as they rang awff that all these men were en, the keeage [cage] dropped laik a stone. An' of course they were daouwn bottom in oother wan. An' the wind was whistlin' through the wheels, an' in seconds [it] crashed through the gates as if 'e was drawin' cool [coal]. 'Cos you draw cool a helluva lot fasster than men. 'E whepped 'em oop, an' when they got aat, they got aat these colliers did, lights still on, joost got aat an: "ah think we'll 'ave 'im for speedin'!" Aw, bloody 'ell! If 't'ad bin me, ah'd 'ave bin 'avin' a shower before mi stoomach go' back! Aw 'e did coom oop fasst!'

This group from Stoke-on-Trent also had some interesting local Potteries usages that turned up nowhere else. The most unusual came from Paul, who's still a relatively young man and quite naturally uses 'mar lady' (with the stress on 'mar', not 'lady') when speaking of his wife. It's a specific term derived from 'my lady' that's also been immortalized in a local newspaper cartoon, 'May un Mar Lady' (me and my wife). Rita, a publican in Mansfield (Notts), says the local equivalent there is to use an old-fashioned name: 'ar [our] Gert, ar Myrtle: my owd man used to coll me that'.

In similar unique vein, only from Kirkby (Notts), Voices heard 'croggy' meaning to piggy-back a ride on a bicycle on the handlebars ('You never bin on a croggy before?'), which appears from other polling information still to be quite common. Then, colourfully, and again quoted by a young man, 'It's black over Bill's mother's': 'There's a cloud in the distance and you know there's a rainstorm on the way; it used to be quite common round here.'

Several respondents mentioned that Geordie words had in recent years made quite an impact in Nottinghamshire. They ascribed this to the arrival in the area of many miners from Northumberland and Durham whose pits had closed and who'd come south in search of work. Acrimony about the 1984/5 strike still sharpens attitudes and tongues as Alf, now a publican but formerly a miner, remembers:

'After all this taam, it's still there in the back of your mind. When ah wen' oop Barnsley, an' thee foon' aat [they found out] that ah wuz frum Notts, straightaway thee coom an' said "scab". Bu' woonce thee foon' aat that ah'd bin aat a full year, they were ove' t'moon. Ah were clear on – everybody wanted to know muh. Ah min [I mean] at foo'ball matches from Yorkshire, thee still shaat aat, "Scab, scab, scab".'

There's a measure of social isolation too to be found amongst some, though not all, of the last groups I'm looking at in this section, the Asian and Afro-Caribbean men and women surveyed across the Midlands by Voices. I've separated them out only because their language story is a rather different one here. Bedworth is a smallish town just north of Coventry and sectioned off from the cathedral city by the east–west sweep of the M6. Here Voices met Anita, Nykita and Kieran, three young women with Punjabi roots. Their speech is only lightly Midlands-accented, with not a hint of their family background, but with many of the today widespread vernacular features that originated in south-east England such as glottal stops ('li"le' for little), TH-fronting ('bovvered' for bothered) and the 'dark l' ('middaw' for middle). Despite sounding in many respects like young people from any corner of any UK city you can choose, though, they've known a degree of isolation:

> 'There's quite a lot of racism goin' around because you're cooloured.'
> 'Because we're cooloured we ge' no'iced more an' it makes like it's an agenda: "Why're you all si"in' togethah?" '

This was even more acute in their parents' case:

> 'My dad was speakin' Punjabi at about ten o' clock a night an' 'e go' attacked because 'e was speakin' Punjabi. Boo' they were droonk. Boo' they were bein' racist really, an' this was in Bedworth.'

These girls have a variety of linguistic backgrounds. One speaks English at home, with parents who are bilingual but, she says, don't have an Indian accent, whereas another's parents tended still to use the language they grew up speaking in India. What's certain is that things are changing, and according to this trio's experience, it's generally for the better, both socially and linguistically:

> 'People are staa'in' to oonderstand, to accept it and [they've] staa'ed to like it as well. I think tha's because of the music. They're making money out of it, like with Jay Sean [Hounslow-born R&B artist, 'the UK's first Asian crossover superstar', according to his website]. I think

the music's the best thing tha's coom out. I' influences people a lo'. It's changed so many people's attitudes towards oos. Programmes like [the BBC comedy] *Goodness Gracious Me* really emphasized on Punjabi and it's becoming more, like, cooltural to actually speak Punjabi whereas thirty years ago it was a bi' of an embarrassment if y'ad tuh speak it at school, boo' nowadays it's a bi' more hip an' a bi' more trendy therefore you can use i' more.'

These young women have a vernacular that marries elements of their historic family Punjabi culture, something of what they refer to as 'street' culture in the Coventry conurbation, and, too, some flavours from the older local dialect. So PE shoes were 'pumps', trendy young layabouts were 'chavs', but for grandmother, they'd use the Punjabi words 'nani' and 'bibi' ('Father's mother is called "bibi", and mother's mother is called "nani"') and for annoyed the word is 'ragoo': 'You're making me really ragoo.' Their source for much fashionable slang is black urban music:

'They're all from rapping now, [like] "phat" – nothing to do with being fat – "phat" is good. Someone said to my friend, "You're phat" an' he was a bit big-built an' he took it the wrong way!'

Coincidentally, not so very far from these young women, Voices surveyed a group of young black musicians, aged between sixteen and eighteen, from the Radford area of central Nottingham, just north of the river Trent. They were Luke, Rebecca, Dwayne, Ryan and Simeon, known as DJ Razor. They spoke a broad patois a long way removed from the old local dialect and in great part based on Jamaican dialect. 'Picknee' for baby, 'bredren' for friend, 'crepes' for trainers and 'crib' for house have cropped up right across the UK. Some words, though, I'd not encountered elsewhere in the survey, such as 'lean' for tired ('When you bin drinkin' an' smokin' too much, when you bin fighting: "He go' leaned oop"'). On the other hand, they used 'mardy' for moody, 'jitty' for alley and 'vex', or 'vexed' for annoyed, all of which are of course local Midlands talk, though 'vexed' was offered by Barbadian respondents (in Reading) in exactly this sense as being pure West Indian usage.

Valerie, Lauren, Rosalind and Amelia are all members of the same family and live south of the Trent, in the Meadows area of Nottingham. Their West Indian roots are in the little paradise island of St Kitts, along, they say, with many other Meadows residents. They speak much less patois than the teenage musicians from a mile and a half away across the river, though their parents retain much more of a Kittician twang:

'Moom an' dad 'ave go' that accent from the Caribbean so they're not fully broadly English. Soom people may find moom hard to oonderstand when she dooz break out in a patois and goes off broad, boot normally we joost talk normal English as far as I'm concerned.'

So they find themselves operating constantly across two registers: 'unwell' would normally for them be 'sick' but:

' "No me feel so good", moom might say that, older black clients would speak like that.'

Like for the Radford men, 'picknee' and 'bredren' are familiar and used terms, though the latter is 'more of a black male thing. We'd say "mates".' In fact, for day to day conversation, these women are most comfortable using the traditional Nottingham vocabulary they've grown up with. So they say 'sucker' for ice-lolly, 'cobs' for bread-rolls, 'jitty' or 'entry' for that household path and use the typical and affectionate verbal cuff-round-the-ear 'You little bogger' or 'Eh, little bogger!'

In the very different linguistic world of the teenage musicians, Simeon was their self-appointed spokesman. He was very conscious of the image they project, as of the linguistic registers available to him. To illustrate the point, he described how he might write a letter of complaint in patois for a failed order in a shoeshop:

'Ah wan' ma trainahs, car, boy, i' seem lak yer messin' me aroun', man, an' chae no' inna tha' [I ain't into that]. Ah'm no' no plom. Ah wan' ma trainahs an' ah wan' 'em nah! Don't ma' me 'aff to ge' fur inta this [don't make me have to get further into this], cos if ah do, yeah, man is gonna ge' 'urt. Lookin forwar' to 'earin' from yer.'

But it was a question of using the appropriate language for the circumstances: he realizes that he and his mates have issues around their image, and has been delighted when he has a chance to surprise people:

'Like when people look a' meh, like, usually ah'm in trainers, hoodeh [hooded top], all bla' [black], an' they look a' meh an' think, "Yeah, 'e's gonna rob meh." Bu' when they speak tchah [to you], most people ask, "Whadjou do, then?" [I reply] "Play the piano, make music, deejay, right, emcee, produce, everything." An ah li' doin' it cos it's li' – you know tha' shocked face on people; they're thinkin': boy!'

So while DJ Razor, with his 'bredrens' talk, is as 'street' as they come, when dealing with the music business Simeon can adopt a much more mainstream register. Not that different, in fact, from the 'telephone voice' that so many people claim to possess, in effect a more neutral idiom that can communicate effectively beyond the narrow confines of the language group. It's the reason most of us today need more than just a local vernacular in our linguistic armoury and one of the reasons dialect is evolving:

'That's why I've learned to, like, change myself. I can act in two different ways. It works. It's joost bein' smart.'

A Midlands Snapshot: Birmingham Salestalk

Gathered in a Birmingham pub are Rachel, Mike, Alastair, Julie and Dave. They work for a big local luxury-car dealership and have a very idiosyncratic take on the world of language and selling, something they do with style and success, not least as a result of their facility with words. They offered Voices a particular insight into the stylistic and regional choices that confront dynamic young men and women when deciding how they'll express themselves privately – and professionally.

First off, they're typical of the supremely mobile young professional – Mike's from Halesowen in the Black Country, has a strong local accent and is very relaxed with it. But he's the only one to sound really identifiably local: Alastair's a Scot, Dave's lived in the south and travelled widely and has only been in Birmingham for a few months, while Julie and Rachel both have loosely northern vowels (Julie's from Nuneaton in Warwickshire and she says 'mooney' not 'munny' for the folding stuff) but there's little to mark them out as Brummies. Mike, who still lives very close to where he was raised, is also aware of the advantages – and disadvantages – of selling cars with one of the country's least favourite accents, and a pretty strong sample too:

' 'Avin' worked in the maow'or tryde [motor trade] for sor' uv ten
yeears, yew becoom a li"le bi' boilingual. An' yew aff ter taown oop
an' taown deaywn [you have to tone up and tone down]. F'rinstance,
if yer dealin' wi' soomb'dy from the Black Coontry, yer gaow: "Aw
roight, myte, 'aouw ye daouwin', ar kid?" loike, blah blah blah [you
go: "All right, mate, how're you doing, our kid", like]. People loik
yerselves, ye speak 'aow thy'd loike to be spaowkin to. This is moy
nawmaw [normal] speech, boo' oi can taown oop an' taown deaywn.'

Mike has no difficulty in exaggerating his natural Black Country vowels
('roight', 'myte' for right and mate) to make a local customer feel at home,
and likewise uses expressions like 'our kid'. Being able and prepared to
'tone up and down' is his secret. When they're not selling cars, they're
typical young Britons, enjoying nights out in the pub ('I belong there,'
said one), hill-walking, going to the gym, diving in the Maldives and so
forth. Mike, who likes to display his ready, very blue wit adds, 'Oi go
doivin' – it's joost a different sawt!'

In fact, the conversation is typified by a flashy jokiness that involves
a liking for drink, and a shorthand for their business some of which is
well known (tyre-kickers, 'toim-wasters', 'cut-and-shut' – a car that's
been assembled by sticking together two damaged vehicles) but also
includes expressions I'd never encountered. A 'chopper' or 'swapper' for
instance is a customer (always a 'poonter' – punter, sometimes rhyming-
slang fashion a 'Billy [Bunter]') who wants a part-exchange; a 'white flag'
they define as 'someone who buys a car without a fight' and if you get a
deal 'back in bed' you rescue it when it seems lost (you'd 'cocked on the
deal').

From then on in, the reference points become more and more edgy:
'meeting a customer up to the knockers' means they can't afford any
more, the 'smelly armpit brigade' are punters who metaphorically come
in with their hands up and don't need much salestalk, and older customers
are 'biscuit-dribblers', 'leg-draggers' or 'Motability punters'.

Mike was particularly fertile with the imagery that he promised he'd
not made up for the occasion, such as his descriptions of old, battered
vehicles with too many miles on the clock:

'More hits than the Bea'les [been in a few accidents]; you could 'ave a
shave in the steerin' wheel [because it's shiny and worn] – it's done

137

that many moils; moondoost on the dashboard [it's been to the moon and back].'

And it's not just a male thing; Julie admits that after five years in the motor trade she's 'one of the lads' as far as language is concerned. On the terms in the Voices survey, Mike's Black Country origins produced, inevitably, the most regional alternatives. So he'd say 'cowd' for cold (a version found across the whole Midlands), 'babby' for baby and 'caggy-' or 'gab-handed' for left-handed, while Julie from Nuneaton would still call an alley by one of the usual Midlands terms, 'jitty'. Beyond these and the occasional expression like 'full of arms and legs' (west Midlands slang for pregnant, Mike insisted) and 'arrye enner' (the Black Country version of 'all right, isn't she'), these young salespeople had a vernacular that was pretty typical of their age group across the UK. Not surprising perhaps as, in Mike's words, 'in the maowtor tryde you've go' sooch a mix uv people'.

Thus attractive is 'mint', 'fit' or 'a minter' – they describe really good-looking cars as 'Alans' (from 'Alan Minter', a form of botched rhyming slang that's not a rhyme, built on the name of the well-known former boxer). Words for broke produced the standard 'skint' but also 'potless', which is London slang (see Chapter 3) and explained perhaps by the fact that the motor trade is:

'full of nootters and wideboys an' you tend to move around. Oi've go' mixed friends, soom from Loondon, you ten' to pick oop stooff.'

Amongst the list of words for friend they quoted 'blud' ('that's like a black term; blood-broother'), now firmly part of the wider younger vocabulary, though still remaining a staple of British Afro-Caribbean speech.

Not surprisingly, for a bunch of people for whom effective words are their trade, they had some lively alternatives too on the Voices list: for unattractive, Mike offered, alongside the now routine 'minging' and 'munter', 'fell outa the oogly tree an' 'it every branch on the way down', whilst for 'hit hard' he suggested 'batter', as in:

' "Oi'll batter im loike a fish." Or "Oi 'it im that 'ard 'e looked loik the Elephant Man." '

As you can see, a great deal of their language is allusive and metaphorical, and this means that a form of rhyming slang – somebody suggested the term 'Brockney' for the Brummie version – runs like a vein (sometimes a pretty rough and ready one) through their talk. 'Shoes', for example, are 'rhythms' (rhythm 'n' blues) and 'sausage' is cash (sausage and mash); but what about 'ge' 'im down the soapy to ge' a dipper'? To decipher this you need to know that a 'dipper' in the trade is a deposit, and that 'soapy' is short for 'soapy tip' and means bank: there's rhyming slang involved, but I draw a veil over exactly how.

To end, a piece of linguistic insight from the much-travelled Dave into the way in which one tiny segment of our current vernacular functions, and a process that's confirmed by Dr Clive Upton of Leeds University, who observes our current language professionally. The choice of words offered by respondents to Voices for 'drunk' has been vast, and indeed the list of potential terms as identified in one dedicated glossary runs to many hundreds. But Dave from the Birmingham car-dealership was the only person interviewed by Voices to articulate what characterizes the construction of many of them: 'any noun with -ed on the end'. So, he suggested:

> 'I'm cabbaged, I'm tabled, I'm completely and utterly carpeted, I'm lettuced, I'm Christmas treed . . .'

It's an exactly accurate observation, as Dr Upton confirms, and explains why there are so many new terms emerging. It also, I think, offers a tiny illumination of the mechanics of language: that's to say that when we hear a noun turned into a verb in the past tense (cabbaged, tabled etc.) and prefaced by 'I'm', or 'last night I got completely . . .', our brains recognize the pattern from existing examples and apply the relevant meaning, i.e. 'drunk'.

Simple really, but quite revealing none the less.

A Midlands Glossary

ar Gert, ar Myrtle the wife; a term of endearment (recorded in Mansfield, Notts)

arn ours. From 'our 'un' (our one)

babby baby

bibi a grandmother (paternal); Punjabi word

Black Country the heavily urbanized and industrialized area beyond the city of Birmingham to the west and north; formerly characterized by buildings blackened by smoke pollution

blart, blarting to cry, crying: Black Country dialect as in 'Stop your blartin'!' Etymology uncertain; the *Oxford English Dictionary* suggests a corruption of 'bleat' (early nineteenth century); possibly regional rendering of blurt: 'to utter abruptly'

bob, bob off to play truant (Stoke usage). Perhaps from 'bob', to cheat, befool, mock (fourteenth century); also 'bob off', 'bob out of', to get rid off by fraud, flout; Middle English *bobben*

bogger term of endearment or gentle reproach: 'little bogger!' (from 'bugger')

bost, bostin to burst, to bust; 'bostin' means by extension excellent, great; 'a face like a bosted clog' means ugly

brummagem cheap-looking or showy, imitation goods; originally a counterfeit groat coin (seventeenth century). From 'Birmingham'

Brummie an inhabitant and the accent of the city of Birmingham

caggy, caggy-handed, coggy left-handed. See also **keggy, gab-handed**

canna, dunna, munna, shanna, wonna old dialectal forms of 'cannot', 'doesn't', 'mustn't', 'shan't' and 'won't'

cap to play truant ('Let's cap it this afto!')

causey a pavement (Derbys). From 'causeway'

cob a roll, round piece of bread; a 'chip cob' is a favourite meal (Notts). 'Cob' originally meant a small, roundish lump of something, such as coal; as a 'small round loaf', first recorded seventeenth century

cob to throw. First noted in this sense in Kent, mid nineteenth century; in Cheshire, late nineteenth century ('cob it away, it's good t'nowt')

cock a term of endearment; especially in the Black Country: ''Ullo cock, 'ow are yuh?'

cowd cold (general Midlands usage)

crimes o' Paris – exclamation, used as expression of exasperation, as in 'Crimes of Paris! Whatsisname?' (Potteries usage)

croggy riding pillion on the handlebars of a pushbike; as in 'You never been on a croggy before?' Recorded by Voices in Nottinghamshire but glossaries also list the term as Teesside dialect; possibly a corruption of 'crossbar'

cut a small canal, an artificial watercourse, cut or dug out. Mid sixteenth century

ey oop 'hey up' (regional interjection)

fow unattractive (also Lancashire usage)

gab-handed, gabby-handed, gaggy-handed left-handed. See also **coggy, keggy**

gennel a narrow walkway, e.g. between terraced houses. Noted as 'ginnel' in Manchester court records, mid seventeenth century; as 'jennel', mid nineteenth century. Possibly a corruption of French *chenelle*, channel

gobbin(g)s coal-mining refuse. From 'gob', a worked-out section of a mine; nineteenth century

if God spares me imprecation (recorded in Wolverhampton, 2004). The phrase has been in widespread use (in letters etc.) in this form for many centuries. James I of Scotland is quoted as using the expression in 1424, but it is noted also in twentieth-century Scottish popular usage

it's black over Bill's mother's wet weather is approaching. Recorded in Nottinghamshire, but claimed by some glossaries as Birmingham usage; one (involved and unlikely) explanation suggests that the Bill in question is (William) Shakespeare

jitty a narrow walkway, particularly at the end of a row of houses

keggy, keggy-handed left-handed. See also **coggy, gab-handed**

kench a lot: 'Ah gorra kench o' pots for 'im' (Derbyshire usage). A kench was a strip of arable land with a number of furrows; eighteenth century

mardy, mardy arse moody, spoilt; a 'mardy arse' is a moody person. From past participle of 'to mar', spoil; originally found in Nottinghamshire in early twentieth century and used in dialogue by D. H. Lawrence in *Sons and Lovers*

mar lady the wife (Potteries dialect = my lady)

mash to brew tea; as in 'mash a cooppa tea', ''Ave you got a mash oop, mi doock?'

mi duck my duck (a term of endearment)

nani a (maternal) grandmother (Punjabi word)

nesh soft, tender, susceptible to cold, squeamish, weak; as in 'You're a nesh, you are!'; quoted (inaccurately) in Voices as meaning 'cold'. Old English *hnesce*, soft, tender

old hundred swearing (amongst miners: 'owd 'oondred'). Derbyshire mining usage

phat excellent, cool; one glossary defines it as 'a cooler way of saying "cool"'. Originally an African-American term, current since the early 1960s; etymology disputed but probably a respelling of 'fat' in the sense of 'rich, abundant, desirable'. The acronymic derivation '*p*retty *h*ot *a*nd *t*empting' is a post-hoc construction

puther to gush, particularly of smoke, as in 'Smoke is putherin' out'; also 'Blood were putherin' out of gash on 'is arm'. Widely as well found in Yorkshire dialect usage meaning 'to make clouds of smoke or dust'

ragoo annoyed (used amongst younger Coventry Asian community). From Afro-Caribbean usage?

settle a seat, bench. From Old English *setel*, *setil*, a seat

snap a miner's meal; carried in a snap-tin, rounded at one end: 'It was a metal box because of the mice and rats down the pit'

snicket a narrow walkway between houses; also used in a colliery to describe an underground alleyway. Of obscure origin, recorded in Kirkby's *Lakeland Words*, late nineteenth century

sofee sofa, settee (Nottinghamshire, Derbyshire, Staffordshire usage)

sorry, sorrey a friend, mate, used as term of address; late eighteenth century. Also quoted in dialogue by D. H. Lawrence in *Sons and Lovers*. From 'sirrah' (which derives from 'sir' – Old French *sire*, from Latin *senior*, elder)

sucker an ice-lolly (Nottinghamshire, Derbyshire)

tag off to play truant (recorded in Belper, Derbyshire)

twitchel a narrow walkway between houses. Variant of Middle English *twychen*, from Old English *twycene* or *twicen*, a fork in a road; first found in modern sense in Nottingham, fifteenth century; cf. also **twitten** (Sussex dialect) with same meaning and probable similar etymology, nineteenth century

up the stick pregnant (as 'oop t'stick')

vexed annoyed; preferred term across the Midlands ('Oh, ah was vexed with meself'). Also Afro-Caribbean usage (see Chapter 3)

watter water (rhymes with 'hatter')

wom home (used in north Midlands area; cf. Lancashire usage)

yowth a term of endearment (= youth). Derbyshire, Nottinghamshire, Leicestershire: 'Ey oop, yowth'

6 : EAST ANGLIA

Language in a Landscape: Long Vowels and Wide Horizons

Funny how the edges of Britain tend to get marginalized. Something perhaps to do with the north–southness of the M1 and the M6, scoring England up and down and carving off the eastern and western extremities. Now this is an exaggeration, certainly, and the motorways are barely fifty years old, but the bulges and curves of the English coastline do lend themselves to being cut off. And so it is with East Anglia, that great swelling out into the North Sea on the eastern side of the island, notched on its northern flank by the Wash. To misquote the novelist L. P. Hartley, Norfolk and Suffolk are another country, they do things differently there; indeed I clearly recall some general election pundit years back refusing to be drawn on the likely result of an East Anglian constituency because the electors of this corner of Britain have, it seems, a habit of bucking the national trend. When, then, I discovered that the Norfolk seaside village of Happisburgh pronounced its name very differently from its spelling, as 'Hazebruh', this corner of England instantly acquired a special linguistic lure.

A horizontal landscape, seemingly as much water as land, crisscrossed by dykes and canals and creeks. Bure, Yare, Waveney and Thurne – the rivers of the Norfolk Broads (or 'Broadland' as the tourist authorities inharmoniously call it) have a poetry all their own, an ancient resonance. Thurne, echoing down from Old English *thyrne*, meant a thornbush; Yare comes from a Celtic root perhaps meaning babbling river; Bure is Old English again, perhaps related to the gap (*byrst*) through which the river passed and Waveney stems from the Old English words *wawne* and *ea* together signifying a boggy river. And given how those slow-flowing waterways gather silt, it's well named.

The Danes came here too in the ninth century, as along vast swathes of England's eastern seaboard. Fair-weather raids at first, no overwintering, no more than a dozen or so miles in from that flat, flat coastline; but then in 879 permanent settlements. Guthrum was their king and in 886 he signed a treaty with King Alfred on how those watercoursed acres from the Thames north across East Anglia were to be carved up. And as always, the Danes left their indelible mark on the map – villages like Hemsby and Scratby, Filby, Thrigby (with their Old Norse -*by*, a village or homestead) and Thwaite (a clearing or meadow) show the typical heritage of the Scandinavian settlement.

But most East Anglian place-names are good Old English, lots of -halls for instance (Runhall, Matishall, Rushall, Kenninghall, Coltishall, Gressenhall, Tittleshall and Tivetshall in Norfolk, Rickinghall, Knodishall, Knettishall and Ilketshall in Suffolk), where the -hall represents the Old English *halh*, a secret place or nook.

Yet to hear people talk of these places, you'd never quite guess how they are spelled – and that's part of the secret of the local speech of this very special corner of England. It's an accent and a rhythm of delivery emulated nowhere else in the British Isles. Because in these parts Coltishall becomes 'Cawle-sil', Rushall, 'Roosh'll' and Tivetshall 'Titsorl'.

And while we're discussing idiosyncratically pronounced local place-names, a short linguistic detour: the delightful oddity to be found in two villages on the river Bure just north of Norwich, Great and Little Hautbois. How (. . . to the sound of *hautboys* or oboes) that noble, apparently ancient spelling momentarily conjures the grandeur of a Shakespearian pageant! Yet the local pronunciation gives it away: it's 'Hobbies'. Dig down into where the name came from and you'll soon find that its medieval spelling was actually Hobbesse, from *hob-wisse*, a meadow with tussocks. Put the woodwinds away; they only started playing because of what's known as 'popular etymology': by 1200 and with a Plantagenet king on the throne the records begin to show the village's name as *Haut-bois* (and even, yet more exotically, *Alta Bosco*!) – the spelling 'improved' to suggest the French 'high wood', or 'haut bois' . . . They still call it 'Hobbies' today, though.

The fact is – with Hautbois, as with Happisburgh where we started – you can no more look at the name on the map in East Anglia and work out the way the locals pronounce it than take an educated guess at what a Norwich man would be talking about if he said he'd got a lot of 'dodmans' and 'bishy barney bees' in his garden (snails and ladybirds).

The speech of these flat lands is idiosyncratic, individual, different – nothing like the accents west of the Isle of Wight. Yet all too often when actors try to simulate the local twang it comes out as some uncomfortable imitation of stage Mummerset, and believe me, there's almost nothing that annoys a Norfolk or Suffolk local more than that ('That sound so false to anyone lives 'ere,' said one). East Anglian discourse is lumpy, jerky and yet richly melodic, and with a range of syntax and terminology still in use that you won't find elsewhere.

For a start, however abraded and standardized the local dialect may have become, even now almost no-one uses the little word 'it': round here, 'it' systematically becomes 'that'. So, in the example I've just quoted, '*That* sound so false . . .' simply means '*It* sounds . . .'; and this formation occurs quite naturally even in the middle of a sentence: one man describing the farming rituals of an East Anglian summer completely unselfconsciously talks about 'haymakin' when *that* was really hot'.

Equally systematic is a pronunciation regime that routinely shifts and truncates the standard vowels of English. So your 'nose' in Norfolk becomes your 'nuzz', good old 'roast beef' is 'russ beef', 'often' stretches to 'awffen' and the 'eye' sound in words like 'like' and 'kind' and 'eye' is twisted into 'loik', 'koind' and 'oi'. 'Get' slims to 'git' and 'hay' becomes 'hi', while a 'box' is a 'baahks' (for more detail see the 'Sound of . . .' section in this chapter). And you can take a filleting-knife to the syllables too – the fishing port of Lowestoft is gutted to 'Low-st'ff' while the wonderfully evocative village of Great Snoring (yes, it really does exist – a couple of miles north of Fakenham) in the mouths of locals is more like 'Griss-norn'. Add in some non-standard stress patterns and 'Hautbois post office' naturally becomes 'Hobbies pusst-*aw*fiss'. No wonder incomers get lost.

Fifty years ago, when Stanley Ellis set out for East Anglia under the rigorous eye of the legendary Harold Orton of Leeds University, who created Britain's first systematic Survey of English Dialects, he visited old farmers and labourers across this corner of the land. From Outwell to Reedham, from Carboldisham to Ashwellthorpe, he gathered stories of rural life that sound today like some distant east of England version of Thomas Hardy's nineteenth-century Wessex countryside. A far-off landscape inhabited by reed-cutters (with long, involved tales of clearing out the waterways and the repeated imprecation 'd'yuh see, loik?') and game-keepers (stories of setting up 'nyess baacksiss' – nest boxes for the 'hins', henbirds) and a speech that today seems so broad and guttural that it takes several auditions even to get the lie of the land in a story.

Thirty years later, by the time Ellis returned with a BBC microphone, the isolation had largely been dissipated. Mains electricity had reached out to the remote pockets of this cut-off corner and David Butcher, a local dialect expert, was opining that much of the true Suffolk and Norfolk speech had been lost. Still vigorous at that time, though, was the use of the apparent present tense to represent the past – 'he say', 'I say' meaning 'he said', 'I said', and the strong imperative form 'Do you go there!' Ernie Armes, a fish buyer from 'Low-st'ff' (Lowestoft) whom Ellis taped, was unabashed in his glorious celebration of the joys of the Suffolk-cured herring:

> 'As the fines' fish in tuh'sea, a hairr'n' is [that's = it's the finest fish in the sea, a herring is]. You can do anything you like with i'. You can kipp'ri', you can bloat'ri' [you can kipper it, you can bloater it], you can smoke i' an' you can tin i' and you can souse i', pot i'; you can do anything you like with a hairr'n' an' tha's still a lovely wholesome fish – boo'iful.

Ernie's speech was littered with a shoal of glottal stops, which I've indicated here with apostrophes; he also had a real sense of the rhythm of his speech with his litany of ways to prepare the herring – kippering, bloatering, smoking, tinning, sousing and potting. Preparation of the fish was the thing, and again Ernie regaled Ellis with an eloquent explanation, in broad Suffolk, of how it was done:

> Scale i' fahst [first], cut the hayid awff [cut the head off], cut the tail awff, pu' a slit in the ven' [vent], pull all tuh gu' ou' [pull all the gut out]. Foive snotches [five notches] each side, lay un in pan, plenty o' noice froy-fat [lay un = it in the pan, (with) plenty of nice frying-fat] an' they're lovely – boo'iful. There y'are, they beat all your bloomin' pork chops, I'll tell yuh!

Ernie was a fine figure of a man, well on in years and long retired from the fish trade, but who had spent his life travelling on the herring circuit up to Scotland:

We use' tuh gaw all up tuh lochs [we used to go all up the lochs] –
Kinlochleven, Kinlochbervie, cross to Stonnoway [Stornoway, Isle of
Lewis]; buy hairr'n's t'ere from t'ese li'l ol' crawf'ters [buy herring
there from these little old crofters]. We us' to go in wha' call lil ol'
puffah [what they called a little old puffer], lil ol' butts [little old boats]
use' to go up in t'ese lochs . . .

Note the repeated use here – and common across the whole of the region
– of the expression 'little old [this]' and 'big old [that]', or simply 'old'
on its own. Ernie's was the typical, heavily stressed and jerky delivery
studded with some classic Suffolk pronunciations – the familiar 'boo'iful'
made infamous by a TV commercial for Norfolk turkeys, but also the 'lil
ol' butts', standard East Anglian pronunciation for the vessels that have
carried so many of them out to sea in pursuit of fish.

Even in the mid-1980s, skippers were lamenting the death of the trade
– the image of Lowestoft harbour quay-to-quay with boats so you could
walk from one side to another is one of past prosperity regretted far
beyond Suffolk, in fishing ports the length and breadth of the British
Isles. So too the loss of local speech, where words like 'beating' (mending)
nets and the people who did the job, 'beatsters', seem destined for the
linguistic museum ('beat' was a very old term once found from the north
to the south of England, though 'beatster' was local).

Suffolk and Norfolk men and women are none the less today passionate
about keeping alive their distinctive accent and lexicon and the enthusiasts of FOND (Friends of the Norfolk Dialect) are dedicated to keeping
the flame burning. It is interesting to note, however, that, even fifty years
ago when the first recordings were made here for the Survey of English
Dialects, an old villager from Carboldisham was sighing into the microphone that 'Vill'ge loif ain't what it wuz then . . .', and thirty years later
another elderly countryman was regretting the loss of 'dodmans' and
'tittamatorters':

When I wuz a boy that dawdimun [dodman = snail] used to be a
pop'lar expression but thass dyin' out. Then my old grandfather used
to say, 'Hare you goin' on the tittamatorter [= seesaw, a widespread
term recorded from Scotland to Worcestershire] when you go down
the pahk?' People think I'm pullin' their leg but I aren't.

As you can see from the 'Voices' section of this chapter, in which I compare the results of the latest survey material, there is still a great deal of rich local talk to be unearthed in East Anglia, without resorting to the linguistic preservation order.

The Voices Survey: Dannies, Dykes and Dwiles

For the 2004/5 survey, Voices recorded a range of interviews across the whole of East Anglia, from Norfolk, down the Suffolk coast to Aldeburgh (see the East Anglian Snapshot), inland to the tiny village of Edwardstone, westwards to Cambridge and ending up in the very south of the region on the Blackwater river and the flat St Osyth marsh a mile or two from Clacton in Essex. And what strikes you straightaway is that despite the inroads that national standardization is making – unsurprisingly, most felt in the university city and in the London fringes – there's a huge degree of regional flavour still to be found in the talk. There's also a perhaps surprising degree of consistency across the whole region. So the watermen of Essex happily distinguish the way they speak from 'the Kentish boys' ('totally different to us, they don't speak the same really; little bi' posher') on the other side of the Thames estuary and repeatedly ally themselves linguistically with the Suffolk talk to the north.

A young woman they would call a 'mawther' ('that's a Suffolk word') and for cold they'd say – like their Norfolk cousins a hundred miles to the north – 'fruzz right through', though 'fair shrammed', which they claim to be a 'Suffolk thing', in fact is widespread across southern England: Voices noted it in Plymouth and in Hampshire. For Rick, Andy and Pat, who spend most of their lives on or around boats, the water and its associated vocabulary were ever-present. Alongside 'bog' and 'loo' for toilet, they offered the nautical 'heads', and while a friend was the national standard 'mate', the crew were 'the lads' ('You an' the lads going to take the barge out?'; and I thought I detected a touch of the Thames lighterman in the accent here).

Streams were 'ditches' for this trio, as they were too for Colin, Bob, Tony, Vera and Jean, who live two counties away at Hingham, ten miles west of Norwich. They're members of FOND and unsurprisingly could summon up a couple more equivalents for these waterways that are so

The Sound of East Anglia

There are many for whom the very idea of dealing with the sound of Norfolk and Suffolk speech within the same breath is a heresy. And it is true that the two extremities of England's eastern bump have distinct differences. Yet the sound of the whole region is so distinct, so very different from what lies to the west and south that it makes sense to take them in one big mouthful. Throughout the region speech has a 'tune' that swings the speaker along on a series of rollercoaster upward inflexions, rather like the so-called 'upspeak' that's become a national standard among young people, perhaps in imitation of *Neighbours*, but especially in Norfolk repeated throughout the sentence.

Combine this tune with a heavier than normal stress pattern and the broadest East Anglian speech begins to resemble the vocal equivalent of cross-country skiing, with a series of swinging upward stresses that's almost melodic. This happens even in perfectly ordinary words, as recorded by Voices: 'That was quite a cold day', has a strongly marked rhythm DA di DA di DA DA: 'Tha' wuz kwat uh koold dye'. Even an ordinary item like 'two pairs o' pants' gets treated to the DA DA di DA rhythm.

In Suffolk, Voices found similar emphases ('knackered' and 'shattered' were 'NECKud and 'SHE'ud') yet much less marked. The rhythms were less melodic too, the vowels sounded further back in the mouth with a sort of vocal gargle and an open 'a' the dominant sound.

This patterning of the speech, combined with a complete game of musical chairs with the vowel sounds are what make the accent of this corner of England so special – and so difficult for outsiders to imitate. So across the

much part of their landscape: 'beck' was interestingly the most common, turning up elsewhere in Norfolk as well (I normally associate the word with the north of England), and 'dyke' – a good East Anglian term, mentioned as the local word for a stream even by the urbanites Voices caught up with in a Cambridge gay bar.

The Hingham quintet had a really rich collection of terminology, much of which they were intent on saving for the nation, so maybe they can't be taken as entirely representative. They had memories of 'tipping the water down the cocky' (heavily glottalized: 'co"ee'), an old word for drain and of 'chopp'n' ou'' sugar beet by hand. They talked of trousers

region the 'ay' sound becomes like the vowel in 'eye' – 'trains' are 'trines' and a 'play' becomes a 'ply'. Short 'a' turns to short 'e', so your 'beck' in East Anglia is what lies below your shoulders, and if you've got a bad one, you need to be more 'rilexed [relaxed]'. Conversely, and again we heard this right across Norfolk and Suffolk, the 'eye' vowel turns to 'oi', so the 'Isle of Wight' sounds more like the 'Oil of Woight'. 'O' also shifts round, to short 'a', so a 'knot' turns into a 'gnat' and the county town of Norfolk becomes that wonderful cathedral city 'Narge'.

So you can see that it's all a great deal more complicated than simply saying, as in the notorious television ads for turkey, 'boo'iful' (the switch of the 'byou' sound in 'beautiful' to a simpler 'boo'). This does certainly happen, of course, and Voices recorded it in Suffolk and Norfolk, as also 'hoomun' for 'human', 'stoodunts' for 'students' and 'awpatooni'y' for 'opportunity'. But conversely we also heard 'kyool' in place of 'cool' and 'whew' for 'who'. People were, as always, quick to point out how local pronunciations can be, with two Suffolk villages a handful of miles apart giving the 'e' in 'together' very different values (one's close to standard, the second more like 'to gather').

Two final overarching features that mark the whole region out are the lack of 'r' sounds and its glottal stops. In the south-west, in Lancashire and in Scotland you can't get away from the mighty 'r'. Not so in East Anglia. The nationwide glottal stop replacing 't', on the other hand, is found here, but also where you'd normally always voice the consonant. The effect is of hitting a momentary air-pocket in the middle, so 'temper', 'jumper' and 'knickers' sound like 'TEM'uh', 'JUUM'uh' and 'NI'az'; add the heavy syllabic stress and the stop sounds even more marked, just adding to the rollercoaster ride that is the sound of classic East Anglian English.

as 'strides' (though that's turned up amongst older speakers right across the UK) and being 'malted' (pronounced 'mawl'id') or 'all of a muck wash' if they were hot. A couple of them also mentioned a word for light rain that's today more commonly found in Scotland and Northern Ireland: 'smirring'. Heavy rain, on the other hand, was that Norfolk and Suffolk standard 'hulling it down' (from 'hurl'). There was a real sense of regret amongst these men and women that 'Thass ge"n' wa'ered down' by the arrival of incomers and that the 'little old' local stories ('li"le ol'' and 'gre' ol'' are regular affectionate regional adjectives) were going to be lost. This one came from personal experience – as so often – of harder times when running water and electricity had not yet reached the neighbourhood.

> 'We 'ad an old boy live nex' door to us in a little town not far from here called A' 'leborough [Attleborough, four miles south of Hingham], an' 'e said to me one day, he said, "Do you know what? Thass my bathday today." An' so I went indoors an' said to my mother, "Tha' old boy nex' door is a dirty ol' devil. He only 'as one bath-day a year". And she said, "Don't tawk su sof', boy [don't talk so soft, boy]; he mean baathday [birthday], no' bath-day". An' there is a difference, you know.'

Though, frankly, I'd have said that in this speaker's mouth 'bath' and 'birth' were virtually indistinguishable.

The fact is that there is still plenty of rich Norfolk and Suffolk talk to be found even now if you get to speak to the right people: locals, not incomers, and the middle- rather than the teenaged. Take the Cromer road north out of Norwich (locally always pronounced something like 'Narge'), veer left on the B1149 and you quickly come to Horsford, where the 2004/5 survey of regional speech met three members of the local bowls club. Rich Norfolk pronunciation abounds here: synonyms for annoyed brought 'foitin' mad [fighting mad]' and 'raa''y [ratty]'; if you were a bit off-colour you 'di'n' feel too sharp'. But nothing brings earthier or more relished memories than talk of the lavatory and the days before indoor sanitation: 'Tha' wuzn' cawld a "toilet", tha' wuz called a "pe"y" [petty – from "petit place" or little place, a word that still turns up right across England]'.

As with the Hingham group, for Wendy, Jim and his friend (Ken) from Horsford, the days when rural East Anglia was beyond main drains, piped water and electricity are still vivid and present. Up bubble stories of having to cope with a 'li'l ol' privy' at the end of the garden, with the routines of emptying the waste and digging trenches to bury it (and, with a gurgle of humour, of the never-bettered tomatoes that flourished there).

> 'I hed a frawthy [frothy] ditch down the side o' my house when I first go' marrid. We had the oul' soukawaey [soakaway]; that di'n' drain too well an' when Shirley did the wash'n' 'at ollays oossed t'overflow

[that = it always used to overflow]. Sou I dug a trench 'tween the soukawaey and the ditch, fill'd i' full o'r ol' faggits [filled it full of old faggots = sticks] an' any other ol' rubbish I could find an' covered it up agin. Washdays, awll the way down beside of th'road it wuz awl frawthy . . .'

As a girl Wendy, an elderly but widely travelled woman (she'd spent some time in Australia yet her rich regional voice remained unaffected), remembered being fascinated by the flora that adorned a fairly primitive house she used to visit:

'They di'n' 'ev a flaour [floor] in deir'ouse, t'at wuz just mud [that = it was just mud], an' t'at alwiz used tu mek me wonder whoi [always used to make me wonder why], 'cuz in one carner of the livin' room there wuz alwiz this roout [root] of stingin' nettles. An' I use' to wonder why di'n' they pull 'em up!'

This anecdote about tougher times, recalled from the creature comfort of a centrally heated twenty-first-century home, has much the same rose-tinted nostalgia as Ernie Armes's description from the mid-1980s of his early life in the then dingy Lowestoft area known as the Grit:

Nearly everybody what lived on t'Grit was connected directly or indirectly with the fish-trade. 95 per cent on' em wahre. Some were either beatsters [= net-menders] or worked on the beat stores or worked on the fish market or fish'men. An' t'at were a very good commoonity. One helped another, I can assure you t'at. None o' t'at lookin' where what' Missis Jones a go' noo clean cartins [none of that looking where Mrs Jones has got new clean curtains], I go' a pu' mine u'. None o' t'at squit [squit = silly nonsense]. Anybody in trouble, t'e neighbours always 'ud help you.

As is the case almost everywhere in Britain, the stalwarts of Horsford Bowls Club claim to be able to detect differences in accent from village to village – between nearby Hevingham, Marsham and Aylsham for example, with barely more than a brace of miles between any of them. Between Norfolk and Suffolk, indeed, they'd have you believe it's a matter of two different languages and different again when you get into Fenland. On the other hand, many linguistic features they see as distinctive are also to be found right across the region and across widely differing age ranges and circumstances. So most of the men and women interviewed for the latest survey naturally described themselves if they got annoyed as 'riled', would normally 'hull [hurl]' something rather than throw it and if they were cold, they'd be 'fruzz' or 'fruzzn [frozen]'.

Most East Anglians know what a 'dwile' is (a floorcloth or mop) and many will still use the term. Though twenty years ago Ernie Armes remembered a famous occasion on the radio when a group of distinguished academics had been mystified by the term: 'Bloody dwile, I say to my missus, dems brainy buggers nahver 'eard of a dwile!' Likewise you'll find people from Kings Lynn to Ipswich dropping the word 'boy' (friend, mate) into their conversation as a matter of course – 'Wass toim, boy? [What's the time, mate?]'. In Arnold Wesker's Norfolk-set play *Roots*, from nearly fifty years ago, the word 'bor' (a shortened form of 'neighbour') is used repeatedly as an alternative interjection to 'boy' and it still got a mention today in the Voices interview from the tiny Suffolk village of Edwardstone, though it seems to be less common.

Widespread, though, is the lament about change, about rich incomers buying up local property, about the decline in traditional employment and the effect of vastly greater social and geographical mobility. Throughout this book you can find examples of a new linguistic order where old words are lost as social and economic circumstances change and new vernaculars develop in their place. In both Horsford and Edwardstone (meaning, incidentally, 'Edward's village' in Old English), a few miles west of Ipswich, Voices heard memories of 'buskins' (that were described as 'leather protectors worn on the shin') – made of velvet or moleskin that the speakers' grandfathers used to wear: 'Old Mr Gant he used to wear buskins. I think he even got married with his buskins on!' was a recollection from the Suffolk village, and from Horsford, Jim remembered, 'My grandfather only ever had one pair of trousers; the rest of the time he wore breeches and buskins. Moleskin ones f' Sundiz.' Buskins and extreme poverty, both, now, largely things of the past in this corner of England.

'Dannocks' were also something farm-workers used to wear for hedging around Edwardstone: 'your left hand would be completely leather and the right hand would be a mitten.' Dannocks have gone too, but it's a word, the group agreed, that's still found in local slang meaning hands:

'The girl behind the bar calls her hands "dannies" and that's where it comes from.' Old Suffolk words for country things – the heron, tadpole and earwig (respectively 'harnser', 'pollywiggle' and 'erriwiggle') – all got a mention, but there was a distinct sense of the linguistic preservation order in the air amongst this group of enthusiasts, as too for their catalogue of terms for hitting something hard – you'd give someone 'a good soling', 'sussicker' and 'wassicker', or 'frosh' something: 'I hoolly froshed it.' The intensifier 'hoolly', conversely, used here where in standard English we'd use a word like 'really' or 'fairly', is still very widespread.

In complete contrast to this time-honoured old talk of the villages it's worth remembering that within this same corner of England and not more than an hour away by car is inner-city Cambridge, where you can find very different yet equally powerful linguistic forces at work. Voices, recording well away from the honeyed stone and honed accents of university life, interviewed a couple of musicians (who feature in greater detail elsewhere in this book) who were eagerly debating the difference between cussin' and swearing – more broad Jamaican than Broadland. Meanwhile in a city pub popular with the area's young gay community, there's scarcely any greater trace of traditional East Anglia – just a faint memory of 'ditch jumping' as a childhood game (leading inevitably to breathless camp repartee about old dykes). Indeed, the only truly regional flavour is contributed by a young Yorkshireman who digs a few northern terms like 'sile' out of his memory.

Out in the region's villages, chips remain firmly on shoulders. There's the widely held belief that the gentle rural voice is seen by outsiders as slow and lacking in intelligence. One Horsford club member recalled being laughed at when she was in Devon 'for sayin' oi wuz gawna heng mi linnin ou' [hang my linen out]' rather than 'put the washing out'. But are these attitudes towards localness really anything new, a product of our greater mobility? As the accompanying 'Snapshot' from Aldeburgh lifeboat station demonstrates, amongst locally born people – even the younger ones – there's still a long way to go before the localness is driven from the way they talk. In fact, dig down and you'll discover that many of these feelings and fears go back decades, as captured in the long tradition of dry Norfolk humour, frequently featuring well-heeled incomers rolling up amongst the locals:

'Ol' boy he leaned over 'is gate one evenin' and the big car drew up an' the chap said, ''My good man, can you tell me where I can get bed and breakfast?'' An' he say, ''Why yes,'' he say, ''down aul' Crown go' good rooms'', he say. ''Bu' I dain' so sure you'll ge' bed 'n' breakfuss this toim a noit.'' And I think that sums Norfolk people and our way of life, little jokes like that.'

An East Anglian Snapshot: All in the Same Boat

Steven, Maurice and John are all stalwarts of the Aldeburgh lifeboat station that has been serving the little Suffolk town and the surrounding coast for well over 150 years. The boathouses on Cragg Path shelter the two vessels – one inshore, one offshore – and the sound of the mortar (always known as 'the gun') fired to bring the lifeboatmen running is so familiar a part of Aldeburgh life that the inhabitants of this achingly picturesque port clamoured for it to be retained in the face of modern technology.

'I mean some o' the older folk in the town if yuh don' use 'em – 'cos we did stawp 'em for a while, di'n't we – they'd moan like 'ell, becoz they di'n' know when you' goin' an' when you' comin' baack. You do two to gou and one for the retarn, an' they always complined that they di'n' know when we're come home.'

This is Steven, aged thirty-five, a handsome young mechanic on the station who was born and raised in Aldeburgh. His view of language in this corner of Suffolk is conditioned by whom he's talking to. When confronted with outsiders, his speech gives little away about where he's from. The intonation pattern is definitely not quite that of standard British English, but it's flatter and less sing-song than many an older Suffolk man. Yet when Steven gets chatting to the full-time lifeboatmen John and Maurice, who's now in his seventies and joined the station from the Navy in 1955, the accent thickens and local words begin to appear as if by magic.

Together the three men get talking about changes to the village – the incomers that are buying up the town, just the latest group of visitors to have taken a shine to this pretty former fishing village with its old brick and timber cottages and handsome colourwashed residences. In recent decades fashionable with London's musical elite, drawn by the town's association with the composer Benjamin Britten and the festival that he founded, Aldeburgh was once a labouring place with its fleet of boats and its building companies and railway connection to the outside world.

'There were uptowners and downtowners. I remember Dad saying [the division] was from the railway, Railway Corner. I think they used to have great battles along the way, uptowners and downtowners; and then go out to Blaxhall and join together to fight – united front.'

And John nostalgically recalls an idyllic childhood of boundless possibility:

'You had total freedom. Used to go fishin' on the marshes, fishin' on the beach, on the river with the boats, across the marshes playin' on your boikes, and when you got older used to meet your friends, bike to Southwold, bike to Orford – every Friday noight it was daown to Orford or Sat'd'y for a sing song in the pub. But that doesn't happen any more.'

And in the 1960s the railway line that connected them to the rest of Suffolk was axed:

'I never imagined them takin' that away; to me tha' was permanent. What we called the "crab an' winkle" – one train engine and two carriages, the "crab an' winkle" – went from here to Saxmundham. All the fish went by train: used to be hundreds of boxes, bushel boxes.'

These men see the changes to Aldeburgh as responsible for a dilution of the dialect: 'Visitors must water the accents down. If you go back a long way in toime everybody had their commoonity here, but naouw you travel all over the plice. So definitely yuh do lose uh [it].'

The septuagenarian Maurice is the broadest of the three men, and he knows and still uses the phrases and terms he grew up with:

'We hed em in ah day, as youngsters, you saawta grew up wi' 'em; bu' naouw I still heng on to 'em, bu' you don' heair them anywhere, hahdly. You're losin' i'.'

When asked to respond to the survey's rigorous rote of terms for left-handed, attractive and suchlike, it's always Maurice who comes out with the older, more distinctive term – so when the interviewer asks what word he'd use for unattractive, it's 'doggo – yes that's what we used to say'. The two younger men evince surprise, but then, when asked for the opposite (the vernacular form of attractive), it is Steven who, to the surprise of the older pair, offers the new nationwide slang term 'fit'. In the end, the inventory for this word is quite rich: 'corker', 'fit', 'cracker', 'shiner' . . . And when it comes to an equivalent for moody, after a little prompting from the interviewer, all agree that 'warspy' is fairly common: 'Gor, 'e's ever so warspy ennee? [isn't he?]'.

And it's Maurice again who unearths the old formulation in response to the notion of being unwell: 'Oi don' fare so good, boy, today'. The others can only reach for standard terms like 'grotty' and 'feel like shit', but acknowledge that 'with Suffolk you still get people asking "how you fare".' For Steven, if you're a bit hot, you're 'a bi' swea'y', though Maurice, under pressure from the younger men to produce the 'old' word or phrase, offers 'Thass a ho' 'un today, boy' – 'a ho' 'un'. Cold, on the other hand, is, Maurice reckons, 'fair frawn' (short for 'fruzzn'), though it's not common these days, he says. All these older formations are clearly part of these three men's experience, though to differing degrees, and it's fascinating to hear as they debate the linguistic currency, how the older, more indigenous expressions tumble out from distant memories – another expression for cold, for example: 'hoolly fraish [very fresh]'.

Steven, though still a relatively young man, can remember being seated on the bar of the pub his parents ran in Aldeburgh and listening to the old village people talk. And it was seemingly this osmotic absorption of a lexicon that reaches back centuries that still keeps him just about in touch with the rural linguistic tradition, albeit tenuously, though one he'll today only use when he's certain he'll be understood. Words like 'yaffle' for a green woodpecker, and 'harnser': 'There are things like that,' says Steven, 'that you use just around people who you know will know what you're talking about. But then with somebody you don't know, I'd call it a "heron" rather than a "harnser". But talking to John or Morry, I'd say, "I saw a harnser this morn'n'."'

'Harnser' is a very old dialectal word meaning 'heron' found notably in Shakespeare, when, in act II, scene ii, Hamlet affirms to Guildenstern,

'I am but mad north-north-west: when the wind is southerly I know a hawk from a handsaw . . .'

So here in Aldeburgh, we have three men whose differing linguistic experiences map the ebb and flow of the vernacular in this corner of Suffolk. They are all local, but as the bar empties of fishermen and fills with incomers ('If you want a two-thaasund poun' paintin', thass ol right: you can go down the street an' buy one tumorruh. But if yuh wanna Brussels sprout, thass no good is tha' – thass the difference,' says Morry), they need their local talk less, a utilitarian, comprehensible English more often:

'But thass the way iss gawn; nothin' yuh can do . . .'

An East Anglian Glossary

back'us back-house or wash-house (Suffolk)

beat, beet; beatster to mend fishing nets; a beatster mended drift nets. From Old English *boetan, betan,* to make good, repair

bishy barney bee a ladybird. Note the rhyme 'Bishy, bishy, barney-bee/When will your weddin' be?'

blust expletive (blast), as in 'Cor blust me'

bor a friend, mate (from 'neighbour')

boy East Anglian interjection = mate

buskins leather leggings or trousers

dannocks a hedger's gloves (nineteenth-century usage). Hence familiarly **dannies** = hands

dardledumdue a daydreamer (old-fashioned)

dickey a donkey (formerly widely used and recorded since 1793)

ding verb and noun: to hit, thump; a blow. From Old Norse and Old English *dingen,* recorded fourteenth century. As in 'U'l ding yu over [I'll ding you over]' and 'a ding o' the lug', a clip round the ear

dodman a snail; origin obscure but variants found across the whole region: **homedod, hodmadod, hoddermedod, dodderman** (by extension, a slow-moving horse)

dudder a shiver. Once used widely, recorded from the fourteenth century. Also **didder**

dwile a floorcloth, mop. From Dutch *dweil*, first recorded 1823. **Dwile flonking** is a pub game

dyke, dike a ditch. From Old English *dic*, a trench

erriwiggle an earwig. Another Norfolk term for earwig is **pishamire barnybee**

frawn cold (also **fruz**), hard-frozen ('A'm frawn a cold' = frozen with cold)

fruz cold (frozen)

harnser a heron. Derived from heronsew, a heron; from Middle English (Shakespeare's Hamlet says: 'I am but mad north-north-west: when the wind is southerly I know a hawk from a handsaw', thought to mean 'hernshaw', 'heronshaw', a heron)

hoolly really, fairly, from *wholly*, thoroughly

hull to hurl, chuck, throw away

jannicking (or **nanniking**) fooling about, obstructing (Suffolk/Essex). Other forms: **annicking, nonnicking, skywannicking**

jaykie a tadpole, young frog

loke a lane or alley, usually enclosed. From Old English *loca* enclosed place

mardle to gossip

mavish a songthrush (also **mavis**). From Anglo-Latin *maviscus*

mawkin a scarecrow; also found as **malkin**. From diminutive of the names Matilda, Maud (seventeenth century)

mawther a girl, young woman (as in 'Hello, my li'l ole mawther')

petty a toilet. From mid nineteenth century, *petit place*, a little house

pingle to play (with food)

plawks hands

pollywiggle tadpole. From Middle English *polwygle*; other old forms **porriwiggle, purwiggy, pollywoggle. Pot-ladle, poddle-ladle, pollywag** were also found in East Anglia

riled annoyed. From *rile, roil*, first recorded in the nineteenth century

smur to drizzle. Origin obscure

sole to hit hard

squit silly nonsense. First recorded in this sense in 1893; origin obscure

tittamatorter a seesaw

tittle-me-fancy a pansy (plant)

titty-totty very small

troshing threshing, and by extension working ('Do you keep a troshin'!'
  – 'Carry on with the threshing', meaning by extension 'Goodbye')

yaffle a green woodpecker; probably imitative of the call. Also recorded
  in 1609 as *yaffingale*

7 : LANCASHIRE

Language in a Landscape: Much More Than Just Coronation Street

In the once grinding industrial centre of Manchester the flags are flying. Gaudy banners hang from the walls of a former pumping station, proclaiming trade union pride – banners that were carried aloft on demonstrations and rallies, public manifestations of workers' solidarity. The building now echoes, though, not with the roar of machinery but with the sweeping strings of heroic music as Glenda Jackson narrates a slick video story of the struggle for workers' rights: we're in the People's History Museum, a celebration and commemoration of hard graft and the sacrifices made by men and women who had to fight for the rights to a decent working life and wage. And the industrial heritage celebrated here is the human story that the dialect of Lancashire has interpreted for the better part of 300 years, language and labouring landscape inextricably entwined.

Yet it's somehow symbolic that this sprightly collection's polish and meticulous layout are far removed from the filthy, deafening conditions in which many Lancashire mill workers had traditionally to labour. The grime of the pumping station's walls has been scrubbed back to clean bare stone and the surrounding streets swarm now with museum-goers rather than clog-shod weavers: the 'dark satanic mills' have been demolished or transformed. So too the dialect that grew from all that industriousness has softened to a more general standard in some areas, yet thickened into something urban and new elsewhere.

The streets were hot and dusty on the summer day, and the sun was so bright that it even shone through the heavy vapour drooping over Coketown . . . Stokers emerged from low underground doorways into factory yards, and sat on steps, and posts, and palings, wiping their swarthy visages, and contemplating coals. The whole town seemed to be frying in oil. There was a stifling smell of hot oil everywhere. The steam-engines shone with it, the dresses of the Hands were soiled with it, the mills throughout their many stories oozed and trickled it ... and their inhabitants, wasting with heat, toiled languidly in the desert ... Their wearisome heads went up and down at the same rate, in hot weather and cold, wet weather and dry, fair weather and foul.

Charles Dickens's description of Coketown in *Hard Times* is the very essence of that old industrial landscape. 'They say about good old days, but I don't think they wurre ...' reflects with a sigh Fred, an elderly Oldham man. From the conversations recorded for the Voices survey in the former industrial heartland of north-west England, it's soon apparent that what the Victorian novelist described wasn't so very far removed from the Lancashire mill-towns that are still part of living memory.

And no question of wearing leather on your feet: it was wooden clogs for mill workers for day-to-day use: 'The clogs for through t'week,' remembers his wife Emily, 'and shoes for weekend – yoou daarr't [daren't] use your shoes through t'week.' Their friend Eliza explains:

'The bottoms wuz made with wood and the tops wuz made with leather ... an they 'ad irons on round the sawls [soles], like, to mek 'em lass' longer. Oh ye 'ad to polish 'em oop an' mek 'em shiyne to goo to school in. An' yuh were looky [lucky] then if yuh 'ad a per [pair] of shoes tuh goo tuh Soondi school in [Sunday school].'

There's a timeless quality to these elderly voices from Lancashire, the strongly sounded 'r' – not flapped or rolled but given that characteristic 'dark' (retroflex) quality that tinges the vowels around it like some oaky fume – so 'dare not' (as above in 'you dare not use your shoes ...') fogs up into 'yoou daarr't'. It's everywhere in Lanky speech this 'r' sound, and as local to the area as cotton mills and cold damp weather. And, by the way, in Lancashire remember to say you're 'starving' if you're cold. As Fred told Voices:

'... we also use "starrving" for "cold" oop here. There's "starrving hungry" and "starrving cold": "Ahm starrved": thass Lancashire "cawld".'

Ubiquitous also is the open 'eh' sound that terminal -y becomes in words like 'pretty', 'pritt*eh*', 'queasy', 'queas*eh*', and in expressions like 'prrawpuh pawrrl*eh*' ('proper poorly' – regular Lancastrian for 'unwell'); while if you were simply feeling a bit temperamental, in Oldham you'd be 'mood*eh* [moody]'.

The distinctive sound and vocabulary of Lancastrians' speech has caught the attention of scholars for literally hundreds of years. Indeed, one of the earliest scholarly dictionaries of Old English, the *Vocabularium Saxonicum*, was written by a Lancastrian, Laurence Nowell (later Dean of Lichfield), in about 1565. Nowell's book is of particular interest because he included 173 words of Lancashire dialect which had Old English roots but which were no longer part of mainstream English. So he quotes the (pretty obscure) word 'racanteth', which, though not known beyond the county, for him was familiar as 'the chayne wher with the potte hangeth over the fire'.

A century and a half after Nowell was catching that first audible breath of Lancastrian localness, a man named John Collier was born in the village of Urmston a few miles to the west of Manchester on the road to Widnes. Collier also was fascinated by the speech of his locality, and though like so many in north-west England he started work as a weaver, he soon abandoned the trade to become a schoolmaster. And he wrote, extensively. Under the pseudonym 'Tim Bobbin', Collier became a notable scholar, recorder and exponent of Lancashire speech and accent. Here for instance are his observations on that pronunciation from 1746:

> In some Places in Lancashire we sound *a* instead of 'o', and *o* instead of 'a'. For example we say *far* instead of 'for'; *share*, instead of 'short'; and again we say *hort*, instead of 'heart'; and *port*, instead of 'part'; *hone*, instead of 'hand', &c . . . 'Al' and 'All' are generally sounded broad, as *aw* for 'all'; *Haw* for 'Hall'; *Awmeety*, for 'Almighty'; *awlus*, for 'always', &c.
>
> In general we speak quick and short; and cut oft' a great many Letters, and even Words by Apostrophes; and sometimes sound two, three, or more Words as one. For instance, we say *I'll got*, (or *I'll gut'*,) for 'I'll go to . . .'; *runt'*, for 'run to . . .'; *intle* (or *int'll*) for 'if thou will . . .'; *I wou'didd'n*, for 'I wish you wou'd . . .', &c.

Spin forward 250 years or so and you can still find Lancastrians cutting and cropping their words; listen to this recollection of a tough Oldham grandfather, recorded as recently as 2004:

'Mi grandad if we misbe'aved ourrselves said, "Ah'll brass thi noouhse fuh thee" – he meant he'd smack ye in the nose, give ye a flat nose. 'E wuz an absolutely loovely gentleman, boot 'e neverr olterrd [altered] 'is accent no matter oo 'e wuz talkin' to. A smarrt man, a proud Lancashuh man . . .'

'Ah'll brass thi noouhse fuh thee [hit you on the nose]' – chopped and cropped, not as much as in Collier's day, but none the less recognizably the same sort of sound. Two and a half centuries ago, when he was writing, the Industrial Revolution was just about to break over Lancashire, transforming the Pennine valleys into centres of intense productivity and trade – a huge churning of society. Collier observed these beginnings and already saw consequences for the dialect:

As Trade in a general Way has now flourish'd for near a Century, the Inhabitants not only Travel, but encourage all Sorts of usefull Learning; so that among Hills, and places formerly unfrequented by Strangers, the People begin within the few Years of the Author's Observations to speak much better English. If it can be properly called so.

In fact, in many ways the effect of industrialization was quite the opposite. By the Victorian age, spinning and weaving cotton in huge factories or mills, powered first by water and then by steam, had become the trade-mark industry of the north-west of England. And as I show throughout this book (compare for instance the pit-villages of Northumberland), there's nothing like the enclosed world of the factory to focus and enrich both the trade's technical talk and the broader dialect: 'flying shuttle', 'water frame', 'spinning jenny' and 'Lancashire mule' became part and parcel of daily life for the mill-girls, together with 'bobbins', 'throstles', 'piecers', 'carding' and 'backing off', not to mention 'barragon' and 'broadcloth', 'calico' and 'camblet', 'drabbet', 'drugget' and 'duck'.

Yet paradoxically anyone who has ever visited a nineteenth-century cotton mill, powered by steam and filled with a thousand or more looms, knows that conversation – whatever the dialect – was pretty near impossible. The Lancashire mule shrieks as its spindles fly round and the vast mechanism trundles forward and back across the floor; in the weaving shed, shuttles fly across the frame in a rhythmical, clattering roar that echoes beyond the walls of the factory round the narrow streets of tiny dwellings. Little wonder that deafness was an occupational hazard:

> 'Yuh cannot tolk in Lancashire without using your hands. That's coom from the mills, because the mills maeid sooch a noise. Mah mootherr wuz a weaverr an' we used tuh gaw a lo' [go a lot], an' all the weavers tolked with their hands across: they could lip-read. They did i' with theeir 'ans – joost 'eld a converseiytion, riyght acrooss the laoums [looms]. An' saw [so] we continue usin' aour 'ans when we tolk, because our moom tolked to oos liyke tha'.'

'Talking with your hands' – the speakers are a group of men and women from teenage to late seventies who've gathered in the village of Mellor Brook, just outside Blackburn, in late 2004, to speak to Voices. The district has been studded with mills for two centuries and even today, when they've fallen silent, cotton spinning and weaving are clearly still a big part of their lives, at least historically. They all speak broadly with classic Lancastrian accents – '*ty*let' for 'toilet'; that ubiquitous 'eh' sound again, 'playing hook*eh*' for 'hookey' (truanting); and the smoky retroflex 'r' voiced by almost all of the group, and nowhere more so than in local terms like 'Ahm jiggerred [exhausted]'.

Yet to the outsider every one of these men and women is perfectly comprehensible. By way of contrast, travel five miles east and fifty years back in time to a February morning in 1954: the linguist Stanley Ellis of the Survey of English Dialects, armed with his tape recorder, is visiting another group of Lancastrians in a place just down the road from Mellor Brook.

Great Harwood (or 'snuffy Arrod' after its onetime reputation for snuff-making) was then still one of Lancashire's busy mill-towns, situated like nearby Mellor Brook on the edge of Blackburn. It's worth pausing in Harwood for a moment to observe just how much broader the speech of this area was then and how it's softened and simplified across those fifty years.

The middle-aged woman Ellis recorded there that Monday – sadly the data doesn't give her name – speaks in a rolling, gentle modulation. Her phrases bubble with delight as she recounts her stories – a tale, for instance, of how someone thought they'd seen a ghost because a man who'd ''a' t'werrk oll neet' in the graveyard hadn't changed his white shirt. Nothing particularly unusual in this – the group in Mellor Brook love their stories too. But here's the difference. The modern listener who's not familiar with old rural Lancastrian speech needs at least half a dozen attempts at the tape even to begin to get the hang of the story, let alone the fine detail of the actual words. By way of illustration, here's my approximate transcription of how she describes an old local character in Harwood in the old days:

> Then there werr another auwt chap when we were ut Finisher's Arms, yuh knaw; Carrters then thee did 'at four 'awses goowin tuh Manchister loowedid with clawth, ye knaw. Thee 'at tu gaw through we' rawd. An' this were a bik toll owd chap: 'e 'ad both is two 'anss toook awff on t'choppin machine . . .

> [Then there were another old chap when we were at [the] Finisher's Arms, you know; Carters then had four horses going to Manchester loaded with cloth, you know. They had to go through our road. And this were a big tall old chap: he had both his two hands took off on the chopping machine . . .]

In this profoundly local talk, it's not so much the words as the accent that makes it hard for modern untuned ears to understand. The pronunciation of vowels is skewed a very long way from the standard such that 'watch' is pronounced to rhyme with 'hatch', 'night' as we've seen becomes 'neet', the first syllable of 'loaded' gets drawn out into two quite distinct sounds 'loowedid' and so on.

And the words are shaped differently too: 'our' here is 'wer' and then chopped to become the almost unvoiced 'we'': 'we' rawd' – 'our road' (cf. Geordie 'wor' for 'our'). In a similar vocal transposition 'home' becomes 'wom': 'they wor koommin *wom*,' says the woman at one point. (Cf. the Cumbrian version of 'home': the not dissimilar 'yem'. Interestingly this sort of 'h' to 'y' shift also turns up in 1950s Harwood, where 'yed' was 'head' and a 'headache' 'yedek'.)

Then there's the time-honoured tradition that John Collier referred to of chopping syllables and running words together: in the tale of the Harwood 'ghost' the woman describes one man as a:

. . . big tawll yoong chap gooin' t'iz werrk, y'naw no' thinkin' ayt ubaei't e's ge' 'n pass' litch geaite . . .

[a big tall young chap going to his work, you know; not thinking about anything . . . he's getting past the litch-gate . . .]

Here are Collier's 'cut oft' letters and 'two, three or more Words' sounded 'as one' – no articles, indefinite or definite ('big tawll yoong chap', 'pass litch geaite'), elided syllables ('gooin' t'iz werrk') and a whole sequence of words smoothly run together where you might expect pauses (as here after 'ubaei't' – 'no' thinkin' ayt ubaei't e's ge' 'n pass' – which she slurs into the beginning of the next sentence: 'he's getting past the litch-gate . . .').

Finally, she mixes in a few local words like the old northern form of 'anything', here pronounced 'ayt' to rhyme with 'bite' but better known in its Yorkshire formulation 'owt' (see Chapter 8, 'Language in a Landscape: Tykes and Tongues') and the linguistic shapes are so removed from the standard that it's almost a different language. And of course there's the intonation. This again is unusual, rising and falling jerkily as the story-teller becomes more animated.

Familiarity is the key to understanding. As I show elsewhere in some of the modern examples from Northern Ireland and in Scotland, it's precisely because, in a tight single-occupation community, almost every-one speaks in a similar way that the local variety is at its most idiosyncratic – it can afford to be. As soon as people need to communicate with a wider set, from beyond the town, the valley, the county, the range of variation from the norm diminishes.

You can appreciate how closed Harwood used to be just by looking at the map. I examined a large-scale late-Victorian Ordnance Survey sheet for this town that at that time lived for and from cotton: *fifteen* mills, many with typically Victorian patriotic names: Britannia, Victoria, Albert, Albion, Wellington, Prospect . . . Here you can actually see the closeness of the back-to-backs (every one individually mapped), in which the dialect of people like the woman Stanley Ellis recorded thrived. Here is the intimacy that people lived every day of their lives – street upon densely packed street built to accommodate a population that grew in the course of the nineteenth century from 1,500 to over 12,000.

Today in neighbouring Mellor Brook, memories of this sort of close-woven living, of back-to-back houses and poverty, of outside toilets and narrow passageways between houses, still have the capacity to bring out regional distinctiveness, though as nothing compared with fifty years ago. People go 'oop ginnel [up the alley, pronounced with a hard 'g' as in 'get']' to cut between cottages, even the not-yet-twenty Matt. 'Once a ginnel always a ginnel,' says Harry, aged seventy-two. Though in Blackburn, his friend Eddie adds, they were called 'back alleys', not ginnels:

'You will have back-to-back houses; they meay be fifteen in a raw and thi' have wonn back alley. A ginnel is between two geybl'en's. That is a ginnel.'

['You will have back-to-back houses; they may be fifteen in a row and they have one back alley. A ginnel is between two gable-ends. That is a ginnel.']

It's curious just how regularly any discussion of local words seems to bring out the scatological in people. From Cornwall to Yorkshire, from Northern Ireland to Norfolk, Voices has heard tales of the privy:

'If it's an exceptionally long terrace house, they used t'ave a ginnel to go to t'communal tylet between the houses, because if yuh needed tuh gaw quick, 't's a damn long weay tuh roon tuh gaw oop back alley, so you gaw through t'ginnel!'

['If it's an exceptionally long terraced house, they used to have a ginnel to go to the communal toilet between the houses, because if you needed to go quick, it's a damn long way to run to go up [the] back alley, so you go through the ginnel!']

Likewise in Burnley, where old Lancashire lives in close proximity to multicultural modernity. Here a highly charged political atmosphere and BNP demonstrations rather than mill closures make the headlines these days, yet it didn't take a lot of prompting to get a group of six twenty-first-century Burnley men and women from the older tradition talking 'privies', 'petties' and 'the long drop' as if they still had to use them every day. Voices asked them what they called the lavatory:

'Tylet, the outside tylet; the priveh – it was the priveh in Lancashuh; "long drop". You' tuh roon uh lotta wawtuh rin yuh kitchin to floosh i'. You sat on the wooden sla' with a hawl in the middle an' did your wha'no' an' yuh had to roon wawtuh rin the skoollery to floosh the tylet. A "tippler toilet".'

['Toilet, the outside toilet; the privy – it was the privy in Lancashire; [the] long drop. You'd to run a lot of water in your kitchen to flush it. You sat on the wooden slat with a hole in the middle and did your what-not and you had to run water in the scullery to flush the toilet. A "tippler toilet".']

I imagine that 'tippler toilets' – a speciality, it seems, of north-east Lancashire (and 'colloquially known as the "longdrop bog"', to quote Hansard of all sources) – are rarely heard of in London these days. They're fresh enough though in the memories of this group of Burnley residents, like the time they had to fish a kitten out of the 'long drop' with a brush, or had to go down the yard in a gale:

'An' i' was all very windy as well bicoss it wen' straiught dauwn to the dreain. Saw the win' would coom dauwn the dreain, woon't i'. An' you'd si' there an' you'd bi windeh. You see they din't 'ave lids on – they joost 'ad a saeyt with an 'ole in, an' my broother use' to frighten me to death becuz 'e use' tuh seay if yuh sit on a long taam, a rat'll coom oop an' bi'e yuh bottom . . .'

['And it was all very windy as well, because it went straight down to the drain. So the wind would come down the drain, wouldn't it. And you'd sit there and you'd be windy. You see they didn't have lids – they just had a seat with a hole in, and my brother used to frighten me to death, because he used to say if you sit on a long time, a rat'll come up and bite your bottom . . .']

These people have a range of accents, some much broader than others; but there's not a trace here of the lilting and unconventional intonation recorded by Stanley Ellis in Snuffy Arrod fifty years ago. Then, it is likely few of these people would have had the telephone, fewer still a television. In that time, they've equipped themselves with the technologies of communication, and likewise with the language. The memories may persist, vividly, but it's no good, when the mills close and you have to go further afield for work, if only those who live on your ginnel or within half a mile of your privy can understand you.

The Voices Survey: Lancs and Mancs

The survey carried out in 2004 for the Voices project may not have uncovered the sometimes impenetrable tracts of rural Lancastrian that the Survey of English Dialects found in the 1950s, but it did throw up some sharp distinctions between town and country, and, inevitably, between young and the not so young. Individual voices, too, displayed wide differences of degree, with incomers from, for example, Scotland and Tyneside maintaining both the accent and many of their regional terms in the teeth of a stiff Lancashire linguistic breeze.

As I've already shown in this chapter, how much you need to converse with those outside your immediate street, village or area affects the degree of variation in your speech. For the Mancunian comedian Mike Wilkinson, connecting with his audience is the essence of what he does – fail and he's heckled off. It's a very particular challenge for local performers like Mike, with gags steeped in local references. As success brings an ever wider public they must subtly adapt their vernacular to a style that works more widely – for example, amending even words that have gained fairly national currency like 'scally' (northern slang for a 'disreputable lad'):

'I think you have to watch a few of your colloquialisms. Because like with scallies, not everybody understands what a "scally" is. And if you're doing material about scallies, you've got to find out what the regional equivalent is – like it's goin' to be "chavs" down south, "neds" in Scotland. You've got to find some common ground or find what the local lingo is. I do a story about a guy who gets stabbed up a ginnel and I went to London and I changed the word "ginnel" to something else because southerners wouldn't have got it.'

Mike and his two stand-up companions John Warburton and Seymour Mace who were interviewed for the Voices survey are wordsmiths by

The Sound of Lancashire

Apart from the ancient rivalry that's pitted white rose against red for generations, the two speech patterns either side of the Pennine hills are distinctly different. Of course Lancashire and Yorkshire talk do share some characteristics – like the northern shortening of the vowel in 'love' to the sound in 'book' which I've rendered here with 'oo': 'Yuh wha', loov?' But the overwhelming sound of the Lancastrian accent is markedly individual, sharply etched with angular vowels. Here's the ubiquitous Lancastrian 'r', dark and brooding that runs like a seam of iron through the talk: 'top u't yarrd' was where the privy was in the old workers' dwellings. I've indicated this with 'rr' in the text, but it's further back in the mouth than, say, a West Country burr.

Then there's the familiar '-y' sound at the end of words, here almost always an open 'eh': 'lucky' becomes 'look*eh*', that 'privy' again is 'priv*eh*'. This open, slightly slack-jawed sound turns up repeatedly: 'shade' comes out like standard 'shared' (I've written it 'shehd'). Contrarily, where you'd expect an 'eh' sound like this in standard English pronunciation, as in the word 'pair', in Lancashire

trade, and revealed an almost dictionary-like sense of the range of meanings when subjected to the routines of the grid of questions. For example, asked for a regional synonym for throw, the responses were 'lob', 'toss' and 'chuck'. Nothing particularly Mancunian there, apart from the accent ('chook' for chuck). But mention of 'chuck' starts the trio on a linguistic adventure that (strangely) ends up sampling bacon butties. Like this:

> 'It's probably the most widely used word in the north-west: "chuck" can also mean be sick, or to be doomped.'
> ' "Arreet chook" – it's a term of endearment as well, isn't it . . .'
> 'It's short for Charlie as well.'
> 'There's a chook-wagon that stops near an industrial park near oos an' iss called Sue's Chook Wagon an' she sells beiykn boohtiz for £1.30. A chicken wagon . . .'

Seymour Mace is from Tyneside, his companions are from Manchester, and though there are distinct regional differences between their speech, there's one linguistic quality that all three share: it's drawn from a distinctly urban setting, complete with that particular (though not exclu-

it gets flattened to something like 'purr' – 'a purr o' shoes'. Cilla Black has this pronunciation, and another typical local accent note she's made her own is the inserted 'r' in a string of words where you'd normally expect a 't' ('a lorra lorra laffs'). We heard that too, though not widely, in our survey.

Perhaps the most distinctive vowel shift from the standard, though, is the 'o' sound, both long and short. 'Know' in Oldham they say like the standard pronunciation of 'gnaw' ('yuh knaw' in my transcription); so when asked for what they'd call someone who's rich, our informants all said 'rawlin' in i' ' – rolling in it. Even the short 'o' of 'pot' and 'posh' becomes lengthened to sound more like 'port' and 'Porsche' ('pawt', 'pawsh' on the page).

In urban Salford, the pace is faster and the old dark 'r' has been eliminated, but all the main features are heard – 'poorleh [poorly]' for unwell and even in this often breakneck ratatat speech, you get the extra syllable in words like 'poor', another typical Lancastrian lengthening: 'poowuh', 'poowuleh'. In the 'Snapshot' section you can find a more detailed account of the intricacies of this very distinctive Mancunian linguistic omelette of well-beaten vowels, sliced syllables and chopped consonants.

sive) city phenomenon, the glottal stop. I've indicated these with a swarm of apostrophes. Perhaps unsurprisingly, their richest regional language stories come from the closed community of the city school playground. Again, it's an environment where accent, a highly specific vocabulary, linguistic codes as well as fast-shifting fine and critical distinctions about which vernacular terms are fashionable and permissible and which are not determine the speech you use. Take to play truant for instance, which was 'playing the wag' or 'wagging it':

> '[I wagged school] only woonce, an' ah fel' really guilty about it because ah lahked the teacher at the taam. I joost did i' coz i' wuz laak a meiyl thing an' you 'ad to wag i' a' soom staeige. Boot Wigan which is ten maal from where ah live they coll i' wack i'.'

> ['I wagged school only once, and I felt really guilty about it because I liked the teacher at the time. I just did it because it was, like, a male thing and you had to "wag it" at some stage. But [in] Wigan which is ten mile from where I live they call it "wack it".']

'Wagging it' was also the unanimous and only word for a group of lively sixth-formers in Salford, west Manchester, that Voices brought together for the survey. Not that all had 'wagged it' though – one girl admitted she was too scared:

> 'Ahd probly wag i', liyke; tell mi moom tha' ah dint feel well when ah fel' well, bu' ah wouldn't, liyke, say ahm goin tuh skyule an' not turn op. Ahd be a' hoaum when ahm waggin' i'.'

> ['I'd probably wag it, like; tell my mum that I didn't feel well when I felt well, but I wouldn't, like, say I'm going to school and not turn up. I'd be at home when I'm wagging it.']

Jak, who's very sensitive to linguistic distinctions, wanted to be more precise:

> 'Bu' thass *blaggin' i'*, though, no' waggin' i'. So you's blaggin' yuh moom an' dad's 'ead [you're blagging your mum and dad's head] an' then you'd 'aff to blag college as well, sayin', "Ahm no' well". So iss liyke a liye [lie], you've blagged i'.'

Jak is an eloquent young man, interviewed here on the eve of his eighteenth birthday. You can read more from him in the 'Snapshot' section, later in the chapter. Jak is proud of where he comes from: Salford was the workshop of nineteenth-century Manchester. Crossed by the Bridgewater canal that brought coal cheaply to Manchester from the pits at Worsley, it was a maze of factories and smokestacks – cotton mills, inevitably, but also dye-works and docks, foundries, engineering and chemical plants. It was the landscape immortalized by L. S. Lowry in his characteristic paintings of spindly figures bent forward into an apparent constant gale of hard graft and misfortune, the lines of factory windows and plumes of blown smoke framing almost every scene. Now Lowry's paintings are on show in the spectacular arts centre that bears his name, one of a string of signature architectural landmarks that today characterize the waterside Salford Quays development. Yet, as this group from Pendleton College prove, Salford's grimy reputation lives on. 'If yu' tell soomwon you're from Solfud, they pu' on this accen',' observes one girl with a grimace. Her friend is quick to agree:

LANCASHIRE

'When ah wuz lookin' for a job ah wen' in the Job Cen're an' [the form] said, liyke, "where was you born?" An' ah was abou' to pu' "Solfud" [and I was about to put "Salford"], an' 'e said, "No. Doan' pu' tha' because they'll absolutely, liyke, pu' you daown" [Don't put that because they'll, like, put you down]. So ah pu' "Manchester" an' ah go' the jawb. Ah asskt if ahd pu' "Solfud" [I asked if I'd put "Salford"] wha' would 'ave 'appened an 'e said, "We turn loawds o' people daown . . ." '

As you can tell from these approximate transcriptions, the Salford accent is broad and quite marked. Glottal stops abound, syllables are dropped and words merged into one fast urban utterance that for once is almost impossible to illustrate on the page. The name of the town itself is cropped to something like 'Solfud'; 'd' sounds are de-voiced to 't' (e.g. 'asskt' for 'asked'); the diphthong heard in RP 'eye' is skewed and lengthened with a 'y' sound that I've attempted to transcribe in words such as 'liyke' – the almost meaningless 'like' that permeates these sixth-formers' talk as it does that of many young people across the country.

This group were asked whether they felt they were discriminated against because of their accent: 'Ah ge' cahlled cawmmon,' says one girl – and called common by her own sister no less:

'She speaks sliyghtly poshuh than ah daow, through the frien's she's graown oop with, daown in Wursleh – theh alwiz class Wursleh as the posher ent [end] uv Swinton.' [Swinton and Worsley are localities to the west of Salford.]

So these youngsters from the Manchester conurbation say they can discern fine shades of accent and social difference within a couple of miles – as often claimed in older, rural dialect areas. Jak, who speaks fast and furiously, slurring words together almost beyond comprehensibility, defends the Salford dialect with passion:

'People feel discriminated against because they can' oonderstan' 'alf uv i'. Iss liyke, "Wha' yuh seayin'? Wha' yuh gooin' on abaw'?" Thass whiy they pu' oll them advices an' 'a'. An' iss liyke yuh fru' Solfu' – yuh're a bad-ass. Yuh go' a kniyfe in yuh ba' pocki'. An iss liyke, "Shood oop! Moope'!" Saw wha' if ah tolk lik' this? 'S no' ma faul'. If

175

ah din' liyke i' ahd change i'. A' th' en' uv the deay this is 'ow ah speak an' ahm no' goin' tu' pu' on a voiyce joss tu' please soombody else. This is 'oo ah yam.'

['People feel discriminated against because they can't understand half of it. It's like: "What are you saying? What are you going on about?" That's why they put all that advice and that [about speaking clearly in university interviews]. And it's like: you're from Salford, you're a bad-ass. You've got a knife in your back pocket. And it's like "Shut up! Muppet!" So what if I talk like this? It's not my fault. If I didn't like it I'd change it. At the end of the day this is how I speak and I'm not going to put on a voice just to please somebody else. This is who I am.']

The discussions that develop around the word choices in the Voices survey have in almost every interview brought recollections of childhood. Yet compare Jak's rapid town speech with that of this elderly couple, Fred and Emily, from Oldham, on the edge of the Pennines at the north-eastern flank of the Manchester conurbation. Childhood for them was the hardship of barely having any decent clothes to call their own. Their delivery is slower, the Lancastrian 'r' voiced throughout, an occasional interpolated 'r' to separate words ('poorr it aweiy' – 'put it away') and a noticeably older-sounding, less urban variety of regional speech that lies a deal closer to the Survey of English Dialect recordings from 1954. Yet from Oldham to Salford as the crow flies is just eight miles.

'Mi bess soot, mi Soonday bess. You worr it tuh Soonday skule or something laak tha'. Then ye had tuh teik it awff, hang it oop an' poorr it aweiy [put it away] till nex' week. Orr, faeilin' tha' [failing that], soom pooer people ha' tuh teik it awff, wrap it oop in t'braown peiper, teik it to the paawn shawp [pawn shop] on a Moondei morning then gaw back furrit [for it] on a Friydei naaight. They were all pooer people wurr [where] ah lived in them days.'

In Mellor Brook likewise it's a more country sound, although the village is only a couple of miles from urban Blackburn, and here the town dweller and the country dweller are seen as almost different species.

Matt, still in his teens and the youngest of the group, can easily spot the incomers:

'We coll 'em a "townie" – [they wear] trackies an Rockies [tracksuit bottoms, Rockport shoes] an a bit of "bling bling" as well. Country people don't wear that. Every Saturday you see that.'

'Townie' is one of the national words used, alongside 'chav', 'trev' and 'pikey' to indicate a trendy guy 'with attitude', as they say. I suspect, though, that in Matt's case, he also means it literally – they come from Blackburn. Julie, aged thirty-six, certainly does:

'We live in Mellor Brook, we're village people, we liyke village liyfe, boot a lo' of townies they coom to Mellor Brook [and] thee dawn uccept [they don't accept] village liyfe, yuh naw. Thee wawn't join in the community centre and things tha' gaw awn in Mellor Brook liyfe. They joost wanna keep themselves to themselves, dawn wanna fit into village liyfe.'

Of all the Lancastrians interviewed for the 2004 survey, the groups in Oldham and Burnley, with their predominantly older informants, offered the richest range of regional variation. So words they used quite unself-consciously included 'gradely' (recorded in dictionaries as long ago as 1894, when Brewer defined it as 'a north of England term meaning "thoroughly", "regularly", as in *behave yourself gradely, a gradely fine day*'), 'vexed' for annoyed, and for to throw (alongside ordinary terms like 'chuck' and 'sling') 'cob it out' – 'throw it away'. 'Frozzen' turns up in Burnley for cold (cf. similar Yorkshire and East Anglian usage) and to 'laik' was play for this group too, again paralleling the Yorkshire term. Other phrases reflected the social circumstances of a community of relatively poor manual workers: an invitation into the sitting room was simply 'Coom in th' owss': 'There were only two rooms to pick fro' an' t'other was t'kitchen!'

Few distinctly regional words had seemingly universal acceptance and usage across the region – from Oldham to Burnley to Mellor Brook and to Manchester – 'keks' was the standard word used for trousers for young and old (alone the youngsters of Salford preferred the widely accepted alternative, 'pants'), though Doris from Oldham maintained a slight difference: 'They're "kegs" an' the one what wears them is boss of the house!' All, however, agreed that PE shoes worn at school were for Lancastrians and Mancunians alike not plimsolls but 'pumps' – pronounced 'poomps':

> 'Children call them poomps an' you were looky if you 'ad any – ah say you were looky if you 'ad any!'
> 'We were poor; we couldn't afford the whitening for the poomps . . .'
> 'Well, now iss trainers, boot they aren't poomps!'
> 'It's down south that they call them [affecting a posh accent] "pleemsoles".'

There was, though, an interesting Manchester variant that cropped up amongst both the folk from Oldham and the Mancunian comedians – 'gollies' or 'galoshes': 'li'l slip-on poompy shoes,' recalled Mike Wilkinson; 'we went to Cornwall woonce an' spen' four hours on this beach a' soonset triyin' to fin' mi dad's galoshes cos 'e'd lost 'em.' For a member of the Oldham group it was city usage: 'In Manchester they're called "gollies" – galoshes – which is rubber overshoes, boot i' got to be a word for poomps: gollies. An' I still use it with my children to wind them oop – "'Ave you got your gollies on?"'

The Mancunians and the Oldhamites also more or less agreed on how they'd say someone's ugly: 'a face like a bag o' chisels, like a bag o' spanners,' said the comics, 'laik a bag uv 'ammers,' offered Fred from Oldham, though this colourful expression was merely one of a selection: 'a face like a robber's dog' and 'fou' (rhymes with 'now' and allegedly derived from 'foul') were two.

Amongst the younger people surveyed, from Salford to Mellor Brook as well as for the stand-ups, the preferred words were the inevitable national standard 'minger' and 'minging', 'skanky' and ''anging', and, very derogatively of women by men, 'dogs'. It's vernacular, certainly, but not what you'd call regional English.

So the picture across rural Lancashire and the Manchester conurbation is a patchy one. Dialect enthusiasts fill the internet with websites celebrating Lanky talk, yet the evidence of the Voices survey suggests that the old Lancashire lexicon is today locked into the memories of the older generation. The vigorous speech of the young people interviewed in

Manchester – broad in accent, rapid of delivery and idiosyncratic in the way they express themselves – is meanwhile using more of the national vernacular, albeit with a very distinctive local Lancashire flavour. As John Collier acutely observed 250 years ago:

> I still maintain that there can be no definitive dictionary for any dialects, by the meaning of the very word it reasons that it is differential. Every individual has his or her own idilect [dialect] to maintain the point.

A Lancashire Snapshot: Jak and Emily

Jak and Emily live within eight miles of each other. They're both Lancastrians and proud of it and within the compass of their very different forms of local speech they illustrate in a nutshell the fascinating complexities that lie within any discussion of regional English in the twenty-first century. Jak we met in Salford (see the 'Voices' section) with his friends from Pendleton College, to the west side of the Manchester conurbation. Emily and her husband Fred come from Oldham, eight miles as the crow flies eastwards, the old cotton town on the edge of the Pennines. Both Jak and Emily share a vivid sense of humour, the laughter cascading throughout their conversation. Each speaks a rich and sometimes opaque local dialect, recognizably similar – the accents, though distinct, are clearly from the same area – but Jak's is flatly urban, quick-fire, glottal-stopping and choppy merging words into mere strings of sounds, Emily's crackling with Lancashire 'r's and vowels that extend into extended diphthongs and triphthongs.

Both the young man and the elderly woman are living in relatively closed communities where language thrives – Emily within the confines of an old stable community, Jak still amongst his peers at school. But there the similarities end. There are touching points in their lexicons, naturally – each agrees that the standard vernacular for hot is 'boiling' (though Jak pronounces it more like 'byling') and they both agree on the more distinctively northern expression as well: 'sweating cobs' (that the Oldhamites claim as specifically north Manchester or Oldham dialect, though Voices found it quite widely in use across the north of England).

For the Salford youngsters this was 'dead old', the sort of thing their grandparents would say. Right enough, from the evidence.

Completely distinctive, though, is the 'reflexive' way Jak and his friends from the western suburbs of Manchester constantly express how they think and do things. It's a form that Voices turned up almost nowhere else in the UK. For example: 'Ahm chufft, me [chuffed = pleased].' 'I don't believe in i', me.' 'I'm knackered, me.' 'It's min' tha'', 'Thass sick, tha' [mint, sick = good].' Combined with an equally regular up/down intonation pattern, falling away on the 'reflexive pronoun', this form peppers the conversation without anyone remarking on it.

Yet Jak is a subtle analyst of the way he and his friends talk. He was fascinated and puzzled by an expression a friend from a handful of miles away used about smoking:

> 'Ah dawn smawk no more [but] I knew this girl from Rochdale; an' you knaw people seaiy, "Saeive me 'alf a cig", an she'd seaiy, "Tooz me oop on tha'" [two's me up on that, i.e. we'll share].'

He's not alone though in being mystified by specific local usage. Back in Oldham, Emily's friend Eliza also remembered a time when she needed a translation for a phrase from Wigan, still in Lancashire, but half-way to Liverpool. Her neighbour said:

> ' "Ahl gaw an' put 'is black bit oop [I'll go and put his black bit up]", an' I used to think what is " 'is black bit"? So shisehd [she said], "Look at Eliza's faiyce! She doesn't knaw what ah mean, do ye?" An' I said, "Naw." She said, "Ah mean 'is loonch [lunch]." She were a Wigan person, she kem from Wigan, an' iss alwiz stook in mi min', tha' [it's always stuck in my mind]: "Ah'll gaw an poot 'is black bit oop." '

At the other end of the age range, Jak's fascinated by the way his group can use the same word in different contexts to mean completely different things, such as 'mint' and 'sick' as current terms of approbation: 'The same words can mean a load of different things depending on where you come from – it's just the context of where you use it,' he points out.

For Jak, it's a particular problem that crops up when he hooks up with friends across the world in an internet chat-room – 'Iss this mad fing; people just sen' yuh pictures an' messages, iss fooneh.' Notice, incidentally, Jak's non-local and now very widespread use of the 'f'-sound to replace 'th' (technically known as 'TH-fronting'), once a London characteristic but now across the country. It's most frequently though not exclusively found in the speech of young people: Emily doesn't say it, for example, though an elderly Cornish speaker we talked to did.

Jak and his friends have a very finely tuned set of vernacular vocabulary, much of which is to be found nationally, but it can trip them up when exchanging messages over the internet. So while 'minging' and 'hanging' are standard-issue derogatory terms found amongst the equivalent age group for instance as far away as the westerly end of the Cornish peninsula (though they were most insistent that the word was 'anging' and that *Coronation Street* had mistakenly featured it with an initial 'h'!), there's no guarantee that the words have *international* currency. 'Buzzing' (Jak says, 'boozzin') is one such:

> ' "Boozzin": thass the meain wuhd [the main word] ah use on th'
> in' 'ne' [Internet], "boozzin". Pe' 'le [people] seaiy, "Whoss tha' min
> [mean]?" Ah seaiy iss jooss "boozzin' ", liyke.'

And when pressed for what it means, Jak offers 'mint' – 'great', 'fantastic'. Words Jak used for the converse of 'buzzing' and 'mint' were 'mank' and 'manky' (again, very common slang) and 'munter', pronounced 'moon'ah' with a heavy glottalized 't'. Jak's glottal stops are spectacular. They give his speech a broken quality which combines with his tendency to run words together to produce an energetic and pacy urban style. He blames where he lives:

> 'Ah coom frum 'Oolton [Hulton] nex' tuh Walkden an' no-one
> pronounces their 't's; ah doan know ahm doin' i', me. Iss jooss tha' ahv
> doon i' for tha' long you jooss pick i' oop, you doan even know i'.'

One of the things Jak's noticed about the way he and his group use words is how context-sensitive they are; so the same term can crop up with a number of quite distinct meanings in different parts of a conversation (it reminds me of that heartfelt appeal of the uncomprehending parent: 'But do you mean "bad" meaning "bad" or "bad" meaning "good" . . . ?'). So Jak employs 'sick' for crazy as well as for terrific and 'peppered' to mean broke ('Ahm peppered, me'), but also drunk (along with more familiar words like 'wasted' and 'leathered').

This is youthful language, spry and on the move, where you have to 'get' it before you can understand it. As Jak and his friend agree, it's a form of coded speech in which, for example, ''Ave you bin baeikin' caeikes?' has nothing to do with cookery but relates directly to buns in ovens, i.e. 'Are you pregnant?' Dialect used as code has always been part of its value – a way of identifying speakers as 'belonging' while at the same time keeping non-users at arm's length. By this measurement, Emily, Fred and their friends from Oldham are, despite their broad Lancastrian accents, relatively open speakers of English. They use few opaque regional terms, and those they do you can usually work out fairly easily. When Fred says he came home 'kettled' or 'kaylied' [pronounced 'kay-lide'], you can guess he wasn't entirely sober. So in one slightly perverse sense, the older folk from Oldham – as the people we interviewed from Burnley and Mellor Brook – could be said to speak a purer English than do the lively youngsters from west Manchester. It just depends what you mean by 'vernacular', 'dialect' and 'accent': take your pick.

Listen to Emily and Fred on what Jak might call a 'sick' night out:

''e coom 'awm kettled lass naat an she give 'im what forr! "Kaylied" we us' tuh say as well. Locally we'd 'ave awll said "kaylied" in the ol' days, because it is a local word.'

['Have you ever been "kaylied", Fred?']

'Now an' again, t'ad bin knawn: niyce feelin' while it las's. Iss the marnin' afterr, thass the trouble!'

A Lancashire Glossary

This list contains old Lancastrian dialect terms, technical language from the textile industry and modern regional slang: I have indicated the relevant context where necessary

backing off in the textile industry, the reversing of spindles on a spinning jenny or Lancashire mule to unwind yarn

barmcake a variety of breadroll or bap. From Old English *beorma*, fermenting froth – barm – used as form of yeast

barmpot a slow-witted person, term used as insult. From 'barmy' (frothing with barm)

barragon, barracan coarse cotton cloth used for workers' clothing (textile industry). Originally from Persian *barak*, a coat of camel-hair, via Spanish *barracan*. A Victorian report on the asylum at Hanwell near London reports 'it was made a regulation in 1835, that strong dresses of *barragon*, or sacking, be procured for the patients who tear their clothes, to prevent necessity of restraints'

bobbin a reel used to hold yarn for use e.g. on looms (textile industry). From French *bobine*

butty a piece of bread and butter; by extension, a sandwich (as in 'bacon butty'). From 'butt(er)y', 'butter cake'. Quoted by Mrs Gaskell in *North and South*, 1855

buzzing in an expectant or excited state: 'something good is going to happen' (contemporary slang)

camblet a woollen cloth (originally from camel- or goat-hair; textile industry). From French *camelot*, pile

chuck a term of endearment. Corrupted from 'chick'; Shakespeare writes, 'Pray, chuck, come hither'

clemmed, clemt hungry. Mid sixteenth century: 'to pinch with hunger'. From Old English *beclamman*, to confine

cob: get a cob on be annoyed. Origin unknown

cob: sweat cobs to sweat profusely. One of the many meanings of 'cob' is a 'large lump or piece of anything'

Corporation pop water

drabbet a drab, off-white coarse linen used for making smocks (textile industry)

drugget a coarse, wool and cotton cloth, used for floor coverings; a mat made of such material (textile industry). From French *droguet*, worthless object

duck a strong linen used for sails (textile industry). From Dutch *doek*, cloth

entry a narrow passage between houses

ginnel a long, narrow passage between houses, either roofed or unroofed. Origin obscure, possibly a corruption of French *chenelle*, channel

gollies sand shoes, plimsolls. Perhaps a corruption of 'galoshes'

gradely very good. Original dialectal meaning: decent, orderly. From Latin *gradus*, grade, step

jiggered exhausted, broken. The word is used to represent an oath (e.g. 'buggered'). Origin disputed, possibly from 'jig', dance, or 'jig', a nautical term

kaylied very drunk. One suggestion is that the word derives from 'kali', meaning a fizzy sherbet sweet like cream-soda

keks trousers. Etymology uncertain. The term is now widely known in the UK and was quoted from many different areas, though usually with reference to north-west England

kettled drunk

mard(y) moody, whining, spoilt; also 'in a mard'. Frequently used in the abusive phrases 'mardy get' or 'mardy cow'. From 'mar', meaning 'to spoil', especially of a child, past tense 'marred'. Hence 'mard' and 'mardy'

moithered annoyed, confused. Origin uncertain; cf. **mithering**, continual fussing

peppered broke (contemporary slang)

piecer a mender of broken threads (textile industry)

proper poorly very unwell. The expression is found widely in northern use and in the Midlands, where it's claimed as a typical Black Country saying

pumps light shoes, plimsolls. Origin obscure

scally a miscreant, chav, trev. From 'scallywag' (contemporary slang, especially in Liverpool)

scrote a dodgy-looking youth, a 'scally'

segs hard lumps of skin (e.g. on the hand), callouses. Used since mid-Victorian era. From Old Norse *sigg*, hard skin

skrike to cry out, utter a shrill harsh cry. From early fourteenth century and found in Chaucer. Of Scandinavian origin, cf. Norwegian *skrika*

spell, speld a splinter (of wood). From Old English *speld*, a splinter

starve, starved, starving to be (very) cold. The term 'starve', from Old English *steorfan*, originally meant to 'die a lingering death', e.g. of cold; from the fourteenth century the expression to 'starve for cold' is recorded, later evolving into 'starve *of* cold'

tarra goodbye

throstle a spinning machine for cotton and wool. From Old English *throsel*, a thrush, named for the singing noise of the machinery

tippler toilet a primitive Lancashire form of exterior water-closet, familiarly known as the 'long drop', flushed by running water in the scullery

townie a chav, trev, scally, undesirable outsider (contemporary slang)

wag it, play the wag, wack it to play truant (contemporary slang). Perhaps related to 'wag', shake, oscillate. First used in the Victorian era

wom home (as in 'going wom')

yat a gate. Found in wordlists from the early eighteenth century

yed a head; **yedache** a headache

8 : YORKSHIRE

Language in a Landscape: Tykes and Tongues

Think of Yorkshire these days and you're perhaps in the land of television soaps and popular drama – of *Emmerdale* and (for those with longer memories) James Herriot. It's odd how these days we filter our experiences of the regions of Britain through the ersatz version peddled by broadcasting and the novel – whether it's Poldark's Cornwall, the Isle of Mull's capital masquerading as Balamory or Postman Pat's Cumbrian 'Greendale'. It's all a great boon to the marketeers, of course, who are all too happy to sell weekend breaks in Brontë or Herriot Country. But somehow it masks the reality.

Every decent cliché worth its salt has its imaginative feet firmly planted in truth. But clichés and stereotypes are uncomfortable guides to the seeker after truth. The Monty Python caricature of northern poverty in the famous 'Four Yorkshiremen' sketch is hilarious precisely because it sends up the image of a sort of miserabilist delight in awfulness combined with the traditional image of the competitive Yorkshireman and spices it with homespun wisdom: 'My old Dad used to say to me, "Money doesn't buy you happiness, son." Aye, 'e was right.'

Thus it's not a bad plan to be careful what dialect we're talking about when we're roaming the fells above Swaledale or walking the streets of Leeds. And dialect, just like the images of a place that we carry in our minds – the smokestack forest of Halifax, for example, that figured in many a geography book of forty years ago – moves, and moves fast.

There's something about Yorkshire place-names that reaches back. Look at any map of the county and the names reek of history. Start with the county's old ridings: originally these were Scandinavian geographical divisions (north, east, west) where *thrithjungr* meant a 'third part'; the opening consonant was lost and the main chunk of the word morphed into 'riding'.

Now pick just a handful of names at random from the former North Riding: Bagby, Thimbleby, Melmerby, Birkby, Melsonby and so on . . . the Scandinavian heritage of the place-name ending in all those ringing -*by*s is an obvious telltale. *By* or *byr* was the Old Danish word for a village or a homestead and so Bagby originally meant simply 'Baggi's farm', Thimbleby – nothing to do with needlepoint or delicate miniatures – was in fact quite prosaically 'Thymill's farm'.

The Danes – and it was principally the Danes, though the Norwegians also got a look-in – first settled in modern-day Yorkshire in the last half of the ninth century. In fact a huge swathe of eastern England came under their influence as part of the huge Viking expansion spreading across Europe and beyond. Through war and peace, the Danes left their stamp on the land and on the people – York became one of their strongholds: the Dane Halfdene was king of York in 875.

The basic language of Yorkshire continued to be a form of Old English, known to us today as Anglian, the northern expression of the speech that had arrived on English shores from Germany and the low countries 300 years earlier. But the influence of those powerful conquerors from the north and the east was strongly felt – in the names of places (as above) and people, and in many of the local words that pepper Yorkshire speech still. In fact it is said that the northern English of the so-called Dark Ages and the Scandinavian dialectal imports weren't so very far apart linguistically – to the extent that the two peoples could understand one another – and that the cross-fertilization and eventual fusion were a natural development.

So it is that all those dales – Swaledale, Thornton le Dale, Arkengarthdale and the rest – also owe their origins not to the English up-hill-and-down-dale tradition of Old English (*dael*) but to the Norse linguistic roots across the water of *dalr*, a valley. (As for the Arkengarth bit, that's a compound name made up from an old Norseman's name, 'Arnkell', very common apparently in Scandinavia, and 'garth' – lots of those in Yorkshire too – meaning an enclosure or farm. Put it all together and you get 'the valley of Arnkell's farm'. Easy really.)

In Leeds, Briggate (pronounced 'Briggut') and Kirkgate ('Kurgut') are not gates, nor in ancient York is Coppergate; the 'gate' was a street to the Norsemen. (Coppergate has nothing to do with copper either, incidentally, as it signifies the 'street of the cupmakers'.) And up on t'fells, the Vikings are never far away because those hills (fells) were also originally Norse, as was the waterfall that to Yorkshire people is a 'force' (originally *fors*). High *Force* waterfall, for example, is a well-known tourist magnet, and the 'foss' in the village of Fang*foss* not far from York comes from the same Norse root. A true local will put you right to the pronunciation, though, which is 'Fankuss'.

Also Scandinavian in origin are the ridge, which here becomes a 'rigg', and the outcrop that's a 'scar' (nothing to do with disfigurement) and those ubiquitous 'thwaites' (Scandinavian settlements) in the valleys – all part of the long and rich linguistic marking that has shaped Yorkshire talk.

If the map is visible testimony to the county's history, the words that live within that landscape offer the same pedigree. Go to picturesque Thornton le Dale on the edge of the North Yorkshire Moors and you'll find – as the local guide says – that the main (and most photographed) feature of the place is the 'beck'. And though you'll not find a 'beck' in Hampshire or the Highlands (that would be a 'brook' or a 'burn'), the word brought to northern England on the tongues of settlers from Scandinavia (as *bekkr*) is now the standard word for a stream.

Then again, when my Yorkshire through and through father-in-law routinely referred to linen being 'in the "kist"', I at first imagined this was a particularly unusual pronunciation of the standard 'chest'. Not a bit of it. 'Kist' is another of those words that made the migration with the Norsemen (*kista*) and took root in northern England, to crop up regularly in dialect still. And when – as it is so often in these parts – it's 'siling down' with rain, some say that the Scandinavian influence (*sila*) is also still to be felt.

Scandinavian linguistic bedrock is only half the story. It's people that make a dialect and in the farms and fields of the Dales, in the woollen mills and coalmines, in the steel foundries of Sheffield across two centuries of heavy industrial labour, were forged the shapes of the Yorkshire dialect that has come down to us. Fiercely proud of their traditions, suspicious of 'offcomeduns' (outsiders) they 'fettle' (make) things well and are strong in homespun philosophy: as the famous proverb has it, 'If tha does owt for nowt, do it for thysen' ('If you do anything for nothing, do it for yourself').

With the evaporation of mining and the closing of the collieries, generations of closely woven communities have been dispersed. The language of the pits has lost its purpose, as have the deputies, overseers and hewers who worked there. Likewise on the farms of Yorkshire, as throughout Britain, mechanization has removed the need for 'hiling', 'shocking', 'stitching' and 'thriving', so eliminating yet another specialist lexicon from the pages of Yorkshire speech. There's nothing too appalling here and nothing to mourn: linguistic change is an inevitable part of social evolution, and one, as this book shows, that's going on in places the length and breadth of the UK. Stanley Ellis, one of the original field-workers for the Survey of English Dialects of the 1950s and 1960s, puts it like this:

> It's no good talking about horse's harness if you haven't got a horse; it's no good talking about parts of an old-fashioned plough if you're ploughing with a modern tractor. But that doesn't stop you identifying almost instantly the pronunciation of a man who's lived in a district all his life and as soon as he opens his mouth you're pretty sure that he comes from that place just over the hill, or far in another country.

Back in the 1960s, the SED uncovered still-rich seams of unchanging Yorkshire talk reaching back centuries. Here, as across the whole of Britain, the social churning of the Second World War had begun to make an impact, yet in the country districts where mains electricity was still a rarity, change was slower and language dawdled. Stanley Ellis heard from farmers about their carts and the individual local terms that they used to describe them, all – like the parts of a plough Ellis refers to above – now long disappeared. Already when these recordings were made, mechanization had arrived in North Yorkshire ('We dawn't do that naouw since we go' mechanized'), although one farmer interviewed described the 'box sledge' he still used for collecting bedding material for his 'beeasts' on the steep fellsides: 'Ooh aye, for rooshes [rushes], for beddin'; rooshes an' bracken . . .'. Asked about what he did to keep warm in winter, the same farmer showed Ellis his store of peat (he pronounced it 'peeyit') cut from the fell – but remarked that peat burns too quickly and it took a lot of it to keep you through the winter. Even so, back in 1963, he could point to 'a fellow on t'tops there, a shepherd, Joy they call 'im, I think 'e burns nowt else boot peeyit'. One can but wonder what became of Joy the shepherd who lived on the tops above Grass-ington forty years ago.

The rural lives and the language that the SED captured in Yorkshire back then were in the process of profound change. The farmer I've quoted was keen to show how modern he was, yet also admitted to indulging in a little propitiation to the gods of agriculture to deliver him from having trouble with calving. In those parts they called it 'picking':

> They use' t'ave soom o' these 'ere wha' the' caall 'looky stawns' [They used to have some of these here what they call 'lucky stones'] and in aa yoonger deays, they used to keep gayse [geese] on t'field, use' tuh stopp 'em pickin': gowse mook [goose muck] the' reckoned. If yuh kep' gayse whe' yuh had a lot o' calvin' cauws [If you kept geese where you had a lot of calving cows] it sorta stoppt 'em pickin'. Ahv 'ad looky stawns an' soochlike to driyve t'evil spirits aweeiy.

From Wibsey, in the West Riding, now just a couple of miles south of Bradford town centre but in days past a separate town, Stanley Ellis heard tales from the once famous Wibsey Fair, where horse-dealers gathered from all over to trade, and occasionally to indulge in a little underhand practice. 'There were these Johnny-boiys, yuh knaw, they usse tuh . . . [well, there was] a lot of physicking gawn awn, yuh knaw. Poot a bit a' pepper into it. Ooh aye.' Pepper in the horses' feed was the trick, I would guess, though this farmer was too full of a wicked laugh to spell it out precisely. 'Physicking' is a word from another age entirely, likewise the reference to 'Johnny-boys' for likely lads: it's worth remembering that this recording was made at exactly the same moment the Beatles were storming the world. Today, the south Bradford suburb of Wibsey is less than a mile from the town's ring-road; then the old horse fair was 'a raight famleh gathering':

> It looked a real trait. It start breakfast time, early on; there'd be hoondreds theeyre bi dinner taam. Aw, there'd be crauwded. Farmers an' 'oss dealers. There wouldn't be many chaik boaks [chequebooks] in them deays, y'knaw. The'd pull t'awd wash-leathe' bag aat [They'd pull the old wash-leather bag out] an' pay awt wi' pounds. An' tuh seal a bargain they joost clopped their 'and and say 'That's it'.

Sealing bargains by 'clopping' hands and no credit cards or cheque-books – just an old wash-leather bag: these are memories that belong fifty or more years before they were recorded, and nearly a century ago now. But in fact, the language in which they're articulated, as too the accent, is far less distant than some of the SED documents that I've listened to in the course of preparing this book, in Lancashire, for instance, and Devon and Northumberland. Is it that our ears are generally more attuned to and familiar with the cadences of Yorkshire speech? Or is it simply that these specific farmers whose stories I've selected just happen not to be the broadest? It's impossible to know for certain, since each individual's speech pattern is his or her own, and for every example there are a thousand exceptions.

Certainly by the 1980s, when Ellis returned to rural Yorkshire for the BBC, most of the broadest talk had melted away out of everyday speech. He was only able to uncover scattered pockets of it, like old snow in spring caught in crevices on the high fells. In this rarest variety (broader still than the Wibsey and Grassington recordings from the 1960s) it isn't simply that the speakers were using a lot of dialect terms: no, this talk had a range of vowel sounds and a rolling rhythm that were miles removed from the standard.

Listen to this old farmer from Pocklington near York talking about the local cricket team he loved and nurtured:

> When ah was a lad we 'ad a village teeyam. And baaye, there was some room gunnins-on [rum goings-on], soom room odd oompires. Baaye gaw, they did cheeyat [cheat]! Fust taam I ivver played, why, t'awd ends 'ad bin sat doown in like mang a lot o' sand [among a lot of sand] – there were greeat big 'oles! You'd never seen owt like it. An' it weer nowt ti 'a' coow mook all aower, ye knaw [and it was nothing to have cow muck all over, you know]. When we started a teeam in t'village, we 'ad a very, very good wickit. An' t'oours [the hours] we spent rollin' it and fettlin' it if there was goin' to be a coop match [cup match]! But I thoroughly enjoyed ma cricketin' daeys – it was champion.

Already in the mid-1980s, when the BBC recorded this reminiscence, youngsters were describing such speech as old-fashioned and uncommon. Ellis noted that the glottal stop (originally an urban, southern phenomenon) was now normal for these Yorkshire children and they used few really local words. One girl said the lads from the country districts were broader: 'The farm boys say, "nowt",' she observed, and don't 'say words fully'. But I doubt even they would resort to the 'by gaw', 'by gum' and 'champion' of Irwin Bielby's speech, though they might still 'fettle' something.

To be completely honest, Irwin had at least two versions of his own speech ready to deploy when the need arose. There was a more gently accented form, with dialectal terms neatly circumvented so as not to confuse the outsider, and then he had his broadest talk, of which the cricket pitch story is an example, which he could turn on at will. Which was his 'natural' speech? Both, probably, since to a greater or lesser degree we all have the ability to switch from one speech-code to another as circumstances dictate: the many examples of people interviewed for Voices who admitted to having a 'telephone voice' simply proves it. In the 'Voices' section of this chapter you can see just how widely contemporary Yorkshire speech varies, from the North Yorkshire Moors dialect, little changed from fifty years ago, to urban Leeds, where words from the Indian subcontinent are being drawn into the web of day-to-day communication.

The Voices Survey: Big County, Bigger Differences

There's a belief, no doubt mistaken, that Yorkshire people think the world pretty well stops at the county boundary. And as far as qualifying to play for the cricket team, that certainly used to be the case. But it's of course an old-fashioned and out-of-date image now and the sort of homogeneity that this notion implies couldn't have been better unpicked than by listening to the range of men and women that Voices interviewed in 2004/5. And before I go any further, let me declare one heresy: I have extended the southern boundary of the area slightly beyond the confines of administrative Yorkshire in order to capture some interesting voices on the edge of the region.

So Voices visited communities deep in the North Yorkshire Moors, in urban Leeds and York, on the coast at Filey and on the edge of the Wolds in the east. From the edge of the Humber estuary, too, are some different yet not so different accents as the region shades south from Humberside into Lincolnshire.

Homogeneity first. The accent throughout the recordings is recognizably out of the same box. Northern 'u' sounds in words like 'shut' and 'come' (I've expressed these on the page as elsewhere in the book by 'oo') are universal and the shortening of 'the' to 't'' ('shoot t'door', 'down t'pit') still widespread. Likewise the ways in which other vowel sounds are modified (see the 'Sound of . . .' section for details) are similar. But the area is distinguished by such huge geographical and cultural differences that to draw too many conclusions about 'the state of Yorkshire dialect' would be pretty unwise. Add to this the variations that I've found right across the UK in the way younger and older people use local language, in town and country, and what you have is a situation where the gulfs between one part of the county, one generation, one social grouping, one type of landscape and another render comparisons less than completely instructive.

For instance, in Driffield, Voices listened in to four elderly people from an area that spread south to Hull and north to Bridlington. These were dialect enthusiasts, one a regular public performer of monologues and poetry in the idiom. How typical were David, Doreen, Dorothy and Don of contemporary Yorkshire Wolds speech? They're certainly broad, and have a huge stock of local words and expressions that they drop quite naturally into their conversation. As they speak to one another, they become less self-conscious about the outsider present (the Voices interviewer) and lapse into still broader forms.

So when David, in his seventies and proud of being able to reach back in his recollections to the 1930s and the freak hailstorm that had occurred when he was only four, ventures the local word for earwig 'twitchbell' at the top end of the East Riding and the southern equivalent 'forky robin' or 'forkin robin', there was just a sense that words were being paraded for their curiosity value. Yes such differences clearly did exist, and amongst farming people such as these no doubt the words and the distinctions persisted longer than anywhere else. But as I have seen across the country, regional talk needs a critical mass, and words like this have surely long lost any real currency among the wider community. However, talk of the creature prompts anecdotes which are told in the broadest

The Sound of Yorkshire

Yorkshire . . . in a few short paragraphs? What an insult! There are dozens of Yorkshire accents – Dales, North Riding, Leeds, you name it. True enough, but then again there are enough shared characteristics to make an overview possible. Listen for five minutes to Geoff Boycott passing judgement (and he'd say 'paessin joodgement') on a batsman's style and you'll certainly hear those qualities soon enough. That long 'u', for one. 'Muck' that emerges rhyming with 'book', and that I've written here with 'oo' – 'mook'. And those shortened northern 'a's: 'brass' that has the same vowel as 'lass' (in the text, 'braass' not 'brahss').

In fact, a lot of what makes Yorkshire *sound* like Yorkshire is in the vowels, baked and tasty like fresh bread. Long sounds that in standard English would be more clipped: 'light', 'pile', 'right enough' all sound more as if someone's stretching them and enjoying the flavour – I've added a 'y' to the transcription to indicate this 'laiyt', 'paiyl', 'raiyt enoough'. The 'ay' sound in 'rake' and 'take'

and most unselfconscious manner. So Dot and Doreen enjoy this exchange about earwigs:

'Ah woonce 'ad one sookin' [sucking] me an' bah golly it got soom gerrin' aout.'
'Ah go' the vacuum to try an gerrit aout, boot we didn't . . .'

On the other hand, the tale of how Don, ninth in a huge family of eighteen children, has never been sure of when his birthday really is, because his mother got the date wrong on the birth certificate, you feel may be a well-varnished set piece of regional vernacular and oft-told, which makes it a bit of a museum-piece:

'Ah wuz yan of a family of twenty. An' ah still daint knaw whether ah wuz born on sixth or tenth a March. [It was] naantin thutty-three. It teik that si lang furra registraa to get aout to village that bi tam I coom aout, 'e cooms into y'oose an' 'e says, "Give us 'is bawthday" an' she says, "Sixth of Maahch": sixth of Maahch is on mi bawth cetificat. Boot as 'e's leavin', she says, "Ahve telld 'im wrang; it wuz the tenth!"'

is more open than the standard and comes out closer to 'wreck' and 'tech' – I've used 'eh' in the text to suggest this quality ('rehke', 'tehke'). Some speakers, particularly the older ones, stretch this out as wide as a Dales horizon (' 'e pickt oop t'rehhke . . .' – he picked up the rake), others keep it tight and short (tek). And they sometimes do the same stretching with 'a' in words like 'water' which I've rendered 'waawtuh'. The open 'a' in terms like 'dark' and 'darling' opens even wider like some Yorkshire dentist's victim to produce a very pure 'a' sound closer to 'daak' and 'daaling' (though the final 'g' in this last word would often be lost – 'daalin' '). The 'r' though in both words isn't sounded, unlike the east Lancashire 'r' as we've seen.

The other familiar Yorkshirism worth noting is the reduction of the word 'the' to 't' ' (the classic 'daouwn t'pit') which in many speakers, old and young, is still a regular feature. It's part of the rhythm of the way people speak in the county which overall has a loping swagger to it redolent of Yorkshire confidence, landing with both feet firmly planted from time to time on a resonant 'but' to start a fresh thought. 'Boot. Then agaiyn . . .'

Don's story is full of East Riding pronunciations: 'yan' for one, 'daint' for don't and 'thutty' for thirty. Similarly Doreen refers to 'chuch' (rhymes with 'such') for church and 'tunn' for turn. This shortening of the longer 'u' sound found in these words ('thirty', 'church', 'turn' and in Don's story above also 'birthday') is clearly typical: all four speakers do it quite routinely, though by listening closely to the full two hours of their discussion, it's quite clear that they have a range of pronunciations they can call on according to circumstances.

But above all what emerges from this lengthy encounter is the fact that this strongly marked regional speech is firmly locked into the agricultural world that fostered it, into the region that gave it its particular characteristics and into the generation that grew up with it. Dot, a farm-worker for decades who's done most jobs on the land, was a particularly unselfconscious speaker, with her explanations of rat-catching beside a stream (beck) and threshing:

> 'When you were thrashin' you'd 'ave 'oondred and soome rats all laid out: the rats used to thrive in the beck and Saturday soom of oos used to gaw and rattle the rats, wait for them to coom out the oyl [hole]

. . . [we'd] clobber them with the stick or owt. An' we were killin'
them as they kem out.'

Trouser-legs had to be tied up at the bottom, or tucked into socks or the
rats would be tempted to run up; which is what happened to one
unfortunate man, the local butcher, who ''ad it 'eld wi' 'is 'and, boorr 'e
dossn't leave gaw 'cos it wuz still wick, you say'. There's nothing forced
or artificial in the way Dot speaks of 'thrashin'' and the 'oyl' (hole) from
which the rats emerged, or indeed of the butcher who 'had it [the rat]
held with his hand, but he doesn't leave go because it was still wick
[alive]'. Each of the group has his or her story of farming in the old days:
Doreen remembers the 'drawvers [drovers] coomin' through' her village
with their beasts and the way they slaughtered a pig and how she and
her childhood friends vied to help out. And there are the almost inevitable
tales of privies: a three-seater for the men, two-seater for the women –
'Baaye golly it dint 'aff stink!' – and the equally inevitable regret about
the outsiders in the villages – that word 'offcomeduns' again. 'Ah can
gaw back ti Barmston any taam,' says Don about the place he was born,
near the coast eight miles east of Driffield:

> 'boot it's different because of the offcoomduns that's coom in – the
> visitors – they're tekkin over all the properties; and the ordinary village
> people can't afford it.'

And Doreen ('braaught up on a faam, hail, snaw or blaw [hail, snow or
blow]; ah couldn't live anywhere else') refuses to go near Hull because
it's too busy, preferring nearby Beverley: 'Ah liyke Bevly cos it's a market
town and ah feel attom there.' Hull, twenty miles south of Driffield,
seems to epitomize for these older people the antithesis of what they are
and what they enjoy, even for Dot, who was born there. David, for
example, has never strayed from the tiny village of Wold Newton north
of Driffield, and wouldn't want to: he likes North Frodingham where he
goes for cricket, but it's too flat:

> 'Ah liyke the hills. Ah would never want to flit [= move]. Aye mayght
> gerr away wi' it i' Driffield bicause ah can ge' ou' an' look a' fields,
> 'ave a li' le waak [walk]; boot ah couldn't go an' live in a pleice
> laak 'Ull.'

Cut to urban Hull and meet Chris, who's a porter at Asda and has high hopes of becoming a dance star. Voices met Chris and a fellow hopeful, Gemma, along with Natalie, a dance tutor, in the town, and what emerged was, naturally, a world away from the agricultural timelessness of the Wolds: 'I work part time at River Island and in my spare time I'm choreographing, watching dance pieces,' explained Gemma. All three have an urban flatness about the way they speak compared to the Driffield quartet: different times, different surroundings, different working environment. And yet, and yet there are points of coincidence. When asked the routine question about what they'd call playing truant, the Hull youngsters offered: 'twaggin'', to 'twag' – 'I got caaught woonce an' ah never did i' again.' Back to Driffield and again 'twag it', 'twaggin'', or simply 'skippin' skeel [school]' were on offer.

For baby, both groups came up with standard northern 'bairn' (or 'bain', a local variant suggested from Cleethorpes), and hot was another shared term, 'mafted'. (You may recall that the Yorkshire-born Emma from the Creations hair salon in Truro (Chapter 1) surprised her colleagues by suggesting 'mafted' for hot.) Inevitably, the older people had another older form, 'yat' (which was also cited by a group from the Dales village of Norton: 'In broad Yorkshire it's "yat"'). The Woldsman David's seventy years of farming experience give him the chance for a bit of extra colourful detail: 'It wuz that yat tedeah ah wuz wet-shad with sweeyat [It was that hot today I was wet-shod with sweat]', i.e. so dripping with sweat that his shoes were almost soaked through.

There were of course other more conventional points in common between the two groups – 'sannies' was the shared word for plimsolls (sandshoes, as in Scotland, curiously), but their vernacular strong points lay inevitably in the most distinctive corners of their respective worlds. So in Driffield the emphasis was on the older world of farm life forty, fifty years ago: father was 't'awd man' (the old man) and even 'fore-elder' (dictionary definition: parent or ancestor). Clothes were 'cleeaz' (a local pronunciation that recalls the Scots 'claes') and 'Soonday Best' or 'Soonday go-to-meetin' clawthes'. Cold was 'nithered', as it is for many older Yorkshire people (cf. the Yorkshire 'Snapshot' of a Castleford family) but also 'cawd' and 'nesh'. In Hull it's 'freezin'' and 'baltic' (widespread modern slang, this).

If one of the dancers is a bit moody, they'd be called a 'mardy arse' (regional, but not uniquely Yorkshire – more a Midlands usage), but they did come up with a distinctively traditional regional term for an alleyway or passage. Unlike the regulation Yorkshire 'ginnel', found throughout the industrial cities and towns around Leeds and Bradford, for the Hull trio it's a 'tenfoot'. Chris even checked:

'I actually measured our tenfoot woonce cos ah wan'id to know if it was ten foo' wide. An' i' actually was.'

And with splendid local accuracy, he added: 'over in Grimsby they have "eightfoots"!' But where the real relish for linguistic distinction came in was in the world of young people and the clothes they wear. This is the territory of the 'chav', the 'trev', the 'pikey' and the 'townie'. Chris calls them:

'A "pog"; a "townie": I think thass coom from gypsies: we used to go "pogs", "gyp-hogs", then i' got shortened to "pogs". "Townie" is quite a popular thing at the moment; it's how they dress. They wear woolly 'ats on the top of their 'ead, they took [tuck] their trousers in their socks, wear trackies, an' they joost coom oop to you. An' it's the weay theay speak – it's always "Aw meiy [mate]; oh can you spare me twenty pee? Ah joos coom outta prison. Ah need mi boos fares awm . . . or ahll deck yer [I just come out of prison. I need my bus fares home . . . or I'll deck you]".'

Head inland from Hull along the A1079, passing south of Irwin Bielby's village of Fangfoss, and make for York, venerable city, ancient market centre and Norman stronghold overtopped by the great Minster. There, Voices met Lee, Nick, Stacey and Sarah, drama students from the city's Stagecoach Youth Theatre. They're socially and vocally mobile – after all they need to be, they're actors. For them, 'Yorkshire talk' is more simply an accent; they have even fewer really local terms in their vocabulary than their counterparts in Hull and readily reach for more or less national slang like 'knackered' for tired and 'chuffed' for pleased. But they're proud to have a Yorkshire accent, being often asked to pronounce words like 'booger' to delight non-Yorkshire friends. A touch of older Yorkshire, though, when asked for their words for cold: 'cawd' (but never 'nithered') and 'frozzen'. They'd heard tell of 'yat' for hot, but didn't use it, though that originally northern but ever-spreading vernacular for trousers, 'keks', they did say.

No, it's in the geographically remotest corners and amongst the elderly that the greatest stock of Yorkshire-isms is still to be unearthed, so Voices gathered Doreen, Eva and Paul at Helmsley in the heart of the North York Moors national park to catch some of the sound of the old North Riding. Their talk was fashioned in the narrow valleys and high fells of Rosedale, Bilsdale and Farndale and around Goathland, though today all three are perfectly able to modulate into perfect and well-articulated (if quite strongly accented) standard English. It's also true that, as with the group from Driffield that you met at the beginning of this section, this North Riding trio are dedicated to keeping the flame of regional speech very much alive, through membership of the sterling Yorkshire Dialect Society.

But theirs is no artificial preservation scheme. As so often in this survey, you've only to get them talking amongst themselves and our trio from today lapse quickly into broad talk, albeit nostalgically. The inevitable recollected joys of a two-hole earth closet, for instance: 'Nice ti 'ave a bit o' coompany if it was caad [cold] an' windy!' Unfortunately this model had a gap at the back that invited pranksters:

'Ye could gan soom neits an' lads'd be aboout an' they would shoove a nettle oop!'

['You could go some nights and the lads would be about and they would shove a nettle up!']

Classic, too, is their assertion of the exquisite localness of this local talk, even within the boundaries of the North Riding: 'Go three miles from here and the pronunciation is completely different' and in this landscape of fells, talk of 'tups' (male sheep) and 'ploughing' is how you judge the localness of someone's speech. So 'toop [tup]' is rendered in Farndale as 'tiup' and 'plieuh [plough]' twists to become 'pleeiu' as in 'Ah wuz 'alpin' mi faathuh ti pleeiu [I was helping my father to plough].'

This bunch will still offer you 'siling down' for pouring rain and 'dowly' for unwell, just as the late Union leader Sid Weighell did for Stanley Ellis when he came to survey Yorkshire dialect twenty years ago.

Paul, Doreen and Eva certainly are 'nithered' or 'frozzen' if they're cold, 'jiggered' if they're exhausted and 'crazed' if they're annoyed; they're just the words that come most naturally to them, still. 'Fettling' is what they do to make or prepare something (you fettle breakfast), just as their counterparts in Driffield do, but no mention here of 'femmer', a word Sid Weighell waxed lyrical about in his interview with Ellis in 1983: 'femmer' means 'fragile'. Nor do we hear now about another of his favourites, 'galluses' (braces and a term formerly found across many areas of England), largely I imagine because few today wear them.

Digging out those older dialect words can take some doing these days, even among people you might expect to reach for them naturally. Heading back east again towards the coast, Voices met Don, Mansfield, Paul and Jim, fishermen from Filey. At first, they tended to produce national standard vernacular forms and were happy to agree that when they're not feeling too well they're simply 'under the weather' or 'off-colour'. It was only when one of them pointed out that, amongst his mates, feeling 'unwell' was more likely to be described as 'being badly', that the others chimed in in agreement. The older, regional form is buried under a topsoil of day-to-day utility, but dig a bit and it's still there to be excavated, though, now, it's not what they most readily use.

As the conversation advanced and the fishermen became more relaxed, just as with the group from Driffield, expressions like 'gallock-handed' for left-handed began to emerge:

> 'When the women had to skein the mussels one by one for bait, they always used to say that a woman who was gallock-handed was never a good skeiner!'

'Gallock-handed' still turns up quite widely amongst Yorkshire people of a certain age, but I was more surprised to hear it (or something like it) from Chris, Gemma and Natalie, the dancers from Hull, who offered 'golly-handed. My nan used to say that. It's joost a word that was made years ago . . .' 'Gallock-handed' is clearly one of the tougher bits of enduring Yorkshire dialect bedrock because it was quoted by an otherwise rather linguistically bland, middle-class group that Voices interviewed at Norton, north of York. They struggled to assemble a dozen true Yorkshire-isms that they'd use unselfconsciously, but here was 'gallock-handed' again, as well as 'dowly' and 'nithered'. Traditional terms like 'laikin'' for playing they knew too, as well as 'nesh [weakly]' and 'mardy' again for moody, together with the familiar 'snicket' and 'ginnel [alleyway]'.

Finally in this whirlwind linguistic tour of Yorkshire, head sixty miles south and west and you're in metropolitan Leeds, and a couple of continents away linguistically. Here, the old Yorkshire is not even a memory, but just a faint shadow on the walls of urban Moortown in the north of the city. In 2004/5, Voices interviewed a group of young men and women from Asia and Africa who have made the district their home. Keranjeet, Mandeep, Charndeep, Tarsem, Inderjeet and Indera are second-generation immigrants, now firmly rooted in Yorkshire. They were full of admiration for the linguistic achievements of their parents but could, with the assurance of complete fluency in both their native and adoptive languages, now smile at the occasional linguistic faux-pas committed by their less English-proficient parents ('When my Dad says "scrapyard" he pronounces it "crapyard"!'). Proficiency in *Yorkshire* talk took a bit of rehearsal, though:

> 'I'll never forget when we first came to England, my two brothers had already been here four years prior to us and they spoke really broad Yorkshire. And me and my sister didn't. We used to sit there and listen, and every night we used to go "borrul uv wodder, borrul uv wodder" [bottle of water] to practise our Yorkshire accent. And that's how we picked it up!'

Their backgrounds are Punjabi and East African, but all had almost uniformly Yorkshire urban accents, though they readily deploy terms from Punjabi and Swahili amongst their English: 'It's amazin' the noomber of languages we've now adopted', but, they added, it's perfectly acceptable to mix and match as required. And they know that, so far, their Yorkshire speech consists of accent rather than vocabulary:

> 'The Yorkshire language is disappearing. OK we've go' an accen', boot what we'd call the sort of Yorkshire . . . your gri' 'y [gritty] manual workers, your factory workers, your gri' 'y Yorkshire people, they'd be the woons that would be communicaeytin' an' usin' the language in tha' weay.'

However, Tarsem remembered how his Yorkshire speech was sufficiently local to prove a bit of a barrier when he was sent to work in Edinburgh with an equally broad-speaking Scottish colleague from the Scottish capital:

> 'I had an experience with another Singh: I couldn't understand a word he was saying to me. Now two Singhs should be able to communicate – but not in English we couldn't, not on your life!'

Dialect, as I say repeatedly throughout this book, both includes and excludes, and clearly in this case the lingua franca was not going to be English. However, a couple of members of this group reported a different and fascinating sort of inclusion/exclusion language that they'd developed. It's a mixture of Punjabi words and English backslang – not unlike the 'eggy language' that's widely known amongst schoolchildren in which the syllables 'eggy' are inserted into the middle of words to render them almost incomprehensible to the casual listener (for a contemporary example, see the 'Snapshot' in Chapter 12). This, I learned from Mandeep, was a way of creating a bit of private space for them as young people in a crowded home:

> '[With Punjabi backslang] you have your own little space where no-one can interfere. It's really hard to have privacy in our household compared to my English friends who have their own rooms: with ours it's compulsory to sit as a family downstairs – so if you want to have your own world without parents, you're sociable by being there in body but in your mind and language you're doing your own thing.'

Finally, in a variation of the lament that Voices has captured across Britain for the older forms of local speech, these new Yorkshire men and women found themselves regretting the loss of their own indigenous songs and traditions within the newly minted mixed culture that's developed amongst their north Leeds community. Now, explained Mandeep, the 'proverbs, etiquettes and morals' within the songs and their lyrics, together with the storytelling traditions, are here heard these days only at weddings: 'and I can mime the actions but I can't sing. And it's sad that slawly it's bein' lost.'

A Yorkshire Snapshot: Family Album

Castleford, West Yorkshire. Take a northward slip off the trans-Pennine M62 and within a mile or so you're in the heart of the town. This is rugby league's heartland, a proud tradition that flourished with the area's many pits. But now with the pits closed the big buzz in Castleford is the new skiing and leisure centre, the designer outlets and the shopping centres. Two worlds and generations apart that inform the lives of one local family. There's Derrick, once a pithead worker, then a greengrocer and now a grandfather and dispenser of old wisdom. His son, Andrew, followed him into the fruit and veg trade but has a less well-defined Yorkshire dialect. Sophie, Andrew's daughter, goes to school in Leeds and has acquired an urban speech-style still less identifiably 'local'; she's not afraid to take on her grandpa when she thinks he's wrong.

Derrick's full of stories of his former life at the coalmine in Fryston, once a thriving pit-village just outside Castleford, all expressed in a colourful traditional Yorkshire dialect:

> 'Yer granddad used to coom oop the shaafft, into the workshops and if ah 'ad a spare ten minutes, [the blacksmith] used to get the awld fire going, t'blacksmith's fire, an' ah used to watch 'im for ten minutes mekkin' 'is 'orseshoes. Dauwn the bottom of the pit we 'ad a marvellous garaage, an' we 'ad all oos diesel engines there, and that's where your granddad worked.'

Derrick's accent's unmistakable, like his frequent dropping of 'the': 't'blacksmith's fire', and elsewhere in the conversation 't'lights' and 't'pit' ('it were dark when they turned t'lights off down t'pit'). Another old Yorkshire form runs throughout his speech too: 'us' in place of 'our': 'all oos diesel engines', 'oos lamp on oos cap', and he regularly uses the older verbal 'it were' rather than 'it was'. Sophie on the other hand speaks pretty much standard English, albeit with a distinctly regional accent: 'Was it dark?' she asks.

> 'Well it was, but where we worked there were all fluorescent laights so we never used to wear oos lamp on oos cap.'

Derrick has an old Yorkshire pitman's ability to tell a spellbinding story; Sophie listens rapt as he recounts the day when 'we 'ad a lat trapt in t'shaafft [we had a lad trapped in the shaft]':

'Ah still see 'im today. They call 'im Jimmy Winterbottom; aye Jimmy Winterbottom. 'E never ever went back dauwn t'pit. 'E were faast eight hours. We 'ad a shaafftsman down t'pit that deay called 'Orace 'Unter and 'e'd gone sixty, seventy foot oop and the manager said to 'im, "Bring thysen down." And 'Orace says, "Ah'm nearly at the cage", and the manager says, "Tha brings thyself down!" '

'Thysen', 'tha brings thyself': this is vintage Yorkshire vernacular. Derrick is by now well into the story of the day they saved young Jimmy, and he brings on the man, a Pit Deputy called Addy, whose heroics were responsible. But this in turn brings about a telling little linguistic confusion, language and culture at a crossroads: 'We 'ad a Deputy . . .' begins the old man. Andrew jumps in to clarify for his daughter:

'Does Sophie know what a Deputy is?'
'Yes I do! It's a person that's lower, like a Deputy Head. It's, like, one lower than . . .'

Not quite: here it's a piece of technical mining vocabulary and Derrick winds himself up to offer the authoritative explanation:

'Listen! If tha's a collier, a collier can tek 'is exams an' becoom a Deputy. An' a Deputy 'as a lamp an' a steeck [stick], an' 'e walks oop an' down t'feace [up and down the face] an' 'e says, "Coo' that loomp o' caoul 'ere [Cut that lump of coal here]; coot tha'; leave tha." A Deputy. An' then if 'e's clever enoof, tha gets an Ovverman [Overman]; an' then tha gets an 'Ead Ovverman, an' then, an' then . . .

– 'An' then!' Sophie chimes in – she's loving this

'. . . you coom to t'Oonder-Manager of a Pit, an' then the Manager of a Pit.'

The hierarchy clarified, it was on with the story: in spite of the fact that the Deputy had somehow saved young Jimmy Winterbottom's life, he wasn't going to go back down: ' 'E said to me, "Dereek, never no more".'
'So 'e didn't go to the mines anymore?' queries Sophie . . .

204

But this stops the conversation dead: why had Sophie called them 'mines' when granddad called it 'a pit'. ('It *were* a pit, it were a pit,' mutters Derrick.) Sophie can't offer any explanation and it clearly comes as a surprise to the family. The vernacular of mining was traditionally as engrained in Yorkshire talk as coal-dust in a hewer's skin. But Sophie, born since coal in north-east England ceased to be an everyday reality and with her dad in the greengrocery business, has no reason to have it as part of her vocabulary. What's happening here is a very audible example of the organic process of language change. Andrew again:

'Sophie, I remember you assking oos not many years ago, "Daddy what is 'coal'?" Was that because at the taaime we didn't have a coal fire, and didn't burn cawl? Had you never coome across it?'

His daughter, unabashed, agrees that she 'probably didn't know what it was'. The cultural and linguistic gulf has begun now to fascinate the whole family:

'Listen to your granddad! When tha's cawld in Yorkshire, tha's "nithered". That means "cawld". If you say to somebody, "Baaye Christ, ah'm nithered", tha's cawld.'

'And why do you say "vexed" instead of "annoyed"?' Sophie asks Derrick.

'Oh, mi granddad Davison used to say that: "I'm vexed",' he replies. Now it's a competition.

'But I know what "put wood in t'oyl' means",' says Sophie, ' "shut the door!" '

'But if ah said tuh thee, "Doost thou want to go to t'midden" [to the midden], dooz tha knaw where tha'd be gawin'? To t'midden. It means "toilet". Because when we'd naw toilets indoors, the toilet were daown the yaard, an' if yuh grandma wanted to go to t'toilet at naight she'd 'ave to bloody get oop an' gaw across to t'midden.'

'A midden was a dry toilet,' explains Sophie's grandmother.

'I think I've worked it out, Sophie,' Andrew adds, 'it was an old fashioned builder's bog!'

Andrew joined his father in the greengrocery business when he was eight, and remembers the laborious sorting and turning of heaps of nuts to keep them in good fettle for the Christmas market, and relishes telling stories of the tough hours spent scrubbing celery in freezing water till it was white to prepare it for sale. His stories of hardship come from the same tradition as his father's: the rigours of a past age recalled with affection from the standpoint of someone who no longer has to suffer them. But while his voice remains richly accented, his language has now the smoothness of broadly functional contemporary English, easily comprehended anywhere in the country.

So his linguistic radar is well tuned to detect when, just for a moment, his father eases away from his own broadest Yorkshire, as when he's remembering his regular visits to the wholesale vegetable market in Leeds:

> 'Ah can remember gawin' daown into Kurgut [Kirkgate] Maarket with my dad an' not seein' a veh'cle; they were aall 'orses an' carts. Big 'orses.'

But Andrew responds by querying his father's pronunciation of 'horses' with a long 'aw' sound ('orses'). Didn't he mean ''osses'?

> ''Osses, aye, 'osses as we seay in Yorkshire, they were 'osses.'

When Derrick's wife enters the room, there's much merriment and rib-nudging about making sure everyone speaks properly in her presence. All three generations of this Yorkshire family seem acutely aware of the fact that they all have very different degrees of Yorkshireness in the way they talk. Sophie has her own code, shared with her schoolmates; her grandfather – broad and relatively unyielding in his dialect vocabulary, syntax and accent – even he moves away from the norm sometimes ('I can speak properly when I want to speak properly'). And Andrew, from the middling generation growing up in the 1960s when culture, language and social mobility were all beginning to shift markedly, has perhaps the broadest range of dialect options, sharing with his father a close knowledge of the old ways, but adopting perhaps first out of necessity and then from habit a more widely applicable version of 'talking local'. Except, says his daughter Sophie, in the privacy of his own phone:

> 'You've got a strong Yorkshire accent but Granddad's harder to understand than you are. But, it's weird because, dad, if he's speaking

on the phone to a fellow Yorkshireman 'e manages to put on this really Yorkshire voice, with words such as "awld lad" and "loov". He can put on a posh voice when he's talking to my schoolfriends but sometimes he can be really Yorkshire . . .'

A Yorkshire Glossary

The list includes old farming vocabulary, contemporary regional slang and more general Yorkshire-isms which I have indicated where appropriate

bail! run for it, leg it! (contemporary young Cleethorpes speech)

beck a stream. Old English *bece*, from Old Norse *bekkr*, a brook

bezz, bezzin' it move fast, go somewhere quickly: 'I just bezz it to my house' (contemporary young Cleethorpes speech)

brass money. From Old English *bras*

by gaw, by gum by God (euphemistic usage). Early nineteenth century

caff chaff (old Yorkshire farming term)

catto'ed drunk (perhaps related to 'KO'd' – knocked out – also used to mean drunk)

champion terrific, wonderful, excellent

chuffed pleased, proud. Originally meant 'swollen, puffed out'. Sixteenth century, origin unknown. This word has now become national standard vernacular

clarty muddy, filthy. Origin unknown; *beclart* is found as early as the thirteenth century

cob, sweat cobs to sweat profusely. A 'cob' is a general word meaning a small (roundish) lump of something: 'sweating cobs, cobbles'. Late nineteenth century

dale a valley. Old English *dael* from Scandinavian roots, including Old Norse *dalr* meaning something like 'a deep or low place'

Deputy an official working underground in a coal-mine charged with overseeing the safe operation of the work

dowly unwell. From Old Scots *dolly*, originally meaning miserable, doleful; origin uncertain

fell a hillside. Northern Middle English *fell* from the fourteenth century, Old Norse *fiall*, a mountain

femmer fragile, weak; sometimes 'fimmer'; also found in Scots with the meaning 'thin' or 'slender'. From Old Norse *fimr*, nimble

fettle to do, make, put in order. Perhaps from Old English *fetel* with the sense of 'gird up'

flit to move house. From Old English *fleotan*, to float; cf. Scandinavian words *flytja*, *flytta*

force a waterfall (also place-names: High Force, Fang*foss*, Wilber*foss*). From Old Norse *fors*

fore-elder(s) ancestor(s), parent(s). Old Norse *foreldrar*, ancestors

forkin robin an earwig. Cf. 'twitchbell', which is restricted to the north of the county (older Yorkshire dialect). One glossary claims Danish *orentvist*, earwig, as a related term

gallock-handed, golly-handed left-handed. Origin uncertain

galluses braces. Derived from 'gallowses' or gallows; Middle English *galwes*

gan, gannins-on to go, goings-on. Also in Northumbrian and Scots usage

gate a street. Found in Yorkshire street-names like Briggate, Kirkgate, Coppergate. Middle English *gat* (thirteenth century), from Old Norse *gata*

ghyll, gill a ravine. The word is found in place-names from the thirteenth century, in general use from the sixteenth. Old Norse *gil*, a ravine

jiggered exhausted, tired (perhaps euphemistic use for 'buggered')

jitty alley, path between houses. Origin unknown

laik, lake, laiking (out) to play (a game), playing: 'laikin' at taws up a ginnel': playing marbles up an alley. From Middle English *laike*, Old Norse *leikr*, to play. The verb 'laiking' is also used in some parts of Yorkshire to mean 'taking a day off work'. Also **laikins**, toys

loppy flea-ridden. Also noted in a 1950s glossary from near Sunderland

mafted hot. Origin uncertain

mardy moody, miserable. Dialectal term originally found in Nottinghamshire in the early twentieth century and used in dialogue by D. H. Lawrence in *Sons and Lovers*

midden a dungheap. Middle English *myddyng*, from Old Norse *mykidyngja*, a muckheap

mullock a mess, rubbish. Used by Chaucer (fourteenth century) and related to Old English *myl*, dust

mun must (verb); as in 'you mun do that'

nesh delicate, fragile, susceptible to cold. From Old English *hnesce*, tender

nithered cold. To 'nither' meant to 'abase' or 'oppress', from Old English *nitherian*; 'nithered with cold' first appears as a specific meaning in the nineteenth century

nobbut badly (of health) not too bad ('middling')

offcomeduns incomers, outsiders

Overman a senior official overseeing the workings of a colliery. A nineteenth-century mining glossary notes: 'an overman is almost invariably a man who has passed through all the gradations of pit work, from the trapper upwards, and who has been raised to his situation on account of his ability and steadiness. His wages in 1849 were 26s. to 28s. per week, with house, garden, and coals gratis.'

owt, nowt anything, nothing. Regional pronunciation of 'aught' and 'naught'. (In the Voices survey, Dot in Driffield says of herself: 'Ahm alwiz doin summat if it's awnly nowt')

oyl a hole: 'put wood in t'oyl' = shut the door

pick to have difficulty calving (of a cow)

pog, gyp-hog a flashy hooligan (contemporary usage, Hull)

reek a smell, smoke. Related to German *Rauch*, *riechen*

riding one of the three divisions (literally a third part) of Yorkshire. From Scandinavian root *thrithjungr*, a third part

rigg a ridge or spur. From Old English *hrycg*, Old Norse *hryggr*, a back or ridge

rive to split or tear apart. Northern Middle English *rive*, from Old Norse *rifa*; cf. Old Scots *ryve*, to tear in pieces

sannies sandshoes, plimsolls (modern usage)

scar a rocky outcrop. Old Norse *sker*, an isolated rock in the sea (cf. Scots 'skerry')

shocking, stitching old Yorkshire farming terms meaning, respectively, to make into a 'shock' or heap and to form land into ridges

sike like suchlike

sile down to rain heavily; originally meaning 'pour or strain milk through a sieve'. Fifteenth century, from the Scandinavian root *sila*

skopadiddle, skopadiggle a mischievous child (reported from Sheffield, 2005)

snap a snack, a worker's light meal. Used in this sense from the nineteenth century

snicket an alleyway, path between houses. Late nineteenth century, origin obscure

tenfoot, eightfoot alleyway, path between houses (Humberside usage)

thee, tha, thysen, thysel you, yourself. One Yorkshire glossary reports that 'thysen' is most widely found whereas 'thysel' is exclusively north Yorkshire

thrashing threshing

thwaite a settlement (found in place-names). From the Scandinavian root *thveit*, a piece of land

tranklements a kit of tools, necessary equipment (Sheffield usage, but also reported more widely)

tup a male sheep. Northern and Scottish usage for a ram. From the fourteenth century, origin disputed

twag, twagging to play truant (contemporary usage)

us our ('us lamp on us cap' – our lamps on our caps)

wal until; as in 'I'm working 9 wal 5'. From 'while'

wesleybob a Christmas tree bauble

whang to throw, hurl (especially Humberside usage). From the Old English *thwang*

wick alive. A northern variant of 'quick' in the sense of 'alive' or 'living'. From the mid eighteenth century

yam home ('ahm gawin' yam' – I'm going home)

yat hot

9 : CUMBRIA AND LIVERPOOL

Language in a Landscape 1: Under the Influence

This chapter is in one sense a bit of a cheat. Better to be upfront with it, I guess. Unlike most of the other subjects in this book, the two dialect areas in this section are linked not by geography or linguistic similarity, but by importance, singularity and the fact that the local speech of both Merseyside in west Lancashire and Cumbria are very much the result of outside influences. What's certain is that they are both hard to ignore – feisty, fun and inventive in the case of the dialect of Liverpool, known as Scouse; rich, historic and expressive in the instance of the vast Cumbrian region which stretches from the promontory of Barrow-in-Furness in the south right up to the Solway Firth. Both are highly distinctive, both started with Anglian Old English and subsequently underwent the powerful influence of the Norwegian raiders, who then settled along this coastal strip of north-west England. Both too have been influenced by the Irish and Welsh, and the Celtic flavour of some Cumbrian place-names is modern evidence of this.

Liverpudlian dialect – Scouse – is a particular brew of influences, with Irish being the most significant. As a seaport, however, with hundreds of years of trade (the notorious 'triangular trade' of sugar and slaves had Liverpool as one of its three ports of call), the city's talk has undergone influences from the Caribbean and Africa, from Asia and from Jewish settlers from many places. However, bringing the two extremes together within the same breath also serves to illustrate just how starkly British local talk can change within an hour's car journey. Thus, although Liverpool is part of Lancashire and has Lancastrian dialect as its bedrock, it sounds nothing like it. Scouse is another of those 'tip-up' dialects where almost every sentence ends with an upward inflexion (see the 'Sound of . . .' section in this chapter). Add to this the remarkable and unique breathiness – aspiration – that is part and parcel of the way a lot of Liverpool consonants are pronounced ('book' and 'chuck' are 'booch' and 'chooch', with a final sound like the one in Scots 'loch') and you have a complete linguistic one-off, very circumscribed and entire unto itself.

A quick belt up the M6 and you're in the heart of Cumbrian speech. This is predominantly a rural area that stretches from Barrow-in-Furness in the south, up through the Lake District, past Carlisle as far as the Solway Firth and the Scottish border, and the talk here, conversely, shows wide variations. In the south, in Barrow, there's a tinge of the dialects of the Wirral. In the country districts near Carlisle, the sounds take on a distinctly Scottish flavour.

So let's start with the map and some place-names. 'Liverpool' comes from Old English: it was indeed a 'pool' or tidal creek, and (according to one etymology at least) the 'liver' refers to the thick or silty water of that inlet – *lifrig* was Old English for 'clotted' or 'coagulated' and became *livered* in Middle English. It would seem distinctly plausible, glancing at the turbid waters of the Mersey today to believe that the city drew its name from a silty creek.

At the other extreme, you have Carlisle, the county town of Cumbria poised at the crossing point of the Solway and a caber's toss from the southern edge of Scotland. Carlisle's name is at least part Welsh in origin. The *car* is the giveaway, being the modern form of *caer*, city. Take another pair of towns in our region and the Old English consanguinity emerges more clearly: Workington in Cumbria (on that bump out into the sea that lies twenty miles west of Keswick) is where Voices spent some of its time canvassing contemporary Cumbrian speech, but its name has nothing to do with hard work. It's Old English again, referring to the '*tun*, or village, of Weorc's people'. Now, head south to the Mersey, and Birkenhead – that town on the south side of the Mersey tunnel that locals are so particular to distinguish from Liverpool – and you can feel the breath of Old English *bircen* (birch-tree) in 'the headland overgrown with birches'. I wonder how many birch-groves there are in Birkenhead today.

If the bedrock of this part of north-west England then is Old English, the Scandinavian influence is also strongly felt from the Wirral north. On the eastern seaboard of England it was the Danes who made all the running. On the west, however, from about the year 900 it was the Norwegians who came raiding. Their base was a Norse kingdom in Dublin, whence they attacked and subsequently populated the Lancastrian coast and beyond through Cumbria as far as the north shore of the Solway Firth. To this day, the dialect, particularly of the northern area of this region, is strongly influenced by these Scandinavian settlers. Professor Katie Wales of the University of Leeds explains what Cumbrian would have sounded like a thousand years ago:

> It would have been most likely to be a mixture of Old English or Anglo-Saxon, very much sounding like Old Norwegian or Old Icelandic, because of the Viking and Norwegian settlements that were happening in the north-west. It would also sound very northern, even lowland Scottish, because there was a distinct northern dialect by then. There would have been a very distinctive kind of speech spoken in Cumbria – a particularly interesting set of vowels that is still very strong in rural Cumberland today that were very much influenced by the Viking settlement, Norwegians particularly, like 'neet' for night (that you find in Scottish English), but also 'leek' for like.

Until his untimely death a few years ago, Dr William Rollinson was one of the greatest champions and chroniclers of the dialect of this part of England. He offered a sizeable list of words that had been brought in those Scandinavian vessels.

> There are a large number of dialect words which are in fact Norse: 'steen' – a stone; 'yek' for oak. And 'lake' – ' 'ast thou been laking now then?' – have you been playing? 'Gannen yem' (going home), that's again pure Norse. Oh there's scores of them. If you're darning and you get that hard skin on your hand it's a 'seg'; it's a pure Norse word *siggy* and it's exactly the same thing. You might think also of 'haver'; we used to eat 'haver bread' which is oat bread. A pure Norse word *hafre* meaning 'oats'. A good percentage of the dialect words are Old Norse and this reflects the fact that here in Cumbria we were colonized in the tenth century by people of Scandinavian extraction and they brought with them their language and that language remains today.

In fact there's a well-attested story about a young man called Harold Manning from the village of Flookburgh in the far south of Cumbria, a little east of Barrow-in-Furness, who found himself stationed in Iceland during the war. Manning, so the story goes, found himself able, by virtue of the wealth of Scandinavian terms still deeply embedded in his Cumbrian dialect, at least to make himself understood with the people there upon whom he was billeted. Similarly, Melvyn Bragg remembers a moment of great personal surprise when he once was on holiday in Norway. In the hotel bar, he overheard a sophisticated woman, sublimely fashionably dressed, saying something that sounded unmistakably like 'Aah's gaan yem [I'm going home].' It was a phrase which he'd last heard from the mouths of his childhood playmates in working-class Wigton just after the war:

> I looked round as if I'd gone back to Wigton, and the incongruity of this extraordinarily handsome woman speaking Wigton dialect was wonderful.

This north-western corner of England has constantly been open to outside influence. Celtic roots are found in a number of place-names: the element *blen* (originally Welsh *blaen*, a rocky peak) is found in a number of Cumbrian names like Blencarn and Blennerhasset, and the Celtic *pen*, a headland (cf. Chapter 1 on the Celtic influence on Cornish) is still recognizable in Penrith and Penruddock. Torpenhow, on the edge of the Lake District north of Bassenthwaite (and, in passing, note the Old Norse *thweit*, a meadow, cropping up here), has a mixture of Celtic (*tor* and *pen*) and Old English (*hoh*, a ridge or spur) and a thoroughly lofty-sounding melange meaning the 'top of the hill'. It's local pronunciation, incidentally, masks the etymology, being 'Trepenner'.

And just down the road from Torpenhow, you come to the little town of Ireby, where you can detect yet another outside influence, as Stanley Ellis of the Survey of English Dialects explains:

> [There are] place-names representing the settlement of not only Celts and Angles and Norwegians, but also the Irishmen who came over from Ireland with the Norwegians in the tenth century: Ireby, the Scandinavian *byr* or farmstead of the Irishmen [cf. Chapter 8, 'Yorkshire']. Cumbrians have Roman remains too at the northern boundary with Hadrian's Wall, though that's given little to the language.

The Celtic influence until recently had another very audible presence on the Cumbrian dialect landscape, though now it's in terminal decline if not completely extinct in practical terms. I'm talking about the vital business of counting sheep. Not to get to sleep, you understand, though maybe Cumbrian sheep-farmers once did deploy it in moments of insomnia. No, this is the genuine business of making sure that you'd not somehow lost a ewe or two across the fells. The old Cumbrian counting system was pure Celtic and went, one to ten: *yan, tan, tethera, methera, pimp, sethera, lethera, hovera, dovera, dik.*

A song written by two Lincolnshire men in the 1930s commemorated this old counting system, once found in fact in sheep-farming areas well beyond Cumbria. The chorus goes:

> Yan, tan, tethera, tethera, pethera, pimp.
> Yon owd yowe's far-welted, and this yowe's got a limp.
> Sethera, methera, hovera, and covera up to dik,
> Aye, we can deal wi' 'em all, and wheer's me crook and stick?

But a few years ago Mary, who farms sheep near Carlisle, told a language survey that although she knew the words, she would never in practice use them, and nor would her husband:

> I don't think it's used as much now. William thinks it's bad luck to count them actually. And sometimes if I'm having a count he'll say, 'No, divvent count them, it's bad loock!' You count seventy-five and maybe next day there is seventy-four because a sheep will come up and say, oh I think it's my turn to die today!

It's therefore a good old Cumbrian linguistic stew that's been brewed here over the past 1,200 years, merging many influences from overseas. And for real dialect aficionados, there's another component to add into the word-stock, one which comes directly from the geography of the area and the old drove-roads that crisscrossed it. Because buried deep in the traditional talk of the area are many traveller terms, from the old gypsy routes that were focused round horsefairs and horse-trading.

Melvyn Bragg, a native of Wigton, grew up with these words and can today still recite them with panache and ease – 'parne' for rain, 'gadgie' for a man, 'mort' for a woman, 'jewkell' for a dog, and many others. George, who's an old friend of Melvyn's from the town, told him for the

BBC series *The Routes of English* about how the words came to be so embedded in the local talk:

> [The horse-fairs are] long established so you're looking maybe at the mid-1800s. At that time obviously everybody was travelling by horse-drawn cart and horse anyway; it was not so much horse sales as a big gathering of gypsy and Romany families from all over the north of England, south-west Scotland, even Ireland. You combine that at Wigton with Appleby Fair, Rothsley Hill Fair which there was in those days, Brough Hill Fair and it was quite a good circuit for them, for late summer early autumn.

George who was a breeder of champion dogs used this Romany code as a way of making sure no-one else but his wife could understand his comments on fellow competitors. His son, though, confessed that while he'd heard his dad use the words and was thus vaguely familiar with them, he'd never bothered to learn and use them himself.

Here in the rural north-west, as in so many places in the United Kingdom, such linguistic evolution is well in train. As you'll see in the section devoted to the Voices Survey, rural Cumbrian is, while still vigorous, inevitably levelling out a bit; Scouse, on the other hand, as a very specialized urban dialect shows perhaps fewer signs of major change.

You can chart some of these developments through the many dialect recordings made over the past fifty years in this corner of Britain. It's been a favourite location for such study – something perhaps to do with remoteness and geography: cut-off valleys and ancient hill-farming communities have long been repositories for some of the oldest and most intense forms of local speech. In the early 1950s, the Survey of English Dialects, with Stanley Ellis wielding the microphone, talked to, amongst others, an elderly woman who'd worked on one of Cumbria's old estates a handful of miles from Gretna and the Scottish border. Ellis sets the scene:

> Locals will tell you that the area still in Cumbria but to the north of Carlisle has a bit of this and a bit of that in the talk, a hint of Scots and more than a hint of a north-eastern twang that slips along the valley of the south Tyne through Haltwhistle, brought along the good communications established along the military road, built from east to west to move troops to repulse the Scots.

The woman's performance was eccentric and somewhat histrionic by any standards and it's therefore not easy to judge quite how typical it was of the local talk even then. But, like so many of these fifty-year-old recordings, even when you've filtered out the disc crackles and poor quality of the tape, this example is so language-locked, so remote in its intonation patterns, local pronunciations and vocabulary, that it takes a deal of listening just to get the hang of what's being talked about. It doesn't help either that the subject matter is likewise pretty remote from most people's experience today. The talk was of her cows (she uses the Scots and northern English old plural 'kye', from Old English *cye*, plural of *cu*, cow), of milk and of making butter:

> Twelve kye . . . An' deese caouws were black caouws, an' we used to get to milk: they had grand paps . . .

She spoke about how 'We got a big tin for to go awee . . .' (the purposive formation 'for to' – 'in order to' – is a local feature of speech still very much alive in the 2004/5 survey) and about her 'doonkey to tek the milk to Netherby – a "jennet" they coll it.' 'Jennet' is an old word for a female donkey, rarely found outside the dictionary these days. The farmer also uses the old familiar 'thee' and 'thou' as well as the Cumbrian form of the verb 'to go', 'gan', that Melvyn Bragg remembers fondly; and her distinctive pronunciation of words like 'dozen' ('dizzen'), 'night' ('lass nayts cream') and 'pound' ('a poon o bootter') are very striking:

> When ah got the speeds [= paddles] an' ah clopped [= slapped] the bootter, layk that [slapping with her hands]. And then after thou'dd got ee', thou would mebbe get aboot that mooch bootter. No salt in, mind!

When she brews up she has to 'mash a coopa tay', and preparing her butter and other delicacies, she 'poot them on a pleit, an' ah med aboot a dizzen oot ont. For ti ha' for mi breakfasst [put them on a plate and I made about a dozen out of it. To have for my breakfast].'

Another speaker was a retired midwife, equally broad and difficult now for an outsider to understand. She spoke with a very clearly north Cumbrian accent – full of Scotticisms of both pronunciation and vocabulary – about the 'bairns' she had 'fetched into the world'. In many cases, her 'r' sounds are gently rolled (though sometimes strikingly *not* as in 'paats' – 'parts') and she uses forms such as 'wasna' for 'wasn't', 'canna' for 'can't', which recall Scots 'wasnae' and 'cannae' (see Chapter 12). She also says 'mind' when she means 'remember' – again Scots usage – but listen to her very distinctive pronunciation of numerals: 'ain' for 'one' (very Scots this), 'twee' for 'two' and 'thray' for 'three':

> Ah couldna tale ye how moonny a fetched in. Ahv gawn aa' paats of the world, fetched the bairrns into the worrld. Aye . . .

> ['I couldn't tell you how many I fetched in. I've gone all parts of the world, fetched the bairns into the world, yes'].

Stanley Ellis ponders her last delivery; a question she repeats and then answers:

> When was the lass [one] ah feshed into the worrld? Ah canna mind who was the lass woon [I can't remember who was the last one]. Ah have two in the toon, thray in the toon, no men an' ain lass [I have two in the town, three in the town, no men and one girl]. 'Er mother's been dead for fotty [forty] year. She'll be fotty-twee yer aal [forty-two years old]. She wasna twee till 'er mother . . . when she dayd, 'er mother dayd [She wasn't two when her mother . . . when she died, her mother died].

The woman has a beautifully gentle way of speaking, neither pure English nor Scots, but a blend that's particularly easy on the ear, with her softened consonants such as 'feshed' for 'fetched'. And again she uses distinctly Scottish words like 'ken' for 'know', and 'lassie' for 'girl'. In a way it all goes to intensify the sadness she evokes when talking of a baby who died before it could be delivered:

> Ah feshed four o' the lads into the world an' then ah feshed the lassie into the world. Ye ken soomthing? The bairn was haff weay cooming down. Ah could say what was the metter [I could see what was the matter]. Ah says: 'Well Ned! If thou 'ad sent for me when shay took baad ay would a coom.'

Thirty-five years later, Stanley Ellis returned to Cumbria and the differences were revealing. Horses on farms had completely disappeared and with them references to 'swingletrees' and 'thribtrees' (drawing gear for horses) and 'yams' and 'blinder-bridles'. The speakers Ellis selected to interview were again for the most part elderly with recollections stretching well back into that horse-shod, slower era. But the speech was already more open, less impenetrable, as always the result of more frequent contacts with a wider world, both in person and through radio and television. Here's John, an old sheep-farmer, recalling his schooldays:

> Ah can niver forgit when a fust started school. There was I with mi shorts an mi clogs, soom sandwiches an' tay [tea] in a tin bottle on mi back. 'Ee!' ah says, 'awer alld rehd coo kalld yesterday; a greet big red bool calf [Hey, I says, our old red cow calved yesterday; a great big red bull calf].' Na what she med of that ah daant knaa [now what she made of that I don't know], boot ah bet she wuz thinkin, 'Ahv got a reet woon here [I've got a right one here].' Brott intuh taan rayt off Carrick Fell [brought into town right off Carrick Fell].

Note the flattened 'ee' and 'i' sounds again – 'tay' for 'tea', 'rayt' for 'right'. This was also a time when it was still normal – and possible – to call a frog by a different name:

> Saw, soom taam letter [So, some time later] she wuz tekkin' oos for a naiture walk to let oos say [see] soom frogspawn. Well when we got dere, dere were the things 'oppin abaout an' she says, 'There: do you knaw what those are?' an' I said, 'Aye, they're *paddicks*.' She says, 'Naw, they're frogs.' I seays, 'They're nawt, they're *paddicks*.' There ah wuz, the better saad of five yerr odd an' tws te fust taam I knew the' colld 'em frogs! [There I was the better side of five years old and it was the first time I knew they called them frogs!].

Many of the people Stanley Ellis spoke to in Cumbria in the late 1980s were already speaking of incomers, radically changing communities and with regret about the loss of charming words like 'lobbilows' for flames that dance up a chimney. Yet as we've seen across the whole nation, sadness about lost ways is just part of the natural conservatism that seems to intensify with age, whatever generation is canvassed. The young, on the other hand, frequently take a much less melancholic approach. When, for example, a decade after those previous recordings were made in Cumbria, a group of very broadly accented sixth-formers from the area around Carlisle were asked how they thought their dialect might shift as they moved on into an adult world of social and geographic mobility, they were both realistic and fairly sanguine:

'You do have to adjust the way you speak when you talk to somebody. Like I went to Oxford to look round the university and I felt bad using my accent in a way because you feel you've got to talk more southern.'

'That's because nobody else talks Cumbrian down there, isn't it. It's just your surroundings, you are influenced by your surroundings.'

'And because you don't stay in the area like a lot of us will move away so we can't keep our accents.'

'You're mixing with people where you are and you've got to make it easier for people around you to understand. But I mean like my grandda he's never been anywhere; he's always been here and the people he talks to, they've always been here as well. So it's quite a deep-rooted community that does talk broad Cumbrian around here.'

'I think we'll always have Cumbrian underneath, we'll just adapt. But come back to Cumbria and you'll easily pick up the Cumbrian dialect because it's within you.'

Language in a Landscape 2: The Roots of Scouse

At the other extremity of the baggy area covered in this chapter lies the port of Liverpool. As a city dialect, Liverpudlian is far removed from the essentially rural tones of the countryside fifty miles to the north. But then again, as I said at the beginning, it's also very different from the speech of the urban Lancastrian hinterland that lies forty miles east along the M62. As a group of former Liverpool dockers explained to the Voices survey, the city's influences, cultural and linguistic, come from a different quarter altogether – from the west:

'It's not a typical Lancashire city like Manchester or Bolton. It's more cosmopolitan. Liverpool looks more to America and the Atlantic than inwards towards Lancashire: we are a different kind of city.'

'My mum's from Preston: her family couldn't understand what I was saying. A lot of our culture comes from America, being a port: the seamen bringing gear back from the United States. And we have the oldest Chinese community in Europe, Germans, Jews, etc.: we're cosmopolitan.'

And while the linguistic substrate may be Old English with a Lancastrian base, those influences, especially that of the many thousands of Irish who settled in the city in the mid nineteenth century at a time when it was in full expansion and growth, have given the language its completely unique character. (For a detailed analysis of the intonation and accent of Scouse, please refer to the 'Sound of . . .' section.)

Professor Loreto Todd of the University of Ulster at Coleraine is an Irishwoman and a linguist who's better placed than most to recognize the way speech patterns from across the Irish sea have influenced Scouse:

> I think the rhythms, the Irish intonation, are more up-and-down and I can hear it in Liverpool. It's exactly not the *same* as any Irish [accent] I'm familiar with but it's certainly got a lot of overtones.

During the potato famine of 1845 and later, a million Irish died and at least a further million sought refuge overseas, in America and across the short sea hop to Liverpool. The effect on Liverpool speech was enormous and lasting; it's one of the few instances in history, as commentators have observed, where a group of impoverished and uninfluential men and women have achieved such a significant effect upon a speech-community:

> But you have the intonation, you have the rhythms, you have the passionate love of words, you have the love of wit, and an awful lot of those Irish people arriving in the middle of the nineteenth century had nothing to live on but their wits. If they didn't use their wits, they died. With regard to some of the words, one of the ones I recognize very markedly as perhaps being influenced by Irish is 'yous', the plural. It's even more interesting because an awful lot of those poor Irish people would not in fact have spoken English when they came. That might account for the fact that you haven't got a huge number of Irish [Gaelic] words in Scouse.

Scouse is a local language that's shared by all the communities in the city, so in Toxteth, known almost equally well by its postal address,

'Liverpool 8', where many cultures find expression, the uniting factor is often that they all express themselves in this highly coloured and vigorous dialect. Voices spoke to Sylvia, Ishmael, Sarah, Winston and Laurence, a group of Liverpudlians with African and Caribbean ancestors. They consider themselves to be Scousers through and through. Sylvie was particularly vocal:

> 'How many generations of oos have to live ere before we're joost either British or even English? Once you're a pairson of colour, you're never joost "British", you're Black British. There are only five generations of black British in my family, but there are people in Liverpool 8 who've been here longer. And I consider my family to be a truly Scouse family. People came from other places to populate Liverpool: the Irish came in the 1840s, *after* my family. We're British and we're Scouse but we are the world in one place, it's Toxteth, Liverpool 8. There isn't another part of Liverpool can say that, and we should say it with pride because that's who we are.'

The pronunciation affirms it too. All members of the group have the hallmark vowels such as 'wairld' for 'world', the breathy aspiration that turns the 'vernacular' into the 'verna*ch*ular' and that upswing intonation that gives Scouse its rollercoaster swagger. You can hear more from Sylvie and her companions in the 'Snapshot' section later in this chapter. But as Loreto Todd points out, unearthing the source of contemporary Scouse can be a veritable piece of linguistic archaeology:

> As a port, Liverpool is almost like a linguistic stratification – you can take a look at the various levels, the native Lancastrian, the influx of the Irish, then the influence of the black communities, the influence of the Asian communities, the Chinese communities, all giving their taste as it were. And that's a feature, I suppose, of modern Britain.

And although most of the Irish who settled in the city were Catholics from the south, the language does bear some of the insignia of Northern Ireland English too:

> 'Dis' and 'dat' are a feature of the south of Ireland, not of the north, so obviously one recognizes that. But also where I come from in Northern Ireland people would tend to say 'durry [dairy] products' and

'furries [fairies]': 'There's a furry at the bottom o my garrden', that's very Belfast. [That] pronunciation 'durry' and 'furry' is quite similar to something you'd get here. So you get a type of amalgam, because it wasn't just southerners coming here it was people from all over Ireland.

The next section of this chapter, on the Voices survey of contemporary Liverpool and Cumbrian speech, goes into greater detail about the way twenty-first-century Scouse is evolving.

Oh, and finally in this (very brief) excursion into Merseyside, an explanation for the name Scouse itself. All the authoritative texts and experts affirm that it's an import too – another of these outside influences that I've been illustrating throughout the chapter. It's Norwegian, they say, from *labskause*, a sort of stew that's on sale today in Scandinavia. It was reportedly being served to inmates of the Liverpool workhouse in mid-Victorian times and I can tell you that its main ingredients are meat, veg and potatoes. I can even offer you a recipe featuring stewing steak and lamb's breast seasoned with Oxo cubes and Worcester sauce. But as to how this popular seaman's dish became *skause* and quite why the Liverpool sailors for whom it was a favourite dish became known as Scousers, there's less clarity. Suffice it to say that as assuredly as the stew stuck to the ribs of those Merseyside seamen, so the name stuck to the people of the city, and thence became the international signature for their unique way of speaking.

The Voices Survey: Local and Proud of It

Take a great loop across the north-west of England: from Workington on the Cumbrian coast, to inland Kirkoswald not far from Penrith, then down to Barrow-in-Furness at the bottom of the loop of land that protrudes into the Irish Sea and then hurry down across fifty more miles to the Mersey. There's one rallying cry that's heard loud and clear above the din of differences from the contributions to Voices 2004/5. It's the cry of local distinctiveness and a sense of injustice in the face of what the locals perceive as national prejudice.

Compare this affirmation from Ann in Workington:

'Way dawn't tawk Quain's English araound 'ere. Naow ahm praoud of the fact that the weay ah tawk is lawcal accent, it's from Wookkiton, an' ahm no' bothered abaout Quain's English. [Southerners] think we're rooff an' riddy, ye knaw; they think we're common fawk, an' we're joost the seeim as them – it's joost awer accents.'

And here's Nathan, a lad from Barrow-in-Furness, on the way he speaks:

'It's natural. It meks people 'oo they are: you've got your blood group, you've got your breain, but then you've got your accent; it makes a person ah think. If you change it you're not being yourself.'

And from Birkenhead, Leigh; same age group, broad Merseyside accent, but hates being thought of as a Scouser:

'We're not from there, we're sep'rate, we're from woon saad of the hwater, an' like the accen' 's different. I heht being compaired to a Scouser.'

To which Tamara, a feisty twenty-year-old from the same group, added:

'Representation for Scousers is tehrrible, I think. It's awful. Every taam I goe to London . . . I'm sorry, I've 'ad the joawk for years: "Oh, whezz mi bag; whezz mi mooney?" an' all of that – an' it's old naow. Oh my God! Makin' oos out to be barbarians an' stoof. But they've alsaw got a reputation, Scousers, of being able to laff at themselves, so I think it's okay.'

Even amongst the group of much older people from Kirkoswald, a picture-book village half a dozen miles north of Penrith, the octogenarian Nora, who spent some time in Surrey in her youth, is gently ribbed for her episode of 'southernness'. And these posh people, she adds, didn't understand her and 'didn't want to knaw. When you got amoong these posh people you had to speak very properly before they would acknowledge yer.' Her friend Les agrees, complaining about the way southerners never talk to you.

More than in any other region of England here in the north-west, there's a real sense of misrepresentation. The Liverpudlians Voices recorded speak loudly of their unique culture and sense of humour and hate the stereotyping that the media caricature of the tracksuited Scally has conferred on them. Ann from Workington – or 'Wookkiton' as she quite naturally calls her town – is fierce about the way people from all over try to impose their own speech on her, whether it's a former colleague from Scotland or people 'down south'. As she explains: 'It's amazin' how many people dawn't knaw where Coombria is. It's the forgotten county ah think.'

The Voices research, however, has thrown up some distinct differences from place to place. In general, the young people both on Merseyside and in Cumbria showed, typically, less affinity with and knowledge of the old dialect terms that, for example, William Rollinson collected in his authoritative dictionary of Cumbrian dialect. As usual, these go back into the horse era and are championed either by those who are language conservationists at heart, or who have little or no cause to converse with those beyond the locality. In urban Liverpool, on the other hand, the bonding quality of Scouse, bringing together the city's diverse cultures and backgrounds, gives the local talk real relevance. Likewise amongst the embattled former dockers, sacked ten years ago in an acrimonious and protracted strike, you sense that Scouse is a natural and very useful handrail through the many difficulties of their lives.

Nora from Kirkoswald has an abiding interest in and concern for the disappearance of local words and phrases; Ann from Workington naturally uses many local words and local syntax (she always uses the distinctive purposive 'for to' do something, for example). Yet neither of them – in fact no-one Voices met in Cumbria in 2004/5 – has the level of old, engrained local lore that a man like Tommy Miller could offer. Tommy, recorded in 1999, had, like Nora, a long memory. In fact they came from much the same generation – he was born just four years earlier. But listen to how Tommy Miller could use his dialect, naturally, unselfconsciously, as he talked about what he did – buy and sell ''osses' – horses.

> I used to tok [talk] to me hosses oll the taam: 'Coom on lass, Bess, get aout of that . . .' It was oll hosses, aye, wookin oll deay, laiyke. Drivin' an' buyin' 'osses oll the time: 'eavy 'osses, caat'osses, for these copperaytions [corporations] and brreweries an' oll that needed 'em, an' de big faam'osses an'at, ye knaw.

The Sound of the Mersey to the Solway

There are two very different soundscapes in this chapter, which I'll deal with separately.

The Cumbrian accent is itself quite diverse, reflecting the lengthy north–south spread of the region, so in the south, there are distinct flavours of neighbouring Lancashire and Merseyside, while the northern area around Penrith and the border has a distinct tinge of Scots. Here you find gently flapped 'r's and widespread use of pronunciations like 'couldna' and words like 'ken'. But throughout the area and almost drowning out such Scottish flavours are the signature features of more general northern English. For example, the 'u' sound that transforms 'luck' into 'look' (and that I have indicated throughout the transcriptions by 'oo'), and the sharpening of flat 'ay' sounds to more like 'eh' ('rake' becomes 'rehhk') and the short 'a' in 'baths' (rhymes with standard 'maths').

In the Workington recordings, though, some quite acute local features do crop up, so the town itself becomes 'Wookkiton', with a shortening of the 'er' sound in 'work'; likewise, 'worse' is 'wooss' (rhymes with standard 'puss'). The 'e' in words like 'never' and 'ever' is frequently shortened to 'nivver' and 'ivver' and in a similar change 'over' becomes 'ovver', while in the broadest speech

Tommy was speaking not at his broadest – he was poshing up a bit for the interviewer – yet notice how, within a year of the millennium, he would still say 'thray' for three and conjure up recollections of the back-end fairs of old in Wigton (Wickton, in his broad Cumbrian). Notice too how he rolls his 'r' gently – 'brreweries', 'Frriday':

> An then there wuz the big thray-days 'oss-sale at Wickton at back-ind, wi' the Frriday was oll the big seasoned 'osses were gitting sawld. Then there'd be the fust prize 'oss sawld, laiyke, an' everybody'd be asking owe mooch [how much] did the fust prize oss . . . ? Well mebbe i' was eighty guineas; tha' wuz a 'elluva price. Eighty guineas, soom brrewery mebbe baawtt [bought] it.

The only speaker amongst the Voices survey who could match Tommy for broadness of accent was Ann from Workington. She displays all sorts of fascinating regional characteristics: I've mentioned her use of 'for to'

you find 'till' being used to replace 'to', as in one speaker's sister who '. . . moved till Australia'.

Scouse on the other hand sounds pretty much like no other accent in the country. Its 'tune' rises at the end of sentences and phrases, it has a breathy aspirate quality that softens hard consonants (like 'k' and 'g') into floaty 'ch' (as in Scots 'loch'). Similarly 't' at the end of a word can drift off into a 'th' (fit becomes a bit like 'fith'). You'll hear many glottal stops, often in places where you rarely find them, like the signature tag 'la . . .' (from 'lad') and 'but' when used to, say, change the subject: 'Booh', on the other hand . . .'

As so frequently in regional accents, vowels play the musical chairs game, turning 'care' into 'cur' and 'burn' into 'bairn'. 'O' can open up to a harsh 'a' (horrible sounds more like 'harrible') and 'u' is famously 'yew' in the name of Liverpyule itself. 'R' is sounded quite markedly in some words – 'verbal' becomes 'vairrbal' – but very much not in places where, for instance, West Country speech would automatically place them: a Liverpudlian 'staatid' school at five, not 'starrted'.

Finally, there's a feature that not every Scouser has, but that sticks out a mile when they do, because it sounds as if they've had (not entirely successful) elocution lessons. It turns the 'o' vowel into 'eyo', so 'no phone' will sound like a posh 'neyo pheyone'.

to represent 'in order to', where in standard English 'to' would be adequate. Ann does it all the time: I noted in quick succession 'for to enter', 'for to do', 'for to use' and 'for to write'. But she also uses 'till' in place of 'to', just as the Irish do (see Chapter 11). Thus talking about fellow interviewee Harry, who comes from five miles up the coast, she says, ''Arry's from Dearham; 'Arry's got a different accent *till* oos.' And Harry does it too:

> 'They'll soomtaams git at me about maa accent; ah seay, '' 'Ave yer ever 'eard yusselves tawkin'?'' Poo' the readio awn [Put the radio on] an' listen *till* yer awn accent an' say [see] wha' iss liyke. You'll nivver ivver git me a cheinge ma accen'.'

Ann is middle-aged and twenty-five years younger than Harry, and yet she's certainly broader of accent, always says 'Wookkiton' for the town and 'wook' for the job, and often adds 'eh' as a tag. She responds to Harry's stout defence of his localness: 'They tawk down till you because soom of them, ah think, they think yerr mook oonder their faeet to be honest.'

The Workington group had some interesting local responses to the survey terms. To 'throw' for Ann is to 'scop' – 'we would ti say ti scop, boot a lot o' fawlk wouldn't knaw what to scop wooz reailly.' Lyn from Carlisle uses 'peelie-wallie' for 'unwell', a word that cropped up in Scots dialect in Edinburgh (see Chapter 12) with the same meaning ('Ah dawn't knaw if ah brought that with me from Carlisle boot ah often say "peelie-wallie"'). For to 'play', there was recognition of the old term most commonly found in Yorkshire, to 'laik', but the usual West Cumbrian word, particularly amongst children and young people, is to 'doss' or 'doss out': 'Are you dossin' out? – a lot of people use it; I don't like it but I use it as well' was one comment.

But the word that provokes the most amusement and comment amongst the group was Ann's pronunciation, as local as you like, of the common or garden 'worm'. It's 'woorrum', in two full syllables:

> 'Ah knaw when mi broother-in-law coom over from Australia we tried to learn 'im 'ow to say a "worm". 'Ow we seeay i' round 'ere, we seeay "woorrum". An' it were 'ilarious listenin' till 'im traaying to seeay this "woorrum". An' aye dawn't think 'e ever got if off right!'

Workington, once an industrial port with iron and steel at its heart, lies almost due east of Kirkoswald. But to reach K. O. (as the locals refer to it) you have to go the long way round the great massif of the Lakeland fells via Keswick and Penrith: Skiddaw is in the way. Nora, Maurice, Les and George, who met in Kirkoswald (it is pronounced 'K'*koz*wuld'), are mainly from farming backgrounds and are middle-aged to elderly. They enjoy a deal of banter and the conversation is constantly interrupted by jokes and consequent gales of laughter. In between these storms, though, a lot of older Cumbrian words tumble out – alongside the predictable 'beck' for stream, they offer a 'gutter' ('gootter' in their pronunciation). Not all agreed though, and this hierarchy seemed to settle it:

> 'Ah would joos caal it a "beck": you've gotta river, then you've gotta beck, then you've got a little stream then you've gotta "gootter".'

Nora mentioned in connection with streams the word 'dub': 'but it's more for a "pool" than running water,' she added. But this prompts recollections of a local pool called Black Dub and of a meadow called Wesh-Dub field:

> 'You weshed your clothes and hung them out to dry. And the
> "Wesh-Dub field" was where the waater was dammed oop to supply
> Gamblesby fields with waater.'

They remembered how 'brossen' used once to be a familiar local word signifying full up with food – 'fair brossen' was how they put it – and in the days when men still wore braces, for Les, George and Maurice, these were 'galluses'. Again this word was still around in Yorkshire twenty years ago but since has vanished along with the article it described. In the group's discussion of what they'd call clothes in general, you can detect that 'linguistic crossroads' quality that traditional Cumbrian possesses. Thus 'Ye'd nae claes awn [You'd no clothes on]' has a strong Scots flavour to it, but an accent that was definitively northern English.

Amongst other Voices terms, the K. O. group offered to 'hadder' for light rain and 'slattering down' for a downpour. And as often, the local word for left-handed produced yet another variant to add to what is a lengthy list: 'bang-handed':

> '[My uncle] used to work on the reilweays an 'e said that a
> bang-'anded fella got another penny an howur becoz 'e could
> shoovel opposite a right-'anded fella. So 'e was worth more.'

Down in the southernmost corner of Cumbria lies the county's biggest town, the industrial and shipbuilding centre of Barrow-in-Furness. There Voices met a group of largely young people, Nathan, Andrew, Clare and Lucy, and Jane, who was middle-aged. Their speech was typically urban and young with few regrets for old words lost, and plenty of relish for new terms, most of them the latest national standard vernaculars like 'minger' and 'munter'.

One of them did offer 'laik' for to play, the old northern word, and they managed to clock up another variant for left-handed too: alongside the regular 'cack-handed' one of them, Jane, mentioned 'caggy' as being her normal word: 'Ah've always been tawld I'm "caggy-'anded"; it's joos what mi moom an' dad always said.' Though, she added, 'they're from Liverpool'. In fact, the word that emerged from two of the groups Voices spoke to in the city – both the former dockers and the multicultural group from Toxteth – was not 'caggy' at all, but 'gammy' or 'gammy-handed'.

Perhaps predictably, the young people of Barrow had greatest variety of terms in the region for truanting: the commonest and most local was to 'jig' – 'jigging', but also the more general 'bunk off' and 'cop off' as well as the inevitable national standard slang, 'skive'. On the Mersey, while for Matt, Leigh, Nicky, Kayleigh, Steve and Tamara of Birkenhead College the norm was again the regulation 'skive' and 'bunk off', on the other hand, amongst the middle-aged ex-dockers the Lancastrian standard asserts itself, to 'sag' or 'sag off'.

But the youngsters from Barrow reserved their enthusiasm – and opprobrium – just as I've found in many places across the country, for the derided 'young person in cheap trendy clothes and jewellery', otherwise known as a 'chav':

'They're in caps and trackies, trackie-tops and tha', lots of bling, Del Boy jewellery. There're a lot down town outside McDonalds; "townies" is the same word, it's interchangeable. It's joost a trend, soombody's beamed them down.'

In Liverpool, of course, chavs have an identity all their own. They're 'scallies', short for 'scallywags'. They've become associated through TV comedy and other programmes with a clichéd image of the city of Liverpool. Unsurprisingly it's not an association the locals like to share: here are the dockers:

'Scallies: a gang o' scallies. Hangin' roun' the chippie, dressed in shell-suits – you'd say it's a gang o' scallies. They think everyone's a rogue and they're all wearing these hoods in the height of soommer.'

And the group from Birkenhead College offer a familiar refinement to the designer image: 'Lacoste trackies and Rockport boots . . .':

'Wears lots of sovereigns, loads of gould and kairly-pairm blonde 'air, orange soonbed skin and a fringe, lahk, thass bloo-dried tuh death . . . that's a scallee.'

'[They've got a] nassty accent we don't lahk, and they'll rip anywoon 'oo doosn't aidentify with them, 'oo isn't similar to them, 'oo doosn't dress just laik them: they'll try and kick off – they're lahk a plague.'

Graphic images these – curly-perm blonde hair, orange sunbed skin and a 'fringe that's blow-dried to death . . .' Worth noting here, too, some inimitable Liverpool pronunciations: extended and modified vowels in 'scally' and 'identify' which I've tried to indicate with 'ee' and 'ai' respectively; in each case, the vowel's lingered over slightly. But more significantly there's a fine example here of the Scouse pronunciation of the 'er' sound in 'curly' and 'perm', which as you can see is flattened to the open 'eh' sound in 'care' and 'pair' and comes out more like 'kairly pairm'. In the survey I noted 'Maïrsey [Mersey]', 'Baïrkenhead', 'thaïrteen', 'waïrd [word]', 'baïrd [bird]', 'skaïrts [skirts]', 'rehaïrsin' [rehearsing]' and many, many others – it's a routine pronunciation.

These young Birkenheaders are full of strong urban slang – 'buzzin'' for pleased alongside the regulation 'chuffed', but also another local expression: 'made up'; the Scouse dockers and the youngsters from Barrow had this one too. For attractive they came up with the completely unexceptional, 'sexy' and 'fit' and for unattractive 'pig' and 'a harrar [horror]' in the local pronunciation. But then came a fascinating piece of young inventiveness:

> 'We've got a code, the "petrol station code", so that if, like, there's a really fat oogly woman walking past, it's, like, "Look at the bargain bin over there", boot if there was soomwoon, like, amayyzin', it's, like, "Look at tha' super unleaded over there". An' then the gehrl, if she's too close an' can hear oos, doosn't know what we're talking about.'

The group of former dockers from Liverpool, two Johns, Mickey, Mark and Tony, were the broadest speakers Voices heard from in the city – their vowels were the most distinctive and they used more breathiness in their pronunciation. They lost their jobs in a protracted dispute in the 1990s and formed a solidarity group. When they talked about their love of their old job, they were at their broadest – 'dochers' ('ch' as in Scots 'loch') and 'sich [sick]'; notice how they also use 'made up' for pleased or happy:

> 'Ahm still sich over getting the sach: there was five hoondred dochers got the sach. Sich o' what happened, we're still sich ower i' although it was nyne years ago. Ah was mehd oop to work down the dochs, so

tha's what makes me sich, is the fact that I reely enjoyed mi job. The laff yer 'ad [the laugh you had] down there, the people you were with as mooch as the mooney you were airnin' makes you miss it an' makes me sich about losing mi job.'

These men say 'bevvied' for drunk (Tamara from the Birkenhead crew came up with a complete original here: 'malletted') and for that ubiquitous walkway beside a house, in Liverpool it's a 'jigger'. Trousers were 'keks' of course – pure Lancastrian – though given a Mersey 'ch' it came out as 'kechs':

'If ye wolked in Bairton's daouwn the rawd said, "Loochin' for a pair o' kechs", 'e'd say, "Awver there, meit". Knawwhat ah mean, layke.'

['If you walked into Burton's down the road and said, "Looking for a pair of keks", he'd say, "Over there, mate", know what I mean, like.']

But I couldn't leave this section without mentioning the Scouse tag, 'la'', short for lad. It's glued on to phrases, dropped into the middle of sentences, rather as elsewhere 'mate' sometimes is. 'La'' is pronounced with that trailing, hanging, slack-jawed sound that you often hear in Scouse speech that isn't quite a glottal stop because it's too breathy, but is something like. (It's a sound you also hear when a Liverpudlian begins a sentence with 'but' – impossible to represent on the page, but you get closest with 'booh'). The dockers, always happy to enjoy a bit of local rivalry, claim that the way you pronounce 'la'' was a north–south thing – north and south Liverpool, that is:

'We're from the North End, we're Northenders. And you got the Southenders and they used to say "law", "right law". It's instead of saying "lad". We northerners go "laa", they go "law". They have a different inflexion, a different way of saying the waird, you knaw. We're more sophisticated from the north, we coll 'em ' 'im' – hello 'im! And they [Southenders] always say we wear trainin' shoes with suits!'

A Scouse Snapshot: Liverpool 8 and Beyond

Getting to the heart of what constitutes a Liverpudlian always makes you something of a hostage to fortune, but two interviews by Voices offered some interesting clues.

Sylvia, Ishmael, Sarah, Winston and Laurence from the Toxteth area of the city, also well known by its postal address, Liverpool 8, gathered to talk about their inheritance as Liverpudlians of colour. First and foremost, they were, they asserted, Scousers – not 'black Scousers', simply Scousers: 'People are surprised that I speak English and that I've been here all my life,' commented Ismail, who often goes on holiday to visit relatives abroad; 'it's a big shoch [shock] when they hear me tawching [talking].'

All the reference points that this group offer are based in Liverpool – they may have cultural and linguistic features that originate within their ethnic community, but it's all filtered through – and contributes to – the complexity of the city's make-up. So Sarah and her companions remember with pleasure the very Liverpudlian experience of street-play in the heart of the city (and, incidentally, notice how Sarah uses the classic Liverpudlian pronunciation of the 'o' sound in 'rope', 'reope' – almost like over-elocuted RP):

'Thur were only about four people with cars in our street and the dockers would coom oop and give oos a reoupe [rope] so we'd 'ave the reoupe right achross the street and our mooms would tairn oop for oos; an' the little songs we 'ad that we used for playing . . .'

And Winston and Sylvia recall the games they loved:

' "Off-ground Tich" (tig), "Knock the Door – Dash": you knoch on soombody's door and then basically you dash! . . . Jacks and alleys, top and whip, "Stope the Pussy", "Stope the Boonny" [bunny], hide and seek – we were always out playin'.'

And the former dockers – the two Johns, Mickey, Mark and Tony – whose ages range from mid-forties to early sixties, recall a similarly street-level childhood. This is the older John:

'There was a huge square an' 600 families were round the square an' we used to be out for hours. You played things like "Tich" (tig), "Kick the Can", "Raaleo": these were chasing games. Kick the Can was the wairst woon. Before you could play ye ad to faind an aal can [find an old can], an aal beans can: there wasn't tha' many cans. An' you'd be there for bloody hours. In the end your moother used to coom an seay, "Geddup for your teay!" You didn't want to coom in.'

In both these illustrations, that Scouse 'ch' sound is very prominent, transforming 'tig' into 'tich'. Notice the pronunciation of 'old', which for the dockers is the distinctive 'aal': perhaps a note of Irish?

The group from Toxteth were very proud of their Liverpudlian roots, but Ismail and Winston were definite they wouldn't use the word 'la'' (lad) – it was just too, well, boring as a tag-word:

'I try not to use "la'" as in "lad".'
'Yeah, that is a bad one – it's either a "kid" or a "lad".'
'It's a Scouse waird; it's like sayin' "man" at the end [of a phrase] – "ey kid", "What are you doing kid?"'

And Sarah agrees, preferring 'love' as her tag, though acknowledging that it doesn't always go down well:

'I say "loov", boot soom people dawn't like it; I wouldn't say, "Hey", I say, "Excuse me, loov". Boot ah realize soom people dawn't like it. Even the customs officer in America I said that to and he said, "I'm not your loov, mam!" and I replied, "You should be so loochy [lucky], then!"'

Voices was interested to find out what the impact of the diverse cultures found in Toxteth is on the broader language. Laurence, whose family roots in Liverpool go back, he says, to the beginnings of the nineteenth century, leads the discussion, asserting that the influence doesn't stop at Liverpool but extends across the whole country:

'Obviously we're using English wairds boot we twist them and bend them. So [thanks in part, he says, to comedian Ali G] these wairds have started to become part of the vernachular of all British people. So for instance only certain people would have used the waird "fit" to describe a gairl who's attractive ten yehrs agoo but now it's a waird which is used almost by everybody. Boot then we 'ave wairds again [that are] particular to our community. So for instance if soomwoon was droonk we'd say "he's liquored". And there are lots of wairds like that.'

And some more of these often Afro-Caribbean terms emerged in response to the Survey questions, so for baby, amongst the normal range of terms, Winston suggested without prompting 'picknee', which Laurence explained came from 'pickaninny': 'That's Jamaican; it just means child. It's a word for a black child used by slavemasters.' For friend, where mate was the regulation term, Winston again added 'spar' and 'bredren'; words, they explained, that 'are used by the younger generation' – ' "bredren" [brethren] means "broother" '. 'The Africans always say "bra" [brother].'

'Duffy' (pronounced 'dooffy') was the suggested local word for unattractive or ugly, from the Jamaican 'duppy' meaning 'a ghost, like a spirit, an evil spirit in Jamaican . . .' And Laurence, when challenged whether these words had made it out of the cultures from which they sprang – like 'trun', which was proposed by Ismail for 'to throw' (along-side the inevitable 'chook') – insisted: 'The white people would under-stand it as well out on the street; the people you hang out with they would quickly grasp it.'

Amongst the dockers, there was little such richness beyond standard Scouse, though I was interested to hear the very strong stand they take on some linguistic matters over which other groups round the country have been much more relaxed. Take swearing, for instance: 'Builders use swear-words,' they claim, 'dochers don't. The older dochers were joost gentlemen an' I never 'eaird ma dad sweair.' I guess it is all relative, though, because this group were happy in the same breath to admit that dockers' language could none the less be pretty rough and ready at times:

'When we're talking we're very abrasive with eachoother an' soom aoutside pairson would think we're gonna kill eachoother each minute, you know 'ave a fight. Boot it's joost vairbal, [something] we've lairnt over the years. Liyke if you dawn't liyke Michey you "wanna smach 'im", liyke [Like if you don't like Mickey, you want to smack him, like]. I mean we've got this sort of insooltin' banter . . . It's Dockology; it's vairy aggressive, abrasive kinda language.'

Their explanation, which sounds pretty likely, lies in the aggressively male culture on the dockside:

> 'There's no women there an' young Andy [another docker] 'e said when 'e staatid 'ere, 'e was absolutely petrified the weay we spoke to eachoother. 'E said it was scairee, an' 'e meant i'. The inflexion cooms from the dochs: ye 'aff to be liyke that down there: if you're not gett'n skittered [ribbed] you're gett'n' left outh, if soomwoon's no' takin' the michey outta yuh.'

So although the intonation of Scouse speech has a natural drawl, there's nothing lacklustre about the linguistic landscape of this diverse city. Aggressive and full of sentiment by turns, spicy and sparky, and the whole under- and intercut with the laid-back sardonic wit that so often bubbles up in tightly bonded and often very poor communities, Scouse is not just one form of local speech but a whole world of tones and colourations: just take your pick. As the Liverpool 8 group concluded:

> 'You can't just speak the one language you speak so that you can entertain all people – we need to be more open and to communicate with people we know and people we don't know and that could be in English, that could be in Somali, that could be in Scouse: you just have to get what you want to say across to them in the best format.'

A Cumbrian and Scouse Glossary

The glossary is divided into two sections: where a word is shared by both Cumbrian and Liverpudlian speakers, I have listed it in either, but not both wordlists

bang-handed, caggy-handed, caggy, gammy-handed, gammy left-handed

barns children (Cumbrian usage); from Old English *bearn*; Old Norse *barn*

bevvied, bevied, malletted drunk. From 'bevie', 'bevvy' (slang: beverage); one glossary records this in British and American army use since late-Victorian times. 'Malletted', recorded in Liverpool/Birkenhead usage in Voices 2004/5, is probably a neologism (from 'mallet'), but note other similarly constructed terms for drunk, 'mangled', 'mashed' and 'massacred'

brossen full (to bursting, with food); 'fair brossen': full up (old Cumbrian usage). William Kendall's *Forness Word Book* of 1867 indicates the word then also meant 'cracked' – a split church bell was said to be 'brossen'. Also found in Lancashire glossaries (also with the meaning 'a fat person') and Yorkshire, where it can mean 'big-headed'; from *borsten*, obsolete past participle of 'to burst'

buzzin' pleased (contemporary Merseyside usage). Slang glossaries and web chatrooms have the term with the meaning 'great', 'excellent': 'one of Europe's most buzzing cities'. Recorded from 1990 onwards

charver a child (traveller talk used in Cumbria). From Romany root *chavo, chey, chiavei, chav*, a child; the dialect expression 'Deek at that charver lowpin' ower t'yat' means 'Look at that boy jumping over the gate'

cleg a horsefly (old Cumbrian usage). Also found in Scots; from Northern Middle English *clege* (fifteenth century) from Old Norse *kleggi*

coo, kye a cow, cows (old north Cumbrian usage). Also found in Scots: Old Scots *ky* (fourteenth century), Middle English *ki*, Old English *cye*, plural of *cu*, a cow

doss out play outside (contemporary Barrow-in-Furness usage)

dub a pond, pool (old Cumbrian usage). Also found in Scots. Perhaps from Low Countries root *dobbe*, a small, stagnant pool; cf. Irish *d'ob mire*, a stream, and Welsh *dwvr*, water

fluke a flat-fish, flounder (old Cumbrian usage). Also found in Scots. From Middle English *fluke* and Old English *floc*, Old Norse root *floke*

gadgie a man (traveller talk used in Cumbria). From Romany terms meaning a non-Roma man: *gadjo, gazhó, gajó*; plural *gadje*, feminine *gadji*

gae, gay, gey very (though one glossary insists '*not* "very" but "quite" '). Kendall offers the definition "considerable", as in "a gae lot", "a gae bit bigger". Seventeenth century

gan, gannen to go, going ('gaa'n yem': going home). Cf. Scots usage where *gan* is a variant of *gae*, to go. From Old English *gan*. Kendall's *Forness Word Book* (1867) lists various parts of the verb: 'ga', to go, 'gaan', going, 'gaes', goes and 'gaen', gone

gripe a three-pronged dung-fork (Cumbrian usage and more generally northern, and cf. Ulster 'grape' with the same meaning). Found in various forms as long ago as the fourteenth century

gutter small stream or trickle of water (Cumbria)

hadder to rain lightly: 'it's haddering'. The word is reported in north Cumbria and on the Isle of Man, though not throughout the region; variants include the noun 'haddy' (mist, noted in Douglas in 1661) and a 'haddery day', drizzly

haver, haver-bread oats, oat-bread (old Cumbrian usage). From Old Norse *hafre*, oats

jennet a small (female) donkey. Cf. 'jenny', an old usage found beyond Cumbria

jewkell a dog (traveller talk used in Cumbria)

jig, jigging to play truant (Cumbria). The word is also reported from Australia

keks, kecks trousers (Lancashire, Merseyside and more widely northern usage). Origin unknown

lake, laik to play. From Old English *lacan*, Old Norse *leika*, to play

lobbilows sparks, flames (spelling uncertain)

mooly beat up (traveller talk used in Cumbria, spelling uncertain)

narky miserable, moody (Barrow-in-Furness). From 'nark', an unpleasant person; late-Victorian usage

nash run (away) (old Cumbrian usage). From Romany term *nash*, early nineteenth century

paddick, puddock, paddock a frog, toad (old Cumbrian usage). From 'pad', a toad; originally from the twelfth century, from various root words, including Scandinavian *padda* and *padde*, a toad

paggered tired, exhausted (old Cumbrian usage). To **pagger** is to fight

pani, parney rain, water (traveller talk used in Cumbria). From Romany *pani*

peelie-wallie unwell, off-colour (Scots, nineteenth century). Imitative of a whining, feeble sound

pissymother a dandelion (old Cumbrian usage)

pumps light shoes, plimsolls. Origin obscure; the term is found throughout north-west England

scop to throw (Cumbrian usage, quoted in Workington in Voices 2004/5). Also reported as meaning 'catch'

slape slippery (Cumbrian usage). From Scandinavian roots *sleppa*, to become free, escape. Cf. Norwegian *sleip*, slippery

slatter to rain (heavily): 'it's slattering down'. Kendall's 1867 *Forness*

238

Word Book lists 'slatter' as meaning 'to spill water or slop', reporting a Scandinavian root word *sletta*, to dash. Other glossaries list **slattery** as 'showery'

sprag a chock of wood (e.g. used as a brake between the spokes of a wheel). Cumbrian but in wider use, of obscure origin, nineteenth century. Kendall records 'sprag' as a verb: 'to stop a wheel by inserting a chock between the spokes'. Origin obscure

stree straw (current Cumbrian farming dialect). Kendall lists it as 'streea', reflecting local pronunciation

swingletrees, thribtrees drawing gear for horses. Old agricultural terms in national use. Also **whippletrees**. 'Trees' were blocks of wood

till to: 'different till us'. Cumbrian usage (recorded by Voices in Workington 2004/5) and found in this sense also in Scots. From Old Norse *til*

yam home; cf. 'hyem' in Geordie dialect. Related to Scandinavian *hjem*

yan, tan, tethera, methera, pimp, sethera, lethera, hovera, dovera, dik cardinal numbers, one to ten, in Cumbrian dialect. Nineteenth century. There are many variants of this old Celtic-sourced counting system and versions are found well beyond Cumbria; cf. **ain, twee, thray**, one, two, three, recorded in north Cumbria by SED

yat a gate

yek an oak tree (old Cumbrian usage). John Brockett's *Glossary of North Country Words* (1846), which drew on several earlier source glossaries, records the term: 'he's as hard as yek and iron'. Cf. Old Swedish *ek*

Some Scouse words

bifter a cigarette. Liverpool usage from 1989, but also found more widely as equivalent of 'spliff'

bredren a friend (Afro-Caribbean usage found in Liverpool). From 'brethren' but used in the singular

docker's doorstep a big crusty piece of bread

duffy unattractive, ugly (Afro-Caribbean usage found in Liverpool). From *duppy*, West Indian term for a ghost or evil spirit: 'The Duppy is a West Indian ghost who can be summoned by a secret ritual to do the caller's bidding' is quoted in one source; eighteenth century

jigger, ennog an alley, pathway between houses

la' a lad (used as a tag-word, Liverpool usage)

Limey Lime Street (railway) station

liquored drunk (Afro-Caribbean usage, found in Liverpool). Cf. alternative spelling, 'likkered up', listed in one glossary

made up pleased

picknee a baby (Afro-Caribbean usage found in Liverpool). From 'pickaninny', a child, in turn from Spanish *pequeño*, small; e.g. 'me sistah-in-law what had a white picknee', mid-twentieth-century Guyanese text

sag, sag off to play truant (Liverpool usage)

scally, scallies scruffy or disreputable person. Now used as local equivalent to 'chav'. From 'scallywag'; origin obscure, but *scurryvaig*, a lout, may be related according to one glossary

Scouse the dialect of Liverpool and Merseyside. Mid twentieth century, from 'lobscouse', a fisherman's stew (first recorded in the early eighteenth century), probably related to Scandinavian, Low Country terms *labskause, lobskause*, a stew; 'lobscouser' is Victorian slang for a sailor

scran (pieces of) food (also listed in Cumbria and Scots). Obscure origin, perhaps related to Icelandic *skran*, rubbish

skitter to verbally abuse, to take the mickey (Liverpool usage)

trun to throw (Afro-Caribbean usage found in Liverpool). An anonymous West Indian carol entitled 'Never Throw a Lighted Lamp at Mother' is recorded with this verse:

Don't never trun rocks on yer mudder
Don't never trun rocks on her head
Don't never trun rocks on yer mudder
Trun bricks on yer fadder instead.

wack a Liverpudlian

whack, bang, chin, smack to hit something/someone hard

yous, yews you (plural)

IO : NORTHUMBRIA

Language in a Landscape: Miners and Marras

I think we Northumbrians have good reason to be proud that after
1,500 years or more we still have that half-wild exclamatory music of
the ancient Anglo-Saxon spirit in our speech: so intimate – crude, of
course, and forthright – but highly expressive.

Shortly before he died in 1985, Fred Reed, a proud Northumbrian, long
a pit-man from Ashington and one of the most distinguished poets
writing in regional vernacular, gave me this passionate affirmation of the
unique character of the speech of his homeland.

Of all the regions of England, it's this north-eastern corner, from
Middlesbrough as far as the Scottish border at Berwick, that's amongst
the richest and most complex in dialect. Here are ancient forms of the
language – the very first records of English were set down by the poet
Caedmon, writing in the local dialect of Old English in the seventh
century at Whitby and a few years later by Bede in his monastery at
Wearmouth and Jarrow in his translations of the Bible, his *Ecclesiastical
History of England* and his hymns.

Maybe it's this antiquity – and a proud Northumbrian is quick to
mention the venerable monk's name when reminding southern visitors
that Bede's is some of the earliest English we have – that puts a linguistic
spring in the step of north-easterners. Certainly this area's talk (and
especially that of the northern Northumbrian valley of the river Coquet,
pronounced '*Coke*-itt') was considered by Stanley Ellis of the Survey of
English Dialects (with superb partisanship) to be 'the loveliest language
to be heard anywhere in England'. A quick browse through the small
avalanche of dialect sites and wordlists that abound online these days

confirms that there is both a huge pride in the linguistic heritage of the north-east and an equally impressive appetite for it.

The trouble is that many if not most people who think 'Northumberland' think 'Geordie'. And of course in some ways they'd not be wrong. Geordie has been put firmly on the national map by popular TV dramas and films and perhaps more than anything else by the earthy humour of *Viz* magazine. A true local though will define the 'Geordie' area very precisely: the club comedian Bobby Hooper talked to Ellis about the exact meaning of the term back in 1983. For him 'Geordie' was broadly urban Tyneside – Newcastle, Jarrow, Hebburn, South Shields, stretching south through Gateshead to his own native Birtley. Much below that, you're approaching Sunderland and you're out of the purest Geordie into Wearside.

> If you take from Ashin'ton down to Durham which is basically the
> north-east, as yees well naah [as you well know], there's at least
> twelve different accents altogither. They vary from Ashin'ton where
> it's very Northumbrian down to Durham where it gets a bit softer. But
> everybody naas you come from the north-east with that accent.
> Anybody listenin' to us would seeay, 'He's a Geordie, hen.'

But true Geordie, Hooper maintained, actually stretches only a few miles north as far as the old pit country at Seaton Delaval. Beyond Seaton, reaching up to Fred Reed's native Ashington, is a very particular dialectal corner. Here the local pronunciation and vocabulary, although clearly from the same stock as pure Geordie, were heavily influenced by coal mining that for so many years was the lifeblood of the area. It's called 'Pitmatic'. I look at that in greater detail in the 'Snapshot' section, 'No Pit, No Pitmatic?'

Joan Beal, of the University of Sheffield, who has been leading an extensive research programme here and knows pretty well everything there is to know about Northumbrian speech, suggests that the misunderstandings about what is Geordie – or *who* are Geordies – are maybe not so surprising after all:

> 'Geordie' 's a term that really has two meanings. It can mean a person,
> and I think if you spoke to quite a lot of people round [Ashington],
> they would be quite happy to call themselves Geordies. I mean my

husband is from Guide Post which is another old pit village half-way
between here and Morpeth, and he is very proud of being a Geordie.
But on the other hand we tend to use the term 'Geordie' as a dialect
to refer to the urban dialect of Tyneside. But I think people down
south think people from Teesside are Geordies; they think anybody
north of Hull is a Geordie. But you do have very different dialect types
up here: this Northumbrian here does have very different
characteristics from the more urban Tyneside of Newcastle, North
Tyneside, Gateshead
and so on.

Whatever you call it though, the Old English that was spoken here –
known as Anglian – has bequeathed to modern Northumbrian and
Durham dialect a goodly stack of words and formations that can be
traced back to the earliest glimmerings of English in the region. 'The
original Northumbrians,' says Stanley Ellis, 'who were the descendants
of Anglian settlers – you've got to remember that you distinguish between
the Anglians and the Saxons – formed a sort of community out of which
came a lasting separate variety that existed within the area.' Joan Beal
quotes 'bairn' (child) and 'burn' (stream) as just two examples of those
direct descendants of original Anglian (northern) words. (Middle and then
Modern English were derived from West Saxon in southern England.)

And if you think that 'bairn' and 'burn' sound as much Scottish as
English, then you'd not be mistaken. Northumbrian Old English was
originally spoken from the River Humber right up to the Firth of Forth
– the political boundary is of relatively recent origin – and the dialect
here was even once referred to as 'English Scotch'.

In fact 'bairn' (in a plural form 'barnum') appears in one of the very
earliest Anglo-Saxon source texts that have come down to us from which
we can trace the connection with modern Northumbrian. It's the hymn
by the poet Caedmon, who was active in the mid seventh century. The
relevant verse reads in Anglian:

He aerist scop aelda *barnum*
heben til hrofe, haleg scepen;
tha middungeard moncynnæs uard,
eci dryctin, æfter tiadæ
firum foldu, frea allmectig.

He first created for the *children* of men
Heaven as a roof, the holy Creator,
Then Middle earth mankind's guardian,
The Eternal Lord afterwards made,
The earth for men, the Lord Almighty.

Beal says you can subsequently trace the route of this one word 'bairn' down to today via a sixteenth-century text featuring a character who's supposed to be a stereotypical Northumbrian for the Elizabethan reader:

> And again he uses this word 'barns', which probably at that time would have been pronounced 'bairns', and that picks him out to an Elizabethan London audience as a Northumbrian. So you can see little threads going right through the history, these isolated fragments of Northumbrian from the earlier times.

Local pronunciations, too, which often appear to stray a long way from the standard, also have deep linguistic roots. A Northumbrian may well pronounce 'house' as 'hoos' and 'down' as 'doon', a direct connection with the speech of 700 years ago. As Stanley Ellis says, 'Here they've hung on to the earlier "oo" sound "hoos", "doon" represented in the spelling of 1300.'

In fact, listening to some of the recordings made by Ellis in the 1950s and 1960s for the Survey of English Dialects, it's quite possible to think that you are quite literally listening to an ancient, very different tongue. At Wark near the Scottish border, an elderly man was interviewed whose speech is set so far back in the mouth that, even after repeated hearings, to the untutored ear only perhaps one word is comprehensible in each sentence, words which tumble out in a jerky stream. This recording is not far removed from the famous sketch from TV's *Fast Show* featuring an incomprehensible Geordie footballer. It's the language of the deep countryside and a deep past that has today certainly disappeared from most corners of the UK, with perhaps the exceptions of parts of Scotland and Northern Ireland.

The linguistic landscape of Northumberland is a little like a grassed-over ancient fortress – it doesn't take much excavation to reveal the basic structure of an ancient language tradition. And as throughout the UK, the map helps us to find our way down to the foundations. Newcastle upon Tyne is a post-Norman Conquest name that first appears in the twelfth century, when we find a note of 'Novum Castellum Super Tinam'. But most Northumbrian place-names are Anglo-Saxon in origin. Ashington, now bereft of its mining and searching hard to find a new role with its growing business park, was a 'valley overgrown with ash' to the earliest settlers (*aescen-denu*) while the market town of Morpeth a handful of miles to the west has a more sinister, though still Anglo-Saxon, origin, meaning 'murder-path' (*morth-paeth*).

Unlike counties further south, Northumberland and Tyneside show little of the Scandinavian influence that is for example scattered throughout Yorkshire: there are only eight places in Co. Durham whose names end with the Danish giveaway -*by* (village) and they are all in the south, while Northumberland counts no places at all with this formation. Linguists take this -*by* index as a sure-fire indicator of Scandinavian influence – or the lack of influence, as in the Northumbrian case. No, the names and the speech here come from Anglian-speaking peoples; though Joan Beal, linguistic archaeologist as she is, can point to occasional words with Danish roots like 'kist', a form of chest or box used in collieries by the Pit Deputy 'wherein he keeps his tools, play nails, brattive nails, etc', to quote a Victorian dialect dictionary. There's a slightly different form of kist on show at Woodhorn colliery, Ashington, that's now a museum of the industry:

> They have the 'kist' which seems to be the sort of desk that the foreman works at, and that's the Scandinavian form of chest. So you do get some Scandinavian words coming in, but fewer than you would in other parts of the country.

'Carrying coals to Newcastle . . .': the saying encapsulates Northumberland's industrial legacy. Yet today it's not mining but the shiny new constructions of Newcastle and Gateshead (such as the new 'winking' bridge and the Baltic and Sage arts venues) that are grabbing the headlines round here: millennium and post-millennium projects have blossomed.

It's a far cry from the poverty, unemployment and hunger marches (Jarrow lies four miles east of Newcastle city centre) – the stories of hardship and hard labour that were for so long the soundtrack of the north-east. The miners' strike of 1984 and its aftermath mean that no coal is fetched from below here. Yet fifty years ago, when the SED visited, the Northumberland and Durham coalfield was one of the UK's principal areas of coal production.

The villages still dot the landscape of course, their houses in tight ranks or 'raas [rows]', but the colliery winding gear is now dismantled, slagheaps greened over, the miners' institute just a social club full of memories. Strings of settlements running along the seams north and south of Newcastle bear names destined by geology for ever, it seemed, to be associated with coal and the men who worked it. Ashington I've referred to but also Cramlington, Bedlington, Ponteland, Guide Post, Seaton Delaval, Blyth and dozens more. Here were born the clichéd images of Northumberland, of whippets and pigeon-lofts and prize vegetables, the lot underscored by a rendition by brass band of 'Blaydon Races'.

This tiny strip of terrain between Ashington at the northern edge and Seaton Delaval in the south has long fascinated linguists, who have dubbed it the 'Pitmatic' area, where a very particular form of Northumbrian dialect throve in the dense clusters of mining communities. Fifty years ago, in the tiny area not much more than two miles square around Ashington you had pits at Woodhorn, Linton and Ellington to the north, Newbiggin and Lynemouth to the east by the coast, and at Ashington itself, with a further eleven immediately to the south. Little wonder these industrious villages bred a very individual vocabulary and accent.

This 'Pitmatic' – the name is said to come vaguely from 'mathematic' or 'automatic' – sprang from a life of shared existence, doing the same job, working in the same place, meeting the same people and suffering the same tough times. Look for a moment at the roll of honour for Woodhorn Colliery and note the thirteen who died in an underground explosion in 1916 which left thirty-four children fatherless. Such tragedies fix and shape societies – and the way they express them in words. 'It was almost manufactured to create the sorts of very tight social networks which tend to preserve traditional ways of speech,' says Joan Beal.

> In the pit village, the pit 'raas' meant that you necessarily lived next door to the people you worked with. You had the miners' social club so you socialized with the people you worked with and that tends to reinforce traditional values.

As I show elsewhere in this book, the tighter, more closed the community with fewer reasons and opportunities to travel beyond a very immediate vicinity, the more intensely local and individualized the language becomes.

The regular Northumbrian coal-cutter is universally known as a 'hewer', who was, as a mines inspector's report explained in 1894, 'the actual coal-digger. Whether the seam be so thin that he can hardly creep into it on hands and knees, or whether it be thick enough for him to stand upright, he is the responsible workman who loosens the coal from the bed.'

'Ah couldn't stan the oonderground. I couldn't stand crawling abawt the luoouw toonnels,' remembered Harry Grieves in 1983, recorded by Stanley Ellis in the heart of the Pitmatic area:

> Two yewers [hewers] in the faave-quaa'er [five-quarter] seam waw wawking at tha' taaim in pleeaices ah think it were two feet eeight haaigh [were working in places I think it were 2' 8" high]. There was a thin skin of water on the bottom suo that they wah lying on their siyde . . . which is wheeah the oould miyner's cracket cooms in. It was a pleein piece of wood with two sheeaipd legs so that the surface was at an angle and they could put thah head on that cracket, d'you see. An' then they could yew [hew] quite coomfortably.

To 'hew', incidentally, derives from the Old English *héawan* and originally meant 'to strike with a cutting weapon'; the hewer of *coal*, however, first puts in an appearance much later, in 1708. Notice in Harry's Pitmatic the typical stretched 'o' vowel, 'luoouw [low]' and 'suo [so]' – you can find more pronunciation details in the 'Sound of . . .' section of this chapter. His old miner's talk of a 'cracket' also amply demonstrates the way the words and the lives are woven into one single thread in these communities – the 'cracket' is an oblong rough miner's stool used down the pit, which subsequently found its way into every home in the area as a useful piece of furniture; unsurprisingly it's a word that's recorded in many period dialect wordlists from right across the region.

But besides the hewers with their crackets, there were dozens of separate jobs down a Northumbrian pit, from bottomers and buttockers, corvers and crutters to horse-fettlers (ostlers) and putters to wailers and trappers, these last being menial jobs done by boys. And then there was, of course, what became that time-honoured Geordieism, the 'marrow', or mate. Though today it's inescapably associated with the region, 'marrow' (or 'marra') is not purely Northumbrian in origin: Bishop Kennet of Peterborough, the author of an extensive collection of dialect words from across England, noted it in late seventeenth-century Yorkshire and Francis Grose's *Provincial Glossary* (1787) lists it in Somerset ('a companion'), while by 1849 a *Glossary of Terms used in the Coal Trade of Northumberland and Durham* defines the term as 'a partner'.

The Victorian era was the moment when the collection of regional forms of speech became a national obsession. Here as across Britain many hundreds of dialect terms were recorded in wordlists from all over Northumberland. Some are distinctly regional, others are found more widely. Many have come down to us in more general speech – 'bait' for example is the common word still for a worker's packed lunch here – but others, like their equivalents in farming, have been swept away as the industry has died and those tight working and living and talking relationships have been dispersed (see the 'Snapshot' section, 'No Pit, No Pitmatic?'). As Joan Beal describes:

> 'Bait' was the word that miners would use for the meal they took down the pit with them (your 'lunch' in the Lancashire coal pit, your 'snap' in the Yorkshire coalfield and so on – it's a different word in every coalfield), but round here it's the general word for the food that you take with you. I don't know to what extent young people talk about their 'marras'; they probably talk about their 'mates' now. But 'marra' is a word that can be used in any situation, outside of a pit. So some of the more generalized terms I think would carry on and find a home, but I think it's inevitable that very specialized words die out

– words like 'keeker' (a surface foreman) and 'kep-clack' (a particular type of valve) and the 'powder-reek', which was what smoke was called following a firing underground. These words have an uncertain present and an unlikely future. In the 1950s, when the SED came to the villages and the pits were working at full stretch, the conversation was thick with them: 'cavil' (pronounced 'kyevvl') for a working place in the mine selected by a draw and 'to howk' for punish were just two. 'Powder-reek' I heard still used by an old pitman in 2002, but it can't be long before to all intents and purposes its only life will be in old glossaries.

Other terms have found new energy away from the industry and are thriving – 'smart money' was originally compensation paid to disabled men and boys who couldn't work any more: five bob for the men, half a crown for the lads, as was explained to me. '*Smart* money' was thus (dark irony, this) money you hadn't actually had to work for. It's of course now a piece of normal vernacular right across the country. On the other hand, down in the detail of the tough lives lived in a mining household, other money-related words like the delightful term for savings – 'keepy-back' – are unlikely to live beyond the generation that needed them and can tell stories about them: like the one about a fellow miner from Newbiggin, 'and his wife, she never springcleaned, she never did nowt', went the old pit-man's tale. 'And he used to hide these "keepy-backs" under the stair carpet. Well, they went there one day and she had put the stair carpet up, and there was all these "keepy-backs". And he never got it!'

At a broader level, words like 'hoy' (throw) and 'dunch' (hit) are still alive and, well, kicking, locally amongst the older generation. For a number of years, cars in Newcastle were emblazoned with a proud sticker declaring 'Divvent dunch us, we're Geordies!', though as you can see in the next section, Voices found patchy evidence of many of these terms amongst today's young Tynesiders. At the grammatical level too there was little to show in the current survey – though its sample was very selective – for some of the more characteristic elements of Northumbrian speech. Joan Beal singled out the so-called 'double modal' construction in which two verbs like 'must' and 'can' (modal verbs) are used together as being unique in English dialect (though found in Scotland and America):

'I must shall come tomorrow' – that to most English speakers would seem very strange. I met a lady from Stakeford, another little former mining village, and I heard her say, 'But you must can do it' and this made me take a step back, but it's obvious when you think about it; you can see what it means: 'You must be able to do it'.

There is one feature of Northumbrian speech which is nationally known and parodied and yet which – perhaps because somehow it marks the speaker out as belonging to an older social arrangement characterized by the whippet-and-pigeon image – is losing ground fast. It's the so-called Northumbrian 'burr', the characteristic 'r' sound that is made at the back of the mouth and that's rather like a Frenchman's 'r'. Stanley Ellis maintains that you can go to Morpeth market and hear any number of people still using it, though Clive Upton of the Survey of Regional English at the University of Leeds is more sceptical. The contemporary evidence we have is thin, though an old pit-man recorded three or four years ago could still 'do it', although in his day-to-day speech he'd adopted the more standard national 'r' sound.

Back at the beginning of the eighteenth century on the other hand it was typical and used with pride. Daniel Defoe, immortal as the author of *Robinson Crusoe* but who also chronicled contemporary life in his *Tour thro' the whole Island of Great Britain* (1724–7) was the first to note the 'burr' in print:

> I must not quit Northumberland, without remarking that the Natives of this County, of the antient Race or Families, are distinguished by a *Shibboleth* upon their Tongues in pronouncing the Letter *R*, which they cannot utter without an hollow Jarring in the Throat, by which they are plainly known, as a Foreigner is in pronouncing the *Th*: this they call the *Northumberland R* or *Wharle*; and the Natives value themselves upon that Imperfection, because, forsooth, it shews the Antiquity of their Blood.

In the Survey of English Dialect material, largely gathered in the ten years from 1953 to 1963, the burr is still widely heard (though it's worth remembering that the sample was deliberately skewed towards older and rural speakers). A butcher talked lovingly about his slaughtering and curing procedures, which sometimes 'went Rang [wrong] . . .' He talked of how he 'gave it a Rubbin with salt . . .' and prepared 'spare Ribs'.

I've used a capital 'R' to indicate in my transcriptions this unusual sound for British English. Twenty or so years later, Bobby Hooper, a Geordie from Birtley, south of Newcastle, remembered being taken aback by the sound when he stopped his car to ask the way to a working men's club where he was due to perform:

> This delightful ol' chap was sittin' on the seat and I pulled up wi' the car, and opened the window. And 'e said, 'You gan doon the kRoo-ad.' He seays, 'Ye coom to a kReet big koose set back in tsaant Rees,' he said. 'Yuh canna missit, cos theer's a kReet big sayn oot theeah.' And ah honestly didn't knaw what he'd said. And I thought this is ridiculous: it's only twenty mile from where ah live.

In fact what the old man was telling Bobby to do was to 'go down the road; you come to great big house set back in its own trees. You can't miss it, because there's a great big sign out there.' Where the burr actually comes from is not clear. It may have originated in Scandinavia in common with the Parisian 'r'. What is certain is that people like the man Bobby Hooper encountered are thin on the ground today: an old miner who became a schoolteacher later in life told me he found it 'difficult to say now when you've been out of practice with it for years'.

Yet twenty years ago it was quite possible to find a number of speakers who still used it quite naturally. One was Bobby Thompson, who spent his early life in the shepherding fastnesses of the Northumbrian valleys but who subsequently became a champion horticulturalist with a busy diary of public speaking engagements. At High Spen in Co. Durham, he encountered a problem:

> Ah wuz just taakin to them at the Women's Institute the same as ah' dee anywar else and even theah wor finnden some of my wawdz difficult in north west DuRham.

'Dee' for 'do', 'finnden' for 'finding', 'wawdz' for 'words' and of course the 'burr' – these factors were impeding comprehension. In his Coquetdale fastness, only Bobby's immediate marras needed to understand him. Now he was ranging through the region making himself understood to a much wider set of people. It's the typical story of dialect change. When the message can't get through, you have to modify the medium to one both sides can understand. Linguists call it 'levelling'. But it isn't all one-way traffic, and as I show in the 'Snapshot' section in this chapter, new vernaculars are always ready to spring up wherever and whenever the need arises.

The Voices Survey: Urban Renewal

What's immediately striking about the recordings made in Newcastle and Wearside for Voices in 2004 is the change that appears to have taken place in the years since the BBC were last in the city making dialect recordings in 1983. As anyone knows who has been half aware of the news since the turn of the millennium, a huge programme of urban

The Sound of Northumbrian

You know you've arrived in a different linguistic land almost as soon as the great arch of Dobson and Stephenson's Central Station in Newcastle, opened to great pomp by Queen Victoria in 1850, hoves into view. As the train doors swing open, from the loudspeakers and the hubbub of voices swirling round the platform, there are the unmistakable peaks and troughs of Geordie talk. There's something about the sound of the speech from here that wants to raise a smile; what Stanley Ellis has called 'the unmistakable singing intonation of the Geordie'. It's rarely dull and uninflected – its playfully non-standard vowels ('oo' in words like 'house' – 'hoos') and well-known roster of endearing terms – 'marrer' for 'mate', 'hinny' for 'honey', 'divvent' for 'don't' and so on are now national favourites, propelled by TV dramas like *Auf Wiedersehen, Pet*. And the wisdom goes that the Newcastle accent shifts more products and is therefore much in demand for call-centres.

So what's the key to the Geordie magic? Actually I think a lot of it lies in the rhythm. Northumbrian speakers tend to sound rather jerky in their speech, with lots of glottal stops, in places where you'd not normally find them. Thus a Morpethian (from the market town of Morpeth) talking about the rich variety of local accents says: 'thah aul differen'' – 'they're all different' – but 'they're' is transformed into a very open 'ah' sound. Rather than eliding ('theyrall') as in standard speech, she then inserts a little hiccup stop in 'thah.aul'. The ubiquitous

renewal has been taking place in the conurbation that spreads along both banks of the Tyne and that is home to three quarters of a million people. To an extent the latest survey suggests that there's likewise been a degree of reconstruction in the language. Broad accents remain, but much of the old Geordie talk is being supplanted by a vigorous, but different blend of humorous metaphor and terms borrowed from other sources or adapted and made new on Tyneside.

The transformation seems vaguely in keeping with the city's recent metamorphosis from a heavy industrial manufacturing and processing centre to a modern thriving city of culture, the spick and span great Victorian municipal buildings newly polished up and neoclassical Grey Street, with its gentle curve and rows of corniced windows so loved by John Betjeman, claiming with some justification to be one of the most

open 'ah' (as also in 'wah' – 'were') also doesn't get modified – another surprise for the uninitiated, this – when followed by an 'r'. Let me explain. In Plymouth, the Hartley area of town would always have a resonant 'rr' sound ('Arrtlee'). New Hartley in Northumberland, by contrast, has a completely silent 'r', a very open 'a', something like 'haahtli' (and a clearly sounded 'h' into the bargain). Two ends of the country, one word and two completely different pronunciations.

Also adding to the jittery rhythm is the tendency to turn 'i' into a more indeterminate 'uh' sound at the end of words, so 'hewing' (cutting coal) can sound (like the first part of 'hue and cry' in RP) something like 'hewun'; likewise that Geordie standard-issue prop, the whippet, is a 'wipput'.

In Geordieland, too, the ayes have it. The word's used universally to replace 'yes' and the vowel, when found in other words, has a very rich, drawn-out quality, which I've indicated in the text by adding a 'y': 'thirteen miyle', 'biykah'. 'O' in 'go', 'so' and 'low' can, in some areas, be twisted into *three* sounds which start with an 'uoo' and drop lower to a sustained 'uhh' – sounds impossible? Listen to an old miner who talks about the cramped conditions: 'it was suoouh luoouh . . .'

This is classic Pitmatic – the dialect of the eastern mining area – now limited to the older generations who knew and lived the hewer's hard living. One final note: occasionally, my transcriptions of Pitmatic exceptionally feature a capital R. This is how I've chosen to notate the Northumbrian burr or uvular 'r', sadly now a truly endangered linguistic species (for details, see Language in a Landscape).

beautiful urban streets in Britain. It's canny nice. In fact, the favourite term of approbation found here is still 'canny'; it's the word that the Victorian local word-collector, Richard Oliver Heslop, described as 'an embodiment of all that is kindly, good, and gentle. The highest compliment that can be paid to any person is to say that he or she is "canny".'

If Newcastle – and the local pronunciation firmly puts the emphasis on a strong open short 'a', New*cassle* – or 'Toon' as it's often referred to, seems to be shaking off some of the pure Geordie that was fermented in the physical and linguistic closeness of factory or mine, that smiling up-and-down inflexion remains. As does the natural humour of the place, a great scatological urban humour, sharp and earthy. Not for nothing is this the place that created and has nurtured *Viz* magazine, in its own words 'a unique mix of rude comic strips, tasteless crap gags and muscular use of sexual swear words'. So the conversations that Voices captured from here – and to an extent from Wearside as well – reflect a pretty earthy attitude to swearing, to bodily functions and to day-to-day life that I heard rarely in other major provincial cities. 'You're about as much use as a one-legged man in an arse-kickin' competition!' was a fair example of the rough and ready wit Voices met here.

Gail, Paul, Ian and Loretta met to talk through their lives and their language in autumn 2004; they're young to middle-aged colleagues working in sales at a city firm. Their conversation was free-flowing and, alongside a ubiquitous readiness to say 'aye' rather than 'yes', consisted linguistically of a mix of the old local (fairly rare), the new national standards, like 'knackered' for tired or broken, and the frankly bawdy. Take this set of responses to the survey question about words for 'attractive': 'as smart as a carrot', 'classy bird', 'fit', 'she's worth a shag' and 'ah wouldn't mind shaggin' that'. The converse was equally rough: 'Ah wouldn't gaw out with a dirty bitch', 'I would kick her outta bed for fartin'', 'Looks awnly her mother would loov', 'She 'ad a face like a smacked arse' and 'I wouldn't crawl over you for him' were the insults on offer. And before anyone levels accusations of sexism against this group, the women were just as outspoken and quick with the dirty repartee as the men. For instance, 'beer-goggled' was an expression they produced for that inability to make sensible judgements about people that overtakes you when (to use their offerings for 'drunk') you're 'hammah'd [hammered]', 'mullered', 'mapped' (they wondered whether it came from 'off the map'), 'leathered' or, in one particularly colourful phrase, 'as happy as a dannsin' [dancing] tramp'.

This alcohol-induced short-sightedness produces its own set of measures of someone's (lack of) attractiveness: 'Men'll say "she's an eight-pinter" or a "ten-pinter".' And with this, Gail and Loretta burst into fits of giggles and the following anecdote:

> 'Like one of the lads ah work with – 'e wen' out, go' pissed, took this bird hawm. When he wawk oop [woke up] the nex' mornun she was that ooglee, he said: "Ah was gonna saw me ahm off rather than wake 'er oop!"'

Bar-talk prompted a torrent of hilarious but deeply scatological expressions for visiting the lavatory and defecating, starting with the pet dog:

'Mi usban when 'es teikin' Norman the whippet out says, "Ahm teikin'
'im down the Green for a "barry" ' and it means 'e's teikin 'im down
the Gracie Field for a Barry White – shite!'

'Drop the kids off at the pool', 'Mr Brown's knockin' at the window',
'the tortoise is poppin' 'is 'ead out' and 'touchin' cloth' were pure *Viz*
talk, but not entirely untypical of the conversations amongst the young
professionals Voices met. Compare this with the talk of a younger group
of students from Hebburn a little to the east and a mile from Jarrow. In
response to the Voices question about words for 'moody' this quintet
were able to offer the regional 'she's got a cob on' and 'mardy' (though
it wasn't a word the speaker would actually use herself – she'd had a
friend at school who was 'very local' she said, who used a lot of dialect
words. ' 'E's a mardy get', or ' 'E's a mardy beggar' would be her typical
comment). But the conversation then modulated into another of these
rather near-the-knuckle discussions comparing notes about vernacular
metaphors for menstruation, like 'on the rag', 'the painters are in', 'Liverpool are playing at home', 'I've got mi friend' and, with a groan of
disgust from the group, 'on the blob'.

'Mardy' was a familiar word in central Newcastle too – 'mardy arse':

'Mi moom would say "stop bein' a bloody mahdy ahse"; or "this kid's
whinged all day – he's a right mahdy arse!" '

Gail, brought up in the Pitmatic zone, is very attuned to the nuances of
regional speech and had several playful alternatives to 'mardy' or sulky:
'she's in one', 'she had her pet lip out', and, by extension, 'is your pet lip
out?'

Neither of these sets of interviewees from the Newcastle conurbation
was particularly broad, but all had a fair selection of words to hand that
appear in most contemporary glossaries of Geordie (the name may derive
from the local engineering giant of the steam age, George Stephenson).
So we had 'marra' for mate while for to throw all knew and used 'hoy':
'stop hoyin' stawns [stop throwing stones]', though with the reservation
that it was 'a bit common'; one of the Hebburn group agreed ('Mi mam
doesn't like me using "hoy" ') but proposed 'it's hoyin' it down' as regular
vernacular for a downpour. To 'hit hard' produced the standard 'smack'
and 'belt' but amongst the slightly older group also 'I'll bray yer – I'll

bray 'er arse' with the comment that 'that was quite common when ah was groawin' oop. If somebody got kicked in, in the village they got "brayed"; we still use that now.' Spin back forty-two years to a woman recorded by the SED in Medomsley, north of Consett on Wearside, and you hear her tell how when her teenage son misbehaved 'we neahly brayed the life out on 'im!' Little change there, then, though the accent was a lot broader four decades ago.

Regular favourites of the Voices survey that frequently throw up strong regional variation here gave, for truanting, 'playing the nick' and for to hit, the classic Geordie 'dunch'. Both Tyneside groups had these. Seeking a local vernacular equivalent for left-handed person brought almost complete unanimity amongst the groups on Tyneside and Wearside: the preferred term was 'cuddy-wifter'. In the words of a member of the Hartlepool and Sunderland groups: 'everybody that was left 'anded wuz a cuddy-wifter'.

But the term 'cuddy' sparked an interesting discussion amongst the Newcastle sales-people, who knew that in Pitmatic a 'cuddy' was a pit-pony: 'Ma grandad used to be a cooddy-keeper,' explained Gail, and suggested the following dialogue:

'What the hell are you puffin' and blaahin at?'
'Ahm not.'
'Tha's puffin' an blaahin' lak a brokkn-winded cooddy! [cuddy]'

Gail was full of colourful expressions that clearly sprang from her family background – she comes from Easington, whose colliery closed recently: 'I'd be brokkn off at the stock'n' tops,' she'd say if she was annoyed, to the complete bemusement of the others. And asked what word she'd use for someone whose name she'd forgotten, she recalled such lapses of memory in her Pitmatic-speaking father:

'When ah use' to coom 'ome from skouyl [school] an' ah use' to listen ti mi mam an' dad uf thehd bin reeidin' the peihpah [if they'd been reading the paper]: ' "Yee, ye nivver guess whee'ees deed [who's dead]?" "Who's that?" "Aw, man, ye narr [you know], aw man, what'sis neim again? Aw man ye narr man. She married 'im wi' woo'n leg [with the wooden leg], lived in Steiation Rawd [Station Road] bifor the war . . ." '

This strong echo of broad Pitmatic – Gail adopts the accent and inton-ation quite unselfconsciously – strikes an odd note amongst the rollicking modern talk of urban Newcastle.

From Hebburn, Voices heard those two local words with attested Anglian roots, 'bairn' (child) and 'burn' (stream), and several people from both Hartlepool and Newcastle offered the classic Geordie word 'bonny' as an alternative to attractive: it's surprising just how often the connections between Geordie dialect and Scots show up in the course of routine conversation. One quality I hadn't expected to hear in the dialect speech of this area is the use of an interpolated 'r' sound to link words. Cilla's 'lorra, lorra laffs' is a Lancastrian example, but several of those interviewed for Voices did it too. So we recorded: 'referring toorra wheel [referring to a wheel]' 'gerr'on the boos [get on the bus]' and in Middlesbrough 'a lorra people feel it' and 'norralf [not half]'.

On the other hand, I was expecting to hear many more instances than the single example recorded in the Voices survey of 'wor' – 'our' in Geordie – which cropped up in Hartlepool: 'We'll get wor glad rags on'.

The most vivid moments of these interviews came in reminiscences of youthful misbehaviour or close-run encounters with undesirables. Ian remembered a prank he and some marras used to play to upset people at a bus stop – and as he did so he grew broader in his speech by the second:

'A greeit geeim tha' we used to play when w' wu' kids, me an a frien' a mine: we woonce go' dressed oop as ooould women, pro'ah ooould women [proper old women] wi' joost the ooould gran's cawht [old gran's coat] on, an' round glaesses an' everythink. An' we'd stan' at the boos stop an' weeit [stand at the bus stop and wait] until everyone was reeady to gerr'on the boos [get on the bus].'

The scene is set, the boys at the bus stop, one dressed as an old woman. The fun's about to begin and Ian's about to drop a classic Geordie word completely uninvited into the story:

'An' we'd push the ooould woman – which would be mi meeit – ou' on' the road an' star' kick'n 'er head in. An' th' all ussd te coom roonin' affter oos [they all used to come running after us], this ooould gadgie [this old chap]. An' mi meeit was laffin soo mooch woonce, 'e go' caugh' by the gadgie. 'E picked 'im oop an' claoutid im roun' the eear [clouted him round the ear].'

'Gadgie' – a man, a bloke – is typical Geordie, though it is also found in Cumbria, a word borrowed from travellers' language. 'Radgie' (angry) and 'radged' were other words the Tynesiders came up with very readily: 'Ma moom would say, "radged as a broosh".' Together, 'radgie gadgie' is Newcastle slang for a madman, and is the name of a proprietary brand of beer.

'Radgie' might also be applied to the Geordie specimen of a pheno- menon that's walking the city streets of the UK at the moment. Call them 'chavs' or 'trevs' or 'pikeys', 'townies' in the north-west, 'Trobos' in Wiltshire: they are, as the Voices survey succinctly puts it, 'young people in cheap and trendy clothes'. The Hebburn students knew what we were talking about:

'somebody with a quite broad accent, really nasal, hanging around
street corners, maybe with a bottle of cider, slightly interesting
bleached hair, in a tracksuit and swearing quite a lot.'

These, to a Geordie, are 'charvers' and usually to be avoided unless you're looking for trouble.

The final word in this section goes not to a Geordie at all, but to an incomer. One of the many correspondents to the Voices project is Liz, a southerner, who wrote to tell her story of arriving in Northumberland to do telephone nursing for the NHS: 'I thought', she wrote, 'I was fairly fluent in Geordie until I started to discuss health matters.' Of the many words that flummoxed her and that are by her evidence still in regular and normal service in this most lively of linguistic areas are: 'starving' for cold (also common in Yorkshire), 'clamming' for hungry or thirsty, 'cockly' meaning nauseous, 'shabby', not very well, 'putting' (throbbing), 'parky' (fussy about food), 'kite' (your belly), 'spelks' (splinters) and 'blebs' for blisters. All but one of these appear in Heslop's *Glossary*, which he compiled nearly a century and a quarter ago. Geordie is even today indeed a most resilient dialect.

A Northumbrian Snapshot: No Pit, No Pitmatic?

Fifty or more years ago when the Survey of English Dialects reported from Northumberland, that cluster of eastern pit-villages north of New-castle were still hard at work fetching tons of coal from below. Dozens of shafts and galleries, thousands of men engaged in hewing to fuel the nation's hearths and power stations. Today, all are closed. Ellington, the last mine in the area, suffered a catastrophic inrush of water in January 2005 and that was it: the final shift had been worked; 340 men and women lost their jobs. It was the end of Northumberland mining; but was it also the end of Pitmatic?

In the summer of 1953, Stanley Ellis came to the very same Ellington colliery and recorded the voice of an old miner speaking Northumberland Pitmatic. The recording is remarkable as, with the recent closure, it now offers us a complete life cycle of Ellington: the man had been there when mining began forty years earlier, leaving his agricultural life to go underground:

> Ah keim off the faahm an ah wen' down the colliery when it was jiss startun, aweeiy from bank, seeiy, to sink the shafft, y'seeiy.

His flat 'a' sounds – 'keim [came]', 'aweeiy [away]', and lengthened 'ee' in 'seeiy [see]' are typical, as is the drop-away of the -ing in 'starting' ('startun'). 'Bank' is pit-talk for the surface. This man was headed straight underground.

> Boot anybody goon doon the pits naoow, the pit's there, y'seeiy. Ye dooan g'straight on tuh cooal feeice. Y'ad to knock aboot an' get use' to woon thing an' another.

He tells of how pit-men have to serve a sort of period of acclimatization ('y'ad to knock aboot') before going to the face. Long 'oo' replaces 'ou' ('aboot' not 'about', and in the next clip, 'Roond' not 'round'); 'going down' becomes simply two syllables, 'goon doon', and open 'o' in 'don't' and 'coal' has the typical flattening to 'dooan', 'cooal'.

> Boot thev go' liyke tRainin' school for byes naouw liyke a tRainin masster an 'i teiks them aal Roond an they get aal instrooctions what's

best fuh saifety and everything else, naouw. Boot they didn't at that partic'lar tame. You wen' doon the pit.

Here's that vanishing feature, the Northumbrian burr (see the 'Sound of . . .' section) – 'tRainin' [training]', 'all Roond [all round]'. The combination of burr and skewed vowels ('boys' becomes fairly and squarely 'byes' and 'time' sounds exactly like 'tame') makes this Pitmatic difficult to follow for the outsider.

In 2001 I asked a trio of schoolboys from two miles away at Ashington whether they knew what was meant by 'bank': ' "bank" as in where you put your money,' was the almost inevitable reply. These three lads had grown up in the area since the miners' strike and the closure of most of the Northumberland pits. Now the Pitmatic with its 'bank' and its 'cavils' – the quarterly lottery for your hewing pitch that was such a determinant in how much you'd make, depending on the richness of the seam – only dwelt in the memories of the retired and laid-off pit-men and in the glossaries. Here's one, the Pitmatic speaker Raymond Reed, son of the poet Fred Reed, recorded at the same time as the lads:

> Ah wuz brote oop [brought up] in a mining cooltchah [culture]: mi faathuh wawked at the pit, mi ooncles an' mi coosins, and everything in this toon rivuhlvd [revolved] aroond the pits; not joost the pits themseeilves but aal the welfare, the sportun facilities, and even one of the picture-hooses was caalld 'Tha Miyners', affter the pitmun.

Twenty years earlier, but critically just before the axe finally fell following the 1984 strike, Harry Grieves told Stanley Ellis in his broad Pitmatic of just how the closeness of these communities bred the very specific and individual patterns of speech:

> Every pleeace was different to every body else. We wah very inwaahrd-looking. Even in two villages like Sea'on Delaval and New Haah'ley [New Hartley] which aah vuhtually woon pleeace; there was a connecting street of houses. If you coom from New Haah'ley you weren't at hoom in Sea'on Delaval. If you belong' to Sea'on Delaval, you wur a streinger visiting New Haah'ley, yuh see. And we knew wheh a man keim from because of his accent.

It's a view that Kathleen from nearby Morpeth thoroughly endorsed: 'Pitmatic's Pitmatic and Geordie's Geordie and Morpeethian's Morpeethian and thah aul differen'.' Mark from Ashington, in 2001 a schoolboy on the verge of making his way out into a much wider and more mobile world, is aware of the rapidly changing speech of this corner of England. He knows that, though he uses plenty of local phrases ('canny nice' is a favourite), he doesn't speak Pitmatic and he's a lot less broad than previous generations:

A lot of the awldah generation, a lot of mah rela'ives, speak like tha'. And you ten' to pick oop odd words off theihm. Boot, ovahrall, things have cheinged a bit and naouw a lot of pe'ple my eige are star'n' a speak maw cleeahly withou' as much of an accent; as things like the industries are cheingin', as you ha' to communicate with different pe'ple in other paahts of the coon'ry, an' still meik yourself un'ahstood.

In fact, Mark and his companions, brothers Dean and Adam, were very broad speakers indeed when the BBC interviewed them, Adam particularly so. He was the youngest and one of a group of lads who didn't care overmuch about what people thought about how they spoke, ''cos like if w'with muh mehts, we understand each other like tha', arr'aye' [all right], so, y'knaa, if I say "now we're gan oot" [going – gannin' – out], y'knaa what I mean.'

Adam's speech, with its rapid-fire delivery, switchback intonation, words slurred together and tic-like tags: 'y'knaa' [you know]' and 'arr'aye' [all right]' is certainly broad. Like that of the old miner recorded in Ellington fifty years before, you'd really find his talk difficult to follow if you weren't a member of his speech-club. Or gang:

If thah's won Ashah and a loa' of Staeekies, you knaa y'wan' to get rannin' [if there's one Asher and a load of Stakies, you know you want to get running], because basically we divven' [don't] liyke each other! Diffrun' liyke, y'knaa. Yaahr either a Staaekie or you're an Ashah, rund heeah.

And, with his talk of bitter rivalry between 'Ashers', the Ashington gang, and 'Stakies' from Stakeford just down the road, you can sense a not too dissimilar dynamic at work here to that which produced the richness of

Pitmatic. It's different, but it's very real. For those who've moved on, like Gail from Easington (see 'Miners and Marras'), Pitmatic may now be little more than a memory of her parents; there may indeed be some degree of 'levelling' of the accent varieties, as the loss of the industries that nurtured them swept away the reasons to be different. Yet certainly within small speech groups, and in school where the need to open a linguistic window on many other worlds is yet to come, in this language-saturated corner of Britain local speech is certainly thriving.

A Northumbrian Glossary

Terms that derive specifically from the mining industry are marked 'Pitmatic'

aye yes. There are many suggested sources for this widespread northern and Scottish usage: a variant of 'I (assent)', or an alteration of Middle English *yai* or *ayye* or *yea* or even a version of an expression of admiration as in Old English *ei*

bairn a child. Originally Old English *bearn*, the word remains part of Northumbrian and Scots usage (see text) in various forms. **With barne** is a mid fifteenth century expression

bait a snack (Pitmatic); 'food taken by a pitman to his work' (Victorian mining glossary). From Icelandic *beita*, Old Norse *beit* and Old English *bat*, food

bank the surface (in a pit); 'at bank', on the surface (Pitmatic). Old English *banke*, a hill

blebs blisters, bubbles in glass. Recorded in several regional glossaries for more than 400 years; variant of 'blob'

bray to hit, beat, as in the expression 'I'll bray yer arse'. Also found in Cumbria often historically 'to beat to a powder', as to 'bray spice' in a mortar

burn a stream. From Middle English *burne*, Old English *burna*, a brook or stream

canny nice, good. In widespread use as an intensifier: 'a canny wad' is a hefty sum; 'canny nice' is also heard. In printed records for more than 350 years as 'cunning' or 'shrewd'; origin obscure

charver, chava Geordie term for a trendy guy with attitude. From the Romany root *chavo, chey, chiavei, chav*, a child

cockly nauseous

cracket a (three-legged) stool, originally an oblong rough stool-like contrivance that allowed a hewer to rest or support himself in a low working (Pitmatic); also *crecket, creckit, cricket.* Found in texts from the seventeenth century; origin obscure

cuddy in Northumberland and Wearside dialects, a horse, especially a pit-pony; also donkey (cf. Scots *cuddy,* diminutive of *cudyuch,* an ass, a small, strong horse)

cuddy-wifter a left-handed person. According to one record, 'cuddy-*handed*' found north of the River Tyne, 'cuddy-*wifted*' to the south

cush, cushty excellent, 'cool'. Geordie slang from Romany sources *kushto*

divvent don't. Geordie usage, widespread in region. 'Divvent dee that' – don't do that

dunch, dunsh to hit, thump, bump, jog with the elbow. Found in English from the thirteenth century; origin obscure, but perhaps onomatopoeic; cf. similar usage in Scots

gadgie a man. From Romany terms, meaning a non-Roma man: *gadjo, gazhó, gajó*; plural *gadje,* feminine *gadji*

gan, gannin to go, going; (especially) Geordie usage, as in the famous song 'Blaydon Races' (1862), the chorus of which begins 'Oh, my lads, you should have seen us *gannin'.* Dialectal form of to 'go'. *Ray's Collection of English Words. Not Generally Used* (1674) records *gang;* cf. Scots usage where *gan* is a variant of *gae,* to go

Geordie a Tynesider, inhabitant of Newcastle upon Tyne (see text); also the dialect of Tyneside. Origin disputed, but the most likely source is from mining: 'Geordie' is a local familiar form of George and was the term given by Northumbrian pit-men to George Stephenson's *Geordie* miner's lamp.

hew, hewer to cut coal, a miner. From Old English *héawan,* to strike with a cutting weapon

hinny a honey: a term of endearment ('my honey')

hoy to throw. Recorded in Victorian wordlists, and later Scots usage. Perhaps from *hoise*

hyem home. Scandinavian origin, cf. Cumbrian dialect *yam,* home

keeker a mining supervisor checking the quality of coal sent to **bank** (q.v.) (Pitmatic). Recorded in Victorian Northumbrian dialect

keepy-back savings (Pitmatic)

kist a Pit Deputy's desk, or chest, in which tools and records were kept (Pitmatic). Formerly 'chest': 'the reliks kyst' (fifteenth century). From Old Norse *kista*, Old English *cist*, a chest or coffin

kite the belly. Widespread northern usage recorded in Ray's 1674 *Glossary*

mackem: a native of Sunderland. Perhaps from a local shipbuilding saying: 'We mackem, ye tackem' – 'We make them, you take them'

mardy moody, miserable. Dialectal term originally found in Nottinghamshire in early twentieth century and used in dialogue by D. H. Lawrence in *Sons and Lovers*

marra a mate, friend (= 'marrow'); especially in Northumbrian pits (Pitmatic). Originally 'one of a pair'. Etymology uncertain, possibly from Old English *mearu*, *maro* or Old Icelandic *margr*, friendly

netty a toilet. Early nineteenth century, origin uncertain, possibly from 'necessary'

Pitmatic a dialect of English used in the pit villages of eastern Northumberland. Formation after 'mathematic' and 'automatic'

pit-yakka an underground worker, hewer (Pitmatic). 'Yakka' is Australian slang for 'work'

proggie mat a Northumberland or Durham miner's home-made domestic mat, made from short strips of cloth pushed through hessian with a *progger* (Pitmatic). From *prog*, to prick or pierce (seventeenth century)

put to throb or palpitate. Noted in the 1880s by R. O. Heslop in his local newspaper articles

raas the rows (of houses in a (pit-)village). The specific meaning and spelling with 'a' is noted in the mid fifteenth century: 'the este [east] rawe' (Pitmatic)

radgy, radgie mad, angry. Of Romany origin

smart money money paid to disabled miners (Pitmatic)

spelk a splinter. From Old English *spelc*, chip, splinter

tab a cigarette. Originally a 1930s term, but still widely used, recorded by Voices in 2004

II : NORTHERN IRELAND

Language in a Landscape: Plantation to Peacetalks

Nothing is quite what it seems in Northern Ireland. The waters of the River Bann flow peacefully under the arches of the old bridge at Portadown. An occasional fisherman checks his line, adjusts the set of his rod. Along the banks of the Bann, fishermen, strollers, pause to sit awhile and watch the swirl of the water. Two hundred yards away a northern sun casts milky shadows across the broad expanse of the high street, relatively empty today – it's not market day – and not so very different, as someone once remarked, from the centre of a town in the Lake District or Scottish Borders with its widely set houses and individual shops.

There's something eerily normal about the place. And normal it is – except it isn't, because this is Portadown, and Portadown means centuries of bitter and bloody history. In 1641 a band of Protestants were driven off the bridge here as revenge for previous massacres and were drowned in this same innocent Bann; just round the corner lies Garvaghy Road – *the* Garvaghy Road, stuff of stand-offs and Orange marches and hate and headlines about Drumcree. These places have a *history*.

Now Portadown's teenagers exchange notes on the best places to hook up and have a good time in the place they call 'Porty' – a good time being downing large quantities of 'Buckie' (Buckfast tonic wine), indulging in minor illegal substances and chilling with their mates, somewhere they're not going to be attacked by the local hard nuts. And one of the best hook-up places apart from the local park is, after nightfall, precisely here on the tranquil banks of the Bann. Or not. 'Get a life! Get a train to Belfast instead!' writes one to an internet chatroom. 'This is Portadown – the home for losers!' responds another.

The fact is that in this beautiful province of the United Kingdom, the outsider has to tread very carefully. Here close reading of the places is essential – you need special tools and can assume nothing. Only perhaps in Northern Ireland does the director of an arts centre – an arts centre, note – have to make a point of saying (as he did once to me in Portadown) that visiting creatives must 'check their sectarian associations at the door'.

Commentators like the writer and broadcaster Gerry Anderson have long remarked upon the fact that nothing here is quite as it seems. Hosting his daily talk show on BBC Radio Foyle in Londonderry, Anderson has evolved his own compromise euphemism for the city he loves – 'Stroke City'. Nothing to do with sudden illness, this, though. Neither Derry (the old Irish name, from *doire*, a grove of oak-trees) nor *London*derry, which it became after the so-called Plantation of Ulster (the settling of many thousands of people from the British mainland in the seventeenth century) will do for an impartial broadcaster. So for Anderson, Derry/Londonderry or 'Derry-stroke-Londonderry' was a neat solution to the partisanship that either individual name suggested on its own. And it wasn't long before 'Stroke City' took wing as a useful and safe nickname. As Anderson has written:

> Northern Ireland is a small country and many people don't like each other. We sense that we are different from other nationalities in that we may be unable to forgive each other for what we have done to ourselves.

The many paradoxes and contradictions that abound here lead to a note of irony that pervades every utterance; there's also a level of savage humour that combines the charm of the south with a sharp blast of northern toughness to produce a hilarious and sour undercurrent. In 1985, Stanley Ellis, veteran of the Survey of English Dialects, came to Belfast for the BBC to listen to the 'craic', pronounced 'crack', of the city. Craic is what everyone enjoys in Ireland: great conversation, banter and gossip, often consumed along with quantities of alcohol; though none of that was in evidence when he met a young schoolboy, Geoffrey. Geoffrey's classic joke epitomizes the mix of dark humour and language that runs like twined threads through the province. Did you hear the one about the little boy sitting on the bridge crying his eyes out? A man goes up to the boy, taps him on the shoulder, asks what the matter is:

An' the wee boy says, 'well, ah've droppt mi meiyt; 's in the revver [river].

Horror! The man takes off his hat and coat and jumps in the water to rescue the young lad's mate, but:

' 'Scuse me, ah can't feind yer wee frieynd [Excuse me, I can't find your little friend].' The wee boy starts to laugh. The maan says, 'Whadd arr ye laughin' at?' He says, 'It's nawt mi frieynd; ah said it's mi *meiyt*.'

And here comes the linguistic punchline:

'Nawt mi meiyt as in "huyman" [not my mate as in "human"],' he says, 'it's the meiyt outta mi sandwich! [it's the meat out of my sandwich]'

The key to the daft schoolboy joke is the fact that here in Belfast 'mate' and 'meat' are homophones – that's to say they're pronounced identically, something like 'meiyt' (see 'The Sound of . . .' section). Jokes like this are harmless fun, but they demonstrate a consciousness of language and a pleasure in playing with it – young Geoffrey's delight as he told the gag was infectious – that pervades this part of the UK. The reason lies in the region's history.

'I think it was Northern Ireland poet Tom Paulin who said that when you look at a language you can see all sorts of layers and interactions and so on,' says the linguist Professor Loreto Todd of the University of Ulster at Coleraine, herself a native of Coalisland, County Tyrone:

and if you think in terms of Northern Ireland and just go back a thousand years, you've got the Gaelic [Irish] speakers from Northern Ireland interacting with the Gaelic speakers from Scotland, interacting with the Viking settlers who came, interacting with the Lowland Scots who came, interacting with the English who came and with the Welsh, and although that type of composite exists in other parts of the world it's not quite that particular mixture. So in a way Northern Ireland is unique.

A thousand years ago, the indigenous language of the north would, according to Professor Todd, have been basically Irish Gaelic. Yet the proximity of the north of Ireland to the Scottish mainland – a mere sixteen miles at its closest point – means that Scotland has always had a powerful influence on the way the people here speak:

> The link between Northern Ireland and Scotland has existed certainly for 1,500 years, and was quite strong even a thousand years ago. So the people in Northern Ireland, in Derry for example, would if they had been contacted by Highlanders or Islanders have been able to understand them. There were differences of course, but there would have been inter-intelligibility between the two. So the link with Scotland has always been very strong.

Now add to the melting-pot the English of the settlers – the legions of Planters as they were called, many from Scotland, but also from all over England – who were granted land in the north. They became the landlords, often the absentee landlords, of vast swathes of the country in the sixteenth and seventeenth centuries, and in this systematic settlement, or 'Plantation', of foreign nationals Ulster is unique: the only place to be colonized within Europe.

As so often, the names – of people and places – give a clue to the history. Thus many towns like Portadown and nearby Armagh have names derived from Irish origins – Portadown was *Port an Dúnáin*, Harbour of the Fortress, in Irish, and Armagh *Ard Mhacha*, Macha's Height. Yet just down the road are Stewartstown and Cookstown, their Scottish or English Planter origins plain for all to see. (Not so evident, perhaps though, when subjected to the vagaries of the local pronunciation: not 'Stewarts-town' and 'Cooks-town', said one indignant interviewee for the Voices survey of the spreading modern pronunciation, but 'the weay the lawcals seaiy the pleice neimes: *Stewston* an' *Cuckston*'.)

The land is drenched in Irish *and* English blood, and massacres like that at Portadown and the brutal 'putting down' of rebellions was for long a familiar tale of distress. Take for example this report by one of the English commanders in Ulster, Sir Arthur Chichester, in May 1601:

> We have killed, burnt and spoiled all along the lough within four miles of Dungannon, from whence we returned hither yesterday, in which journeys we have killed above one hundred people of all sorts, besides such as were burnt, how many I know not. We spare none of what quality or sex soever, and it hath bred much terror in the people.

When the outsider despairs of the way Ulster politicians of all colours refer to history that is in many cases 300 and 400 years past as if it were in living memory, a quick study of the brutalities visited upon those who lived and settled in this land goes some way to explain why. The hurt lives on. It's interesting that in the Voices survey, one of the most fruitful areas of enquiry was equivalents for to hit hard – words like 'slinge', 'dunt', 'blatter', 'blarge', 'clash' ('ah'll gi' ye a clash'), 'scally' ('gi' hem a scally in the lug [ear]') and 'dunter', not to mention a 'steimisher' (spelling very approximate here), as in the expression 'I gave him a *quare steimisher* at the Turnip Fair.'

When Stanley Ellis came to Belfast in the 1980s, fighting talk was also a constant in his conversations: young Elaine told the story about a clash she'd had with her twenty-year-old brother. 'Fayt' and 'rayt' are her strongly urban Belfast pronunciations of 'fight' and 'right':

> Whan me an' ma braa fayt we really fayt. Rayt? He's twenty; near tar th' neck o' me th'aw week [near tore the neck off me the other week]. Ah had 'em by the hair an' he was chewin' at ma nack [neck]. Mi ma [mum] near keilld the two of us . . .

The punch-up ended with Elaine's mother clocking her son over the head with a plate. Not funny, though Elaine none the less had a dark Belfast chuckle as she recalled the incident.

There are places throughout the world where language is a weapon in a struggle for superiority – the Walloons and the Flemish in Belgium, to take one familiar continental example. In Northern Ireland, the linguistic battle lines are differently drawn: here are hair-trigger sensibilities about shades of meaning within one language, English. It's a place of nuance in which political statements are a high art form of leaving unsaid the real meaning, where the explicit is so often a red-herring, when a community stand-off is defined by terminology – so many of the sticking points of the Good Friday Agreement have been interpretations of words, after all (what exactly does 'beyond use' mean?). Language is one of the most effective weapons in the struggle as it doesn't, at least at a superficial level, cost lives. Yet which language, where it comes from and who speaks it is – unsurprisingly in this country where nothing is quite what it seems – a complex and tangled story.

Although, as we've said, there are three discrete sources for the amalgam of Northern Irish English, Professor Todd emphasizes that it would be foolish to think of them as being separate entities. Gaelic speakers have long integrated with English speakers, producing what's known as 'Hiberno-English', carrying over into English their Gaelic sound patterns, their idioms, their rhythms and their pronunciations. Likewise, words that originated in Scotland are deeply embedded in the talk of more or less everyone:

> The three communities have lived together, not always in harmony, but they have lived together for three hundred plus years, and so they have rubbed off on each other. I mean the 'wee' that you hear for 'small' which if you like many people think of as Ulster Scots – everybody in Northern Ireland uses that, so it's not just the Ulster Scots who have it: I couldn't live without having 'wee', it's part of my ideolect [personal language style].

Listening to samples taken in the very recent past in 2004 and 2005, it's quite astonishing to a non-native speaker just how rich and varied the talk is in the six counties. Perhaps it's because this is still predominantly a rural area. Sure there are factories and highways, but the repeated images of the Falls Road and the Shankill and the rest over the years have maybe conveyed an erroneous sense of ubiquitous urban grit. In fact in the green of field and hill – old Planter castles and ancient Irish forts nestling in woods, the Mourne Mountains in the south and out west the Sperrins and the loughs of Fermanagh – the deep rural still predominates. This too is a land of great family dynasties, of clans – and clannishness: another spur to dialect survival. As I've found repeatedly throughout the UK, the wider the dialogue with the outside world, the less it's possible to adhere to a resolutely local vocabulary, pronunciation and syntax. You have only to compare the speech of the 88-year-old resident of Rathlin Island off the Antrim coast who's never left with that of his daughter, thirty years a nurse in Belfast. The old man retains his strong local accent and range of dialect terms while his daughter's English is much closer to the standard, albeit accented.

So although there's been a lot of stirring of the regional language melting pot over the centuries, intense pockets of sharp difference do remain. What often surprises the newcomer to regional speech here is that these are not particularly marked along sectarian lines. Both Unionist and Republican share more or less the same ranges of vocabulary and, with tiny, barely detectable details (like the way the letter 'h' is pronounced), the same accent.

Some recent research in Derry does suggest that the Protestant community may be acquiring aspects of Belfast pronunciation in a few of its vowel sounds and this could be due to some form of solidarity or alignment. On the other hand it's just as likely to be the result of exposure to particular TV and radio programmes. Gerry Anderson maintains that he simply can't determine the background of the many working-class callers to his local radio programme in 'Stroke City', though he says he hears amongst the more middle-class listeners distinct anglicisms that only Protestants would be likely to use.

> Middle class Catholics tend to use the same vocabulary as working class Catholics but middle class Protestants tend to use words like 'colleague' and describe something as being 'fun' that you wouldn't hear middle class Catholics use. It's as if middle class Protestants are looking towards England for their reference points, whereas middle class Catholics don't tend to do that.

But these tiny shades of difference aside, the major distinctions here come from the national origins – Irish Gaelic areas along the border are rich in Hiberno-English with syntactical elements and a colourful use of language drawn from the indigenous language. Take this anecdote recorded around the turn of the millennium by a Londonderry woman, though she was born in County Galway:

> A honeymoon couple had moved in next door to us and my friend Kathleen used to say she was 'broke to the bone' – very, very embarrassed – by the antics that she witnessed in the neighbour's garden as the young bride rushed through the garden gate to greet her husband when he came home in the evening. And then she said, 'She'd be as wrapped around him like a wet flag *till* a pole!' And I don't think you can get any closer than that, you know.

Then there are localities where even the briefest of samples gives off a strong scent of Scotland across the water: 'When ah wuz a weiyn [wain = child]' is the habitual opening to reminiscences here. Scottish people settled in the north of Ireland in huge numbers, says Loreto Todd, from the sixteenth and seventeenth centuries on, 'and they brought with them their Lowland Scots, which is still a feature of quite a number of areas in Northern Ireland'. The specific dialect known as Ulster Scots – you can sample numerous examples of it in the 'Voices' section of this chapter – is a variety over which people are still divided. There are many who maintain that it has sufficient unique characteristics to qualify as a separate language, though there are many others who disagree.

Of the three major influences on the development of regional speech here, only the English – RP English – rarely puts in an appearance, at least in the sound of the dialect. But in this clan territory the language-origin detector has another very simple tool up his or her sleeve: your name. You just have to know the key – as the Tyrone native and expert on the language of Northern Ireland, Loreto Todd, does:

> You can tell the aboriginal Irish in names like O'Neill, O'Connell, O'Donnell, McGuire, that sort of thing. You can tell the Highlanders in names like Macdonald, Macdougall, Macduff, and the Lowland Scots in the Paisleys or the Stuarts. There are hundreds of these Lowland Scottish families around. English settlers bear names like Church or Dudley or Ellis or Upton or many, many names like that. And you can get little Viking remnants, a name like McKettrick, which sounds so Irish but is actually Mac Hetric – Citric – 'son of Citric'. Often they're hidden, and as you start excavating and taking away the layers, you begin to see that each of these communities has added to what I would regard as a unique amalgam.

It's a shame that the Survey of English Dialects of the 1950s and 1960s never attempted such an excavation of Northern Ireland. There are of course less systematic, historical wordlists of local terminology here and there, but one of the most interesting that's worth spending a moment to look at was drawn up in the very earliest days of the Victorian era's fascination with regional English.

Its author, William Lutton, was born in 1807 and was a man of some culture, having studied medicine in Paris before changing career to that of highway surveyor working alongside bands of Irish 'navigators' or navvies constructing the Great Northern Railway. Lutton compiled in 1840 an extensive lexicon of nearly one thousand terms he had collected in his native area north of Portadown in the boggy area near Lough Neagh known as the Montiaghs.

In his 'Montiaghisms' very local words jostle shoulder to shoulder with more widespread Ulster terms, many of them now lost altogether in the course of the 160 years separating his book and today's Voices survey, not least because the agricultural methods from which they sprang have vanished with mechanization. (How many farmers, I wonder, still speak of *clokes*: 'those grains of wheat which, after winnowing, retain the husk'?) In fact, already by 1924 the editor of the second edition was moved to remark that 'numerous entries [are] not now in use [and] some have even passed from recollection'.

However, *blairney* is there, recorded as 'frothy conversation; ridiculous nonsense', *brae* as a 'steep hill' and to *clout* as 'a blow struck upon the head with the unclenched hand' (common enough today across the whole of Britain, but none the less also cited for Voices by speakers at Kilwaughter as local vernacular). Lutton also lists the word *quare* (we also heard that in Kilwaughter) and *daunder* (to walk about slowly and idly; to saunter) much as young people in Belfast today say they're 'daundering about'.

He has country words like *loanin* (a narrow lane leading to fields or private dwellings; a bye road), and *smurr* for 'a small rain', which turned up in the latest survey too. Similarly in Armagh, Voices, surveying in 2004, found the word *grape* (a three-pronged dung fork) not so very far from where Lutton recorded it 160 years ago. Today it's cited as part of a farmer's colourful expression to encourage slackers:

'If ye werren't warrking harrd enough he wud turrn rynd un seiy ti ye
[If you weren't working hard enough he would turn round and say to
you], "Put a bit morre nya greipe, ye boye yuh [Put a bit more in your
grape you boy, you]", meanin' wurrk a wee bit harrder, ye knaw.
"Grape" – it's a dung forrk. I doan know anny otherr neim furrit!
[I don't know any other name for it]'

Contrast, incidentally, the Ulster 'grape' with the Cumbrian 'gripe' (also meaning a three-pronged fork), which youngsters near Carlisle were still familiar with at the new millennium.

But perhaps the most attractive language to be found in Lutton's fascinating list is in some of the turns of phrase rather than single words: thus under 'h' he records:

> *hear my ears*: ' "I can't hear my ears", is an exclamation frequently uttered when a number of sounds makes it impossible to hear any one thing distinctly.'
> *heart-scald*: 'that which causes grief or uneasiness of mind; anything vexatious.'
> *heel o' the evenin'*: 'the latter part of the evening twilight just before night sets in.'

Coming much more up to date, Stanley Ellis tackled an overview of *urban* Ulster speech in Belfast in 1985. Belfast is a modern city more fought over than most in the UK. For as long as most people can remember, the accents of politicians from the city have been associated with atrocities reported, heated cries of injustice done, with accusation and counter-accusation. For an outsider it's hard not to think 'problems' when the lilting tip-up interrogative inflexion of the Belfast accent hoves into earshot. Yet Belfast is changing, and as heavy manual manufacture has languished – Belfast has long had aircraft and shipbuilding at its heart (the *Titanic* was built here, remember) – so a shiny new Belfast has sprouted. Even so, amid the cranes and the chrome, an old-fashioned warmth of spirit that typifies close-knit industrial communities still thrives.

In this capital city, Ellis found a rich seam of city talk with what he called a 'running commentary of repetition' in tag-expressions like 'so she is', 'so it is', 'so he did', 'so they would', 'so I am', 'so you wouldn't', 'so I do', all of which turned up quite naturally within a few moments of conversation. There's an exciting beat to the language here, unmatched elsewhere in Northern Ireland – a combination of city sharpness and tough living that, as in Liverpool and Newcastle in England, give a real savour to the talk. Only amongst the young people interviewed in Craigavon did Voices catch anything like the energy to be heard here. Even young Geoffrey, he of the daft joke about his mate who'd fallen in the water, was full of it, with his descriptions of his mother's plates of food 'piled up like the Mourne Mountains', and the hated cups of scalding tea she insisted he drink 'like lava from a volcano; roastin' so it is, terrible so it is'. In Belfast, there's a quick-fire pace to the rattle of the syllables that tumble out on top of one another, sounds twisting to turn breakneck linguistic corners: so the 'bottom of our street' comes out something like 'boddummy arr street', a 'y' sound now representing the word 'of'. It's a routine transformation here: 'follow' becomes 'folly', 'into' is 'inty' and 'window', 'windy'. Amongst other terms, 'deadly craic' and 'craic ninety' were the terms of approbation here in the mid-1980s, and Voices caught the latter still in regular use in Craigavon twenty years later.

As in Derry, there's very little in Belfast to differentiate the way the different sectarian communities speak, though in the south and west of the city linguists have noted a slightly greater occurrence of pronunciations like 'kyar' and 'gyarden', and possibly the more southern Irish 'tord' and 'torty' for third and thirty. In the north and the east, conversely, Ellis reported that there was a tendency to use more Scots terms. But the differences are tiny and hard to attribute to any particular cause. On the other hand, Belfast usages like to 'mitch' or 'on the beak' (play truant) and to 'lift', meaning to 'take up' are common everywhere. One speaker for instance told of the sad day when she had to bury her schoolboy brother:

> 'He had a terrible big funeral for the whole school come till. It was really sad when you saw all the school children taking a lift of the coffin.'

The grammar of the first sentence in this example is truly a wonder, the sort of meaningful yet impossible linguistic construction that really adds zest to local talk. Compare, too, the Belfast observation 'I've felt worse many times when I was half as bad', which again sounds quite odd, though you know what they mean, and in which, they say, the Gaelic influence is clearly to be felt. Whatever the source, it's further evidence of what Stanley Ellis called:

> a continuing ferment of language that is forming, adding to and losing little bits as time goes by; picking up traditional words and adapting them and taking on new slang forms that – who knows – may stay in the local language, or may be transient.

'It's a life that's vibrating and it's friendly,' a local headteacher told him, 'and the Belfast accent is a strange one. It is harsh, it is a paradoxical kind of accent because in one sense it is aggressive and in another sense it is warm and humorous and friendly.'

This final observation, gathered from a feisty and funny middle-aged woman, seemed in those pre-Agreement times to epitomize both something of that fighting spirit as well as the sound of the place:

Dey arr a wee bi' temperr'd, but ah leik anybody wi' a temparr, ah duy [They are a little bit 'tempered', but I like anybody with a temper, I do]. Ah don' leik anybody too smooth oll the teim [I don't like anybody too smooth all the time]. Ah duy, ah leik anybody wi' a temparr!

The Voices Survey: Good Craic, from Craigavon to Kilwaughter

Where the mountains of Mourne come down to the sea lies the small fishing port of Annalong. Annalong lies in the shadow of these gentle blue granite peaks that stride across the horizon in that lump of land between Carlingford Lough to the south and Dundrum Bay in the north. We are here less than twenty short miles from the border with the Republic of Ireland, which runs through the lough, and you'd expect the influence of Irish Gaelic to be particularly strong. What Voices found, however, was a strong taste of Scots in the speech of the locals they interviewed in late 2004. According to Maynard, a fisherman born just down the coast at Kilkeel, these are very closed communities and the way they speak is in some ways locked into the tightly knit social structures: 'Annalong people have always kept themselves to themselves and marry amongst themselves.'

And they have a word for it – 'gadgie' – of traveller origin that's found in many places in the north of the UK, including Tyneside and Cumbria and meaning 'a man'. For these fishing folk from Annalong, 'gadgie' is an affectionate term they use to define people who indeed keep themselves to themselves, loners – albeit in a very positive way: 'a gadgie fisherman was hard to beat', they insisted. Outsiders were 'blow-ins' even if they ended up marrying into the locality. Said Maynard:

'People haven't moved too far away from here and that's why we would use the term "a blow-in" if somebody got married to somebody from Belfast or Carrickfergus or Cookstown. A large part of

the surnames that existed 400 years ago still form 80–90 per cent of
the bulk of the surnames that you'll find in this area.'

And again Ulster's long history of identity, roots and clannishness is un-
erringly back on stage. Maynard and his friends enjoy Scottish dancing
and fiddling and travel to watch Glasgow Rangers. They are keen to claim
Scots origin for many of the local words they use, and it's clear that the
linguistic roots across the water of much of their speech constitute a significant aspect of their identity. 'Minging', for example, now found across the
UK with the sense of 'bad' or 'unattractive' is how they describe bad or
stale fish and is a modern word with its roots firmly planted in Glasgow.

On the other hand 'thrawn', meaning 'moody', 'awkward' ('moody' is
one of the standard enquiry points of the Voices survey), are part of an
older Scottish lexicon. As fishermen, they know full well that 'a traan
perrson aboard a bouyt's harrd tuh thole [a moody person aboard a boat's
hard to put up with]'. 'Thole' or 'thoil' by contrast is an Old English
word that also forms part of classic Yorkshire dialect meaning 'to bear'
or 'put up with' but that has been recorded widely in Northern Ireland
over the years and also turns up in Scottish lexicons. In Annalong, Voices
also experienced a time-warp moment when 'duds' was offered as the
preferred local word for 'clothes': 'duds' is another of the terms that
William Lutton listed ('ragged, worn-out clothes') back at the very beginning of the Victorian age (see the 'Language in a Landscape' section) and
here still going strong in the twenty-first century.

This group of middle-aged men and women had a rich range of
vocabulary and an accent to match: herrings were 'harrns', 'sweltering'
hot came out as 'swaellrrin', while the reverse – 'it's a cold day today' –
sounded very close to 'kyle dayaday'. But their accent and range of
vocabulary were as naught compared with those of the quite remarkable
group that Voices surveyed in the tiny Antrim village of Kilwaughter –
'Kill-water' to most, yet for these strongly Scots-influenced speakers it's
'Kill-wochter' (cf. Scots pronunciation of 'daughter' as 'dochter').

Kilwaughter lies, like Annalong, at the foot of peak, in this case
Agnew's Hill, just south of Larne on the road to Ballymena. Here stands
ruined Kilwaughter Castle, a romantic pile whose 'demesne, richly
planted with oaks, beeches, sycamores' according to a Victorian guide-
book was once a favourite haunt of the area.

The Sound of Northern Ireland

Of course, there's no single 'Northern Irish accent'. There are literally dozens: from the angular, flinty talk of young people in Craigavon to the rattle of Ulster Scots in Antrim and the softer island speech of Rathlin.

Nevertheless, there are a number of points that most speakers share. The feature that strikes the outsider immediately is the intonation pattern – almost song-like at times, and marked often with a refrain of 'so it is', 'so it was', 'so she did' and so on. The actual sound of the words is distinctive too. Vowels shift routinely from the standard, so 'brown' becomes 'brine', 'vine' becomes 'vane' and 'pin' becomes 'pen'.

And as anyone who encounters a Belfast schoolboy or schoolgirl knows within about ten seconds, the 'oo' sound in 'school' emerges from the lips curled into a French 'u' sound (as in *tu*), represented in this chapter by 'uy', since there's no direct English equivalent. So 'school' looks like 'skuyle' on the page and rhymes with standard English 'mule'.

Another distinctive feature is the quality of the local 'r'. It's not dissimilar to a West Country burr, but when combined with the other sounds acquires a very

---

The elderly group from the village we talked to are amongst the strongest speakers of dialect recorded in the present survey. Their delivery is maybe stiffened and slurred a little by age, yet the spins and curves they impart to their linguistic deliveries would impress the world's most ambitious cricketer. This, for example, was an anecdote about an expression for 'unattractive':

> 'Mi fella yusst tuh seiay when th'were praisin' the brad uttuh woddn an' th'were goin' a but ourr the tap: "she's nae beauty te kip 'err awff 'err work." ' ['My friends used to say when they were praising the bride at a wedding and they were going a bit over the top: "she's no beauty to keep her off her work".']

'Bride' becomes 'brad' and 'wedding', 'woddn' ... it's hard for the uninitiated to keep up. The speech of this group abounds with overt Scotticisms – 'nae' for 'no' and 'ourr' for 'over' in the above quotation are both closer to the mainland of Scotland than to Northern Ireland, as is the casual remark to the interviewer elsewhere in the session, 'ah dinna

particular feel ('word', for example, sounds more like 'wurrd'). Likewise the vowel in words like 'some' and 'come' has something in common with the way a northerner in England might say it, yet in context sounds nothing like it. I've rendered it here as 'oo', to echo the vowel of standard English 'book'. The short 'a' in 'man' gets lengthened to a flatter 'maan', and the short 'o' in 'log' to something like 'lawg' (to rhyme with 'morgue').

Many of the regular vowels have extra qualities too. The double e of 'feel', for instance, sounds more like 'feeil', the word acquiring a little sweeping pinch at the tail of the sound.

There are some other very particular features that crop up not entirely uniformly, like the insertion of a 'th' sound alongside the 't' after an 's', as in 'straight', which can sound like 'sthreiaght'. Another pretty typical, though not universal element also features the characteristic Irish 'th' which in the south becomes classically a simple 't' – 'I *tink* therefore I am' – yet in the north is often simply 'h' – 'I *hink* therefore I am'. 'Kinda hing' for 'kind of thing' is widely heard. Another common sound is the extra 'y' that some people (influenced maybe by southern Irish connections) add after a hard 'c', where 'car' sounds more like 'kyarr'.

think aa've much tae add [I don't think I've much to add]'. And at a lexical level, too, Scots words are everywhere: a 'wain' is a child, a 'burn' is how they refer to a stream (cf. the Annalong response, 'straim', simply a heavily accented version of 'stream'). Clothes here are 'claes', as Voices heard in Torry near Aberdeen, a long shift is a 'sirk', while 'troosers' are 'draaz [drawers]' and 'breeks [breeches]'. When they fell to quoting and counter-quoting the poetry of Robbie Burns it came as little surprise.

They had many of the standard Northern Irish regionalisms though, too: 'smurr' for light rain (a word found also in Scots), and as in Annalong the main room in the house was certainly neither a living room, a lounge, a sitting room or a parlour, all of which we've found quite widely across Britain in 2005, but simply the 'ketchn'. Plimsolls here were 'gutties' (pronounced 'gaaddiz'), as everywhere in Northern Ireland, from Craigavon to Annalong ('give 'err the gaaddy' – give the car a bit of acceleration – was a colourful motoring example the latter group proposed), and if you're suffering from a 'hirsel' near Larne, you have a sore throat, whereas if you're 'hershellin' a lot in the Mourne Mountains, you were asthmatic, undoubtedly the same notion in both locations.

Just by listening to the men and women talk in Kilwaughter, you get a strong sense of just how intensely rural this part of the United Kingdom is, with its easy references to farming ways. Paths through fields are 'pads' or 'fouyt-paads [foot-pads]', and cows didn't just have one equivalent but multiple forms that sounded almost like the different cases of a Latin or Old English noun: 'keiye ... kye ... kooz ... kettle [cattle]', while bullocks were rendered in the local accent – no blushes offered – exactly as 'bollocks'. One speaker here even went out of his way to chart words from flax-farming ('lint' in Kilwaughter parlance) that have today completely disappeared with the local industry ('nae loonger therr'), a classic process of dialectal evolution, this. A stack of 'lint' was called for example a 'burrt', 'sheeg' or 'havel'. My spellings here are very approximate but, to judge by their murmurs of agreement, these were clearly terms others in the group recognized. It's a throwback to the sort of agricultural community that's almost completely vanished from mainland Britain.

This lively and passionately local group were able to cite a wide range of words to describe parts of the human body: your 'neb' is your nose throughout Ulster (and beyond) and 'oxters' (armpits) is widely known and was another term quoted back in 1840 by William Lutton well west of here. But yet another Lutton entry, 'farenticles' (freckles), which was volunteered here as 'ferntickles', I came across nowhere else these days.

From parts of the body to a discussion of aches and pains was but a step for these elderly folk and elicited some now rare but once typical expressions: 'ma arthreitis's gaouypin' ('gowping' = throbbing) proposed one contributor, together with 'stoon' ('a terrible stoon') a subtly different variety of pain:

'Eff somegdy'd gevven ye a gauf on the jaa and the pein lengerrd furra whaiyl tha' wuz stoouynen yet.'

['If somebody'd given you a blow on the jaw and the pain lingered for a while, that was hurting still.']

This 'stoon', according to Lutton, is 'a violent throbbing, jaculating pain' and is one that lingers – note the use of 'yet' to mean 'still', another Scottish echo.

From Kilwaughter north up the coast to Ballycastle is a matter of thirty miles as the crow flies, though it's a lot further via the winding A2 coast road. There the ferry crosses the short sleeve of water to Rathlin Island, the closest point in Northern Ireland to Scotland – the southward bulb of the Mull of Kintyre is just sixteen miles distant. It is a place of spectacular 500-feet-high cliffs, wild seas and views across the water to the Scottish coast, and where electricity, mains water and drainage have only arrived in the last twenty years. The inhabitants canvassed by Voices told of the remoteness and of an island culture with a deep and long-maintained rivalry between inhabitants of one end of this boomerang-shaped stretch of land and the other.

Their talk was far softer than that of the Kilwaughter group, easy for an unpractised ear to follow without straining, yet they used many of the regional words we've heard already – 'smur' for drizzle ('"a wee fine smur" nearly like wet fog – it's a lovely soft word'), 'pad' for field-path ('though if it was round the house it was the "loanin"' – originally a Scots word) and 'back-kitchen' for the principal room in the house. Here too they 'clod' a stone (recorded also in Annalong) when they throw it, and also like the Annalong group were treated as 'culchies' ('they're counthry people, they arre') in Belfast.

But here too were memories of an old Irish-speaking fisherman who used to make all sorts of mistakes in his English and of other words of Scottish origin that were in regular use on Rathlin. 'Cope' (to blow or knock over) was one: 'If a cow tumbled the wall you'd say she's after "coping" the wall'. 'She's after coping . . .', incidentally, is pure Hiberno-English syntax used to indicate something that has just happened which some linguists call the 'hot news' perfect tense. To 'slipe' is a local word that derives from the island's lack of roads – a 'slipe' was a form of sleigh, they explained, to transport farm materials over rough ground and thus if you're a youngster on the island you're told off for 'sliping [dragging] your feet'.

The sea and seafaring is a continuous thread through these people's lives – drunken sailors in the pubs in Ballycastle, the local word ('shores') for a heavy surf and a rich cargo of superstition connected to boats and fishing: it was bad luck to meet a red-haired woman on the way to the fish – unsurprisingly Voices collected similar tales in Annalong, another fishing community. Then there's the word 'scud', common enough on Rathlin for to hurry but not noted elsewhere and deriving apparently from 'to scud before the wind' – they call the spinnaker the 'scudding sail'. Inevitably perhaps, we were also regaled with colourful stories of priests and fishermen with a classic Irish punchline, as recounted by an 88-year-old lifetime Rathlin dweller, Lochie, in his soft, heavily accented local brogue. Note his soft 'd', 'dthrunk', which we've tended to find in areas where the Gaelic influence is strongest:

'There wuz an ale [old] boy here, used te ge' t'boot an gaw te Ballykyastle [used to get the boat and go to Ballycastle] an soons 'e ge' tuh Ballykyastle e' ge' dthrunk [and as soon as he gets to Ballycastle he gets drunk]. S'w ast cotoff the boot [So he's got off the boat] an' e's walkin' op the road an' the priest met em an' pries' sez t'wim "Dthrunk todeiy again, Jawhn?" [And the priest says to him: "Drunk today again, John?"] "Oh indid. An' bi Christ an' so am I, Father!" ["Oh indeed. And by Christ and so am I, Father!"]'

To close this comparative look at the sound of Northern Ireland today, Voices' visit to the 1960s new town of Craigavon couldn't have been more different. Craigavon lies at the centre of a sprawl of population speared by the M1 highway that runs from Belfast to the west of the province, with Lurgan to its east and Portadown on the west. The craic here is urban, sharp-tongued and deeply scored with black humour. At the Drumgor Youth Centre a group of young people talked about their lives and the words they used to describe them – in an accent they called 'Belfast with a hint of country'. Many Belfast terms turn up in this sometimes troubled place – 'hoods' (pronounced 'houyds', naturally) for the young hoodlums involved in drug trafficking according to one of the group: 'Lurgan people would call us "dump rats," ' said Michael, a youth-leader at the centre, with a big laugh. The hoods normally keep away from the centre, but sometimes 'they snik in furra carryouyt' (sneak in for a take-away). Yet for Megan, another team-leader who also works in the centre's bar, Craigavon was 'dead-on' (a very common urban term of approbation in Northern Ireland). 'Beezer,' added Michael as an alternative now sunk into unfashionable obscurity: 'I always used to say that.' Everything tends to get shortened, he added, in this fast-paced shorthand that's typical of towns throughout the UK, so 'Hello, how're you doing?' here is simply 'About you?' ('Bouyt ye'), as in 'Bouyt ye, whass the craic?'

As we've seen elsewhere in this chapter, the local craic is shot through with irony and colour; 'Sarcasm is unbelievable here,' says Megan, 'you can say the complete opposite and people would know what you mean – you don't even have to put on a sarcastic tone of voice. You just say it and they know!' One of Megan's favourite expressions that she thinks she may have made up reflects this dynamic linguistic energy: 'I would always say it's "crazy like a bottle of chips"' (except of course it sounds more like 'creeizi laak a battla cheps'); 'I mean a bottle of chips is pretty crazy!'

There may be few points here in common with the talk of the rural areas, but these young people's talk is a fascinating mixture of old and new English. Friends are 'meits' or 'mackarrs [muckers]'; trendy youngsters are sometimes referred to as 'spides' (probably a Belfast import), 'messers' and 'hoods', all characterized by their trademark 'houydihtaps [hooded tops]'. They'd tend to refer to the police as 'the pigs' ('peggs' – or as another of the youth workers, Martin, offered with a sniff of the air, 'I can smell some bacon' – his easy wit typical of this group's talk). But at the same time for these laid-back youngsters they're also 'the peelers' – a throwback of 200 years to Sir Robert Peel that's long vanished from slang elsewhere in Britain.

It's interesting to compare the degree to which these young people from urban Northern Ireland have adopted national vernacular idioms: 'be-atch', a derogatory term for girlfriend ('bitch') imported from their music of choice, turned up here as in Salford and in other urban areas across the country. So too common slang words for drunk – 'stocious', 'paralytic' ('parrluttek') and 'hammered' – but here you can also get 'rubbered' ('you know you're "rubbered" when you can't say "rubbered"!'). To describe someone as ugly they would likewise use the young person's national standard 'minging' or 'rough', yet of a woman they say they'd more likely use 'dump rat' or 'mowgly' (pronounced 'moe-gleh' – source unknown).

But even if some of the vernacular used by young people in Northern Ireland is no longer particularly local, what the Voices survey has shown is that there is still a huge bank of linguistic variation amongst the under thirty-fives, and an energy to play games with it, turn it inside out for comic or ironic effect and thereby develop new words and shorthands that mark the province out as still having among the liveliest local speech in the nation. And all of it delivered, from Kilwaughter to Craigavon, in an unbelievably rich accent that has on occasion defied transcription for this book. I mean, where else – apart perhaps from Glasgow – would 'my dad's old ties' turn into the sing-song 'muh daayz auyl taiyz', or a simple, day-to-day term like 'brother-in-law' emerge from a young man's lips as two syllables, 'brraanlaa'?

A Northern Ireland Snapshot: Planting the Inox

Rosie, Annie, Catrina, Marie, Margaret and Biddy are travellers. They are also exceptional in a number of ways, not least within the context of the Voices survey in that they speak not with an Ulster accent but with tones everyone recognizes as originating south of the border: 'very southern' is the universal comment. In reality two at least come from *west* of the border, from Letterkenny (Leitir Ceanainn) in the Irish Republic at the head of Lough Swilly, just seventeen miles beyond Derry. This group of travellers – the terms 'gypsies' and 'tinkers' are today both strongly frowned on – may come from what they still refer to as the 'Free State' (the name Ireland bore until 1937), but they've been resident on the outskirts of Belfast for more than ten years. Yet they've not absorbed an ounce of the angular speech we've illustrated elsewhere in this chapter as typical of the Northern Irish capital.

Voices brought the six women together at the Belfast Travellers' Support Group, which mediates between what they know as the 'settled' community and travellers. In their gentle sibilant Irish tones, full of distinctly different pronunciations ('t' for 'th' and 'sh' replacing 's' in many cases) they talked passionately about their language and about the discrimination they face:

'Soom peiple ten' to class trav'llers all the seim; if won [one] trav'ller's bad, they tin' te tink tat [they tend to think that] all are t'seime, steal tings [steal things]. Bot day're nat oll leik dat [but they're not all like that].'

This group stick together ('We're a very clawse-knit communidy') and have their own rules and customs which they abide by in the face of huge social change elsewhere – they were very shocked when the interviewer for Voices asked what they would call a 'boyfriend'. Such a concept was inconceivable, they said, because there's 'no courtin' – courtin's not allawd'. You won't get a traveller girl going out with anybody before they're married, they assured us, it's just a tradition. Like the frequent references to the 'Free State', there's an old-fashioned quaintness about the use of the word 'courting' when just down the road in the heart of Belfast, as we've heard elsewhere in this chapter, the spides are out on the town enjoying craic ninety with their be-atches. In this community, attraction is a more chaste affair: 'Mebbe they would have alwiz had a wee sparkl' in therr eye fu' th'm.'

These women share a very sing-song intonation pattern too, running their words together in strings of sibilance that can be quite difficult for the uninitiated ear to disentangle. It's been a feature of our findings throughout Northern Ireland that the more closed the community, the less clearly articulated the speech – on Rathlin, in Kilwaughter and amongst the fishermen of Annalong – and these travellers are more self-reliant than most. They don't need to make themselves clear to outsiders, and know it: 'In de shawp, ei ten' tu poot an this pawsh voishe [In the shop, I tend to put on this posh voice],' said one, 'ei trei, bot i' dozzn't wurrk [I try, but it doesn't work].' And they smiled to tell the story of a mother who went into a shop in Donegal, forgetting that she was speaking to a non-traveller, and asked for a 'tit [teat]' for a baby's bottle to great amusement. On another occasion she wanted to buy some bath linen and asked the shopkeeper, 'Whezh yuh tawls? [Where's your towels?]' with a broad traveller accent. 'He was lookin' at her: "You what?" An' she jus' said, "Forgetd abow tet [forget about it]." '

Life on the road for the travellers is full of hardship and many prefer these days to live in a house rather than a caravan, particularly when the weather's bad. Notice the repeated sibilant 'sh' here:

' 'Specially wheniss shnown an everyting on the real bad weather;
ye've more comfurrts in a housh complately than ever you would have
in a caravan. You've praper wash'g f'cilities 'na house, but in a trailer
it's jusht hardship.'

['Especially when it's snowing and everything in the really bad
weather; you've more comforts in a house, completely, than ever you
would in a caravan. You've proper washing facilities in a house, but in
a trailer it's just hardship.']

But what distinguishes this group of Irish speakers more than their way of life, their somewhat archaic turns of phrase or their closed linguistic community with little interaction with 'country people' (ordinary 'settled' or non-travelling people – nothing to do with rural affairs) is the fact that they pepper their conversation – old and young – with words and expressions drawn from Shelta, Irish travellers' parlance. Also known as 'Gammon', this language is thought to be centuries old and is unique to travellers in the island of Ireland, though it does share certain elements with English travellers' cant. Most of the words derive from Irish Gaelic and in written form it even includes non-standard alphabetical signs. The women interviewed in Belfast spoke it to varying degrees – the youngest had a few words, the older women a good working knowledge.

As with backslang, with Liverpool Wej Patter (a form of cant spoken amongst the Jewish community) and other very specialized forms of speech, Gammon is used to keep outsiders out just as much as to communicate with other initiates. In Cumbria, there are those to this day who use English travellers' cant to make sure that secrets are kept secret even when overheard, and here in the Belfast group Margaret explained, for example, that you'd be quick to whisper 'plant the inox' – 'hide the thingummyjig' – if you wanted your 'childer' (not child*ren* in traveller dialect) not to discover a Christmas present. Similarly, if the police turned up when someone was indulging in a bit of light-fingered activity, the cry would go out: '*Mishly* an! Quick there's the *wabs*!' 'Wabs' and 'shades' are both Gammon terms for what elsewhere in Ulster would be the 'peelers' (police), and 'misli' (pronounced 'mishly') is listed in the Gammon lexicon as meaning 'to go', 'walk' or 'depart'.

Other common words are 'byor' for a woman, 'fin' for a man and 'goya' for a child, also sometimes written 'gawthrin' – spellings of Gammon are very variable as it is above all a spoken language and heavily accented. Here's Margaret with a typical observation in cant: 'Dat *byor* dere *an asher* [that woman over there] she lives in a *ken* up the *tober* [she lives in a house up the road].' While the precise origin of many Gammon words is difficult to determine, 'tober' derives, it's said, from the Irish word 'bothar' (road, street), and the Gammon lexicon lists 'Do the shades misli this tober?' as a sample phrase meaning 'Do the police patrol this road?'

Perhaps unsurprisingly with all this talk of police and hiding things, there are several terms in the language for stealing or 'lifting', including 'yock', 'hump' and 'cloy': as in 'What did you yock today?' or 'What did you hump today?':

> 'Ef a chail lifted a sweed an a shahp sheilf [If a child lifted a sweet on a shop shelf] you would say, "Putt tha' back ur the *shades* is goanna crush yuh [Put that back or the police are going to get you]. Putt et back! Yur goanna get yu'self inna whool laadda baathurr [You're going to get yourself into a whole lot of bother]. The police'll come and lift [= arrest] yuh."'

The Belfast support group interviewed for Voices had a stack of stories of how travellers had been persecuted over many years and suffered continual discrimination, but were enthusiastic about their current circumstances in the city. And though they regretted leaving the cosiness and the decorated interiors of their caravans, they can create, as they pointed out, much the same atmosphere by filling their settled housing with their crockery ('delph' – the standard Ulster word, from the Dutch city famous for its china) and their lace:

> 'Ye c'n still bring parrt uv that wid yuh [You can still bring part of that with you] – say yuh crystal, your delph an' your leice – whatever it is youh've had in de car'van – you'll trey ti do someh'n sim'lar in de heouse dat'll indikeite [that will indicate] you're back t'when ye lived in de caravan. You neverr lose yourr identety.'

But on the open road or settled in a city development, Rosie, Annie, Catrina, Marie, Margaret and Biddy, whom Voices met on the outskirts of Belfast, were certain that, whatever their outward appearance, one thing would always mark them out and confirm them in their traveller identity, and that's their individual and characteristic voice:

> 'Uf the' wuh dreisst en tahp qualetei clawz [If they were dressed in top-quality clothes] the minute they open theh meouth paple audomadically awpens their eiyes weiderr [people automatically open their eyes wider] as much as t'saeiy – well iss nat what shiz wearin' bot iss the waeiy shiz taak'n [as much as to say, well, it's not what she's wearing but it's the way she's talking] – so you still arre edentifiyed.'

287

A Northern Ireland Glossary

This list contains a mix of items from contemporary regional slang, older dialect terms which are still heard, though infrequently, and finally a few colourful words from old Ulster dialect that are simply good fun.

A short selection of traveller (Gammon) terms are listed separately at the end

(a)bout ye! Hello! How's tricks (contemporary usage)

bangster a bullying violent person (old Ulster dialect). Lutton lists it among his Montiaghisms (see 'Language in a Landscape' section). Scots records the term from the mid sixteenth century in the same sense

beezer a term of approbation: 'good', 'great' (contemporary usage)

blarge, blatter, clash, dunt, dunter, scally, slinge, steimisher all meaning 'to hit', 'to thump' or 'a blow'. Exact spellings and distinctions uncertain, all recorded by Voices in 2004; 'dunt' is a variant of 'dint', to beat, from Middle English *dynt*

brae a steep hill. Lutton (1840) records the word. Contemporary dialect use in Northern Ireland and regular use in Scotland. Originally from Old English *braew*, eyelid (there is a connection between 'eye*brow*' and '*brow*' of a hill)

breeks trousers, breeches (current older dialectal usage). Originally from Old English *brech*

broke to the bone very embarrassed; **broke** is recorded as meaning 'crest-fallen', or 'vexed' in south-west Tyrone amongst other places (current dialect)

Buckie Buckfast tonic wine. 'Buckie' is a popular alcoholic drink amongst young people in Scotland and Northern Ireland; the recipe is said to have arrived in the UK with the monks who settled at Buckfast Abbey in Devon in the nineteenth century and who manufacture it (contemporary usage)

burn a stream. From Old English *burna*; see Chapter 10 on the transmission of this word in Northumbrian English

carry-out alcohol bought from an off-licence (contemporary usage)

cat melodeon appalling. According to one anonymous attribution, originally a musical term referring to a cacophony, like a cat on heat plus a badly played accordion (contemporary usage)

claes clothes. Via Old Scots *claes* (fifteenth century), variant of English 'clothes'

coup (pronounced 'cowp', still in occasional usage) to knock over or hit. Recorded by Lutton in 1840, the word existed in Old Scots as *cowp* in the mid sixteenth century. From Old French *colper*, to strike

craic entertaining talk (often fuelled by alcohol); also simply 'fun'. Sometimes spelled 'crack'. Lutton defined it as 'enlivening conversation; merriment'. From sixteenth-century English

craic ninety terrific, beezer (q.v.), dead-on (q.v.)

culchie a country bumpkin. A derogatory contemporary Belfast term. The 'Culchie Homepage' on the web explains: '. . . usually found in rural areas, apart from about once a year when they venture into big towns and cities . . . They spend most of their day in muddy fields feeding their herds. They speak a language which can only be understood by other culchies . . .'

daunder, dander to wander aimlessly about. Lutton records it and it is still in regular use amongst young people: 'I'm away for a dander'

dead-on fantastic, cool (contemporary usage)

duds clothes, 'worn-out clothes' according to Lutton; also regular Scots use. From Middle English *dudde*, a coarse cloak. Of unknown origin

dump-rat a hooligan

ferntickle a freckle. Older Northern Irish dialect though quoted in Voices. The word exists in Scots in various spellings; Lutton has it as 'farenticles'. From Middle English *farntikylle*, resembling the seed of the fern

fog, prog to steal (apples – Lisburn usage)

gowp, goup to throb. Also found in Scots with the meaning (of the pulse) to beat strongly or palpitate; imitative usage

grape a three-pronged fork. Also found widely in northern English and Scottish dialect from the mid fifteenth century. From Middle English *grape, graype*. Voices recorded a farming exhortation to work harder: 'put a bit more in your grape'

gutties plimsolls, soft shoes

hallion, halyon Lutton defines the word as 'a lazy, worthless person'. Also found in Scots in various spellings, and used by Robert Burns in 1787. Of obscure origin. Voices recorded the usage 'dirty old hallion' in Armagh in 2004

hirsel, hershelling a cough, coughing. One of many meanings for this word found in Scots, where the *Dictionary of the Scots Language* defines it as 'to wheeze, breathe noisily through bronchial congestion'. Possibly from Old Scots *hirsill*, to graze, though uncertain, perhaps onomatopoeic

hood a hooligan, lout

keoboy a cheeky character, scoundrel (also spelled 'cheoboy')

lint flax

loanin a lane leading to fields. This word is related to 'loan' (see Chapter 12) and is of Scots origin; from Old Scots *lonyng* (fourteenth century) and Middle English *lonnynge*. 'Loan' meaning 'an open space through which cattle are herded' is related to English 'lawn'

mowgly ugly (modern Northern Ireland slang)

mucker a mate, friend

nae no. From Scots (fourteenth century). Old English *nan*

neb a nose. Widespread usage, also in Scots, from 1400 meaning a 'beak'. Old English and Old Scots *neb*

pad, footpad a path through a field. Dialectal use of 'path' (Old English *paeth*)

peeler a policeman. From Sir Robert Peel (1788–1850), founder of Britain's first police force in 1829 (still in contemporary use)

poke an ice-cream

quare very. A reinforcing word, recorded by Lutton, and still used widely in Northern Irish dialect, especially before adjectives: 'that was quare good', 'it was quare craic' (it was a lot of fun)

rubbered very drunk

scud to hurry. Recorded from the sixteenth century. Etymology obscure, likely Scandinavian, Germanic in origin

sirk a shirt. Also Scots, northern English 'sark' with same meaning (cf. the celebrated tea-clipper named the *Cutty Sark*). From Old English *serc*

slipe sleigh or sledge used for transporting farm materials. Fifteenth century, of Germanic origin. Recorded by Lutton in his *Glossary* (1840) and on Rathlin Island in 2004. Verbal use ('to slipe') means to drag

smur, smurr, smirr drizzle, fine rain. Widespread dialect usage, including Scots and East Anglian. Lutton calls it 'a small rain'. Origin obscure

spide an unattractive man (with bad hair, dress and music sense, according to one glossary of contemporary Northern Irish slang)

stoon a throbbing pain. Recorded in 2004, but of older dialect use, recorded by Lutton

thole, thoil to bear, put up with. Old English *tholian*, to suffer, found in *Beowulf* (ninth century). Also still found in Yorkshire dialect

thrawn moody. Originally meaning twisted or deformed, past participle of the verb 'thraw', from Old English *thrawan*, to twist; so, of the features, 'twisted with pain or anger'. Found in Scots with the meaning 'sullen' from the early nineteenth century

till to. Used where Standard English would use 'to': 'I'm away till the shop'

wain a child. From Scots usage: a combination of 'wee' (little) and 'ane' (one) or perhaps from *wain*, to wean

wee little, but constantly used as reinforcing or affectionate word. From Scots *we*, a small measure. Originally an Old English word, *wey*, a weight, thence Old Scots 'a lytil we' (fourteenth century)

whang a leather thong

Gammon / Shelta

byor (phonetic) a woman. From *blewr*?

cloy, hump, yock to steal

fin a man. From Irish *fian*

goya, gawthrin a child. Shelta has many forms of this word

inox a thing, thingummyjig

kam'ra a dog. From Irish *madra*

ken(a) a house

misli to go, walk or depart. Perhaps from Irish *siubhal*, to walk

plant to hide; as in 'plant the inox', 'hide the thingummyjig'

shades, sheids, wabs the police. Sometimes spelled *shed*. Perhaps from English 'shade', cf. 'to shadow'

tober a road. From Irish *bothar*, a road, street

12 : SCOTLAND

Language in a Landscape: Wir Ain Leid (Our Own Language)?

On the old scratchy newsreel film, complete with heroic soundtrack, gleaming steel cylinders lie in different attitudes in what look like doll's house buildings, some toybox filmed in scratchy black and white. It takes a moment to realize that what's on the screen are real locomotives – steam trains, each dozens of yards long and being assembled in what are in effect vast factory production lines, each beast at a different stage of completion. Because this is where they made the locos that powered the Empire's railways: this is the North British Locomotive Company of Springburn in Glasgow. Now only Albert Hodge's 95-year-old classical sculptures – allegorical figures of Speed and Science and of the front ends of several locos – remain adorning the old NBLC building, part now of Glasgow's artistic heritage rather than its industry.

In Dundee, you can find very similar films celebrating the development of the town's yarn industry: 'jute for bags and jute for sacks, jute for hessian, jute for carpets and jute for tailors and upholsterers . . .' Thanks to jute, proclaims the commentary, Dundee had by 1878 a population of 160,000. By the middle of the twentieth century the jute trade was gone and the docks were dying. These images of the industrial cities of Scotland as workshops of the world aren't wrong. It's what helped build the prosperity – and the poverty – that shaped the grain of people's lives, and the way it expressed itself in language.

> Ye knawkt yerr pan en oll dee, knawk yerr pan en is ye wurrk lak a horrse – ye know what heed doon errse up is? Yerr knawk'n' yerr pan ooyt ferr th'employerr!

The speaker is broad Glaswegian speaker Agnes McLean, a veteran socialist and trades unionist in this industrial landscape, who talked about the language of poverty and hard work – 'knocking your pan out' (or 'in') – to Stanley Ellis in his 1983 survey of the city's language. 'You work like a horse,' she said, 'head down, arse up, knocking your pan out for the employer.'

Well ye knawked yerr pan ooyt oll dee, an' en ye wen' awee te danss ti' tyu a clawk ina morrnin'. An' then ye werr back at yerr werrk Sat'dee morrnin' knawk'n' yerr pan ooyt ageen.

Dancing was Agnes's passion that she'd do in her young days till two in the morning, regardless of the fact that she'd to be back knocking her pan out next day. Agnes spoke with an accent that was so broad that despite the clarity of her diction, it took the inexperienced ear several minutes to tune in. And when she spoke of 'baikies' and 'middens', of 'cludgies', 'dunnies' and 'oxters' as a matter of course – just part of her daily experience in a Glasgow tenement, or 'close' – you knew that this was a very particular world with a lexicon all its own. Some of the words are modern – 'cludgie' appears to be relatively modern, 'dunny' is listed as coming from an eighteenth-century English cant term 'dunnakin', a privy, 'midden' (dungheap) and 'oxter' (armpit) are still fairly common dialect words in northern England, but 'baikie' (a sort of bin for ashes and rubbish) appears to be pure Scots.

The fact is that Scots is a wonderful mix of elements and influences. Some are recent words stemming directly from that tough life that Agnes personified and the newsreels commemorated, others brought about by wider historical movements. Scots does begin, though, from the English language. It's wrong to think – as some do – that it's a branch of Gaelic (which, incidentally, is pronounced in Scotland like 'gallic' and not to be confused with Irish *Gaelic*, 'gaylic'). As you can see from the section on Scottish rural speech, the Highlands and Islands have a completely different feel and sound to their talk which stems from Gaelic. No, though there are plenty of Gaelic words that have made their way into Scottish speech, it's Old English that's at the root of Scots. The linguistic mainline, however, divided early on and the Middle Ages saw Scots thrive as a distinctively different variety of the language, with a vigorous and distinguished literary tradition, as J. Derrick McClure, senior Lecturer in English at the University of Aberdeen, explains:

In the mediaeval period, although Scots was the official national language and Scots was the language of a great literature, the mediaeval Scots poets like Henderson and Dunbar and even ardent patriotic poets seemed to have felt no hostility at all to English as a cultural force. Although their language was different – their language was Scots – culturally there was no hostility corresponding to the very real political hostility that there was between the Scottish and the English monarchies.

With the two varieties of English co-existing for centuries, it's not surprising that there are many formal differences – for example, words that are cognate (have the same root) yet that have ended up as noticeably different in modern English and modern Scots.

However, with the union of the crowns of Scotland and England in 1603, southern English became the norm in the written language according to Stanley Ellis:

> When James VI of Scotland became James I of England he took his court with him off to London, and the language that had just been emerging over the previous couple of hundred years or so as *Scots* was given a blow that struck it down, nigh destroyed it. Until a rather weak resurgence about the time of Walter Scott and Robbie Burns.

But in vernacular spoken language, the distinctively different grammar, syntax and vocabulary of Scots remained vigorous and present, says Derrick McClure:

> The mass of the people continued to speak Scots. With the departure of King James the ruling classes, many of the aristocracy, went south with them and got into the habit of spending part of the year in England, part of the year in Scotland. When they were in England they started speaking English and when they came back to Scotland, talking with their tenants and their dependants, they would talk Scots. And so they became bilingual. The ruling classes, the educated classes, the literate classes in King James VI's time certainly were able to read and speak English as well as Scots, but there was no suggestion that they should adopt English in place of Scots and still less that they should force their tenants and their dependants to do so. Scots continued as the language of the mass of the people.

As a result of these many influences, social and political, the speech of Scotland is today one of the most markedly different from standard British English in the United Kingdom. And these differences exist at every level. Take a word like 'outwith'. Unknown in the English of England, it's completely normal usage amongst Scots, with a long and distinguished pedigree dating back to the Middle English of the thirteenth-century words *utenn with* and *utewith*. It means 'beyond' or 'outside of' and it's a remarkably useful word for which standard English has no equivalent that's quite as neat. Remember the Easter hymn 'There is a green hill far away/ *Without* a city wall . . .' that always left me and my fellow schoolmates bemused when we had to sing it? What was this hill that didn't have a wall round it? Well, 'without', in this sense, is merely as close as the regular user of English south of the border gets to 'outwith'.

There are many, many similar words that exist only in standard Scots, like 'kirk' for 'church' and 'dreich' for 'dreary' (see 'Street Talk in Scotland: Three Towns'). According to one authoritative dictionary there are as many as 20,000 separate and distinctive Scotticisms. Some of the words have the same form but a different meaning, like 'scheme' – in the 'Snapshot' you can read about life on a Dundee housing estate or 'scheme' – and even a simple word like 'stay' can have a completely different meaning ('I stay in Leith' doesn't indicate that you live elsewhere but spend short periods in the Edinburgh suburb: it's actually where you live).

As well as from the language's separate development, this very diverse lexicon derives from outside influence, from the Celtic nations and from other countries with which Scotland has traditionally had close historical connections. Derrick McClure explains:

> Scots has words derived from Gaelic, like 'ingle' for fireplace [from *aingeal*, fire, light], Scots has words derived from French, from Dutch. If you look at the vocabulary of [the poets] Robert Burns, or nearer our own time, Hugh MacDiarmid, you find that there are a vast number of words which don't occur in English. Or Scots has preserved words that used to belong to English, like 'bide' for example, 'stay', or 'throw', 'endure', which you find in Chaucer's English, but which disappeared from standard literary English but survived in Scots. It's partly because Scotland as an independent nation of course had close

political and diplomatic relations with France, and with the
Netherlands, and so Scots was influenced by French and Dutch to
an extent that English was not.

It's perhaps not surprising that among the vocabulary that most distinguishes Scotland are words with origins in Gaelic, for which standard
English has no natural equivalent (partially for reasons of geography). So
a 'loch' is pure Gaelic (similarly the rasping 'ch' sound), so are 'glen' and
'sporran', and so too 'whisky' (deriving from Old Scots *iskie bae*, which
in turn comes from Gaelic *uisge beatha*: 'the water of life'). 'Kilt', incidentally, arrives via another route, northern Middle English out of the
Scandinavian fastnesses where they spoke variously of *kiltre op*, *kiltra sej*
and *kilting* (verbs meaning to 'swathe' or 'swaddle') depending on which
bit you came from.

> So the vocabulary of Scots is very distinctive. The ten-volume *Scottish
> National Dictionary*, which includes, or purports to include, all the
> words that are unique and distinctive to Scots, has got over 70,000
> entries.

So much so, according to Derrick McClure, that Scots is claimed by
many as a distinct and separate language. Just as in Northern Ireland
(with Ulster Scots) and to an extent in Cornwall (with Cornish), there
are those in Scotland who for nationalist or separatist and literary ends
stress the differences rather than the similarities between Scots and English and who like to speak of 'wir ain leid' (our own language). You only
need to sample some of the offerings on the elaborate and thorough
website that bears the name to begin to get a flavour of the arguments
and the passions that language nationalism excites.

Speaking as a *Sassenach* (or Saxon – Gaelic *sasunnaich*, i.e. a non-Scot),
I don't intend to enter this fray; yet listening closely to the conversations
captured by the Voices team in 2004/5, there seem to me greater struc-
tural, syntactical and lexical differences between the English used, say,
by the young men I've written about in the 'Snapshot' section ('Jutetown
Blues') and national standard British English, than by almost any other
speakers I've heard, and I include those extraordinarily broadly accented
voices recorded in Kilwaughter in County Antrim. It gives their speech
more than simply a flavour; it has true individual texture and robustness:

when Gary says he's 'fae Fintry, where I stay now' you get a real sense that he's not simply saying 'from' and 'live'. This is a different way of expressing yourself that is clearly much more than simply English with an accent. If the old adage that a language is 'a dialect with an army and a navy' has any validity, then clearly Scots doesn't quite qualify. Though having a Parliament might be half-way there.

Has this individuality undergone any of the sorts of changes during the last fifty or so years that I've recorded across parts of England – very marked in the Thames Valley for instance, less so in parts of rural Cumbria and inner-city Bristol or Manchester? The Survey of *English* Dialects of the 1950s and 1960s made no excursions into Scotland, but Stanley Ellis recorded there for his series *Talk of the Town, Talk of the Country* in 1983. He took a trip down Byres Road in the heart of Glasgow's West End. Byres Road runs roughly north–south, with fashionable and spacious leafy suburbs at its most northern point, the Clyde a stone's throw from its southern 'with downtown views of the ship-yard cranes, standing like ossified sentries over the largely empty yards: the men who once worked them now sitting in the bars making their pints of lager last . . .'

Ah was redundant ou' the shepyarrds – ah wuz a cuikboy in a canteen, ye know – ahm redundan', ahm levvin' on Maaggie Thaatcherr's haandouiyt she giz me, twenty-three pouynd sexty-feiyve a week, an' ahm tuiy aul' ti ge' awn mi biyke.

Al was a redundant shipyard worker, cookboy in a canteen, he explained, 'living on Maggie Thatcher's handout she gives me, £23.65 a week' – too old to get on his bike, he added with a characteristic Glaswegian hard-up smile. Ellis wrote:

Nowhere I've been has had any more rotten time of it than Glasgow. And yet there's no doubt that through everyone I spoke to here there has run a thread of humour. Wry, self-mocking at times, most often springing out of adverse conditions, but always there.

All the men and women Ellis encountered had broad Glasgow accents, notably Agnes McLean, whom I quoted at the beginning of this section. Back in 1983 Agnes was closer by at least a generation than most these days to the serious hardship of living in a 'close' or tenement: her memories of the 'baikies' and 'dunnies' were still fresh; she lived those tough times. For today's Voices interviewees, while this level of poverty was also still a reality they'd experienced personally, particularly for the elderly trio from Carlton, it was now receding into a softer, more distant memory.

But the language is still as vigorous as ever. There are telltale signs of the spread of now standard British national vernacular terms like 'knackered' for tired out and 'chuffed' for pleased (surely the most ubiquitous words found by Voices), and amongst the young Taysiders you can detect the influence of television and national slang ('mental' for insane, 'chuck' for throw, 'loaded' for rich). Yet, as I pointed out earlier in this section, they have at least as much if not more individuality than most in their strong local accent and Scots lexicon, used naturally and utterly unselfconsciously.

To judge by the evidence of the latest interviewees, I'd still go along (with the odd nod to the language of Del Boy and Big Brother) with the local expert who more than twenty years ago assured Stanley Ellis:

> I have not from the inside detected any real change in accent and dialect words caused by post-war developments and the decline of industry and the scattering of the population to the suburbs. They have taken that culture with them and in spite of the fears of many Scots linguists that we are all being homogenized by television and radio and films I personally don't see a lot of evidence for it. People in Glasgow sound the same to me as they did when I was ten years old.

The Voices Survey: Street Talk in Scotland – Three Towns

During the autumn of 2004, Voices travelled all over Scotland and captured the sound of Scots talking in town and country, north and south. It's a rich and complex picture and I can only hope to scratch the surface in these pages. What emerges most strongly, however, from all the recordings is the vibrant nature of the varieties of the English language spoken in Scotland. I don't intend to engage here in a discussion of the validity (see 'Language in a Landscape: Wir Ain Leid?') of the claim of Scots to the title of 'language' rather than 'dialect'. In this section I simply set out to offer the evidence of the Voices material as proof, if proof were needed, of the vitality of Scots as heard on the streets of three urban centres, Edinburgh, Glasgow and Dundee.

I shall not attempt either to draw too many firm conclusions from the evidence of Voices; just as I found in Northern Ireland, there is such individuality and local variation – sometimes between one street, or at least one 'scheme' (housing estate), and another – that this sample should be treated with some care. One of the Dundonian interviewees for Voices put it most succinctly when discussing the local term for left-handed, 'pally-juykerrd' (local pronunciation of 'pally-dukered', probably from 'dukes', Victorian slang for hands – 'molly-duker' is a similar Australian expression with this suggested etymology): 'It juss dipens where yurr fae in Dundee, as well. The language even varies within the toon – fae different schemes as well.'

'Toon' is how people from all three cities referred to where they live: standard 'town' has no currency in Scotland and 'toon' is a historic throwback to before the major vowel changes that began in southern English in the early fifteenth century. The original 'oo' sound in words like 'town', 'house' and 'down' have all been retained in Scottish speech. But if they're agreed on 'toon' you can take your pick when it comes to words for left-handed. Within Dundee, in the Lochee area to the west that was once known as 'Little Tipperary' because of the large number of Irish immigrants who settled there in the nineteenth century, the term is 'paddy-handett [paddy-handed]', 'and ahm fae tha' end of the toon,' said Joe.

Go beyond Dundee and one of the most widely known phrases is 'corrie-fisted' – indeed, many informants told Voices the colourful story of the corrie-fisted defenders of Ferniehirst castle near Jedburgh in the Borders. In the early sixteenth century they were required to wield their axes in their left hand by the left-handed laird, Andrew Kerr, as it was thought to offer an advantage in battle – and in consequence they were known as 'kerr-' or 'corrie-handed'.

'Corrie-fisted' turned up in Glasgow right enough, but Voices was also offered 'cloddy-handed' and 'coddy-fisted' (pronounced of course 'festid') by several interviewees together with 'corrie-duke' and simply 'corrie'. In the port of Leith on the northern side of Edinburgh, Voices captured 'corrie-dukit' (pronounced 'jukit') again and a new one, 'carrie-pod', this

The Sound of the Scottish City

In this and the following sections, I'm concentrating on the sound of the cities of Scotland's Central Belt, and Tayside. Raw Glasgow speech, made nationally famous by Billy Connolly, has a rasp and a rawness to it that speaks of the rough side of town. It's all open 'a's, and when combined with the harsh Glaswegian 'r' that rattles the sonic fibre of every sentence, it becomes aggressive, fists-up talk. Cliff Hanley, a broadcaster and connoisseur of Glaswegian dialect, once observed that 'There's a very strong sense of community in Glasgow, defensive and aggress-ive, and our language is part of our determination to be distinct and to exclude other people: it's almost like a rampart', so words are spat out with heavy emphasis and a growly delivery littered with glottal stops.

Vowels tend to lengthen under pressure – short 'e' becomes more like the sound in 'air'; 'i' when stressed becomes a distinct 'eh' so 'rich' makes you 'retch'. The vowel in 'house', 'town' and 'around' is lengthened to 'oo' ('hoos', 'toon' and 'aroon'), though 'ground' is not 'groond' but 'grund' (rhymes with regular 'fund'), a carry-over from Old and Middle English. The sound 'oo' is brought right forward in the mouth in both Glasgow and Dundee to one very close to French 'tu'. As usual, I've added a 'y' to indicate this narrowing in the transcriptions: 'muydy [moody]'.

from Jimmy, the most elderly of the Leith group, who'd grown up in Loanhead, in south Edinburgh. By contrast, take a quick dip into the Borders to check what country folk – not that far from the Kerrs' corrie-fisted family seat – made of their southpaw cousins: the town of Hawick has its own very distinctive southern uplands speech and they came up with 'skelly-jukey [dukey]', 'geggy-handed' and 'cairy-handy' (pronounced incidentally, Hawick fashion, 'honded' and 'hondy').

It's worth, I think, observing that, merely by interviewing twenty or so people from the southern half of Scotland, Voices managed to record, in November 2004, at least twelve different dialectal variants for this one idea of left-handedness. It puts the almost ubiquitous 'cack-handed' and very limited 'cuddy-wifter' that the survey found south of the border into sharp perspective.

Then there are the words that are locked firmly into Scottish society, which have an existence here in a very different way from other parts

The working-class Dundee accent Voices captured has a similarly harsh urban tone but more of a lethargic drawl: the game of Kick the Can is pronounced 'Keck the Caan' with markedly lengthened vowels. 'Fae' meaning from is clearly sounded 'fay' ('ay wuz fae Fin'rae'), and long 'oo' (school) gets a real local twist with a long 'e' to add to that narrowed 'French' 'u' – 'skeeyl'. The vowel in 'eye' flattens to 'ay', so that our informants could comfortably talk of 'may skeeyl [my school]', but a 'boy' at the school would metamorphose into a 'bye'. ('Boiling' here is 'byling' and a 'joiner' a 'jyner'). Amongst verbs, 'can't', 'wasn't' and 'didn't' here routinely become 'cannae', 'wasnae' and 'didnae', and 'doing' a simple sound not far from 'dean'.

On the other hand, Edinburgh talk as captured by the Voices microphone is an altogether gentler matter, with more of a sing-song rise and fall. Maybe it was something to do with the fact that all the speakers had long left the hardship of tenement life behind, but even the guttural talk of dockland Leith was softer than that of either Dundee or Glasgow. One interesting pronunciation point across all three cities is that stress and sentence position make a lot of difference to the way vowels are pronounced such that the same vowel can have two differing sounds within the same sentence: one speaker from Edinburgh (talking about fixing something in her hair) said she'd to 'pen i' wi' a hair-pin'.

of the United Kingdom. Some are geographical features, like a 'loan' (cattle-track). Loanhead, pronounced 'Loanheed', is as I've mentioned a district of Edinburgh, but 'loans' are to be found on the map all across Scotland and the term forms part of the deep culture of the country. Likewise, tenement blocks and 'single entries' (one-roomed dwellings – to my surprise the interviewees from the market town of Hawick also claimed they had 'a lot' of tenements) are familiar social realities, even to a generation that didn't know them first-hand. And when they were demolished, the 'schemes' that replaced them also helped define who you were, along with the vernacular that flourished there: for Mark, Kevin, Joe and Gary from Dundee, the 'scheme' is 'where yurr fae'. It is therefore perhaps no surprise that when asked the regulation question about what they'd call a passageway between two houses, all the urban groups were able not only to tap into a rich word-hoard but also a well-stocked bank of experiences.

The terms they came up with were legion and demonstrated some very fine distinctions. Just compare the relative thinness of English responses that I've written about elsewhere in this book – the ubiquitous 'alleyway' leavened by the rare 'ginnel', 'twitchel' and 'backsie'. Here in urban Scotland, Voices found a whole rack of different words, each with its long history that tells a story of close-living in tough slum conditions. Many are Scots standards: like 'pend' and 'close' (both mean an alley or passageway), though in Dundee the young men gave them an affectionate ending: 'pendie' and 'closie':

> 'There used to be a lo' o' pends on the cent'ra tuiyn an' up the hull [in the centre of town and up the hill]. Ma oul maan was borrn in Norrays [Norrie's] Pend – that's knawked doon noo, it's not en the Ould Toon. Bu' ah think pendies ell be disappearen' fae the language . . .'

And as you can read in the 'Snapshot' section, 'Jutetown Blues', these young men got up to some high jinks in the 'pendies' and 'closies' of their youth. Cut to Glasgow and a much older trio, James, Charlie and Iain. All are in their sixties and all were brought up in the Carlton district of the city near the Clyde. They offered Voices another old Scots term for an alley, a 'wynd' (pronounced 'wined'), a word that's come down to modern Scots from Old English roots and meaning a 'winding, narrow street or alley, chiefly in towns and cities': 'There's stell wiynds un the toon,' they commented.

They also – erroneously – offered 'haugh' (pronounced 'haw') as an alternative. 'Haugh' is a solid Scots word that's part of the standard lexicon, though meaning not an alley in fact this time but a piece of level ground beside a river; Flesher's Haugh is a prominent open space in Glasgow where famously Rangers football club had its origins.

The group from Leith, with a different accent and skew to their linguistic traditions, came up with 'row' (e.g. Hatter's Row and Parsonage Row) and a 'vennel'. 'Vennel' is yet another 'alley' word with a solid pedigree. The Scots dictionary records it from the beginning of the eighteenth century meaning a 'narrow alley' or 'lane between houses' – interestingly exactly what a Yorkshire man or woman would refer to as a 'ginnel'. 'Vennels' are to be found in Dumfries, Forfar, Perth and, naturally, Edinburgh.

'Close', though, is universally understood, with its associated images of social deprivation, families living on top of each other. (John from Edinburgh added the distinction that 'when you're in Glasgow you would talk about a "close" but down in Leith we'd always call it the "entry" when you went up a tenement stair,' a further fine linguistic distinction.)

Originally a courtyard, 'close' then became applied to the passageway that led to it: 'A clawse is no' a public thoroughfare; a clawse . . . it's something you gaw up to . . .' – a narrow lane, in fact. And with the words come flooding back recollections of the tough conditions of working-class family life in a 'single end'. No sitting room, living room or parlour, here, just a kitchen. These were single-bedroomed, sometimes single-*roomed* apartments with no lavatory, and housing a whole family:

> 'A rruiymen ketchn [rooming kitchen] we alwiz colld [called] i'; a
> ketchn. Ah mean therr wasnae such things as scalleriz [sculleries] an'
> louynges – it wuz a roomin' ketchn wi' a bed reeceiss [with a bed
> recess] – a ketchn wi' a reinge ennut [with a range in it] an' we oll saet
> roond i' on a Sa'urday. Some of the faemily sleipt in et an ye ate in et,
> an' tha' wuz yerr ketchn . . .'

These memories bring out the broadest Glaswegian in the Carlton group, words running together in strips of language slipping effortlessly off the tongue: 'slep' enna rruiym, ate enna ketchen, sa' enna ketchen [slept in the room, ate in the kitchen, sat in the kitchen]'. In this fast delivery, 'the' can become elided simply to 'a' ('ate enna ketchen'), and notice, too, the typical 'i' vowel that here, as in Dundee, is firmly voiced as a very open 'e', 'ketchen'. These older men remember ('mind' in Scots) quite distinctly as well the era before electricity – 'Ah caan meind the gaas leit' – and for the children they were at the time, fragile gas mantles meant breakages ('a man'le fragmen'id') and the inevitable parental punishment.

As I note elsewhere, there's something satisfying for the older Voices interviewees in looking back from a position of greater social security to a time of extreme hardship. In Lancashire, it's the tippler toilet they remember with affection; in Glasgow, it's the journey down the hall or 'lobby', filled perhaps with boxes of produce waiting to be sold or a basket of coal, to the 'cludgie' or 'lavvy'. These words recurred through-out the urban areas as standard (older) vernacular for lavatory, though national formulas like 'bog', 'shethoouyse' [shithouse] and 'loo' were also mentioned:

'The bet [bit] betwin the ketchen an' the ruim wuz the lawbby. The lawbby wuz the holl [hall]. The ootsiyde toile' wuz oot on the steir heed [stair head].'

Your friend was always your 'pal' – still the word of choice across all the groups – and drunkenness was common, recounted the group from Leith, Millie, John, Jimmy and John, particularly meths drinkers who'd fetch up in the hallways and smash the gas mantles, whom they'd have to step over on the stair. Millie, who was rehoused when the Leith slums were demolished, remembered her home:

'There were six houses in Admirality Street as they say in Leith – we all know it's "Admiralty" but in Leith they give an extra "i" – and there were four single ends and four rooming kitchens and on the half-landing they'd call the mezzanine floor now, that was where the one lavvy was – a sink wi' a cold water tap that's all there was. And the range the fire range and everything went on in that one room. And people had six, seven bairns . . .'

Hard living, often leavened by hard liquor. Scots is famed for the wealth of words it records for being drunk, but one came out on top every time amongst the Voices interviewees: 'blootered'. 'Blooter', though, also means to 'thump hard':

'Ye talk aboot "bluy'erring" a ball: "Watch i'! Ye'll ge' bluy'errd." An i' also refairrs to a drrunk. Ef someone wurrey [were to] "bluy'err" somebody, they'd become rubberr-legged an' het the deeck [hit the deck] same as ef you werre drinkun', so a suppose et comes from the same thing.'

'Blootered', 'stocious', 'steamin'', 'staggerin'', 'fleein'', 'happy drrunk', 'faytin' [fighting] drrunk' . . .

'Ye ge' haappy drrunks, ye ge' faytin' drrunks an ye ge' singin' drrunks. Somebody tha's steamin' is a haappy drrunk. "Stocious" means paraletic: ye'rre rubberr-legged; ye joost cannae muyve [you just can't move]; ye doan' know the tame a dee [time of day], ye doan know where ye'are, ye cannae stand, ye joost lie there in the gu'err [gutter].'

These observations are from George of the River Clyde Lifeboat Station and his sister Ann.

There was one further word for 'drunk' which had very widespread use amongst these urban speakers – 'stoting'. There's an interesting web of concepts here. 'Stot' and 'stotter' are old Scots verbs for to bounce and to stagger, with short and long 'o' forms and connections to a teutonic root meaning 'to strike or hit'. A 'stoater' (sic) is a strikingly good-looking woman (a 'wee stoater' is a familiar expression), and *The Stoater* even became the name of a popular Scottish newspaper column. Seems like all the terms and meanings have merged into one glorious word – 'stoatin' ':

'. . . and if the rain's coming heavy it's sto'un; i' stotes [bounces] off the grund; "stoating stuff" is "good" and she's a stoter is a laassie who's attractive.'

And for the group from Carlton (with broader accents, hence 'stawturr'):

'she's a stawturr, she's a beautiful, you knaw, burrd, a lassie; thass a righ' guid y'un – applies tae a lo't of things – stawtn game of football, stawtn cuppa tea . . .'

Of course, if it's not stoting with rain, it's likely to be just damp. Rare, alongside the standard-issue 'drizzle', amongst these city groups was the Scots vernacular 'smirr' – I also came across this in Northern Ireland. More common was 'dreich'. Originally meaning 'long drawn out', 'tedious' or 'wearisome' it's a Scots word related to Old English that's now come to mean that sort of unrelenting, penetrating rain that's not entirely unknown in Scotland: 's'smurrn [it's smirring],' said one interviewee. 'It's fiyne, fiyne rain. Drezzle's a wee bet heavier rein affter tha'.'

'Glaikit' was a good old Scots word that most of the city groups Voices spoke to quoted as normal usage. Meaning 'stupid' or 'foolish' it's a term that goes back several centuries. Similarly, still as the standard words for children (of differing ages) we found 'bairn' and 'wain' or 'wean', though the distribution varied. Among the older interviewees, a 'dub' was still a puddle, and 'breeks' or 'strides' were trousers, though amongst the young men from Dundee, the Mancunian 'keks' had become regular usage: ' "Get yurr keks aff!" Ye'd see [say] tha' ti a laassie ef ye werr awn good terrms wi' err.' Or get a smack where it hurts, he added.

That wonderfully variable mundane item that people remember with snorts of pleasurable distaste all around the UK, the school plimsoll, found unanimity across the Scottish towns – 'sandshoes' they were, though commonly abbreviated to 'sannies'. James, Charlie and Iain from Carlton painted a fetching portrait of a Glasgow childhood where sannies were only one and six (7½p) a pair: 'Ye drreeist up furr the furrst Sundi 'n Meaiy: nyu sannies an' a nyu sneik bel' [You dressed up for the first Sunday in May: new sannies and a new snake belt]'.

If you're tired, in urban Scotland as almost everywhere in Britain now, old, young, rich, poor, you're 'knackered' (though it's fascinating that here, as often, there was a slight reservation about using it too publicly, its connections with knackering or gelding horses still too vivid for some to admit the word for polite use). But Voices was offered some interesting alternatives: in Dundee, it was 'puggled'; a Fifeshire expression, it was asserted, though the dictionary records it as having possibly a Hindi origin via army slang. In Leith on the other hand Millie suggested 'wabbit', a late-nineteenth-century word meaning exhausted and without energy.

All agreed that there was a degree of standardization going on even in these vigorous speech communities, though to what extent the norm was a *Scottish* standard or a British one was less clear. Most of the informants were passionate about their language and several of them write verse in a swaggering vernacular that celebrates working lives and the challenges they face. They see themselves in some way as the custodians of a greater past vernacular richness. John, a teacher from Edinburgh, said:

> 'I tried to check out some of the words from my youth with my grandchildren, and words that we would have used in the house would have been "press" for a cupboard, "bunker" and it's worktop now; a "tallboy" that's just a chest of drawers now.'

John was, however, also quick to point out the simultaneous growth in vernacular terms amongst the city's drug misusers: words like 'twirls' for keys, 'mort' for woman and 'screeve' for a car. 'Highers' are money, 'porris' is pocket and 'barri' is great. My spelling here is approximate: these are spoken forms, though in several cases (e.g. 'mort', 'barri') they seem to stem from travellers' cant.

Finally, in this section, a pair of delightful expressions from an old

Leith resident, Millie, that catch the spirit of tougher times, when rising up the social ladder was longed for, but had its own perils: 'One skittery coo likes another', meaning something like 'Birds of a feather . . .' but applied to 'somebody who's drunk and loose and bad':

> 'And there was granny's great one that was for somebody that gets [above themselves] and forgets where they came from: "when dirt rises it blinds you".'

Dundee Snapshot: Jutetown Blues

> 'It's liyke mi meit seayz, wuh arr wha wuh arr, nae airrs nae greicez, brough' u' wi' worrkin' class feicez, levvin fae han' ti muyth, tellin the truyth tuh wha' really me''errs yooursel . . .'

The speaker is a poet, Mark, from Dundee. The passion with which he speaks of an ordinary working life – 'we are what we are, no airs no graces, brought up with working class faces' – runs through the words, the strong Dundonian accent and the confident, defiant delivery.

As I've noted elsewhere in this chapter, Dundee's is a history of industrial wealth and decline built round textiles and the ships that traded them with the world. 'Jute, jam and journalism' was the old rather pat summary of the city's history, and if today the jute's gone, the jam and the well-known titles of the D. C. Thomson newspaper organization (not least the *Beano* and *Dandy* comics) are still a force to be reckoned with.

When Kevin, Mark, Gary and Joe spoke to Voices, though, the picture of the city that emerged was one of poverty and tough living on the streets and 'schemes' (a uniquely Scots usage meaning 'housing estates') of districts like St Mary's, Fintry, Mid Craigie and Lochee. The words and the accent are distinctive: 'bowk', to be sick, to retch, and pronounced here 'bawk' (from Middle English *bolken*, to belch), and 'skelp', to hit (from a northern Middle English word *skelpe*), are just two fine words that crop up in the conversation; as for the accent, you'll need to have a look at the 'Sound of . . .' section to be able to make your way through the very individual quality of the Dundonian brogue.

The stories though are what make this conversation both entertaining and linguistically interesting. Take this account of Dundee street-life not long ago when these young men – they're now in their late twenties and thirties – were teenagers, members of a gang from their local 'scheme', the Fintry Shams:

> 'Yu affullia'ed youyrsel wi what gaang came fae yourr scheme. An ay was fae Fin'rae an' the Fin'rae Shaams were the local gang, an ye sti' see tha graffi'i an the waaz bu' it's no uz promenen' as it was.'

The gangs move on but their insignia remain graffiti'd on the walls. Notice how Mark's speech is dotted with glottal stops ('Fin'rae' is Fintry and 'affullia'ed' is 'affiliated' where the 'i' sound has also moved closer to the 'u' in 'up'). The shift elsewhere in the sentence of 'i' to open 'e' is very marked when the men talk of the district of town known as Mid Craigie, where 'mid' becomes a very definite 'med' sound.

Each gang had its insignia, its salute and uniform coloured jumpers: 'Med' (Mid Craigie) was green and red, Fintry black and red, Whitfield white and blue:

> 'Ye had carrdigans or jumm'errs to associate yourself wi' your scheme – an' there were gaang signs as well – ye'd see guys an' tha' on the bus on the tap doin' their gaang signal ta the diffrun' schemes. An' just to wind up the people in the schemes the buses would ge' breckd [bricked] as well.'

They kept their secrets secret by using a form of backslang, what they called 'eggy language': 'The' pu' "eigg" on the end of everything they'd go' ti seay so "Whatrefeggin youegg on abooteggin [What the f— are you on about] . . ."' And life for these lads was tough – they played hard, fought hard and threats of punishment meted out at home tended to be pretty hard too – 'skelp your puss' (pronounced 'pus') and 'kick your doup' are the expressions here ('smash your face' and 'kick your arse'):

> '. . . atherrise I'll skelp ye riyght in the meth. Ahl skelp yer puss; mi mum an' da said "ahl keck yurr doup!", which is yerr arrse.'

> ['. . . otherwise I'll skelp you right in the mouth. I'll skelp your "puss"; my mum and dad said . . .']

'Doup' (sometimes written 'dowp') has two meanings (it's unclear whether they're related) – the bottom of an eggshell . . . and of a human being:

the Dundee da' who threatened to kick his son's doup was invoking a long and literary linguistic tradition, as the expression is recorded in poetry as far back as 1721.

On the schemes, the lads' favourite games (pronounced with a very short 'e': 'ghems') were: 'Waak the Plank ar Jyne the Cruyw' ('Walk the Plank or Join the Crew'), 'Under-errm Teg' ('Under-arm Tig') and 'Kick the Can'. 'Ye needed a beg heavy ten [big heavy tin], so ye couyd bouyt i' as farr as ye couyd [boot it as far as you could].' Gary laughingly remembered one particularly cruel practical joke they played during a game of 'Kick the Can':

> 'This is horrible, right, but "keck the caan", right. Ye ken a young guy, arright: "gie ye a fevver [give you a fiver] ef ye can keck this caan as far ye caan, eh?" Bu' wha' 'e didna ken [But what he didn't know] was tha' we fund [found] this beg, twelve-ench rusty nail – we'd haammered this ento the grrund. An' basically ye ken the rest: raan up fest [fast] as 'e can, bluy'urrd e' [blootered it], thingied is ankle, caan didnae muyve an' a wuz ou'a t' ghem [can didn't move and he was out of the game].'

Gary's account of the game is fast and furious like the encounter it described. He slurs his words together in a mix of strong accent ('can', 'hammered', 'ran' all are stretched to a very long flat 'a') and Scots terms ('ken', to know; 'grund', ground; 'blootered', hit).

Another favourite trick was to frighten neighbours in a close (tenement – here Mark uses the diminutive 'closie') with a jam jar of bees whose wings they'd removed. It was called 'Canny Annie', which was the name St Mary's boys gave to the bumblebee. Where he lived, says Mark, they were known as 'yellow-noses':

> 'We callt them "yella-noseys" up in Fin'rae, bu' ower un Lochee I think they called them "fogies", in Lochee, aye. It was the ains [ones] that ye could catch an' taak the weng aff them an' keep them as wee pets; tha' was a "yella-nosey". '

And why 'Canny Annie'?

> 'We called it a "Canny Annie" 'cos she couldna sting – 'cos she cannae!'

The game consisted of taking a jarful 'while they were still fresh' as Mark puts it, get them agitated with a hefty shake of the jar and bang on the front-door of a tenement flat. They'd remove the lid and the insects 'ud aa' be uit' – would all be out – and then you'd take off smartish:

'We used to ge' a jarful of wassps an' bees whiyle they werr still fressh, an' sheik them ap ge' them a bu' wiyld, djap on somebody's doorr – had to be up the closie where the bees couldnae ge' awa – an' le' the led aaff an' the bees an' wassps ud aa' be uit when the perrson opened the doorr. An' ye'd ta' off.'

'Skeeyl' – 'school' in its distinctive local pronunciation – was often to be skipped, or as these young men put it 'plonked' (pronounced 'plunked'): 'plunk' is no geein' ti skeeyl; no' go'n' in at aa' [not going to school; not going in at all].' Those essential items of every pupil, plimsolls for PE, here are, in keeping with many places across Scotland, neither 'pumps' nor 'daps' and certainly not 'gutties'. They're 'sand-shoes' or, colloquially, 'sannies'; though these lads knew them more readily as 'borstal breakouts'.

Like the accent with its myriad glottal stops (Mark was insistent that 'mental', that ubiquitous term for insane, would never be heard in Dundee carrying its 't': 'very definitely not "men*t*al"; it's a sort of "uh" sound'), the language of working-class Dundee is pretty uncompromising. If you were to see someone unattractive, they'd be (as widely in the UK) a 'dog', or, more graphically still: 'If you were unattractive you'd gie me the bawk ['bowk', to retch; for its etymology, see above, and the glossary], you'd be bawking.' And if you were feeling particularly uncharitable, you might even go so far as to say that a woman had a face 'like a joiner's nailbag' – 'She's go' a puss like a jyner's nailbag'.

This group of enthusiastic and talented performance poets from the rough corners of town are very attuned to the language they hear about them in their native city:

'When you'rre en a pob, oor wurrk en a faactory the laanguage is as couyrrse as Hell. We've go' a laassie therre wha' wurrks on the liyne an' she would 'a' fe''id ba' en the ju' mulls. She'll tawk abuyt anything jus' liyke any o' the boys – just any sexual innuendoes an' a'. She's go' other wurrds tha' the boys 'ud yase, an' yeer liyke crengin' some'imes!'

['When you're in a pub, or work in a factory, the language is as coarse as Hell. We've got a lassie there what works on the line and she would have fitted back in the jute mills. She'll talk about anything just like any of the boys – just any sexual innuendoes and that. She's got other words that the boys would use, and you're like cringing sometimes.']

It may not be the norm, says Mark, the poet, the man of words, but it's real enough and belongs to the world they know and grew out of, and all the more genuine for it:

'It's no' stuff ye'll hearr usual laassies en Dundee socie'y spea'in' liyke bu' ah thenk in the faactory environment ye do ge' people tha' steck [stick] to the language they've been bro' up wi' and ken [been brought up with and know].'

And in his poem 'The Mither Tongue', which he delivers with a passion that galvanizes a room, Mark writes:

'There are some that say it's a wee bit raa', ay dinna think so at aa'. Ay think it's braa, it's fine an' dandy, it's loose an' free when ay talk in broad Dundee.'

Rural Scotland: Remote Control

The car certainly wasn't going anywhere. It was beached, motionless and overheating, beside the mirror waters of the Kyle of Tongue. The empty, single-track road (with passing places, as the signs reminded careful drivers) stretched pitilessly away into the drizzle. It was raining. Again. This was my first experience of real remoteness, or at least of the reality of remoteness within the British Isles. It was nearly fifty years ago; even main roads beyond the tourist trails around the Trossachs and Loch Lomond were in those days ribbon-thin bands of grey tarmac – or less – winding effortfully over passes and along lochsides, hugging contours and skirting watercourses they couldn't bridge. Caithness and Sutherland (as the counties that constituted the northern part of Scotland were then known) were a very, very long way from anywhere. And the car, an ageing Ford Popular – not even a Harry Potter Anglia but the preceding sit-up-and-beg model with flapping indicators that sometimes didn't flap

– the car wasn't moving. It was, my mother assured me, part of the adventure. A sodden tent going mouldy for shelter – it had rained literally every day for a fortnight – my disabled mother's wheelchair sticking ungainlily out of the boot, and a slightly frightened child, and we were stuck thirty miles from a telephone. Some adventure.

I tell the story only because it burned into my child's mind just how remote 'remote' could be, even in Britain. The Kyle of Tongue has long been bridged and cars have for many years not had to take the grand detour round the sealoch. But then – and in linguistic terms it really isn't long ago at all – to travel from one settlement to another in this part of Scotland meant a very long and slow journey. I remember marvelling that the map marked post offices, lodges, hotels and AA boxes as major landmarks. There was little else. Even towns like Oban, with its sea connections and important role as a ferry hub, was an arduous drive from the nearest next town.

This is the linguistic cradle for much of Scotland's rural speech, in these villages and settlements, tiny, thinly scattered across the map and self-sufficient. Self-sufficient in language too. Here, as perhaps nowhere else in the United Kingdom, there are closed communities that remain, even with modern communications, to a degree closed off – by relatively irreducible elements like geography: island fastnesses, remote valleys accessible only over difficult passes. And, of course, all parts of Scotland are susceptible to extreme weather which can, at worst, suspend the ferries, destroy the power lines and sweep away causeways. In the so-called Long Island, that eyebrow-shaped pattern of lumps of peat and rock that curves down the west side of the Highlands, I remember the inhabitants of North Uist – Uibhist A Tuath in Gaelic – telling Stanley Ellis and me of the 200-kilometre-an-hour hurricane that had recently swept caravans half way across the island. Here the wind rarely doesn't blow, and the living is hard.

About half of the Scottish landmass – essentially the west and the north – is historically a Gaelic-speaking area, while the south and east, along a very rough diagonal line but looping a lot further south of the Great Glen, speaks Scots in a number of distinctive dialects, each markedly different from one another. On the Kyle of Tongue, that wet August day in 1961, our feelings of remoteness were compounded by the accent of the locals when eventually they rescued us. It's a sound that once heard

is never forgotten, the gentle purr of Gaelic-accented English. To Sassenach ears it has a wonderfully melodious, susurrating quality, full of
devoiced consonants and emphasized sibilants, so sharply different from
the gruffness of urban Glasgow or yet again from the upended vowel-
scheme of the so-called 'Doric' dialect heard in the east.

The Survey of English Dialects of course never made its way to
Scotland, though the riches of Scots in its many different forms have
been well documented by a number of academic and other enquiries,
notably the *Linguistic Atlas of Scotland*, published in 1975. One of the more
interesting recent reports was that carried out in 1996 by the General
Register Office of Scotland with a view to assessing whether a question
should be included in census returns about the speaking of Scots. It
concluded:

> The language used in Scotland today retains a lot of traditional speech
> forms, though there is a continuum of speech type in the Scottish
> population ranging from clearly English to clearly Scots.

The report suggested that at a conservative reckoning at least a third of
Scots considered themselves as Scots speakers. That's to say that their
speech was more than simply a Scottish-accented version of English, but
included words and syntax that was dialectal and distinctly different.
Perhaps not surprisingly, the very marked pronunciation and vocabulary
of Doric – the word itself when pronounced by a native speaker comes
out something like 'Dourech' – gave the Grampian region where it
flourishes a very high score of 60 per cent. The south-west corner of the
country also scored well at 40 per cent. Again, perhaps predictably, it
was the older segment of the population that contained the greatest
numbers of self-confessed Scots speakers. Coming up to date, the contemporary Voices survey, which I'll come back to later in this section, has
taken language snapshots from over 160 individuals from Coldstream in
the Borders, to Stornoway in the Western Isles, to Whalsay on Shetland
and St Andrews on the east coast. It's a major record of the way Scots is
being spoken in all areas, and not just in the well-trodden and easily
accessible Central Belt.

Ten years before that GRO report, Stanley Ellis, long the field-worker
for the Survey of English Dialects, investigated for the BBC the interplay
between Gaelic and English in the Western Isles. It's a complex boundary,

scarred by long and painful history: the so-called Highland Clearances of the native population of the northern mainland and islands by Lowland landlords and their frequently English agents in the eighteenth and nineteenth centuries eventually drove native Gaelic-speaking crofters from their land. Many emigrated and the displacement irretrievably reduced the population, diluted the culture and had a lasting effect on the viability of Scots Gaelic. The songs and the speech of the Uist people are still touched with a yearning sadness that translates a deep and poetic attachment to the land that is theirs. As John MacDonald told Ellis:

> I feel the strong Gaelic roots we have are firmly embedded in the soil right round about us. I think if theess stoune dykes could talk they would talk to me in Gaelic. I'm cerrtain of that.

The Uists, North and South, and the little islands of Benbecula and Grimsay that lie between them (and today also Eriskay to the south), are all joined by a winding road that becomes a causeway over the thin inlets between the islands. It's forty or so miles from Lochboisdale in the south where the ferry arrives to Lochmaddy in the north: a landscape of horizontals – the few trees blown that way by the scourging winds, the water lying in long slivers of silver-grey across the landscape interrupted by a handful of bleak peaks. Stanley Ellis called North Uist:

> A piece of *broderie anglaise* with the shores of an apparent 1,000 freshwater and seawater lochs delicately and randomly filling in the landmass especially in the east. The wind, arriving at land after 3,000 miles of ocean, seems to blow endlessly.

The famous 'black houses' – *tigh dubh* in Gaelic – with their thick stone walls and thatched roofs, are built strong and low to resist the insinuation of the wind, yet even twenty years ago most of the islanders lived in comfortable bungalows and many black houses were ruins or uninhabited. Back then one crofter (a small-scale farmer living at the shoreline) spoke of the still strong place Gaelic had in the island. But he hinted, too, at the change that was already afoot:

> We are a string of islands: that does protect Gaelic. If we were joined to the mainland of Scotland, Gaelic would have died a death a long time ago. Ninety-nine per cent of those still in the island, especially in

the crafting, they speak Gaelic. But there is a very strange situation: you hear the parents speaking Gaelic, but all the younger generation seem to be speaking English.

Now that younger generation are themselves parents and living twenty-first-century lives in these now less-remote islands. Voices caught up with four of them in Stornoway, the capital of Lewis, in this string of peaty pearls the next but one island-mass north (Harris is in fact not an island at all but linked to Lewis by a tiny finger of land). Innes, Kevin, David and Alasdair are young men from Lewis with a very modern outlook on life. There's Gaelic in the offing – they'd use the indigenous words when they were speaking the language – but these men, you can tell in an instant, are comfortable in English. Not for them the fractional pause as they render their thoughts from Gaelic into schoolroom English that Stanley Ellis heard from the Uist men and women in 1985. There's talk of snowboarding: they know the special 'left-handed' and 'right-handed' terms for the sport, but stick to the standard English elsewhere. And listen to this string of mainstream English terminology when they were asked the standard Voices question about words for drunk:

'Pissed, steamboats, hammered, trousered, ripped, rat-arsed, got a good glow . . .'

You could be anywhere. So how about that telltale that's been a pointer from the very first chapter of this book? What do these lads call someone who's unattractive? They're 'minging', 'a dog' or – and this for me is the most revealing, because clearly it's made its mark via humour – they 'walked through the ugly forest and got hit by every branch'. Now, don't get me wrong, these men (to varying degrees) are fluent and comfortable Gaelic speakers. (There are, according to the statistics, nearly 60,000 Scots who claim to speak the language.) And when they say familiar English words like 'bonkers' (the Voices question about words for 'insane') it comes out as 'bonkersh' with that arresting Gaelic-English sibilance. They also preferred 'allt', the Gaelic word for stream, to any English term:

'We used to say, "We're going down to the allt!" I would call it an allt even to people who [didn't understand Gaelic].'

But within English discourse, the old Celtic words were few and far between. Compare them with Iain MacDonald, a crofter recorded by Stanley Ellis around a quarter of a century ago, as he flips in and out of Gaelic while he describes peat-cutting. Peat is the natural fuel of the islands, cut and stacked often just above the shoreline in black piles drying into scented briquettes ready to burn through the long, bleak Hebridean winter. Peat-cutting is a job Iain carries out 'in Gaelic'. As Ellis commented: 'they describe the whole thing as a Gaelic activity . . . because that's how they think and speak, even when they're working alone.'

> Turfing is where you skin the top to a depth of eighteen inches to get to the good burning fuel below that. The implement is known as a 'tairsgeir' ['treisgeih'] – peat iron – *tairsgeir* in Gaelic: *buain na mònach* ['buanvonnach'], literally cutting the peat. In Gaelic *mhòine* ['vawnye'] is the Gaelic for peat.

Cut to the mainland in 2005 and the small town of Inveraray near the head of Loch Fyne. When I travelled this way as a youngster (before the catastrophic breakdown) it was already remote territory. Not now. The M9 today peeks into the other corner of the map, and the speech captured by Voices is Scots, rather than Gaelic and as often as not hales from the Central Belt conurbation: 'This used to be a Gaelic-speaking area, not so very many years ago,' lament Donald, Laura, Dorothy, Colin and Malcolm, 'fifty to sixty years ago it was all Gaelic.' Now English is spoken in the post office (the redoubt for older speech, seemingly). One man admits he was taught Gaelic in school:

> 'but I didn't listen. I can think of very few fluent Gaelic speakers who were born and brought up in Inveraray. Most of them have been incomers from either Jura or Raasay. If you go into the paper shop, the lassie there's from Eriskay. Now she addresses you in Gaelic every dee about the weather; you know she's got wonderrful worrds for the weather – you get that, and 'How are you?' Words like 'bodach' ['bottach'] for the old man would be used a lot and 'cailleach' ['kayach'] for the old woman and 'how's your health?' would be discussed, in Gaelic probably.'

I feel there's a deep longing to connect with the Gaelic roots of the town, but a realization that they've now gone too far to get back.

'You always felt coming down over the Rest an' Be Thankful [Pass] that you were coming into a different world but it's bin diluted. It's still not spoilt completely but it's bin diluted an' not for the best.

Today, almost all the reference points of this group belong in a sort of general Scottish territory that's loosely located round the culture further south: when they're annoyed, they're 'Scunnered – you're scunnered wi' yeself – ragin': ah'm reigin'; fair beelin' [boiling].' And if they were not feeling too well, it was a Scots term rather than a Gaelic one that sprang to mind – that delicious expression heard earlier in this chapter in Leith, 'peelie-wallie'. (Incidentally, according to this group, 'wallie' meant china-white and was applied to such things as 'ornamental ducks': 'wallie ducks' were either side of the fireplace, 'wallie closes' were superior tenement buildings decorated with tiles and 'wallie teeth' were dentures.) Drunk brought a cascade of similarly non-specifically local words, a 'bidie-in' was what they'd call a live-in partner (Voices heard this somewhat derogatory Scots term in several locations) and truanting was 'dogging' or 'plunking':

'The awld man colled me in an gae me sex [six] of the best with the awd belt. Told me to tek ma hands out of ma pockets an' he gaeve me sex of the best over the legs. An I desairrved it. Bu' tha was for plunkin' the school.'

Their Gaelic was very limited indeed: food terms like a herring and tattie supper, 'sgadan buntàta'; and 'tha mi sgìth' for 'I'm tired', 'seanmhair' for grandmother ('used a lot around here'), 'bùrach' for a mess and 'fliuch' for a rainy day.

Many of these words cropped up, particularly 'tha mi sgìth' and 'seanmhair' in Scots conversation across the country as regular and routine borrowings from Gaelic. I'm not sure whether it's purely chance, or something more atavistic at work, but I've noted that within Scots the Gaelic words that almost everyone borrows are *seanmhair* and *seanair* (grandmother and grandfather), and the same is true of the respective Welsh and Punjabi terms in Welsh English and the English of Punjabi-speakers (in Bedworth, Midlands).

But these little fragments of the old language of the Highlands are mere crackles in the ether compared with the full-blown language. The people of the Outer Hebrides could see it coming, twenty years ago. Parents 'don't teach their children Gaelic. The children are speaking English in the playground. My wife is from the mainland so she's an English speaker.' This man was a Gaelic-speaker and though his eldest son spoke 'fairly fluent Gaelic, the youngest doesn't speak much Gaelic at all'.

> Gaelic is on the decline, over the last twenty years, anyway. People have lost the art of conversation, particularly the younger ones, who sit and watch television and don't do much to provide their own entertainment as they used to, when they used to sing Gaelic songs and tell the stories and recite the stories among themselves and perhaps do a wee bit of "bàrdachd" [= poetry writing] here and there.

On the far eastern side of the country, the dialect of Scots known as Doric (a name with a classical origin but disputed rationale) flourishes in the Grampian area, and Voices caught up with it in the 'Bloo Toon', local slang for the old fishing port of Peterhead (or Peter*heed* as it's always said locally). It's probably too soon to tell whether the crippling impact EU fishing controls have had on the local industry ('there are boarded up and empty shops in the high street . . . and a definite air of depression about the place,' observes one recent guide) will affect the dialect. The rule I've found throughout Britain is that industrial decline spells the dilution of the talk that close-working fosters.

Certainly amongst the elderly speakers Voices met there was a vigorous articulation of the 'Dourech' as they called it. To the untutored ear, this is a quite remarkable form of Scots, and as different from Glaswegian or Stornowegian as the Dundee talk I've described elsewhere in this chapter. This is by any standards one of the most singular sounds in Britain: 'Ah could turn my tongue as bawnie [bonnie] as ye like'. Listen to Wilma, Bob, Margaret, Sheila and Peggy's list of words for 'playing truant': 'didnae turn up', 'jinkin'. There were the usual tales of the warden (the 'snappy'), whose job it was to report and catch truanting children: 'The parents were tellt; ah got put throuygh to the dominie [teacher].' Many of their words were not unusual, but the pronunciation was strongly skewed away from standard English, so 'expecting', the group's word for 'pregnant', is said as 'ixpectan'.

But Doric is also notable for a number of distinctive words, so the Peterhead quintet did come up with 'wee abearin'' as an alternative for 'expecting' and a young teenager was 'just a strechel bruyt [brute]': a Doric glossary offers such delights as 'strushel' for untidy and 'waldies' for Wellingtons.

Perched almost at the very top of the British Isles, in that bit of the map that's almost always too far north to fit in properly and usually turns up in an inset, is the archipelago of Shetland. Whalsay, pronounced locally as 'Whaalsa', is the tiny island barely more than four miles long where Voices met Paula, Joan, Jimmy and Mary, whose ages range from twenty-five to sixty-seven. If Doric did very special things to the vowel structure of the language, then the English of Whalsay is very different again: this was how they reported on their questionnaire response to the Voices question about words for 'pleased': 'What I've putt deen far "pleeuzd" is "bliythe". I'd say, "I'm bliythe".' 'Putt deen' for put down, 'far' is for, and pleased has at least one extra syllable. And that's before you encounter the actual word 'blithe' that they all preferred. For cold it got better:

> 'feelin brally caalt; waneeshin; really caalt, affa caalt; waneeshin: we stell use that werrd yet . . . Sterfen: sterfen wi caalt.'

There have been times when it's been hard deciphering dialect, particularly older examples from the SED, but the Whalsay speech left me bereft of reference points: Shetland dialect ('Shetlandic') is said to be one of the most distinctive of all those to be found in Scotland, with roots in the Norn language (an offshoot of Old Norse) that was spoken here in the fifteenth century and died out some 400 years later, and a superimposed layer of Scots. Whatever the full story, when Joan was asked for her equivalent for throw, it sprang a whole outpouring of words and examples. It is worth mentioning that amid the very different vowel values of the Whalsay accent, some words barely stray from a standard form:

> 'We don't "trow", we "bell": we'd bell a ba'. Ye wuh "heuff" onnytheng: heuffin' a ba'. But if ye werr gaan to bell something awa,

ye wud heuff it awa. Means te sem b't et's sloitly defferent, ah wd soy. B't we w'd nehverr spik about "traowin".'

['We don't "throw", we "bal" [= throw]: we'd bal a ball. You would "huff" anything: huffing a ball. But if you were going to baal something away, you would huff it away. Means the same, but it's slightly different, I would say. But we'd never speak about "throwing".']

Then came the business of digging up potatoes, cleaning off the mud and chucking them into a basket – what Joan called 'hentin' taaties':

'Wi' the taaties, we dell them op with a speade, an' Jimmy usually dells an' I hent them. Eence he dells em op, then you shaak dem affa show, we caa it. An' then you hent the taaties inte a baskit.'

['With the potatoes, we dig them up with a spade, and Jimmy usually digs and I throw them. Once he digs them up, then you shake them off, we call it. And then you put the potatoes into a basket.']

Finally in this grand and very rapid tour of Scottish rural speech, and as if to show that you don't have to disappear over the edge of the map to find amazing dialectal riches folded in the hills and valleys of Scotland (and indeed that you don't have to be in the middle of nowhere either), a whirlwind visit to the Borders and the little market town of Hawick, pronounced as is I think well known these days, 'Hoik'. Hawick is not more than fifteen or twenty miles as the crow flies from England, and yet again the mix of switched vowel values and some distinctive vocabulary render the speech a tough nut to crack for the uninitiated visitor passing through.

They use Scots words like 'vennel' and 'pend' for alleyway, and 'stoting' and 'stoter' for heavy rain, familiar from the urban dialects I've described elsewhere in this chapter. But as Dave, Madge, Ian and Robert told Voices:

'At yin tiym the' hid muckle big barries, an' the' putt ther sleits on therr [at one time they had great big barrows, and they put their slates on there], the' putt therr leatherrs ontit [they put their leathers on to it] an' a' the diffrun' things. An' aye can min' mi paal sayn' ti mi [and I can remember my pal saying to me], "Young Dave, when aye were an apprrentice plumber . . ." '

It was just the very start of a long and involved tale about pushing 'muckle big barries [great big barrows]' round the town, loaded with slates which were in danger of slipping off. Separated by hundreds of miles of the wildest countryside in the UK, there are, though, surprising moments of concordance in the fragment above and the samples of Shetlandic that I've just been quoting: 'yin' for one (Hawick speech has a very particular set of cardinal numbers) tallies quite closely with 'eence' for once in Whalsay. And 'putt' is the same pronunciation of put in both places. They're both Scots, for a' tha'.

There's another familiar sound in Hawick too, the Scottish lament for the loss of richness, of a constant dilution of the ancient speech, of spreading Englishness. They worry here about 'trying to keep it up; a lot of people come into the area' and about the infiltration of Glasgow pronunciations like 'yous'. One of the group says:

'[I] heard my grandson talking about "eyes" – we didn't speak about "eyes", we spoke about "een". It's getting seriously diluted and lost.'

Well, I suppose everything is relative. Personally, I'd say there are still huge mountain ranges of old local speech to be climbed all round the country. In some places, the dust-bowls of uniformity have scoured away some of the more individual features, yet at the same time, new heaps of as yet incompletely recorded or legitimized local talk are being thrown up by young people chatting away nineteen to the dozen on mobiles or furiously tapping away to their friends in Argyll or Argentina via world-wide chatrooms and instant messaging.

Local talk will remain local because we *need* it to be local. We need a badge that says 'I belong here – and you don't', and though the forms won't necessarily be those of Shetlandic or Shropshire, of Cornish or Cumbrian, there will, as long as we wish to be individual and have a distinctive and different voice, be a particular word to use, a pronunciation that's special and another word that's never used. It's as natural as the streams that pour off those Scottish mountains . . . or are they burns, or brooks or becks . . . or cuts . . . or dykes . . . or ditches . . . ?

A Scottish Glossary

An Urban Glossary

Where relevant I have indicated old/new usage and the cities in which the words were recorded by Voices

baikie, bakey a sort of (originally wooden) bin for ashes and rubbish (found in a tenement). Perhaps from French *baquet*, trough

bairn a child. Originally Old English *bearn*, the word remains regular Scots usage

bide remain, stay. From Old English *bidan*

blooter, blootered to hit hard, drunk. Regular contemporary Scots usage, perhaps related to 'blouter', a blast of wind, and 'blootering', meaning 'boasting'; these stem from Old English *blawan*, to blow

bourach, boorach a muddle, messy heap; originally a small hill, a heap of stones. From Gaelic *bùrach*, a mess

bowk, bolk, boak to retch, be sick. Recorded by Voices in 2004/5; from Middle English *bolken*

bunker a kitchen work-surface; the word is applied to many forms of flat surface, such as a window seat, often with nautical connections (cf. 'bunk'). Old Scots *bonker*, sixteenth century

byre a cowshed. Middle English *byre*

champ to mash, crush (as potatoes). Originally muddy ground, related to English 'champ'; also figuratively as in the expression (recorded by Voices 2004/5) 'away and champ your tatties', said to someone who's annoying you and meaning broadly 'get away with you'

clatterbags a gossip

close an alley, especially one leading to a tenement, a courtyard. Originally from Latin *clausum*, an enclosed space

cludgie an outside toilet

corry-handed, corrie-fisted, corrie-duke, cairy-handed, Kerrie-fisted, carrie-pod, cloddy-handed/fisted, coddy-fisted, skelly-dukey, geggy-handed, pally-dukered, molly-dukered, paddy-handed left-handed. These many terms are found across various areas of southern and central Scotland. Those including the element *corry*, *corrie*, *cairy*, *Kerrie* and *carrie* are most likely related to the Kerr family of Ferniehirst Castle and their predilection for left-handed warriors (see p. 301). 'Dukered' appears to refer to 'dukes' or fists (as in the expression 'put up your dukes') and is often pronounced 'jukered'. All were mentioned in the Voices survey, 2004/5

couthie pleasant, sympathetic

crabbit bad tempered, grumpy; cf. Middle English *crabbed*

dinnae, cannae, willnae don't, can't, won't

dominie a school-master. A widely used term in regular usage; from Latin *domine*, 'sir'

doup the backside (pronounced 'dowp'). Origin uncertain, perhaps from *dolp*, the bottom of an eggshell, as in the expression 'I'll kick your doup!'

dreich dreary, as in 'a dreich day': miserable wet weather. Regular Scots word in national use. Original meaning: protracted, wearisome. From Old English *dreoy*

drouthy thirsty; originally 'dry', as applied to weather. Related to English 'drought'

drum a long, narrow hill-ridge. From Gaelic *druim*, ridge

dub a puddle. Recorded in Scots since the mid fifteenth century and by Voices in 2004/5

dunny a privy, earth-closet; underground cellar in a tenement. Meaning 'privy' from the eighteenth-century English cant term 'dunnakin'; second meaning possibly from a different root

endure to last, continue to exist. This specifically Scottish meaning remains from Middle English usage

erse the behind, arse

flit move house

forby, foreby besides, in addition to; often used in phrases like 'forby that . . .', with the sense 'besides the fact that . . .' From Old Scots *forby*, beyond

f(r)ae from; Old English *fram*, thirteenth century

gallus bold, daring, rash, mischievous, cheeky

gawkit stupid, awkward. Of uncertain etymology

glaikit stupid, foolish. Fifteenth century but of obscure origin

glaur mud, clay, mire, slime. Used widely in Scotland, the term is found from the fifteenth century; origin uncertain

grun(d) ground. Standard Scots usage, from Old English *grund*

haugh a piece of level ground beside a river. Twelfth-century usage in Scots as *halch*, from Old English *healh*, a corner

howk dig. From northern Middle English *holk*, hollow out

ingle fireplace. From Gaelic *aingeal*, fire, light

knock your pan out work tirelessly

law a rounded, conical hill, often found in place names (e.g. Berwick Law, Dundee Law). From Old English *hlaw*, a hill, mound

loan a cattle-path. From Old English *lone*, a road (which word also yielded modern English 'lane')

messages shopping

mockit filthy

outwith beyond, outside. Middle English *utenn with*, *utewith*, thirteenth century; but used subsequently only in Scots

peelie-wallie sickly, unhealthily thin. Probably imitative of whining sound; early nineteenth century, recorded by Voices 2004/5

pend an alley leading to the back-court of a block of houses or tenement; originally the arch of a bridge. Early nineteenth century

piece a slice of bread, sandwich, packed lunch

plonk, dog off play truant

press cupboard

puggled exhausted, out of breath. Possibly from Hindi *pagal*, mad, angry, but also possibly a euphemism for 'buggered'

puss a face (rhymes with 'fuss'); *skelp your puss* - smash your face

sannies sandshoes, plimsolls. Standard Scots usage

scheme, schemie housing estate, scruffy person (who lives there: contemporary Scots usage)

single-end a tenement

sinnot a vest

skelp to hit, smack, spank. From northern Middle English *skelp*, to strike

smirr, smur, smurr drizzle. Of uncertain origin

stay to live, e.g. 'I stay in Leith': I live in Leith

stote, stoting, stoating, stoter, stoater to bounce, stagger; 'sto(a)ting' – both spellings are found – is the present tense of the verb, e.g. 'it's stotin' down' (with rain). It can also be an intensifier meaning simply 'very good' (e.g. 'that's a stotin' cup of tea'). By extension, a 'stoter' is someone who is 'very good', thus a Glaswegian male might say of an attractive woman: 'she's a stoter'. 'Stoting (drunk)' comes from the word's second meaning, 'to walk in a staggering manner as the result of drink'. Old Scots *stot*, a bounce, perhaps from teutonic root, *stut*

strides trousers. This term, recorded by Voices 2004/5, is found in many parts of the UK in older usage

vennel an alleyway, passage between houses. Old Scots, fifteenth century, from Old French *venelle*, small street

wabbit exhausted, twentieth-century origin

wain a child. Standard term in national use; formed from 'wee' (little) and 'ane' (one); sixteenth century

wir ain leid 'our own language' (Scots)

wynd a winding, narrow street or alley, chiefly in towns and cities. Found in Old Scots, thirteenth century, cf. Old English *yewind*, a winding ascent

A Short List of Gaelic Words

allt a stream, burn

bàrdachd poetry-writing

bodach an old man

bùrach a mess

cailleach an old woman

cò tha sin? who is that?

crùbach lame

dè tha thu ag ràdh? what are you saying?

dubh black

fliuch a rainy day

gàidhlig nan ceàrdaidhean 'Tinkers' Gaelic' (abusive term describing the speech of Lewis)

mòine peat; **buain na mònach** cutting peat

muladach sad, woeful, sorrowful

norrag a cat-nap, 'forty winks'

pàisde a baby, child

seanair a grandfather

seanmhair a grandmother

sgadan buntàta a herring and tattie supper (literally the words for herring and potatoes)

sgìth tired; **tha mi sgìth** I am tired

sgleog a thump, blow

taigh beag the small house (= toilet)

tairsgeir a peat iron (a sort of spade specially shaped for cutting peats from bog)

teth hot
tigh a house
uisge water; **uisge-beatha** whisky

Index of regional words

Page numbers in **bold** denote an entry in the glossary that appears at the end of each chapter. Alongside English dialect words, a few familiar Welsh and Scottish Gaelic words are also included.

borstal breakouts 310
bost, bostin 127–8, **140**
bourach, boorach **322**; *see
also* bùrach
bowk, bolk, boak 307,
310, **322**
boy 154, 158, **159**
brae 273, **288**
brass 193, **207**
brassic *see* boracic
bray 255–6, **262**
bredren, bredrin 72–3, **75**,
134, 135, 136, 235, **239**
breeding 75
breeks 279, **288**
breh *see* bredren
broke to the bone 271, **288**
brossen 229, **237**
bruck up 71, **75**
brummagem 119, **140**
Brummie 108, 116,
120–21, 122, 123, 124,
136, 139, **140**
buckie 265, **288**
bunker 306, **322**
bùrach 317, **325**; *see also*
bourach
burn 188, 243, 257, **262**,
288
buskins 154, **159**
butcher's 75
butters 62, 71, **75**
butty 103, **183**
buzzin', buzzing 181, **183**,
231, **237**
by gaw, by gum 192, **207**
by gum *see* by gaw
byor 286, **291**
byre **322**
caff **207**
caggled 20
caggy, caggy-handed 129,
138, **140**, 229, **236**
cailleach 317, **325**
cairy-handed 300, **322–3**;
see also corrie

camblet 165, **183**
canna, dunna, munna,
shanna, wonna 99,
140, 218, 250
cannae *see* dinnae
canny, Canny Annie 253,
261, **262**, 309–10
cap 130, **140**
carrie-pod 299–300,
322–3; *see also* corrie
carry-out 282, **288**
cassn't *see* cast
cast, cassn't 33, **44**, 82
catchy 35, 44
cat melodeon **288**
catto'ed 207
cauchy *see* coochy
causey 107, **140**
champ **322**
champion 191–2, **207**
charver **237**, 258, **262**
chava *see* charver
cheal *see* cheel
cheel, cheal 10, **20**, 35,
44
cheoboy *see* keoboy
chin *see* whack
china 76
chuck 171, **183**
chuffed 36, 66, 92, 180,
198, **207**, 231, 298
chwarae 90, 95, **103**
cidered up **44**
ciff, cyff **103**
CJ *see* common Jack
claes 197, 229, 279, **289**
clarty **207**
clash 269, **288**
clatterbags **322**
cleg **237**
clemmed, clemt **183**
clicky-handed, clicky 11,
20, 41
cloddy-handed/
fisted 299–300,
322–3; *see also* corrie

close 297, 302, 303, 309,
317, **322**
cloy, hump, yock 287,
291
cludgie 293, 303, **322**
clunk **20**
cob 135, **140**, 177, **183**,
207
cock 114, 126, **140**
cockly 258, **263**
Cockney 28, 48–50, 51–2,
53–4, 56, 57, 58–60,
61, 62, 63, 66, 67, 69,
76, 101
coddy-fisted 299–300,
322–3; *see also* corrie
co-dee 73, **76**
coggy, coggy-
handed **103**; *see also*
caggy
coginio 93, **103**
common Jack, CJ 94, **103**
coo, kye 217, **237**, 280
coochy, couchy,
cauchy 41, **44**
coopy-down **44**, **103**, **105**
Corporation pop **183**
corrie, corrie-fisted, corry-
handed, corrie-duke,
corrie-dukit 299–300,
322–3
cotch 71, **76**
cò tha sin? **325**
couchy *see* coochy
coup, cope 281, **289**
couthie **323**
cowd 138, **140**
crabbit **323**
cracket 247, **263**
craic 266, 275, 282, 283,
285, **289**
craic ninety 275, 285, **289**
cream-crackered **76**
crepes **76**, 134
crib 12, **20**
crimes o' Paris 126, **140**